THE CAMBRIDGE COMPANION TO DAVID FOSTER WALLACE

Best known for his masterpiece *Infinite Jest*, David Foster Wallace reshaped literature for a generation with his groundbreaking and original work. Wallace's desire to blend formal innovation with the communicative function of literature resulted in works that appeal as much to a reader's intellect as they do to emotion. As such, few writers in recent memory have matched his work's intense critical and popular impact. The essays in this Companion, written by top Wallace scholars, offer historical and cultural contexts for grasping Wallace's significance, provide rigorous individual readings of each of his major works of fiction and nonfiction, and address the key themes and concerns of these works, including aesthetics, politics, religion and spirituality, race, and posthumanism. This wide-ranging volume is a necessary resource for understanding an author now typically regarded as one of the most influential and important of his time.

Ralph Clare is Associate Professor of English at Boise State University and specializes in post-1945 American literature. He is the author of *Fictions Inc.: The Corporation in Postmodern Fiction, Film, and Popular Culture* (Rutgers, 2014) and is currently at work on a study of emotion and affect in contemporary fiction of the neoliberal era.

D1553071

THE CAMBRIDGE
COMPANION TO
DAVID FOSTER WALLACE

EDITED BY
RALPH CLARE
Boise State University

CAMBRIDGE
UNIVERSITY PRESS

University Printing House, Cambridge CB2 8BS, United Kingdom

One Liberty Plaza, 20th Floor, New York, NY 10006, USA

477 Williamstown Road, Port Melbourne, VIC 3207, Australia

314–321, 3rd Floor, Plot 3, Splendor Forum, Jasola District Centre,
New Delhi – 110025, India

79 Anson Road, #06–04/06, Singapore 079906

Cambridge University Press is part of the University of Cambridge.

It furthers the University's mission by disseminating knowledge in the pursuit of
education, learning, and research at the highest international levels of excellence.

www.cambridge.org
Information on this title: www.cambridge.org/9781107195950
DOI: 10.1017/9781108553902

First published 2018

Printed in the United States of America by Sheridan Books, Inc.

A catalogue record for this publication is available from the British Library.

Library of Congress Cataloging-in-Publication Data
Names: Clare, Ralph, 1975– editor.
TITLE: The Cambridge companion to David Foster Wallace / edited
by Ralph Clare.
DESCRIPTION: Cambridge ; New York, NY : Cambridge University Press,
2018. | Includes bibliographical references and index.
IDENTIFIERS: LCCN 2018003682 | ISBN 9781107195950
SUBJECTS: LCSH: Wallace, David Foster – Criticism and interpretation. |
Postmodernism in literature.
CLASSIFICATION: LCC PS3573.A425635 Z58 2018 | DDC 813/.54–dc23
LC record available at https://lccn.loc.gov/2018003682

ISBN 978-1-107-19595-0 Hardback
ISBN 978-1-108-45177-2 Paperback

For all those who continue to put the post-(post) in modernism.

CONTENTS

NOTES ON CONTRIBUTORS

MARSHALL BOSWELL is Professor of English at Rhodes College. He is the author of two works of literary scholarship: *John Updike's Rabbit Tetralogy: Mastered Irony in Motion* (2001) and *Understanding David Foster Wallace* (2004). He is also the author of two works of fiction, *Trouble with Girls* (2003) and *Alternative Atlanta* (2005). With Stephen J. Burn, he is the coeditor of *A Companion to David Foster Wallace Studies* (2013) and the editor of *David Foster Wallace and "The Long Thing": New Essays on the Novels* (2015).

RALPH CLARE is Associate Professor of English at Boise State University, specializing in post-1945 American literature. He is the author of *Fictions Inc.: The Corporation in Postmodern Fiction, Film, and Popular Culture* (2014). His latest book project, *Metaffective Fiction: Structuring Feeling in Contemporary American Literature*, explores the role of emotion and affect in post-postmodern fiction and the neoliberal era.

JURRIT DAALDER read for a DPhil in English Literature at Oxford University, focusing on the work of David Foster Wallace, Jonathan Franzen, and Richard Powers in relation to the Midwestern regionalist tradition. His essays have appeared in *Critical Insights: Midwestern Literature* (2013) and *George Saunders: Critical Essays* (2017). He is currently a Supernumerary Research and Teaching Fellow at Oxford's Rothermere American Institute, and he teaches at the Georg-August-University in Göttingen, Germany.

CLARE HAYES-BRADY is a Lecturer in American Literature at University College Dublin and the author of *The Unspeakable Failures of David Foster Wallace* (2016). Other research interests include the interaction of literature with film; transatlantic cultural heritage; performative sexuality (both normative and queer), resistant gender modes, and the history of burlesque; digital humanities and modes of transmission; adolescence in contemporary fiction; and dystopian narrative.

DAVID HERING is a Lecturer in American Literature at the University of Liverpool, United Kingdom. He is the author of *David Foster Wallace: Fiction and Form* (2016) and editor of *Consider David Foster Wallace: Critical Essays* (2010). His writing has also appeared in the *Los Angeles Review of Books, Orbit*, and *Critical Engagements*.

ANDREW HOBEREK is Professor of English at the University of Missouri, where he teaches courses in contemporary fiction and other media. He is the author of *The Twilight of the Middle Class* (2005) and *Considering Watchmen* (2014), and the editor of *The Cambridge Companion to John F. Kennedy* (2015), as well as the coeditor (with Daniel Worden and Jason Gladstone) of the volume *Postmodern/ Postwar and After: Rethinking American Literature*. He is also the Comics/ Graphic Novels Editor at the *Los Angeles Review of Books*.

MARY K. HOLLAND is Associate Professor of English at the State University of New York–New Paltz. She is the author of *Succeeding Postmodernism: Language and Humanism in Contemporary American Literature* (2013) and the coeditor, with Stephen J. Burn, of *Approaches to Teaching David Foster Wallace* (forth-coming from MLA). She has published essays on Wallace, Steve Tomasula, John Barth, A. M. Homes, and others. Currently she is working on a book tentatively titled *Contemporary Realisms: Literary Form and Function in the Twenty-First Century*.

ADAM KELLY is lecturer in American Literature at the University of York. He has also taught at Harvard University, where he was a postdoctoral fellow, and at University College Dublin, where he completed his PhD. He is the author of *American Fiction in Transition: Observer-Hero Narrative, the 1990s, and Postmodernism* (2013), and has published widely on contemporary fiction, includ-ing a number of articles and book chapters on the work of David Foster Wallace.

LEE KONSTANTINOU is Associate Professor of English at the University of Maryland, College Park. He wrote the novel *Pop Apocalypse* (2009) and the literary history *Cool Characters: Irony and American Fiction* (2016). With Samuel Cohen, he coedited *The Legacy of David Foster Wallace* (2012). He is currently coediting a collection of essays on the comics of Art Spiegelman and is writing a monograph on Helen DeWitt's 2000 novel, *The Last Samurai*.

ROBERT L. MCLAUGHLIN is Professor of English at Illinois State University. He has published many articles on postmodern fiction, especially the work of Thomas Pynchon and David Foster Wallace. He is the author of *Stephen Sondheim and the Reinvention of the American Musical* (2016), coauthor (with Sally E. Parry) of *We'll Always Have the Movies: American Cinema during World War II* (2006), and editor of *Innovations: An Anthology of Modern and Contemporary Fiction* (1998).

MATTHEW LUTER is on the English faculty at St. Andrew's Episcopal School in Jackson, Mississippi. He is the author of *Understanding Jonathan Lethem* (2015). His articles, on authors including Don DeLillo, Ellen Douglas, Willie Morris, and Bret Easton Ellis, have appeared in journals including *Critique*, the *Southern*

Literary Journal, *Genre*, and *Orbit*. He is a founding board member of the International David Foster Wallace Society.

MATTHEW MULLINS is Assistant Professor of English and History of Ideas at Southeastern Baptist Theological Seminary and author of *Postmodernism in Pieces* (2016). His academic and public writing has appeared in *Callaloo, Arizona Quarterly*, the *Los Angeles Review of Books, American Book Review*, and other places.

JEFFREY SEVERS is Associate Professor of English at the University of British Columbia. He is the author of *David Foster Wallace's Balancing Books: Fictions of Value* (2017) and the coeditor of *Pynchon's* Against the Day: *A Corrupted Pilgrim's Guide* (2011). His writing has appeared or is forthcoming in *Critique, Modern Fiction Studies, Twentieth-Century Literature, MELUS*, and *Approaches to Teaching the Works of David Foster Wallace* (eds. Stephen J. Burn and Mary K. Holland).

JOSEPH TABBI is Professor of English at the University of Chicago at Illinois. He is the author of *Cognitive Fictions* (2002) and *Postmodern Sublime: Technology and American Writing from Mailer to Cyberpunk* (1995). His biography of William Gaddis, *Nobody Grew but the Business* (2015), received an award from the Chicago Society of Midland Authors. The editor of the *electronic book review*, Tabbi is also the founding member of the *Consortium of Electronic Literature* (www.cellproject.net/).

LUCAS THOMPSON is a research fellow at the United States Studies Centre at the University of Sydney, Australia. He is the author of *Global Wallace: David Foster Wallace and World Literature* (2017), along with numerous other publications on contemporary US literature.

ANDREW WARREN is John L. Loeb Associate Professor of the Humanities in Harvard's Department of English. He codirects the Mahindra Humanities Center's Seminar in Dialectical Thinking, and teaches and writes about Romanticism, poetry, philosophy, critical theory, and contemporary fiction. He is the author of *The Orient and the Young Romantics* (2014). His new project, *Romantic Entanglements*, is about entanglement (its figure, its concept, its use, and its problem) in the long eighteenth century.

ACKNOWLEDGMENTS

That Cambridge University Press has published a companion to David Foster Wallace is an acknowledgment in and of itself, but an occasion such as this was a long time in the works. In short, a big shout out is in order for the twin pillars of DFW Studies, Marshall Boswell and Stephen J. Burn. Their careful and exacting work was the first that I, and many a budding Wallace scholar, encountered when existing scholarship was at a minimum. They provided the first substantial framework for understanding Wallace. Their book-length studies contain careful and rigorous readings that still open up Wallace's texts in compelling ways, and they ultimately helped to legitimate Wallace as a writer worthy of increased academic attention. That there is a thriving DFW community of scholars today is because of their foundational, and continuing, work.

In addition to thanking all of the contributors in this volume, thanks especially to all of the Wallace-heads out there whom I've met over the years at conferences in various cities, in the United States and abroad. To name (and, inevitably, to forget) a few: Nick Maniatis, the three Matt's – Luter, Bucher, and Mullins (the last of whom once strolled around Harvard incognito with me and kicked back in Emerson Hall, where we decided we liked our league best, be it more bush than ivy). To Lee Konstantinou, the irrepressible and energetic Marshall Boswell, Adam Kelly (whose clean Irish chin will never sport the dreaded neoliberal beard), Mike Miley, David Hering, Jeff Fisher, and Mary Holland (who let me convince her to "Return to *IJ*" in this volume and who has suffered the slings and arrows of outrageous panels!) – we'll always have Paris. Jeffrey Severs, whose paper on "Westward" blew me away at the first DFW conference at ISU and whose *David Foster Wallace's Balancing Books* virtually eviscerated me more recently, many thanks for talking me down from a very iffy introduction to this volume and for a number of discussions over the years. Stacey Olster has once again helped me immensely and saved me from myself more than once. If I were to give all the thanks I owe to her, it would run longer than a Bruce Springsteen concert, of which she has attended her share.

A tip of my editor's hat goes to Boise State's computer-savvy students working at "The Zone" for helping a certain Luddite prepare an entire electronic version of the manuscript – section breaks, roman numerals, end-notes, and all. The online bibliography compiled by the DFW Research Group at the University of Glasgow that I consulted saved me near the very end. Many thanks to the Boise State English department for granting me a course release to pursue this project, to BSU's Arts and Humanities Institute for providing the funding to attend the DFW Paris conference in 2014, and to the Idaho Humanities Council for providing a research fellowship that also gave me time and space to edit this volume.

A final word to one who will never read it: James Rother, in whose class I first read Wallace – the story "Lyndon" – as an undergrad at San Diego State in 1997. During one of several two-hour-long lectures I found myself in the middle of after visiting Rother during office hours (where he was inevi-tably trying to nap before our three-hour evening class), the towering man paused his furious tirade on the death of literature and handed me an essay he'd written on Wallace, a dense if stylish piece that I did my best to fathom later on. That time encapsulates the first Wallace and Wallace criticism I read. It's somewhat dizzying to think back upon it now. Back then I didn't know what graduate school was, and a not-so-simple college degree was an amazing thing. But despite Rother's rage and red-faced glare, his weekly jeremiads and the spittle that followed them, occasionally flecking my face, there came a consecration of sorts. Here I clutch the covenant.

CHRONOLOGY

1962	David Foster Wallace is born in Ithaca, NY, on February 21, to James D. Wallace and Sally Foster Wallace. The family soon moves to Champaign-Urbana, IL, after James secures a professorship in philosophy at the University of Illinois.
1967	John Barth publishes "The Literature of Exhaustion," an essay heralding the ascendance of, and helping to define, postmodern American literature. Barth will become a touchstone of Wallace's early work.
1971	Don DeLillo, a major influence on Wallace and with whom he will eventually have a long correspondence, publishes his first novel, *Americana*. Wallace has a fairly normal and happy childhood but will later trace the origin of his depression and anxiety to around this time, though his family did not notice.
1980	Wallace enrolls at his father's alma mater, Amherst College, MA. He majors, like his father, in philosophy, though he chooses to pursue logic. Excels in his studies from day one.
1982	After experiencing a number of anxiety attacks and phobias, Wallace has a breakdown, marking the first acute bout of the depression that he will suffer from his entire life. He puts his studies on hiatus and recuperates at his parents' house in Champaign-Urbana. Returns to Amherst in the fall.
1983	Back in Illinois for the summer, Wallace suffers another attack of depression. He is prescribed Tofranil as a result. Begins reading another major postmodern influence, Thomas Pynchon. The depression continues, causing him to withdraw from the fall semester at Amherst. During this crisis, Wallace makes a commitment to becoming a fiction writer.
1984	Wallace publishes what is considered his first work, a semiautobiographical story dealing with depression,

"The Planet Trillaphon as It Stands in Relation to the Bad Thing," in the student-run *Amherst Review*.

1985   Graduates from Amherst with two theses, one in philosophy, one in literature. Begins MFA in creative writing program at the University of Arizona in the fall.

1986   *The Broom of the System*, a revision of Wallace's undergraduate literature thesis, is accepted for publication by Viking Penguin. Wallace meets Bonnie Nadell, who will become a longtime agent and friend.

1987   Publishes *The Broom of the System* to mixed reviews. Completes MFA in creative writing at the University of Arizona in the spring and receives Whiting Award, which allows him to attend the Yaddo writer's colony in Saratoga Springs, NY, to finish work on his first collection of stories, *Girl with Curious Hair*. Returns briefly to teach at Amherst.

1988   Returns to Tucson to teach at the University of Arizona. Strikes up a correspondence with Jonathan Franzen after reading the author's galleys for *The Twenty-Seventh City*. Begins attending drug and alcohol sobriety meetings. Consequently, ceases to take the antidepressant Nardil and has another serious breakdown. Returns to Champaign-Urbana. Attempts suicide by pills. Tries electroconvulsive therapy. Publication of *Girl with Curious Hair* by Viking Penguin is held up because of legal issues regarding the use of celebrity personages in some stories. Wallace, following his editor Gerry Howard's move to W. W. Norton, changes publishers.

1989   Publishes *Girl with Curious Hair* with W. W. Norton. Receives O. Henry Award for "Here and There," a story in the collection originally published in *Fiction*. Reads David Markson's *Wittgenstein's Mistress* and soon starts up correspondence with the author. Moves to Somerville, MA, and enrolls for a short period as a graduate student in philosophy at Harvard, where he takes courses from Stanley Cavell and John Rawls, among others. Checks himself into McLean Hospital for rehabilitation after struggling with alcohol and marijuana addiction. Stays for four weeks.

1990   Moves into a halfway house in Brighton, MA, which will serve as a model of *Infinite Jest*'s Ennet House.

1990   Coauthors *Signifying Rappers: Rap and Race in the Urban Present* with Mark Costello, one of the earliest publications to take rap music seriously as a topic of political, cultural, and societal interest.

1991 Suffers another breakdown that leads to a two-week hospital stay. Begins working in earnest on *Infinite Jest*, pieces and scenes of which he had conceived and written as early as 1986.

1992 Michael Pietsch of Little, Brown contracts *Infinite Jest*. Wallace moves to Syracuse, NY, to pursue a relationship with memoirist Mary Karr, whom Wallace had become obsessed with since meeting her in 1989. The tumultuous relationship lasts about a year.

1993 Wallace accepts job teaching literature and writing in Illinois State University's English Department, a bastion of postmodernist theory and fiction at the time, in Bloomington-Normal, IL, an hour from where he grew up. Continues work on *Infinite Jest*. Publishes the first version of his now famous "E Unibus Pluram: Television and U.S. Fiction" in the *Review of Contemporary Fiction*. A revised version will appear in *A Supposedly Fun Thing I'll Never Do Again*.

1996 *Infinite Jest* published to great acclaim. Wallace begins grueling book promotion tour.

1997 Publishes *A Supposedly Fun Thing I'll Never Do Again*, a collection of essays and journalism Wallace had been writing over the years. Receives Lannan Literary Award and a MacArthur "Genius Grant."

1999 Publishes *Brief Interviews with Hideous Men*. Receives O. Henry Award for "The Depressed Person," a story in the collection originally published in *Harper's* magazine.

2000 Publishes "The Weasel, Twelve Monkeys, and the Shrub," an article exploring John McCain's presidential campaign run, in *Rolling Stone*. The piece will eventually become "Up, Simba" in the essay collection *Consider the Lobster*. Receives Lannan Foundation Residency Fellowship.

2001 Franzen publishes *The Corrections* to high acclaim. The book becomes a bestseller. After 9/11, Wallace publishes "The View from Mrs. Thompson's," an essay examining regional American reactions to the terrorist attacks, in *Rolling Stone*.

2002 Accepts "The Roy E. Disney Professorship for Creative Writing" at Pomona College and moves to Claremont, CA. Begins a relationship with Karen Green, a visual artist. Receives O. Henry award for "Good Old Neon," a story later

	collected in *Oblivion* and originally published in *Conjunctions*.
2003	*Everything and More* published, Wallace's book on Georg Cantor, infinity, and mathematics.
2004	Publishes *Oblivion*, his third story collection. Marries Karen Green in Urbana, IL.
2005	Publishes essay collection *Consider the Lobster*.
2006	Tenth-anniversary edition of *Infinite Jest* published by Little, Brown with an introduction by Dave Eggers. Eggers's publishing house, *McSweeney's*, founded in 1998, would publish some of Wallace's works in its literary magazine.
2007	Wallace guest edits *The Best American Essays 2007*, reflects upon the differences between nonfiction and fiction in his introductory essay, "Deciderization 2007 – A Special Report." Tries to stop taking Nardil again and suffers another breakdown and severe depression.
2008	Wallace takes his own life in Claremont, CA, on September 12, 2008.
2009	"Infinite Summer" multimedia, multiplatform, online reading group commences, draws a large number of participants. *This is Water*, Wallace's 2005 Kenyon College commencement address, is published. The first two academic conferences on Wallace's work are held, in Liverpool, England, and New York, New York, respectively. John Krasinski's film adaptation of *Brief Interviews with Hideous Men* released.
2010	Wallace's archive opens at the Harry Ransom Center at the University of Texas, Austin. *Fate, Time, and Language: An Essay on Free Will*, Wallace's undergraduate philosophy thesis, is published. David Lipsky's book-length interview *Although of Course You End Up Becoming Yourself: A Road Trip with David Foster Wallace* published.
2011	Wallace's unfinished *The Pale King: An Unfinished Novel*, edited by Michael Pietsch, is published by Little, Brown. Wallace had been struggling to write the novel for more than a decade, even attending accounting courses for research as early as 1996.
2012	*The Pale King* is nominated for the Pulitzer Prize. *Both Flesh and Not*, an edition of previously uncollected essays, is published by Little, Brown.
2013	Karen Green publishes *Bough Down*, a book of oblique elegies and collages for her deceased husband.

2014   The first annual David Foster Wallace conference is held at Illinois State University.

2015   The controversial Wallace biopic *The End of the Tour*, directed by James Ponsoldt, is released. The script is based on Lipsky's interview *Although of Course You End Up Becoming Yourself.*

2016   Twentieth-anniversary edition of *Infinite Jest* published by Little, Brown with a forward by Tom Bissell.

RALPH CLARE

Introduction: An Exquisite Corpus: Assembling a Wallace without Organs

"The words of a dead man / Are modified in the guts of the living."
W. H. Auden, "In Memoriam of William Butler Yeats"

For David Foster Wallace, good writing establishes a "living transaction between humans."[1] As Auden's elegy of Yeats reminds us, however, the words of the dead are not excluded from this transaction, for there exists, in a very special way, a kind of symbolic exchange between reader and writer that occurs beyond the grave. That words lodge in guts, that they change them and are changed there, is the very stuff of mutual recognition. Yet the way in which those words are received and interpreted or prepared and contextualized matters as well, especially if the author is no longer living. *Infinite Jest* (1996), for example, twice alludes to an absent scene in which Hal Incandenza and Don Gately dig up James Incandenza's body in search of the antidote to his "failed entertainment," a film so diabolically compelling that it causes permanent catatonia in its viewers, as if only the auteur's posthumously willed revision can offer an egress from the infinite regress of his art. What appears to be a satirical poke at conflating the author with his work (the dreaded intentional fallacy), however, is actually more ambivalent than it first seems, particularly since James will return in the novel as a wraith (a point to which this essay will itself return). Wallace appears to be suggesting that, even after actual, physical death, the author remains unavoidably symbolically invested in the work, revealing an underlying anxiety regarding a promised literary afterlife that may or may not await the deceased. A host of questions thus arises: Just what is the relationship between the author's body and the body of her work, between the corporeal and the corpus? How should one go about treating the body of an author's work after her death? Does it deserve the same kind of consideration as when the author was living? And what ought to be the ethical parameters in undertaking such a critical practice?

Nowhere are such questions more pertinent than when considering the life and work, the corpus, of Wallace, for whom the critical preparation for the author's hereafter was a concern that warranted frequent reflection.[2] For instance, in Wallace's damning review of Edwin Williamson's *Borges: A Life*, which he finds reductive for its "dishonest kind of psychological criticism," Wallace laments that the readers of such biographies will "usually be idealizers of that writer and perpetrators (consciously or not) of the intentional fallacy."[3] Yet Wallace's review of Joseph Frank's biography of Dostoyevsky hails Frank's flouting of the intentional fallacy in part because of the biography's basis in historical and cultural fact and its tone of "maximum restraint and objectivity."[4] Evidently for Wallace, the road to critical hell was not paved with a proper and good use of the intentional fallacy. Taking into account an author's intentions in regard to her work's meaning – equating, to some degree, the corporeal with the corpus – could be critically illuminating if done with the proper care and attention. In turn, after Wallace's rapid rise to literary canonization, a conscientious assessment of his work must aim to strike a similar balance between an appreciation of the author's method and a rigorous analysis of the work.

Maximalist Restraint

To be sure, David Foster Wallace is one of the most important American writers of the twentieth and twenty-first century. Wallace's stunningly original work broke away from the often insular and claustrophobic world of 1980s literary minimalism, shunned the trendy pop culture–infused and arguably nihilistically inclined literature that marked the tail end of postmodernism, and suggested the ways in which the passé metafictional forms and linguistic play of postmodernists such as Thomas Pynchon, John Barth, and Donald Barthelme could be wedded with fuller characters and imbued with a meaningful, affective charge to create a unique kind of fiction. His was to be a fiction that would, like the novels he loved best, "make heads throb heartlike."[5] Perhaps most importantly, Wallace's fiction expressed a desire and yearning for the communicative and restorative function of literature. To that end, Wallace ultimately crafted a self-reflexive fiction that nevertheless prompted self-reflection by putting formal innovation at the service of connecting with and not distancing the reader. Wallace's innovative approaches to multiple genres of writing inspired an entire generation of writers who, directly and indirectly, have responded in some fashion to Wallace's literary interventions. Wallace's influence can be detected in the work of Dave Eggers, Zadie Smith, George Saunders, Jennifer Egan, Junot Díaz, David Mitchell, Jeffrey Eugenides, Jonathan Lethem, and Tao Lin, as well as in the nonfiction writings and journalism of Leslie Jamison, John Jeremiah Sullivan, and Chuck Klosterman, among others.

Wallace's writing functioned as an important hinge between Generation X, which spanned the stagflated 1970s to the slackered 1990s and was perceived to be cynical and lethargic, and the Millennials, whose wired-era ambitions and optimistic outlook on life signaled a shifting generational ethos. Wallace has been embraced by members of Gen X largely because of his diagnosis of debilitating, cultural irony; his call for sincerity in a media-saturated, consumerist world; and his ability to reveal a core sadness that persisted in a post–Cold War would-be utopian America. As Wallace argues in his 1993 essay "E Unibus Pluram," contemporary televisual culture and postmodern fiction are indicative of "the oppressiveness of institutionalized irony, the too successful rebel," whereas "the next real literary 'rebels' ... might well emerge as some weird bunch of *anti*-rebels ... who have the childish gall to endorse and instantiate single-entendre principles."[6] *Infinite Jest*, which would herald Wallace's arrival into the literary big time, earnestly addressed Wallace's concerns of this time and crafted a fiction that diagnosed and, to debatable degrees of success, sought to ameliorate these ills through fiction. Alternately, the Millennial generation, in keeping with its penchant for connectedness, civic engagement, and positivity, has especially taken to Wallace's pronouncements that empathy, attention, and awareness are qualities that we should nurture in order to negotiate our data-infused, socially mediated world. In *This Is Water*, his 2005 Kenyon College commencement speech that would eventually be published, Wallace urges his audience to become "conscious and aware enough to *choose* what you pay attention to and to *choose* how you construct meaning from experience."[7] His unfinished, posthumously published novel, *The Pale King* (2011), would explore these twinned themes of attention and awareness in a much more complex fashion. Rarely does a writer's work speak so directly and profoundly to multiple generations of readers.

At the same time that Wallace helped to revolutionize American literature, he was transforming the cultural and moral sensibility of America too, as his nonfiction pieces – often published in popular, mainstream magazines and later collected during his lifetime into the well-received *A Supposedly Fun Thing I'll Never Do Again* (1997) and *Consider the Lobster* (2005) – reached an even wider audience than his fiction initially did. Wallace's work is thus notable for having been embraced both inside and outside of academia by professional (the critic, the scholar) and nonprofessional readers alike.[8] Indeed, there has arisen a robust worldwide group of scholars whose busy publishing has created a veritable Wallace industry. The first annual David Foster Wallace Conference hosted by Illinois State University, where Wallace once taught, was held in 2014, and there is now an International David

Foster Wallace Society that oversees *The Journal of David Foster Wallace Studies*. Equally of note is the vibrant nonprofessional readership that maintains a strong Internet presence, typified by the longstanding Wallace-l listserv, The Howling Fantods website, and by 2009's Infinite Summer and 2016's Infinite Winter, two multiplatform (including blogs, Facebook, Tumblr, Twitter, etc.) international reading groups that read *Infinite Jest* "together." Here is proof that Wallace readers need little, if any, institutional prompting when it comes to forming networked communities, virtual and actual, dedicated to reading and understanding his work. It takes a singular kind of writer, and a singular body of work, to galvanize readers in such a way.

Yet Wallace is much more than a foundational figure of the post-postmodern era. Beyond its more immediate impact, Wallace's writing also participates in the *longue durée* of American literature and cultural criticism that directly and self-consciously reflects upon and questions American values and democratic ideals. In both his fiction and nonfiction one can detect the occasional horatorial echoes of Emerson and a philosophical indebtedness to William James that joins him with a tradition of writers and thinkers who suggest a distinct kind of pragmatic idealism that is thoroughly American.[9] At a time when American society and politics appears to be so divisive, Wallace's call to listen and be attentive to others and the world around us, and his ability to engage deeply and open-mindedly with pressing concerns about individual and shared American values, make his work more relevant than ever. The roots of Wallace's work run deep in the American psyche and thus his relevance to American literature and culture will be a lasting one.

Long after the Thrill

Wallace's corpus has also grown considerably in the decade since his death, and literary critics, editors, and readers have all the while been picking up the pieces by way of posthumous publications. These include Wallace's final, unfinished novel *The Pale King* (2011), his Amherst College undergraduate philosophy honors thesis *Fate, Time, and Language: An Essay on Free Will* (2011), his 2005 Kenyon College commencement speech *This Is Water* (2009), the anthology that is *The David Foster Wallace Reader* (2015), and an edition of previously uncollected essays, *Both Flesh and Not* (2012). Add to this the discovery of Wallace's first published story, the film adaptation of *Brief Interviews with Hideous Men* (2009), D. T. Max's revealing biography *Every Love Story Is a Ghost Story* (2012), several books of single or multiple interviews, David Lipsky's book-length interview *Although of Course You End Up Becoming Yourself: A Road Trip* (2010), as well as its adaptation into the controversial film, *The End of the Tour* (2015), and a forthcoming edition of Wallace's letters edited by Stephen J. Burn. Of major significance was the 2010 opening of the Wallace archive at the Harry Ransom Center at the University of Austin, which allowed Wallace scholars and devotees the opportunity to scour over numerous drafts of Wallace's works, as well as his letters, notes, and the marginalia recorded in the books of his personal library. We might say, then, that since all of Wallace's work has now been exhumed, the real critical autopsy has begun.

With these publications, moreover, has come a wave of posthumous fame for a writer who was already well established and critically lauded. Tending to Wallace's corpus, therefore, must be undertaken with foresight and due diligence. For a writer's reputation in the Internet era is subject, more so than ever, to the whims of rapid media cycles in which memes, hot-takes, and instantaneous commentary trend today and are gone tomorrow. Wallace is a fascinating case study in this respect. Wallace has at times been subject to near deification, via the creation of what Christian Lorentzen calls the image of "Saint Wallace," which persists even after D. T. Max's biography clearly showed that, when at his worst, Wallace could be much like one of his own hideously drawn men.[10] One need only peruse the recommended-reading note taped to the Wallace shelf of many a bookstore to find an earnest and heartfelt quote from a young Wallace declaring what fiction is supposed to be about, thereby transforming it into a veritable back-cover blurb by Wallace about Wallace. As a result, Wallace's themes of empathy and attentiveness have too often been boiled down to pithy slogans that may generate lots of likes and followers in a short-form–social media and Twitter-saturated culture in which spectacle trumps substance, but the actual embodied readerly experience in grasping and understanding these themes, as some readers find, is another thing altogether.

Wallace's fiction, however, is quite often demanding of the reader, who Wallace felt had to "put her share of the linguistic work in" to get something back in return.[11] Such an aesthetic vision aspires to communicate openly with the reader, but the reader must actively engage with the text as well. Further, while Wallace believed that "a piece of fiction can allow us imaginatively to identify with a character's pain," he also stated that "true empathy's impossible."[12] There is a mix of hope and desperation pulsating through these twinned assertions, and they serve as a reminder that Wallace's corpus is at once as dense and complex as it is revealing and profound. For Wallace's supposedly "human centered" texts are often filled with inhuman characters, challenging linguistic playfulness, torturous stylistics, and densely packed, multilayered forms. Readers and critics would do well to appreciate how Wallace's corpus is seamless here, patchworked there, oftentimes enlivening, sometimes deadening, and simultaneously both a wondrous and monstrous thing.

E Pluribus Wallace: One or Infinite Wallaces?

In kind, we should not forget the way in which different kinds of readers and institutions attempt to organize and create not *the* but *a* or at times *our* Wallace. David Hering warns that, "As the unitary persona 'David Foster Wallace' becomes ever more defined, and with it the implicit collapsing together of author and style, the possibility of the monologic text increases."[13] The images of Wallace the Genius, Wallace the Tragic, Wallace the Depressed, or Wallace the Saint are essentially one-dimensional, reductive, and often supersede the work itself. In other words, everybody wants a piece of Wallace, but would it really be so bad if all of Wallace's scholars and all of Wallace's readers couldn't put Wallace back together again? To this end, I desire a sort of Wallace-without-Organs as Deleuze and Guattari might conceive of it.[14] Wallace's readers and critics would then be taking part in a vast, shared project of becoming-Wallace, a Wallace in flux, a Wallace that we never fully know. It may seem somewhat strange to argue for a decentered notion of Wallace, a writer whose moral vision and earnestness were expressly tied to his notion of what it means to be human. Yet, at the same time, nobody understood better than Wallace the difficulty and sometimes pain of self-consciously trying to assemble a unified front, a public persona, Eliot's "face to meet the faces that you meet"[15] that contemporary society demands of us but that, if we reflect upon the attempt to do so, makes us realize that the heady, roiling mix of emotions, memories, images, desires, and dreams that we daily imprint with the impermanent stamp of what we call a "self" is anything but cohesive. Both the tragic ends of *Infinite Jest*'s Hal, trapped inside his own mind and unable to communicate, and of the narrator of "Good Old Neon," a suicide who believes himself a lifelong fraud, remind us of the dangers not only of falling prey to presenting an external self that we imagine others want to see but in believing that the internal self that is not fixed is somehow unreal or inauthentic. In turn, we ought not to embalm Wallace as what once was but instead point out that Wallace is still "becoming-Wallace." If in the process Wallace comes to contradict himself, then let it be of the Whitmanian variety, both generative and generous.

For the opening of the Ransom Center Archives has complicated, if not outright disproven, a Unified Wallace Theory. The archive now "supplements" Wallace's published work and has revealed Wallace's composition process to have often occurred piecemeal and over a long period of time in which different projects overlapped one another. Thus, the fact that *The Pale*

King is an unfinished novel should not be an occasion to lament what may have been but instead should remind us that the oeuvre of any writer is always unfinished and never truly complete, even when it appears so. Every oeuvre is really just an hors d'oeuvre.[16] *The Pale King*, portions of which, according to Wallace's editor Michael Pietsch, were left by Wallace for potential publication and arranged into book form by Pietsch with the help of Wallace's notes, suggests a final meta-authorial move by Wallace that lays bare the writing and drafting process as pure process. Wallace thereby calls attention to the writer–editor relationship, ultimately accepting it as one based on trust and mutual exchange – and one that takes place between the living and dead. All of this is to say that our notion of Wallace's writing has been complicated in intriguing ways. It is, in Deleuze and Guattari's terms, more rhizomatic than arborescent and, like *The Pale King*, could be said to be a kind of assemblage as opposed to a proper book.[17]

It is no surprise, then, that the question of mapping Wallace's career and thematic development is a concern of recent studies, such as David Hering's *Fiction and Form*, which employs a "genetic 'map'" and abundant archival material in demonstrating how Wallace's composition process mirrored his concern with creating dialogic texts.[18] While these maps may not be as wild as a Wallace-without-Organs, each nevertheless reflects upon and traces new and compelling genealogies in and throughout the once-familiar Wallace narrative terrain that begins with the young, earnest anti-ironic and anti-cynical crusader and ends with the more mature, ethically and politically reflective Wallace. In *The Unspeakable Failures of David Foster Wallace*, for example, Clare Hayes-Brady argues for the nonteleological character of Wallace's work by looking at its ideological and aesthetic "failures" that are, paradoxically, ultimately generative, productive, and make the work "coherently plural."[19] For Hayes-Brady, "Perhaps, ironically, the central feature of this coherence is the failure to cohere, characterized by a persistent, multifaceted and systemic resistance to conclusion."[20] Similarly, Jeffrey Severs's extraordinary *David Foster Wallace's Balancing Books: Fictions of Value* argues that the inability of Wallace's fiction to achieve "balanced states" does not preclude the balancing acts that they attempt to achieve in weighing neoliberalism's narrow prescription of value as tied solely to economic exchange against the value to be found in shared spaces of communicative transaction, where one might learn "what other forms of valuing (and thus loving) there are."[21] Severs's Wallace, the most thoroughly historicized Wallace to date, is thus "more attuned to the history of political economy than previous critics have noticed" and the seemingly radical thematic shifts in Wallace's later work actually "masks an ongoing value project."[22] And in *Global Wallace: David Foster Wallace and World Literature*, Lucas Thompson makes claim to "a revisionist account of Wallace's work" by radically deterritorializing our notion of Wallace's writing and its national literary roots through a rigorous comparative examination of the rhizomatic influence of world literature on Wallace, including the French existentialists, nineteenth-century Russian writers, and twentieth-century Latin American authors, among others.[23] Wallace's corpus, it seems, is still evolving, still becoming, and in the hands of the conscientious critic, it is truly an *exquisite corpus*.[24]

Getting Yourself Organ-izized

The overall structure of this companion provides both a substantive introduction to Wallace's most important works and themes and enhances existing critical conversations about them, thus allowing different Wallaces to emerge. To this end, Part One considers Wallace's work in his immediate present, the longer literary past, and as it has resonated since his passing; Parts Two and Three present helpful overviews of his major and minor works, both the fiction and nonfiction; and Part Four offers several frameworks for understanding some of Wallace's most significant themes and concerns.

Part One begins with Marshall Boswell's essay "Wallace and Generation X," which provides a thorough cultural and historical grounding of Wallace's work by exploring his relationship to Generation X and its attitude toward pop culture, politics, and literature. Boswell traces the emergence and history of Gen X and reveals the ways in which Wallace's early work tapped into a zeitgeist detectable in both mainstream and so-called alternative culture that traded in irony and at times a near encyclopedic knowledge of pop-cultural references.

Significantly broadening the scope of inquiry, Andrew Hoberek's essay situates Wallace's work within a longer history and tradition of American literature. According to Hoberek, Wallace can be seen as one of a number of contemporary authors (such as Cormac McCarthy, Toni Morrison, and Stephen King) who helped to renew the American romance tradition as famously defined by Richard Chase. Hoberek discovers, on the one hand, thematic resonances between Wallace's work and that of Willa Cather, Flannery O'Connor, Hawthorne, Melville, and Emerson. On the other, Hoberek finds echoes of Whitman and the Beats in *Infinite Jest*'s messy style and argues that the novel's excessive footnotes, digressions, and generic hybridity place the novel in the tradition of the encyclopedic narrative.

Closing this section is Lee Konstantinou's provocative exploration of what he calls Wallace's "bad influence," or the way in which Wallace's seductive public persona and literary style has effected a generation of writers, critics, friends, and family who seek, in one way or another and whether they admire Wallace's work or reject it, to break free from Wallace's seemingly gravitational pull. Konstantinou explores literary reactions by Karen Green, Jonathan Franzen, Mary Karr, Jonathan Lethem, Jennifer Egan, and others, and charts the different ways in which they negotiate Wallace's influence. Indeed, Wallace's messy, maximalist style and uniquely crafted vernacular persona, Konstantinou shows, have given rise to a veritable contemporary subgenre in which the roman à clef becomes the roman à Wallace.

Part Two focuses on Wallace's story collections and nonfiction. It begins with Matthew Luter's essay on Wallace's earliest work, *Broom of the System* and *Girl with Curious Hair*. Luter sees these texts as indicative of Wallace's struggle toward becoming a mature writer as Wallace incorporates ideas from Ludwig Wittgenstein and Thomas Pynchon in *Broom* and seeks to overcome and challenge the fiction of John Barth, Brett Easton Ellis, and others in *Girl*. Nevertheless, Luter argues that these works are not simply a rehearsal for the more mature work to come but complete works unto themselves.

Building upon feminist and gender readings of Wallace's work, Adam Kelly reads *Brief Interviews with Hideous Men,* with its catalogue of misogynistic and verbally dominating male characters, through the lens of French feminists such as Julia Kristeva, Luce Irigaray, and Hélène Cixous, whose psychoanalytic theories of a feminine logic and writing challenge male phallocentricism. Analyzing a number of stories, such as "B.I. #28," "Forever Overhead," "B.I. #20," and "Octet," Kelly deploys these theorists' concepts – including Kristeva's "abject" and Cixous's *feminine écriture* – to suggest how, although women are silenced in the collection, a feminine logic of writing often destructures the narrative, blurs boundaries and hierarchies, and calls attention to the relationship between (male) language and mastery.

David Hering's essay on Wallace's final story collection, *Oblivion,* explores the theme of "embodied suffering," both mental and physical, with reference to two direct philosophical influences on the collection, E. M. Cioran and Nietzsche. Drawing together Cioran's idea that "consciousness is nature's nightmare" with Nietzsche's notion of active forgetting, or "oblivion," Hering notes how "disembodied oblivion is positioned against a sense of embodied suffering" in stories such as "Mister Squishy," "The Soul Is Not a Smithy," "Another Pioneer," "The Suffering Channel," and "Oblivion." Despite such "scenarios of failed oblivion and self-aggrandizing suffering" that typify Wallace's most pessimistic book, Hering argues that "Good Old Neon" offers "a communicative model of shared consciousness" that suggests the possibility of transcending the self and the nightmare of consciousness.

Jeffrey Severs's overview of Wallace's major nonfiction focuses on the evolution from *A Supposedly Fun Thing I'll Never Do Again* (1997) to

Consider the Lobster (2005) and the ways in which Wallace treated subjects such as aesthetics, consumerism, ethics, and politics in his reviews, essays, and journalism. Severs detects "Wallace's own fiction being mapped out in negative" in many of his early book reviews, provides close readings of Wallace's "tours of outlandish consumer spectacle" in "Getting Away From Already Being Pretty Much Away from It All" and "A Supposedly Fun Thing I'll Never Do Again," and argues that what Wallace called his "service essays" in *Consider*, such as "Consider the Lobster," "Host," and "Up, Simba," comprise a "late-career effort to place civic questions at the front of the reader's mind."

Part Three contains essays on Wallace's two major novels. First, Mary K. Holland, refusing to see *Infinite Jest* as the be-all-and-end-all of Wallace's oeuvre, argues that the novel is "at once pinnacle, pivot point, and through line." Holland finds *Infinite Jest*'s depiction of a media-saturated society, in which communication is hampered by irony and solipsism is the result, as continuing themes from Wallace's earlier work. Yet the novel also weds these themes to innovative formal and structural techniques, such as recursivity, fragmentation, open-endedness, the use of multiple points of view, an experimental authorial/narrative voice via the "wraith-narrator," and a penchant for encyclopedic narrative. Despite all of this, Holland nonetheless posits Wallace as a "radically" realist writer, who meant to reproduce the data-infused, chaotic milieu of contemporary life and what it feels like to live in it. Following Holland's situating of *Infinite Jest* as pivot and through line, Clare Hayes-Brady reads Wallace's unfinished, posthumous novel, *The Pale King* (2011), as a mature work that both continues and rejects the themes of his earlier work as it takes up the subjects of attention, boredom, and choice. Structuring her reading through John Keats's "La Belle Dame Sans Merci," an influence on the novel, Hayes-Brady argues that Wallace presents a new-form of heroism for the contemporary age, one that "combines the figure of the Romantic hero with that of the ironic hero" and makes for a "reflective Romanticism."

The essays collected in Part Four address and respond to some of the most important and recurring topics in Wallace studies and augment existing critical conversations. Robert L. McLaughlin's essay opens the section with an outline of Wallace's expressly stated aesthetic principles to move beyond postmodern literature, cynicism, and culturally destructive irony and to replace it with a literature that would "relieve and redeem" instead. McLaughlin presents two of Wallace's most metafictional stories, "B.I. # 20" and "Octet," as well as the treatment of AA discourse in *Infinite Jest*, as cases in which Wallace aspires to create a sincere, communicative relationship between reader and author that nevertheless respond to the lessons of self-reflexive and self-aware postmodern notions of language. Wallace's aesthetic thus emerges not merely as a penchant for rehabilitating postmodern metafictional techniques but as a moral stance on the value and function of literature as well.

Wallace's fiction was not about aesthetics alone, however, and Andrew Warren argues not only that Wallace was long interested in political ideals and theory but also that his work has always been political, though often in an indirect fashion. While recognizing Wallace's belief in "American-style liberalism," Warren conducts readings of *Infinite Jest* and *The Pale King* through Étienne Balibar's notion of *"politics' other scene,"* or the "space between ideology's imaginary and economics' real social function." Wallace, in Warren's account, engages in *"politics' other scene"* throughout his fiction and nonfiction in his imagining of new communities, new ways of rendering the peripheral sensible, and in creating new literary forms and styles.

Matt Mullins's essay on Wallace as a writer who took matters of spirituality seriously adds to a growing critical concern as to how religion and spirituality are figured in Wallace's work. Mullins argues that Wallace's spiritual vision is exemplified in "three themes shaped largely by Christian practices voided of their particular meaning: conversion, worship, and community." Mullins shows how Wallace's concerns with empathy, solipsism, and belief in something larger than the self are often figured in and through these Christian practices, thereby forging a secularized form of spirituality.

Lucas Thompson's essay on Wallace and race urges readers not to dismiss Wallace for his problematic representations of race nor to exonerate him, but to keep a balanced view of how race plays out in his work. Through readings of Wardine's section of *Infinite Jest* and the essays "Authority and American Usage" and "A Supposedly Fun Thing I'll Never Do Again," among other texts, Thompson notes that as troublesome as Wallace's treatment of race can be, it "often shifts the interpretive demands relating to issues of race onto the reader." Thompson also links Wallace's tendency to universalize a (readerly) subject to the author's reading of Joseph Campbell's pop anthropology in which the world's myths are whipped up into a single, essentialized topping and racial, ethnic, and cultural differences are elided – leaving Wallace's work open to charges of colorblind racism. For, as Thompson puts it, "while this strategy makes his work accessible to a diverse audience, it also leads to a problematic approach to racial difference."

Wallace's problematic take on race also arises in Jurrit Daalder's essay on Wallace and regionalism, which analyzes Wallace's ambivalent use of the "Heartland Myth" in his work. Daalder places Wallace in a tradition of Midwestern regionalists, typified by the "Main Street U.S.A." of Sinclair

Lewis and the sympathetic grotesques of Sherwood Anderson, and draws from archival material to aid his readings of "The View from Mrs. Thompson's" and *The Pale King* to show how Wallace at times both reinforced and challenged the Heartland Myth. Wallace's imagined Midwest ultimately emerges as an ambivalent intertextual space or an example of what Daalder calls "geographic metafiction."

Finally, Joseph Tabbi expands upon earlier critics' identification of Wallace's *Infinite Jest* as a systems novel (characterized by "first-order cybernetics theory") in an enlightening reading of *The Pale King* as an instance of "second-order cybernetics theory," which is distinguishable from first-order theory in its move "away from informatic and dispositional communication toward more cognitive exchanges." Drawing upon the thought of Niklas Luhmann, Tabbi argues that Wallace's characters do not actually communicate with one another, for even the most seemingly sincere and open moments of communication or autoaffection are entangled with numerous semiautonomous systems that end up "employing human consciousness for mostly operational, not communicative purposes." Such a surprising and provocative assertion contradicts Wallace's, and many of his critics', claims regarding the restorative and communicative function of Wallace's fiction and provides potential openings for new and radical posthuman readings of Wallace that move away from the more humanist or guarded posthuman readings of his oeuvre.

Every Wallace Story Is a Ghost Story: or, Don't Forget Wallace Likes Investigating Various Ectoplasmic States

Whatever the fantasy of Wallace that forms in our minds when we read his texts, whatever the Wallaces that might be traced in this companion's pages and elsewhere, every story about Wallace is finally a ghost story. Reflecting upon Wallace's use of ghosts in his fiction – such as the strange wraith-narrator of James Incandenza in *Infinite Jest*, the séance-like evocation by a nested narrator of the dead Neal's voice in "Good Old Neon," and the two specters that appear in *The Pale King* – David Hering keenly argues that Wallace's ghostly authorial presence refutes post-structuralism's "death of the author" by creating a dialogical text aimed toward communicating openly with the reader.[25] Wallace is thus present in his absence. And this is precisely because of Wallace's belief in language as engendering a "living transaction" between people and serving as a "medium," according to Andrew Warren, not only in terms of communication but also as an "occult" vehicle for the author's ghostly presence.[26]

In other words, the author's resurrection means the reader isn't exactly alone anymore, for even the writer ends up with the reader, "down here quivering in the mud of the trench with the rest of us," as "Octet" puts it in an image that recalls the series of isolated mud-bound bodies in Beckett's *How It Is*.[27] The voices of Beckett's catalogue of sufferers, however, must endlessly address the self that will (have) be(en), and their incessant chattering is heard by the sequential self alone. The voices spiraling in the heads of Wallace's caged characters, who exist in media-maximalized cultures instead of abstract minimalist tableaux, are nevertheless ultimately aimed by Wallace to point away from such interiority. Wallace turns the inward outward. Channeling Wallace through Beckett, we might say: I can't go on, you must go on, *let's* go on.

So let's do this. How should one properly approach Wallace's corpus, contribute to this dialogue that seems at once part séance, part communion, and part wake? Who ends up hosting whom? It's the stuff of emperors and ice cream, paradoxes and oxymorons. Perhaps it is only a dream, then, to create a Wallace-without-Organs, just as it is to imagine that you can slip into an/other's skin as easily as you would an old pair of sneakers to go walk a mile, for such identification may simply be narcissism, as Wallace knew well. An ethically aware criticism is one way to proceed, of course. Because in the end Wallace's writing is not merely a "living transaction between humans." It is the "transaction" itself that lives on and courses through bodies – living or not, human and institutional – that it traverses, connects, and communes in myriad ways. This exchange, it turns out, has already been made, perhaps when you first picked up a book by Wallace, or after you read a page or two, or as you looked up from a word or a passage that resonated deeply within you, that settled softly under the skin. And suddenly Wallace is there as well. So come on in, take a load off, and turn the page. Welcome. We've been waiting for you. It's time to share a few words.

Notes

1. David Foster Wallace, "An Expanded Interview with David Foster Wallace," by Larry McCaffery in Stephen J. Burn (ed.), *Conversations with David Foster Wallace* (Jackson: University of Mississippi, 2012), p. 41.
2. Wallace provides a thorough sounding of his thoughts on the poststructuralist ideas about "the death of the author" – which he ultimately rejects – in "Greatly Exaggerated," his 1992 review of H. L. Hix's *Morte d'Author: An Autopsy*, collected in *A Supposedly Fun Thing I'll Never Do Again: Essays and Arguments* (Boston: Little, Brown, 1997), pp. 138–145.
3. David Foster Wallace, "Borges on the Couch," in *Both Flesh and Not: Essays* (New York: Little, Brown, 2012), p. 285.

4. David Foster Wallace, "Joseph Frank's Dostoevsky," in *Consider the Lobster* (New York: Little, Brown, 2005), p. 259, n. 7.

5. While the quote is from Wallace's review, "The Empty Plenum: David Markson's *Wittgenstein's Mistress*" in *Both Flesh and Not*, p. 74, it clearly applies to his own artistic vision, as D. T. Max makes clear in *Every Love Story Is A Ghost Story: A Life of David Foster Wallace* (New York: Viking, 2012), p. 172.

6. David Foster Wallace, "E Unibus Pluram: Television and U.S. Fiction," in the *Review of Contemporary Fiction*, 13.2 (Summer 1993), pp. 184, 192.

7. David Foster Wallace, *This Is Water: Some Thoughts, Delivered on a Significant Occasion, about Living a Compassionate Life* (New York: Little, Brown, 2009), p. 54.

8. See Adam Kelly, "The Death of the Author and the Birth of a Discipline" in the *Irish Journal of American Studies*, http://ijas.iaas.ie/index.php/article-david-foster-wallace-the-death-of-the-author-and-the-birth-of-a-discipline/; and Ed Finn's "Becoming Yourself: The Afterlife of Reception," in Samuel Cohen and Lee Konstantinou (eds.), *The Legacy of David Foster Wallace* (Iowa City: University of Iowa Press, 2012), pp. 151–176.

9. For Emersonian and transcendentalist connections, see Paul Giles's "All Swallowed Up: David Foster Wallace and American Literature" in Samuel Cohen and Lee Konstantinou (eds.), *The Legacy of David Foster Wallace*, (Iowa City: University of Iowa Press, 2012), pp. 3–22. For a detailed look at William James's influence on Wallace, see David H. Evans's "The Chains of Not Choosing: Free Will and Faith in William James and David Foster Wallace," in Marshall Boswell and Stephen J. Burn (eds.), *A Companion to David Foster Wallace Studies* (New York: Palgrave Macmillan, 2013), pp. 171–189. Also see my essay, "Wallaceward the American Literature Survey Course Makes its Way," in Stephen J. Burn and Mary Holland (eds.), *Approaches to Teaching David Foster Wallace* (MLA, forthcoming).

10. Christian Lorentzen, "The Rewriting of David Foster Wallace" in *Vulture* (June 30, 2015), www.vulture.com/2015/06/rewriting-of-david-foster-wallace.html, accessed 15, February 2017. See also Max's account of Wallace's tumultuous relationship with Mary Karr in *Every Love Story*.

11. McCaffery, "An Expanded Interview," p. 34.

12. Ibid., p. 22.

13. David Hering, *David Foster Wallace: Fiction and Form* (New York: Bloomsbury, 2016), p. 8.

14. I am following a line of flight here from Gilles Deleuze and Felix Guattari's notion of the "body-without-organs" in *Anti-Oedipus: Capitalism and Schizophrenia* (Minneapolis: University of Minnesota Press, 1983) and in *A Thousand Plateaus* (Minneapolis: University of Minnesota Press, 1987) to call attention to the potential "unorganized" or virtual dimensions that underlie, so to speak, various organizing bodies or principles that shape Wallace and his work. Thus, one might remember that we can always "free," dis-organize, deterritorialize, or virtually multiply "Wallace" and his corpus against the seemingly unifying force of the author function as various discourses or institutions might seek to shape and calcify it.

15. T. S. Eliot, "The Love Song of J. Alfred Prufrock," in *The Waste Land, Prufrock, and Other Poems* (Mineola, NY: Dover, 1998), l. 27.

16. See Jacques Derrida's "Hors Livre," translated by Barbara Johnson as "Outwork, Prefacing" in *Dissemination* (Chicago: University of Chicago Press, 1981), pp. 1–59.
17. Deleuze and Guattari, *A Thousand Plateaus*, pp. 3–25.
18. Hering, *Fiction and Form*, p. 10. In addition, see Stephen J. Burns's "A Paradigm for the Life of Consciousness: *The Pale King*," in Marshall Boswell (ed.), *David Foster Wallace and "The Long Thing": New Essays on the Novels* (New York: Bloomsbury, 2014), pp. 149–169, and D. T. Max's *Every Love Story*.
19. Clare Hayes-Brady, *The Unspeakable Failures of David Foster Wallace: Language, Identity, Resistance* (New York: Bloomsbury, 2016), p. 4.
20. Ibid., p. 8.
21. Jeffrey Severs, *David Foster Wallace's Balancing Books: Fictions of Value* (New York: Columbia University Press, 2017), p. 31.
22. Ibid., p. 5.
23. Lucas Thompson, *Global Wallace: David Foster Wallace and World Literature* (New York: Bloomsbury, 2017), p. 11.
24. An "exquisite corpse" is a creative exercise or activity developed by the surrealists. It refers to when any number of persons collaborate on a single text, whether literary, visual, etc., by each adding something sequentially to a text they cannot see. Wallace participated in an exquisite corpse, *The Fifth Column: A Novel*, in 1996, although each author was able to see the text immediately preceding her section. See "David Foster Wallace: The Fifth Column: Week Eleven," *The Village Voice* 41.7 (Feb. 13, 1996), pp. 50–51. Of course, critics do something similar in regard to the author's corpus.
25. See Hering's *Fiction and Form*, pp. 5–40, 140–147. For a succinct summary of this growing conversation on the wraith-narrator, also see Mary Holland's essay in this *Companion*.
26. See Andrew Warren's "Modeling Community and Narrative in *Infinite Jest* and *The Pale King*," in Boswell (ed.), *David Foster Wallace and "The Long Thing*," p. 79.
27. David Foster Wallace, *Brief Interviews with Hideous Men* (Boston: Little, Brown, 1999), p. 160.

PART I

Historical and Cultural Contexts

I

MARSHALL BOSWELL

Slacker Redemption: Wallace and Generation X

For the last ten years or so, Wallace critics have tended to regard the one-two punch of "E Unibus Pluram: Television and U.S. Fiction" and the 1993 *Contemporary Fiction* interview with Larry McCaffery as David Foster Wallace's attempt both to situate himself firmly in the tradition of American postmodern fiction, a tradition represented by such luminaries as John Barth, Thomas Pynchon, Robert Coover, and Don DeLillo, while also carving out a new direction for postmodernism that simultaneously honored postmodern self-reflexivity and affirmed what Wallace famously called "single-entendre principles."[1] After the publication of *Infinite Jest* (1996), one could not help but read "E Unibus Pluram" as a blueprint for the unique mixture of self-consciousness and dogged earnestness that characterized Wallace's masterpiece, a doubleness that marked the novel as a clear advance in the development of American postmodernism. Yet as sound and useful as that reading has been, it has nevertheless excised those two key documents in the Wallace corpus from the concrete particulars of their historical and cultural movement. And for those readers who first encountered "E Unibus Pluram" and the McCaffery interview in the pages of the summer 1993 issue of the *Review of Contemporary Fiction,* there was very little sense that David Wallace was setting the groundwork for a masterpiece still three years in the distance: rather, Wallace was talking about, and bringing a fresh and exhilarating perspective on, our contemporary moment. And that contemporary moment was the late 1980s and early 1990s, when the Reagan-Bush era yielded to the Clinton years; when the recently collapsed Berlin Wall compelled neoconservative political theorist Francis Fukuyama to declare that history as we know it was over; when the generation that followed the baby boomers was finally emerging into a tentative adulthood and acquiring a coherent cultural identity to boot, an identity crystalized by the term Generation X; and when alternative culture, represented by white rock bands such as R.E.M., The Cure, and the Replacements, and by indie filmmakers such as Stephen Soderberg, Spike Lee, and Quentin Tarrantino, was about to take over the mainstream. Although twenty-first-century US culture is now indelibly changed and marked by Wallace's intervention, I wish to reverse thrust here and resituate Wallace in the culture from which he emerged, and I also wish to contextualize his work before *Infinite Jest* in relation to postmodern fiction and mainstream and alternative popular culture of the late 1980s and early 1990s.

Wallace was born in 1962. As such, he must be reckoned on the older end of the Generation X spectrum. Most cultural theorists and social scientists identify Generation Xers as born between the early 1960s and the mid-to-late 1970s. As the generation that immediately followed the baby boomers, Gen Xers were originally dubbed "babybusters or boomerangers" before novelist Douglas Coupland applied the already existent term Generation X, which was in fact the name of Billy Idol's original late 1970s punk band, to his own generation in his novel of the same name. The *Oxford English Dictionary* defines Generation Xers as "a generation of young people (esp. North Americans reaching adulthood in the 1980s and 1990s) perceived to be disaffected, directionless, or irresponsible, and reluctant to participate in society." In her pop economics study *Slackernomics* (2008), Lisa Chamberlain provides an account of Generation X's birth that is fairly representative and hence can serve here as a shorthand way into the world that Wallace inherited. As the baby boomers settled into middle age and embodied the very same establishment they once sought to overturn, a backlash against the 1960s counterculture resulted in the mainstream "reasserting itself with a vengeance: anti-hippy, -feminist, -homo – against all identity politics in general – but mostly against the notion of anticonsumerism and antimaterialism."[2] Earnestness, now identified with the discredited politics of the 1960s, gave way to cynicism. Generation Xer's, the inheritors of this new ethos, were offered two competing responses: they could embrace the new yuppie dominant, a class represented in Chamberlain's account by *Family Ties* character Alex P. Keaton, a teenage conservative heartthrob who, week after week, made a national mockery of his parents' 1960s liberal pieties; or they could reject the Reaganized mainstream for the apathetic periphery inhabited by Coupland's disaffected slackers, where yuppie success was scorned in favor of low-paying, low-ambition "McJobs," to use Coupland's own syllogism, and "pop culture" was elevated to a form of intellectual currency.[3]

The latter demographic encompasses Wallace's early readership, which he identified in 1993 as "people more or less like me, in their twenties or thirties ... who've been raised with U.S. commercial culture and are engaged with it and informed by and fascinated with it but still hungry for something commercial art can't provide."[4] Wallace was hardly alone in noting his generation's keen, and not entirely ironic, fascination with US commercial culture. In *Generation X: Americans Aged 18 to 34,* a 2001 reference work on consumer trends, author Susan Mitchell found that "popular culture is 'The Arts'" for this generation.[5] Wallace himself observed, in "E Unibus Pluram," that the "U.S. generation born after 1950 is the first for whom television was something to be lived with instead of just looked at"; he goes on to say that "where we are different [from our fathers] is that we have no memory of a world without such electric definition."[6] In a convoluted recursion that sounds like a David Foster Wallace invention, by the early 1990s Hollywood script writers had clued in to Generation X's love-hate relationship with the disposable artifacts of pop culture and began portraying that attitude in such self-conscious "Gen X" films as *Reality Bites* (1994), in which the characters reference everything from School House Rock to the Brady Bunch, and *Singles* (1992), Cameron Crowe's grunge-era romantic comedy, and in *Friends,* in which the character Chandler Bing, at least in the show's early seasons, was clearly intended to embody that peculiar Gen X creation, the encyclopedic pop-culture ironist. As Rob Owens observes in *GenXTV: The Brady Bunch to Melrose Place* (1999), "The use of pop culture references is the biggest difference between *Friends* and its predecessors ... This device is clearly a trademark of Generation X."[7]

While such mainstream trafficking in pop-culture references sounds old hat now – in fact, it is the very air we breathe – the trend was still *new* in the early 1990s and represented a shift in attitude toward television and pop culture that Wallace was instrumental in capturing and analyzing. And, as is usually the case, whereas popular culture itself was late in picking up on this shift, the fiction of Wallace's generation, and Wallace's own early work as well, was already embodying the new pop-culture reality, as witnessed by *The Broom of the System*'s (1987) scattered references to *The Bob Newhart Show* and *The Munsters* and the "convex mirror" preoccupation with television that anchored his first story collection, *Girl with Curious Hair* (1989), whose fictional representations of such pop-culture figures as Pat Sajak, Alex Trebek, and David Lettermen were intended, Wallace explained in the book's elaborate copyright-page disclaimer, not to "denote, or pretend to private information about, actual 3-D persons, living, dead, or otherwise" but are "meant only to denote figures, images, the stuff of collective dreams."[8] As a testament to how groundbreaking Wallace's pop-infused stories were, the book was held up for publication for nearly a year as lawyers for Norton tried to work out the possible libelous implications of fictionalizing ostensibly "real" celebrities.[9] "The belief that pop images are basically just mimetic devices," he argues in "E Unibus Pluram," "is one of the attitudes that separates most U.S. fiction writers under c. 40 from the writerly generation that precedes us, and designs our grad-school curricula."[10] Wallace goes on to describe a workshop wherein his professor insisted that the students' stories should avoid "trendy mass-popular-media" references, at which point "trans-generational discourse broke down."[11]

What was particularly prescient in the context of the early 1990s was Wallace's analysis of the complex love-hate relationship members of Generation X had to their own encyclopedic knowledge of, and affection for, the pop culture of their childhoods. As he observes early in "E Unibus Pluram," "much of the pleasure my generation takes from television lies in making fun of it. But you have to remember that younger Americans grew up as much with people's disdain for TV as we did with TV itself."[12] And, as Wallace's now famous argument has it, lavishing derision on disposable entertainment that one nevertheless loves leads to a lonely form of meta-watching that is the source of "a great despair and stasis in U.S. culture" that for "aspiring fiction writers ... pose[s] especially terrible problems."[13] He was also the first serious social critic to have argued that, by the early 1990s, television had found a successful way to address the otherwise troubling fact that its most sought-after advertising target – namely, that cherished 18 to 34 demographic, which in 1993 meant Generation X – watched television with tender, ironic derision. The solution was for television, and televised adver-tising, to apply that same brand of ironic, self-conscious derision to itself. Wallace was also the first serious social critic to connect his generation's brand of ironic metawatching, and television's then new embrace of self-consciousness, to "post WWII literature, namely U.S. postmodernism." In his most ringing statement of the situation as he saw it, Wallace writes, "For at least ten years now, television has been ingeniously absorbing, homogenizing, and re-presenting the very same cynical postmodern aesthetic that was once the best alternative to the appeal of Low, over-easy, mass-marketed narrative."[14]

But Wallace was not content with merely locating the source of his gen-eration's discontent. Rather, at the exact moment when US commercial culture discovered, and began exploiting, what was unique about its prized demographic – the irony, the disaffection, the obsession with pop culture – Wallace was looking for a way forward. In this effort he was certainly not alone. Once again, writers of literary fiction were well ahead of the zeitgeist curve. Richard Powers, in his 1988 sophomore novel *Prisoner's Dilemma*, accepts, and also finds problematic, the fact that irony is the primary mode for thoughtful people confronting the hollow simulacrum that is contempor-ary existence, a situation one character defines as "the antieverything infection"[15] For Powers, one way forward was to adopt an attitude he terms "Crackpot Realism," whereby one realistically confronts the enormity of late twentieth-century desolation while willfully, and naïvely, pushing through one's default irony toward a more redemptive approach to contemporary existence. Similarly, Jonathan Franzen's second novel, *Strong Motion* (1992), risks sentiment and earnestness in its startlingly direct and angry approach to such complex political issues as gender equality and ecoterrorism. The novel's style also represented a clear break from that of his first novel, *The Twenty-Seventh City* (1988), wherein, according to Franzen's own description, the author sent his rhetorical bombs "in a Jiffy-Pak mailer of irony and understatement."[16]

Both novelists, whom Wallace overtly identified as his closest peers, were seeking to embody the irony and disaffection of their generation while also looking for a way to reaffirm what Franzen called "humane values." Franzen makes this affirmation in an essay Wallace commissioned him to write as part of a 1996 special issue of the *Review of Contemporary Fiction* devoted to "The Future of Fiction." There, Franzen lists four articles of faith that characterize "serious fiction": a belief in the individual; a "pessimistic" conviction that things will not improve any time soon; a strong "commitment to mediating between the author's subjectivity and the world"; and an affirmation of "honesty," "responsibility," "love," and "significance," the latter of which constitute "humane values."[17] In short, Wallace's innovative call for a fiction that combines self-reflexivity and earnestness, that joins "cynicism" and "naiveté," was by no means a lone cry from the wilderness.

Whereas both *Prisoner's Dilemma* and *The Twenty-Seventh City* explore the limitations of neoliberalism in the context of real political change, Wallace's early work is conspicuously apolitical, and in this aspect he can also be seen to embody a uniquely Gen X ethos. In the context of our current hyperpartisan, thoroughly politicized era, it is easy to overlook the fact that Wallace's ascent to the top ranks of the US literary establishment took place during a rare, brief, and, as these kinds of things always turn out to be, false period of relative historical complacency. The collapse of the Soviet Union occurred two years after the 1987 appearance of *The Broom of the System*; by September 11, 2001, Wallace had published *Infinite Jest*, *A Supposedly Fun Thing I'll Never Do Again* (1997), and *Brief Interviews with Hideous Men* (1999). Beginning with his *Rolling Stone* essay on the 9/11 attacks, "The View from Mrs. Thompsons,'" and continuing through to his blistering portrait of right-wing radio host John Ziegler and, of course, his unfinished novel *The Pale King* (2011), Wallace's work became more political, and more pointed, the political partisanship of the new century replacing pop-culture irony in his work as the source of our isolation and failure to find real meaning and purpose in our life. Had his work not developed and matured in these various ways,

Wallace might have joined his bête noire Mark Leyner among the ranks of forgotten writers-of-the-moment. The key point is that, before 9/11, his work treated politics, if at all, as *farce*. What's more, both of his first two novels are set in an imagined future, quarantining them even further from direct engagement with the contemporary politics of their time. And it was in that precise atmosphere of relative calm in the West that Wallace, a middle-class white male, had the luxury to work out his ideas about information overload, addiction, entertainment, solipsism, and loneliness.

Numerous Wallace scholars have already contextualized Wallace's critique of late 1980s hip irony against the backdrop of Francis Fukuyama's neoconservative tome, *The End of History and the Last Man* (1992), which expanded upon a 1989 essay of the same name that first appeared in *National Interest*. Both Samuel Cohen's *After the End of History: American Fiction in the 1990s* (2009) and Lee Konstantinou's *Cool Characters: Irony and American Fiction* (2016) survey the work of Wallace and his 1990s literary peers within the context of Fukuyama's optimistic reading of the Soviet Union's collapse. Put briefly, Fukuyama reads the end of the Cold War and the so-called triumph of liberal democracy as the fulfillment of a Hegelian concept of history – that is, history as "a single, coherent, evolutionary process, when taking into account the experience of all people in all times."[18] Liberal capitalism had won, while all other models had been obliterated as ineffective and no longer operative. Although we know from D. T. Max that Wallace did vote for Reagan once, no one is arguing that Wallace was a neoconservative. Rather, Fukuyama's thesis helps us understand the prevailing national mood that inspired Wallace to imagine Johnny Gentle's O.N.A.N. As Konstantinou puts it, "When history ends, we face nothing less than 'centuries of boredom'"; and that aura of boredom led, at the time, to a broad sense that "life in post-industrial democracies [was] listless and without flavor; loneliness and a kind of bland sadness were all one could expect of the new world order."[19] What is equally emblematic of this time period is Wallace's approach to history and politics. Whether or not he imagined himself writing fiction after the End of History, as Fukuyama and Hegel have it, it is nevertheless true that he tended to view both history and politics as theater, and, even more important, as something *manufactured* in the absence of real historical change, real political exigencies.

In *The Broom of the System*, for instance, politics rears its head in only one instance, namely, via the creation by Raymond Zusatz, the governor of Ohio in Wallace's fictionalized 1990, of the Great Ohio Desert, or G.O.D. for short. Worried that "the state is getting soft" and becoming "one big suburb and industrial park and mall," Zusatz proposes that the state construct a vast desert made of black sand to serve as "a point of savage reference for the good people of Ohio. A place to fear and love. A blasted region.... A place without malls. An Other for Ohio's self."[20] Similarly, Konstantinou has shown us the remarkable degree to which Wallace's postmillennium O.N.A.N. reflects Fukuyama's post–Cold War vision. In a passage Konstantinou also quotes, Wallace contextualizes the world of *Infinite Jest* as a "post-Soviet and -Jihad era when – somehow even worse – there was no real Foreign Menace of any real unified potency to hate and fear, and the US sort of turned on itself and its own philosophical fatigue and hideous redolent wastes with a spasm of panicked rage that in retrospect seems possible only in a time of geopolitical supremacy."[21] Against this Fukuyama-esque backdrop emerges President and former lounge singer Johnny Gentle, who is "totally up-front about seeing American renewal as an essentially aesthetic affair," and who, once in office, must manufacture, in the absence of a genuine global enemy, "some cohesion-renewing Other," which, in the novel, turns out, comically, to be Canadians.[22]

Although it is now almost axiomatic to regard President Johnny Gentle as an eerily prophetic harbinger of President Donald Trump, the Gentle material, when read in the context of the first Clinton administration, discloses the degree to which politics at that time was viewed as largely inconsequential, a view best typified by the fact that Bill Clinton's 1997 State of the Union address was broadcast on split screen to make room for the conclusion of the O. J. Simpson civil trial. This same sense of inconsequentiality prevailed all the way until September 11, 2001. The most pressing story on cable news networks on September 10, 2001, the day before the attacks on the World Trade Center towers and the Pentagon, involved the murder of a DC intern named Chandra Levy and the possibility, breathlessly floated for months by cable news pundits and legal celebrities, that her murderer might have been Democratic Senator Gary Condit. The story preoccupied the cable news networks 24/7 for the entire summer and early fall of 2001 and instantly disappeared from the national consciousness on September 11. The *Time* magazine front-page story during the week of September 11 was titled "Where Have You Gone, Colin Powell?" and explored why "the man many thought would walk in to the presidency himself a few years ago, [was] leaving such shallow footprints."[23] Salman Rushdie's novel *Fury*, published in August 2001, depicts "the first hot season of the third millennium" as a prosperous but empty "golden age," or a decadent, directionless modern-day Rome, to be exact, in which politics is dismissed as a circus and New York is visited by "the motorcades of two largely interchangeable and certainly unlovable candidates" whom Rushdie calls "Gush" and "Bore."[24]

Wallace himself captured this same mood of empty inconsequentiality in his lengthy *Rolling Stone* piece on the John McCain campaign of 2000, a piece whose first subsection after its playful prologue is titled "Who Cares." There he asks,

> Do you even give a shit whether McCain can or ought to win [?] Since you're reading *Rolling Stone*, the chances are good that you are an American between say 18 and 35, which demographically makes you a Young Voter. And no generation of Young Voters has ever cared less about politics and politicians than yours. There's hard demographic and voter-pattern data backing this up … assuming you give a shit about data.[25]

More importantly, Wallace goes on to include himself among that same demographic, admitting in full that the real subject of his essay is less McCain's campaign than "the enormous shuddering yawn that the political process tends to evoke in us now in this post-Watergate-post-Iran-Contra-post-Whitewater-post-Lewinsky era" – the era, in other words, that defined the politics, or apathetic lack thereof, of Generation X.[26]

But Wallace was not content to accept this apathy, no more than he was content to embrace the *Beavis-and-Butthead* slacker irony that characterized his generation during the last decade of the twentieth century. As D. T. Max correctly observed, Wallace's McCain essay wasn't just about contemporary politics: rather, he used "his unaccustomed ringside seat at American history to further preoccupations that dated back to his 'E Unibus Pluram' essay."[27] For Wallace, US politics had become another self-reflexive, and hollowed-out, simulacrum that people of his generation in particular viewed with a cynical sneer, and, as warranted as such an approach might be, that cynicism had real-life consequences that Wallace is at pains to reverse. Midway through "Up, Simba," Wallace breaks from his narrative to explain,

> If you are bored and disgusted by politics and don't bother to vote, you are in effect voting for the entrenched Establishment of the two major parties, who please rest assured are not dumb, and who are keenly aware that it is in their interests to keep you disgusted and bored and cynical and to give you every possible psychological reason to stay home doing one-hitters and watching MTV on primary day. By all means stay home if you want, but don't bullshit yourself that you're not voting. In reality, there *is no such thing as not voting*.[28]

Wallace would later reprise a similar argument in his Kenyon Commencement Address, and in very similar language, when he affirms, "In the day-to-day trenches of adult life, there is actually no such thing as atheism. There is no such thing as not worshipping. Everybody worships. The only choice we get is *what* to worship."[29] The essay's final move also parallels the final section of "E Unibus Pluram" in that both essays, after conceding that cynicism and suspicion are warranted responses to the dehumanizing emptiness that is contemporary culture, nevertheless appeal to the reader's capacity for earnestness and sincerity. As regards McCain, Wallace suggests if his readers have started "fearing [their] own cynicism almost as much as [they] fear [their] own credulity," then they should try to remember McCain's four years in solitary confinement during the Vietnam War. "There were no techs' cameras in that box," Wallace reminds us, "no aides or consultants, no paradoxes or gray areas; nothing to sell. There was just one guy and whatever in his character sustained him. This is a huge deal."[30]

The Pale King, which is set during the early to mid-1980s, and hence serves as the only Wallace novel set in the recognizable past, contains Wallace's most direct and detailed portrait of Generation X apathy in the form of Chris Fogle. A self-proclaimed "wastoid" and "nihilist," Fogel shamefully recalls an episode when his father, who is clearly delineated as being part of an earlier, more conformist, and more civic-minded generation, finds Chris and his friends recovering from a three-day debauch, which memory Fogle identifies as "being the worst confirmation of the worst kind of generation-gap stereotype and parental disgust for their decadent, wastoid kids."[31] Similarly, at the end of his McCaffery interview, Wallace describes his generation's relationship to the 1960s counterculture as "a bit like the way you feel when you're in high school and your parents go on a trip and you throw a party.... For while it's great, free and freeing ... but then time passes, and the party gets louder and louder, ... and you gradually start wishing your parents would come back and restore some fucking order in your house."[32] But Wallace also leads Fogle out of his nihilistic abyss by having him stumble into an accounting class, wherein the stern Jesuit professor proclaims, "Gentlemen, you are called to account."[33] Fogle abruptly abandons his "wastoid" ennui and becomes an IRS agent. As a creature of the Reagan years and the complex coopting of rebellion that characterized his political education, Wallace consistently arrived at relatively conservative solutions to the problems arising from the dead end of irony and cynicism, a tendency he shared with Franzen as well, who concluded his 1996 essay on "The Future of the Novel" by arguing that "when the times get really, really awful, you retrench; you reexamine old content in new contexts; you try to preserve.... The day comes when the truly subversive literature is in some measure conservative."[34] Franzen's words anticipate those of Glendenning, who observes in *The Pale King:* "There are all kinds of conservatives depending on what it is they want to conserve."[35]

In much the same way that Wallace's core themes and concerns were shaped by the political culture of the Reagan years, so, too, were his vaunted literary innovations largely a byproduct of the late 1980s literary landscape, a landscape Wallace himself analyzed and cheerfully skewered in his 1988 essay, "Fictional Futures and the Conspicuously Young." Wallace quietly suppressed this essay, or at any rate chose not to reprint it, during his lifetime largely because he would reprint, almost word for word, large chunks of it in "E Unibus Pluram," an essay that productively builds upon the earlier essay's somewhat tentative exploration of the impact of television and pop culture on his generation's fictional production. Nevertheless, when read on its own, "Fictional Futures and the Conspicuously Young" provides an accurate portrait of the literary marketplace that Wallace had to navigate with his first two books while also offering fascinating insight into the forces that helped shape Wallace's groundbreaking early fiction.

When *The Broom of the System* first appeared in 1987, it was published in paperback as part of Penguin's "Contemporary American Fiction" imprint. The previous year, Penguin published the paperback edition of Bret Easton Ellis's *Less Than Zero* to much commercial success, a novel Ellis wrote while an undergraduate at Bennington and published when he was all of 21. Meanwhile, Random House had launched its flashy new paperback imprint, Vintage Contemporaries, with glossy book jackets that looked like 1980s new wave album covers, the big success from this latter venture being Jay McInerney's *Bright Lights, Big City*. Other writers who emerged during this period while still in their early 20s were David Leavitt, Mona Simpson, Lorrie Moore, Michael Chabon, and the aforementioned Powers and Franzen. Wallace began his publishing career, in other words, during a brief moment when "writers' proximity to their own puberties seemed now an asset."[36] While the popular media of the time referred to this group of young writers as the literary Brat Pack, Wallace preferred the term "the Conspicuously Young." He goes on to divide the work of this generation into three categories: "Neiman-Marcus Nihilism," which encompassed the zombie yuppie fiction of Ellis and McInerney; "Catatonic Realism," by which he meant apprentice fiction in the Raymond Carver tradition; and "Workshop Hermeticism," which referred to the sort of polished, but unchallenging, work that was taught, revised, and promoted by the MFA workshop industry.[37]

While Wallace is happy in this essay to ponder his aesthetic affiliation with writers such as David Leavitt and Jay McInerney, who, the charge went (and Wallace made this charge twice, here and in "E Unibus Pluram"), had a "habit of delineating characters according to the commercial slogans that appear on their T-shirts,"[38] he is adamant about separating himself from the workshop writers of category three, a virulent section of the essay that provides a window into Wallace's own fractious experience as an MFA student at the University of Arizona in Tucson, an experience that no doubt shaped him into the most original and trailblazing fiction writer of his Brat Pack generation.

D. T. Max's account of Wallace's years at Tucson confirms, and probably draws from, Wallace's portrait in this early essay of the writer's workshop experience of the mid-1980s. Max argues that Wallace's professors were suspicious, or at any rate tired, of postmodernism, which they "associated with a different era," and of minimalism, either of the Catatonic or the Neiman-Marcus variety, which "smelled trendy to them"; rather, what they wanted was "the well-made realist short story."[39] As Mark McGurl persuasively argues in *The Program Era*, the dominant status of "realism" in creative writing workshops can be seen as a product of the "write-what-you-know" dictum, which favors a "crudely empiricist conception of knowledge as that which the author has directly observed"; this valorization of "auto-biographical self-expressivity" is then tempered by "the professional impersonality of craft."[40] Thus has emerged the workshop formula of self-expression ("find your voice") plus self-discipline ("show don't tell").[41] Wallace's early work aggressively flouted both dictums. According to Max, one of Wallace's professors, after reading "Solomon Silverfish," a flamboyant Gass-influenced piece that Wallace submitted for workshop, "took Wallace aside and told him that if he continued to write the way he was writing, 'we'd hate to lose you.'"[42]

This experience clearly colors Wallace's critique of the writing workshop ethos of the late 1980s that he spells out in "Fictional Futures." First, he points out that, for the program staff, "every minute spent on class and department business is ... a minute not spent on their own art."[43] The members of the staff then "take the resentment out in large part on the psyches of their pupils," and in particular those students endowed with a "basic willingness to engage his instructor in the kind of dynamic back-and-forth any real creative education requires."[44] His next complaint is that the workshop situation rewards students who play according to the rules of the "school game," which are as follows: "(1) Determine what the instructor wants; and (2) Supply it forthwith."[45] Conversely, Wallace insists, the "practice of art" by its very nature "always exists in at least some state of tension with the rules of its practice, as essentially an applied system of rules."[46] Speaking obliquely of himself, he concludes this section by arguing that the "'next' generation of American writers" should move past the "relatively stable air of New Criticism and Anglo-American aesthetics" that still controlled the workshop ethos and write fiction that demonstrates "long-overdue appreciation for the weird achievements of such aliens as Husserl, Heidegger, Bakhtin, Lacan, Barthes, Polet, Gadamer, deMan."[47] To be sure, ambitious writers are generally prone to describe the literary landscape of their time in such a way as to make space for their own artistic agendas – whether the author in question is the T. S. Eliot of "Tradition and the Individual Talent" or the John Barth of "The Literature of Exhaustion" – and so Wallace's pointed depiction of the late 1980s penchant for the Conspicuously Young hardly breaks new ground in this regard. Nevertheless, Wallace's portrait provides fascinating insight into not only the literary landscape that Wallace hoped to transform but also how specifically he planned to render that transformation.

More so than Powers and Franzen, Wallace, for all the intellectual heft and ambition of his work, remains a "young person's" writer. His most successful and popular texts not only feature students and twentysomethings – a cast of characters ranging from Lenore Beadsman and Hal Incandenza to Chris Fogel and Meredith Rand – but also address the issues that matter intimately to readers on the cusp of adulthood. Today's college students were all born in the early 1990s, just when Wallace was putting together the body of fiction and nonfiction that would culminate in *Infinite Jest*. They have never known a world without the Internet, without e-mail, without cable television. They were still in single digits when Napster introduced the MP3 and ushered in the streaming revolution. Nevertheless, many of Wallace's contemporary readers experience *Infinite Jest* as if it were written just for them, so perfectly does it depict and diagnose their world, and their experience with information, entertainment, and the pursuit of pleasure. The book's future is their present. A sizable part of Wallace's genius lies in the reach and accuracy of his prophetic vision, the seeds of which were planted in an alien soil, in a world that was only just beginning to become the world we live in now.

Notes

1. David Foster Wallace, "E Unibus Pluram: Television and U.S. Fiction," in *A Supposedly Fun Thing I'll Never Do Again: Essays and Arguments* (Boston: Little, Brown, 1997), p. 81.
2. Lisa Chamberlain, *Slackernomics: Generation X in the Age of Creative Destruction* (Cambridge, MA: Da Capo, 2008), p. 10.
3. Douglas Coupland, *Generation X: Tales for an Accelerated Culture* (New York: St. Martin's, 1991), p. 5.
4. David Foster Wallace, "An Expanded Interview with David Foster Wallace," by Larry McCaffery in Stephen J. Burn (ed.), *Conversations with David Foster Wallace* (Jackson: University of Mississippi, 2012), p. 22.

5. Susan Mitchell, *Generation X: Americans Aged 18 to 34* (Ithaca, NY: New Strategist, 2001), p. 51.
6. Wallace, "E Unibus Pluram," p. 43.
7. Rob Owens, *GenXTV: The Brady Bunch to Melrose Place* (Syracuse, NY: Syracuse University Press, 1999), p. 119.
8. David Foster Wallace, *Girl with Curious Hair* (New York: W.W. Norton, 1989), p. vi.
9. See D. T. Max, *Every Love Story Is a Ghost Story: A Life of David Foster Wallace* (New York: Viking, 2012), pp. 106–109.
10. Wallace, "E Unibus Pluram," p. 43.
11. Ibid., p. 44.
12. Ibid., p. 27.
13. Ibid., p. 49.
14. Ibid., p. 52.
15. Richard Powers, *Prisoner's Dilemma* (New York: Harper Collins, 1988), p. 170.
16. Franzen quoted in Stephen J. Burn, *Jonathan Franzen and the End of Postmodernism* (New York: Continuum, 2008), p. 72. Burn similarly connects *The Twenty-Seventh City* to *Prisoner's Dilemma*.
17. Jonathan Franzen, "I'll Be Doing More of Same," *The Review of Contemporary Fiction* 16.11 (1996), p. 37.
18. Francis Fukuyama, *The End of History and the Last Man* (New York: Free Press, 1992), p. xii.
19. Lee Konstantinou, *Cool Characters: Irony and American Fiction* (Cambridge, MA: Harvard University Press, 2016), pp. 167, 168.
20. David Foster Wallace, *The Broom of the System* (New York: Penguin, 1987), p. 53.
21. David Foster Wallace, *Infinite Jest* (Boston: Little, Brown, 1996), p. 382.
22. Ibid., pp. 383, 384.
23. Johanna McGeary, "Where Have You Gone, Colin Powell?" *Time* (September 10, 2001), p. 24.
24. Salman Rushdie, *Fury* (New York: Random House, 2001), pp. 4, 6.
25. David Foster Wallace, "Up, Simba," *Consider the Lobster* (New York: Little, Brown, 2005), p. 161.
26. Ibid.
27. D. T. Max, *Every Love Story,* p. 260.
28. Wallace, "Up, Simba," p. 207.
29. David Foster Wallace, *This Is Water* (New York: Little, Brown, 2009), pp. 98–101.
30. Wallace, "Up, Simba," p. 233.
31. David Foster Wallace, *The Pale King* (New York: Little, Brown, 2011), p. 170.
32. Wallace, "Expanded Interview," in Burn (ed.), *Conversations,* p. 52.
33. Wallace, *The Pale King,* p. 233.
34. Franzen, "I'll Be Doing More of Same," p. 38.
35. Wallace, *The Pale King,* p. 132.
36. David Foster Wallace, "Fictional Futures and the Conspicuously Young," in *Both Flesh and Not: Essays* (New York: Little, Brown, 2012), p. 37.
37. Ibid., pp. 39–40.
38. Ibid., p. 43.

39. D. T. Max, *Every Love Story*, pp. 60, 61.
40. Mark McGurl, *The Program Era: Postwar Fiction and the Rise of Creative Writing* (Cambridge, MA: Harvard University Press, 2009), pp. 95, 102.
41. Ibid., p. 81.
42. Ibid., p. 64. Tellingly, Mark McGurl ignores this episode in a recent overview of Wallace's artistic project, "The Institution of Nothing: David Foster Wallace in the Program," *boundary* 2 41.3 (Fall 2014), 27–54. McGurl sees Wallace as not only a figure of "the Program Era" but one "whose situation marks a further step toward the *normalization* of the emergent conditions of the institutionalization that that term tries to name," p. 31.
43. Wallace, "Fictional Futures," p. 58.
44. Ibid.
45. Ibid., p. 59.
46. Ibid.
47. Ibid., p. 63.

2

ANDREW HOBEREK

Wallace and American Literature

The third section of David Foster Wallace's 1995 essay "A Supposedly Fun Thing I'll Never Do Again," about a week-long Caribbean cruise on assignment for *Harper's* magazine, begins with the story of a 16-year-old Chicago boy who, several weeks prior to Wallace's trip, had committed suicide by leaping from the deck of another cruise ship. Wallace suggests that official accounts of this suicide, which linked it to "a shipboard romance gone bad," left out "something there's no way a real news story could cover." Noting that "there's something about a mass-market luxury cruise that's unbearably sad," Wallace relates this something else to his feeling of "despair" during his own trip, describing this feeling as "a weird yearning for death combined with a crushing sense of my own smallness and futility that presents as a fear of death."[1]

In a way typical of Wallace's fiction and nonfiction alike, this story epitomizes the dark underside of the essay's admirable attention to social detail – its incisive commentary on the class relations between the cruise's passengers and the ship's "preterite workers,"[2] for instance, or its lengthy descriptions of the fixtures in Wallace's cabin's bathroom. Wallace is so familiar with those fixtures, he tells us, because, as "a kind of semi-agoraphobe,"[3] he feels compelled to remain in his cabin for much of the trip. As the opening narrative of the boy's suicide hints, and the rest of the essay makes clear, this condition is not, or not merely, psychological. Rather, it is an existential grappling with a sense of the emptiness underlying life. In what follows I'd like to argue that this dialectical relationship between social detail and existential dread succinctly encapsulates, perhaps better than any other passage in Wallace's writing, his profound connection to and reliance upon a certain version of classic American literature.

In a compelling reading of Wallace's posthumous novel *The Pale King* (2011), Mark McGurl argues that this dialectic is what prevents us from reading Wallace as a latter-day regionalist, insofar as in Wallace's novel "the landscape of the Midwest is not embracing after all, but only, given time, an occasion for terrifying exposure, like something out of Alfred Hitchcock's *The Birds*."[4] McGurl argues that we must read Wallace's work "as practicing an existentialism of institutions – which is to say, a commitment to the necessity of institutions in making and maintaining a 'meaning of life.'" McGurl finds "a clear, if partial, literary precursor" for this move in Ernest Hemingway's 1933 story "A Clean, Well-Lighted Place," which juxtaposes the "light" and "cleanness" and "order" of the titular café to the horrifying and suicide-inducing "nothing" and "nada" invoked multiple times in a famous passage parodying the Lord's Prayer.[5] "Wallace," McGurl writes, "takes Hemingway's mostly empty existential shelter and fills it with people, giving them rules to follow and things to say to each other."[6]

McGurl is exactly right about Wallace's "existentialism of institutions"[7] – and Wallace's ambivalent commitment, in particular, to the institution of the creative writing program – but his account of Wallace's literary lineage could be extended well beyond Hemingway. There is, for instance, a much stronger case than McGurl acknowledges for describing Wallace as a Midwestern regionalist.[8] Consider, for instance, the passage in *My Ántonia* (1918) in which Willa Cather's narrator, Jim Burden, recounting his Nebraska boyhood, writes that "trees were so rare in that country, and they had to make such a hard fight to grow, that we used to feel anxious about them, and visit them as if they were persons. It must have been the scarcity of detail in that tawny landscape that made detail so precious."[9] This passage anticipates Hemingway's modernist dialectic of detail and nothingness, although it locates both sides of the dialectic outdoors. In this respect Cather anticipates the sense of landscape-induced existential dread familiar to readers of *The Pale King* and Wallace's essays about the Midwest. In his 1993 essay about the Illinois State Fair, "Getting Away from Already Being Pretty Much Away from It All," for instance, Wallace writes,

> I suspect that part of the self-conscious-community thing here has to do with space. Rural Midwesterners live surrounded by unpopulated land, marooned in a space whose emptiness starts to become both physical and spiritual. It is not just people you get lonely for. You're alienated from the very space around you, in a way, because out here the land's less an environment than a commodity.[10]

The issue here, as in Cather's Nebraska, is not just vastness but a peculiarly Midwestern lack of differentiation; as anyone knows who's ever driven through Cather's Nebraska, or through Kansas and eastern Colorado on the way to Denver, the Midwest is scary because it is so *empty*.

If it is thus largely accurate to see Wallace as (among other things) a Midwestern regionalist, this in turn points to an even deeper lineage for his concerns and strategies – one he himself tells us about in "A Supposedly Fun Thing." Mentioning his very DFW-like childhood habit of "memoriz[ing] shark-fatality data,"[11] he brings the subject around to American literature:

> In school I ended up writing three different papers on "The Castaway" section of *Moby-Dick*, the chapter where the cabin boy Pip falls overboard and is driven mad by the empty immensity of what he finds himself floating in. And when I teach school now I always teach Crane's horrific "The Open Boat," and I get bent out of shape when the kids find the story dull or jaunty-adventurish: I want them to feel the same marrow-level dread of the oceanic I've always felt, the intuition of the sea as primordial nada, bottomless, depths inhabited by cackling tooth-studded things rising toward you at the rate a feather falls.[12]

Melville and not Hemingway here lies behind the feared "nada," a point driven home even more clearly by Wallace's subsequent description of cruise ships as intensely "white and clean" in a way "clearly meant to represent the Calvinist triumph of capital and industry over the primal decay-action of the sea."[13] If the point were not already clear, Wallace concludes this section of the essay by telling us that what cruise lines sell is not simple relaxation but, on the contrary, a form of "death-and-dread transcendence."[14]

In "The Castaway" chapter of *Moby-Dick*, as for Wallace in "A Supposedly Fun Thing," it is the sea that provides the sense of undifferentiated vastness that Wallace's writing more frequently attributes to the Midwestern landscape. Pip goes mad as a result of an acute case of the agoraphobia Wallace claims to share. Thrown from his whale boat and left at sea to learn a lesson before being rescued "by the merest chance," the cabin boy's "ringed horizon began to expand around him miserably," and the sea "kept his finite body up, but drowned the infinite of his soul ... He saw God's foot upon the treadle of the loom, and spoke it; and therefore his shipmates called him mad."[15] Resonating with this chapter of *Moby-Dick*, "A Supposedly Fun Thing," like much of Wallace's writing, cultivates a vertiginous sense that, as Ahab says in another passage from the novel, "All visible objects ... are but as pasteboard masks" – that they might fall away to reveal an existential horror or, perhaps even worse, that "there's naught beyond" and that the horror is just a projection of the beholder's psyche.[16]

From this perspective, it begins to seem like more than mere biographical coincidence that Wallace's most well-known novel takes place just west of Boston, ground zero for the philosophical and literary movement associated with Ralph Waldo Emerson and those, like Melville, whom Emerson influenced and/or antagonized. Paul Giles has convincingly described Wallace as updating the American Transcendentalist tradition for the digital age, locating distinctly Emersonian resonances in the "hortatory" tones of the 2005

Kenyon College commencement address that Wallace subsequently published as *This Is Water* (2009).[17] And in fact the imbrication of nature, psyche, and transcendence that leads to horror in "The Castaway" derives from Emerson's writing. In his 1836 essay "Nature" Emerson writes, "One might think the atmosphere was made transparent with this design, to give man, in the heavenly bodies, the perpetual presence of the sublime."[18] Emerson's essay provides a famously idiosyncratic figure for this moment of encounter between the physical and the spiritual: "Crossing a bare common, in snow puddles, at twilight, under a clouded sky ... I become a transparent eye-ball; I am nothing; I see all; the currents of the Universal Being circulate through me; I am part or particle of God."[19] Wallace, in a 1997 interview with Charlie Rose, echoes this figure in his description of his essayistic persona as "basically an enormous eyeball floating around something, reporting what it sees."[20]

Henry David Thoreau takes up this dynamic and marries transcendental speculation to the kind of detailed description that also figures largely in Wallace's essays. In *Walden* (1854), for instance, Thoreau sounds the depths of the titular pond to refute rumors of its bottomlessness. He confirms that "the greatest depth was exactly one hundred and two feet; to which may be added the five feet which it has risen since, making one hundred and seven." But then, in a seeming reversal of his attention to concrete detail, he declares, "I am thankful that this pond was made deep and pure for a symbol. While men believe in the infinite some ponds will be thought to be bottomless."[21] As I have suggested, this alternation between the physical and the symbolic is central to what Wallace calls his "sensuous or experiential essays."[22]

Placing Wallace within this genealogy helps us to see beyond the useful, but in some ways limiting, account of his work in relation to postmodernism. For instance, the section in *Infinite Jest* describing the enormously complicated game of Eschaton played by Enfield's students is frequently understood as an homage to postmodernist writers like Thomas Pynchon, Don DeLillo, or Jean Baudrillard – a reading rendered plausible by, among other things, the game's investment in a Cold War context of missile defense that was anachronistic by 1996. But as a set piece, the Eschaton scene also bears comparison to the many chapters of *Moby-Dick* dedicated to conversation among the crew, the anatomization of recondite activities, or both. These chapters provide a social counterpoint to *Moby-Dick*'s numerous descriptions of existential isolation, from Pip's time as a castaway to Ahab's monomania and "The Mast-Head"'s account of how sailors "given to unseasonable meditativeness"[23] might forget their purpose and fall into the sea. And in a similar way, the Eschaton scene and the others at Enfield Academy counterpoint the spiral of Wallace's own "absent-minded young philosopher"[24] Hal Incandenza into solipsistic isolation as he retreats to the academy's basement to smoke dope – "his bigger secret . . . that he's as attached to the secrecy as he is to getting high."[25] If we want to understand how Wallace moves beyond what he came to see as the limitations of postmodernism, this suggests, we can learn much by tracing his debts to the American literary tradition more generally.

****

Indeed, one might argue that as a novelist Wallace can be understood as a late exponent of the romance tradition influentially described by Richard Chase as the American answer to the European realist novel. The romance tradition is invested, in Chase's formulation, in "action" rather than "character"; in "mystery" rather than social "class"; in "astonishing events" rather than realistic "plausibility"; in "mythic, allegorical, and symbolistic forms" rather than "the immediate rendition of reality."[26] We can see this tradition – whose proponents include not only Melville but Nathaniel Hawthorne and, at a later date, Chase's contemporary Flannery O'Connor – across Wallace's writing. Wallace's existential concerns, his openness to nonrealistic genres, and his interest in allegorical situations rather than finely detailed social description all place him within the romance tradition.

Wallace's participation in this tradition thus combines the thematic and formal, and its formal dimensions help us to understand how "mystery" can be cultivated in forms (fiction and the essay) seemingly more fitted to realistic representation. Consider, for instance, the veil that Joelle van Dyne wears as a member of U.H.I.D. (Union of the Hideously and Improbably Deformed) in *Infinite Jest*. Joelle's acquaintance Molly Notkin tells Rodney Tine that Joelle was deformed by a bottle of acid thrown by her mother with the intention of hitting her husband, who had just confessed his sexual attraction for his beautiful daughter.[27] But the veil itself becomes a source of fascination for the people with whom Joelle interacts, from Orin and Hal's father Jim to Don Gately and the other residents of Ennet House Drug and Alcohol Recovery House, in which she resides during the novel's present. The clear antecedent for this subplot of *Infinite Jest* is Hawthorne's 1835 story "The Minister's Black Veil," in which a cleric named Parson Hooper dons a black veil in his youth and subsequently refuses to take it off – even for the woman who loves him and even in his life's final moments, when a fellow clergyman pleads with him, "Is it fitting that a father in the church should leave a shadow on his memory, that may seem to blacken a life so pure?"[28] As Hooper tells his would-be wife Elizabeth, "This veil is a type and a symbol, and I am bound to wear it ever, both in light and darkness, in solitude and before the gaze of multitudes, and as with strangers, so with my familiar friends" (IJ, 194). As he does with the even more famous "material emblem"[29] at the center of his 1850 novel *The Scarlet Letter*, Hawthorne leaves the meaning of the veil purposely ambiguous, and inserts it into the story so as to highlight its effects on and within a social world. "From beneath the black veil," Hawthorne tells us, "there rolled a cloud into the sunshine, an ambiguity of sin or sorrow, which enveloped the poor minister, so that love or sympathy could never reach him," even as the awful gravity it lends him enhances his abilities as a clergyman.[30]

Wallace puts Joelle's veil to similar use in *Infinite Jest*, while also explicitly linking the veil to the mysterious, catatonia-inducing Entertainment created by James Incandenza and sought by various parties throughout the book. Pestered by Gately to describe her deformity, van Dyne finally responds that she is "so beautiful" that once people have seen her "they can't think of anything else and don't want to look at anything else and stop carrying out normal responsibilities."[31] This statement draws an implicit parallel between van Dyne and the Entertainment, one that Wallace makes explicit later in the novel when van Dyne tells Hugh/Helen Steeply that when the elder Incandenza

> talked about this thing as a quote perfect entertainment, terminally compel-
> ling – it was always ironic – he was having a sly little jab at me. I used to go
> around saying the veil was to disguise lethal perfection, I was too lethally
> beautiful for people to stand ... So Jim took a failed piece and told me it was
> too perfect to release – it'd paralyze people.[32]

Of course this statement adds an additional layer of ambiguity, floating the proposition that the Entertainment is just "an ironic joke."[33] At the same time, it reminds us that Joelle's own ambiguous position between deformity and dangerous beauty is built into the Entertainment itself, in which she plays, among other roles, the mother figure who – face blurred by camera work – looks down at the camera, as into a crib, and repeats variations on "I'm so sorry."[34]

Like Hawthorne, then, Wallace uses his "material emblems" to generate and multiply ambiguities experienced both by characters and the reader. As Joelle tells Steeply of her role in the Entertainment, "My face wasn't important. You never got the sense it was meant to be captured realistically by the lens."[35] This formulation is only partially accurate: van Dyne's face is vitally important, both in *Infinite Jest* and in the Entertainment – but because, rather than in spite of, its interruption of realist representation. The Entertainment captures, moreover, precisely the ambiguity between pleasure and sadness/despair/death that drives Wallace's account of his Caribbean cruise in "A Supposedly Fun Thing." As Molly Notkin (or the narrator's summary of Molly Notkin) describes the film, Joelle sits naked "explaining in very simple childlike language to whomever the film's camera represents that Death is always female, and that the female is always maternal. I.e. that the woman who kills you is always your next life's mother."[36] Of course Notkin is a graduate student, given in her interview with Tine to no-doubt parodic excesses of literary-symbolic interpretation, including the idea that the Entertainment is "little more than the thinly veiled cries of a man at the very terminus of his existential tether."[37] On the other hand, later in the book Gately, lying in his hospital bed, has a dream that recapitulates this account of the Entertainment: in it, Joelle appears both naked and "inhumanly gorgeous," but also modulating into "the figure of Death, Death incarnate."[38] And one of the veil's last appearances in the book, when van Dyne visits Gately a little later, evokes the same nothingness that drives Pip mad in "The Castaway": "What was disconcerting was that when her head was down the veil hung loose at the same vertical angle as when her head was up, only now it was perfectly smooth and untextured, a smooth white screen with nothing behind it."[39]

These scenes, that is to say, participate in Wallace's typical strategy of both affirming and subtly mocking or calling into question his existential preoccupations. Lee Konstantinou convincingly relates this strategy to Wallace's efforts to reestablish a form of qualified sincerity in the wake of postmodern irony. Wallace's goal in imagining the Entertainment, Konstantinou contends,

> is not, therefore, to furnish the reader with a higher-order irony or a deeper critical knowingness. Deepening such irony would only, in Wallace's view, deepen the chasm between the writer and the reader, intensifying the loneliness of both. Rather, Wallace means to exhaust the reader's reflexive irony, to take the reader to the limit of critical thought in order to prepare the way for her willingness to believe in the sincerity of the author.[40]

In Wallace's efforts to move beyond the limitations of postmodern irony, we can again see the influence of the romance tradition exemplified by Melville and Hawthorne. On the one hand, Joelle's veil and Wallace's other material emblems work like the titular object in Wallace Steven's 1923 poem "Anecdote of a Jar," giving aesthetic shape to the otherwise featureless material around them. On the other hand, however, they also function like Melville's pasteboard mask, at once raising and calling into question the possibility of a world beyond the phenomenal one. This world can be existential, or it can consist of the simple but ultimately unknowable content of other people's subjectivities.

Wallace's interest in representing the unrepresentable helps to explain the insufficiency of strictly realist fiction for his purposes. Yet his departures from realist strategies do not always involve nonrealist incident, as they do in his novels. His short stories show the quieter but no less significant influence of Flannery O'Connor, whom he listed among his favorite writers in a 1996 interview with Laura Miller.[41] The Catholic O'Connor associated what she called "mystery" not with existential dread but with theological truth. Nonetheless, O'Connor's 1960 essay "Some Aspects of the Grotesque in Southern Fiction" offers a useful roadmap for how the author in the "modern romance tradition" may approach mystery within prose fiction:

> In these grotesque works, we find that the writer has made alive some experience which we are not accustomed to observe everyday, or which the ordinary man may never experience in his ordinary life. We find that connections which we would expect in the customary kind of realism have been ignored, that there are strange skips and gaps which anyone trying to describe manners and customs would certainly not have left. Yet the characters in these novels are alive in spite of these things. They have an inner coherence, if not always a coherence from typical social patterns, toward mystery and the unexpected.[42]

O'Connor's short stories work numerous variations on this formula, often ending with an ambiguous action or mysterious image meant to point to rather than specify some revelation of mystery: the murder of the vacationing family in "A Good Man Is Hard to Find" (1953), for instance, or the titular lawn jockey at the end of "The Artificial Nigger" (1959).

Wallace's short story "The Devil Is a Busy Man" reads almost like a parody of O'Connor, not only in its title and rural setting but also in its conclusion. After a rural man fruitlessly attempts to get people from town to take away various unwanted items – "a freezer or a [sic] old tiller"[43] – for free, he succeeds by charging small sums. In the story's final sentence, the narrator tells us, "I asked Daddy about what lesson to draw here and he said he figured you don't try to teach a pig to sing and told me to go on and take the drive's gravel back out of the ditch before it fucked up the drainage."[44] If this is parody it is the sort that borders on tribute, since O'Connor has her own suspicion of overly neat endings. Wallace's story "Think," whose fifth sentence is "What cleared his forehead's lines was a type of revelation,"[45] seems much more directly engaged with O'Connor's characteristic technique. What spurs the character's revelation is not only the sight of "the younger sister of his wife's college roommate"[46] standing before him braless, but also his own action of kneeling in response. The brief story concludes with the man telling the woman, "It's not what you think I'm afraid of," and then wondering: "And what if she joined him on the floor, just like this, clasped in supplication: just this way."[47] "Think" is even more denuded of "the customary kinds of realism" than O'Connor's Southern regionalist writing: we know nothing about the man or his family, or about the events leading up to the situation the story describes, except that "everyone else has gone to the mall."[48] Nor do we know the nature of the "revelation" that "cleared his forehead's lines" after "he thinks to kneel,"[49] or even the nature of the "It" that is the subject of his final line of dialogue.[50] "Think" thus seems like an exercise in boiling down O'Connor's technique to its purest form.

Wallace also shares with O'Connor (and with another author that he mentions to Miller, Cormac McCarthy) a darkly comic penchant for the cruel, the violent, and the grotesque. The stories of abusive men in the titular cycle of Wallace's 1999 collection *Brief Interviews with Hideous Men*, for instance, might be read as variations on O'Connor's 1955 story "Good Country People," in which a traveling salesman named Manley Pointer pretends to seduce the philosophy PhD Joy Hulga Hopewell only to steal her artificial leg – although Wallace is arguably more interested in critiquing masculine pathology than is O'Connor, who seems to side with Pointer as an agent of the snobbish and secular Hopewell's comeuppance. Or again, we might adduce the numerous grotesque stories that populate *Infinite Jest*, from the catalog that Wallace presents in his account of Boston Alcoholics Anonymous meetings to the tale of how Joelle van Dyne's mother kills herself, after accidentally disfiguring her daughter, "by putting her extremities down the garbage disposal – first one arm and then, kind of miraculously if you think about it, the other arm."[51] The final story in the Boston AA sequence, told by a young woman who becomes a stripper and an addict after years of watching her father have sex with her disabled and immobilized sister, may be particularly apt. The audience for this story, Wallace tells us, turns away in "empathetic distress" – not because of the story's content but because of "the look-what-happened-to-poor-me invitation implicit in the tale, the talk's tone of self-pity itself less offensive ... than the subcurrent of explanation, an appeal to exterior *Cause* that can slide, in the addictive mind, so insidiously into *Excuse* that any causal attribution is in Boston AA feared, shunned, punished by empathetic distress."[52] As a kind of metaliterary cautionary tale, that is, the audience's reaction suggests that Wallace, like O'Connor, indulges in the grotesque not to generate sympathy but to short-circuit the "coherence" of "typical social patterns" and thereby push beyond the limitations of representational realism.[53]

****

In the 1940s and 1950s, when critics were retroactively formulating the idea of the American romance tradition, it was common to end books of literary history by demonstrating the ongoing relevance of the tradition in the work of contemporary writers such as O'Connor, Saul Bellow, and Ralph Ellison. The rise of postmodernism put a halt to this motif, as modernist experimentalism and other international traditions began to seem more relevant to recent fiction. But, I would argue, the romance experienced a quiet renewal in the late 1970s and 1980s in the works of such authors as McCarthy, Don DeLillo, Toni Morrison, and – not least – Morrison's fellow gothicist Stephen King. Both Wallace and his mutual admirer Jonathan Franzen wrote first novels widely recognized as influenced by DeLillo: Wallace's *The Broom of the System* (1987) and Franzen's *The Twenty-Seventh City* (1988). This was seen at the time as establishing the authors as the latest young heirs of the postmodern tradition. But it's worth noting that in "E Unibus Pluram," the 1993 essay in which he stakes his claim to be moving beyond postmodernism, Wallace suggests that the famous "Most Photographed Barn in America" scene in DeLillo's *White Noise* (1985) can be read as a subtle critique of postmodern irony.[54] With this in mind we might see DeLillo not only as a postmodern forebear to be overcome but also as an important precursor of the blend of postmodernism and realism that, according to Stephen J. Burn, identifies Wallace and Franzen as post-postmodern writers.[55]

I would go further, and argue that while Franzen, as his career progresses, moves increasingly in the direction of the European novel of manners, Wallace devotes himself to the romance tradition that opposed this form of realism, and which explored the existential questions and motifs central to Wallace's own thought. As with everything, Wallace both undercuts and takes seriously these questions – undercuts them, if we follow Konstantinou's formulation, in order to take them seriously. Here too the romance tradition provides a model, since – as D. H. Lawrence was among the first to note – even Melville, in *Moby-Dick*, could combine profundity with seemingly sloppy or bad writing:

> And Melville really is a bit sententious: aware of himself, self-conscious, putting something over even himself. But then it's not easy to get into the swing of a piece of deep mysticism when you just set out with a story.
> Nobody can be more clownish, more clumsy and sententiously in bad taste, than Herman Melville, even in a great book like *Moby Dick*. He preaches and holds forth because he's not sure of himself. And he holds forth, often, so amateurishly.[56]

This could easily stand as a description of Wallace's style, which I would argue purposely courts infelicity as one of his strategies for simultaneously addressing and putting quotation marks around his existential preoccupations.

Elsewhere I have discussed Wallace's style in relation to another American literary tradition, exemplified by figures like Walt Whitman and the Beats, that was committed to defying conventional rules of good writing as a technique for connoting sincerity.[57] The following nonsentence from *Infinite Jest* provides one example among many:

> And then but by tenth grade, in one of those queer when-did-that-happen metamorphoses, Mildred Bonk had become an imposing member of the frightening Winchester High School set that smoked full-strength Marlboros in the alley between Senior and Junior halls and that left school altogether at lunchtime, driving away in loud low-slung cars to drink beer and smoke dope, driving around with sound-systems of illegal wattage, using Visine and Clorets, etc.[58]

If Mildred's "unlikely"[59] name and her story's wildly digressive quality (Mildred will become the wife of another minor character, Bruce Green, who shows up in Ennet House) suggest Wallace's debt to Pynchon, the rest of the nonsentence is unmistakably Wallace's in ways signaled by its violations of the rules of good writing: the opening variation on Wallace's signal "And then but" combination; the inefficient use of a hyphenated string of words and an "of" construction as adjectives; the petering out on "etc." These elements function on the sentence level in the way the book's notorious footnotes do at a higher one, interrupting the flow of reading and generating – as in the contradiction between "and" and "but" – the purposely excessive "junk text" that David Letzler calls "cruft."[60] Letzler draws the term from computer programming, and McGurl, who stresses Wallace's commitment to the precepts of the writing program, would no doubt rightly argue that Wallace's stylistic violations only become visible in relation to these precepts. But Wallace's style also belongs to a tradition, running from Whitman's rejection of standard meter and rhyme schemes through Jack Kerouac's own slangy digressiveness, of eschewing literary conventions for the purpose of cultivating a more intimate and authentic-sounding voice.

For Letzler, Wallace's cruft-laden footnotes, in particular, place him in another literary tradition, the one dubbed by Edward Mendelson, in his 1976 essay on the topic, "encyclopedic narrative." In Mendelson's (distinctly gendered) account, encyclopedic narrative "attends to the whole social and linguistic range of [the author's] nation," it "makes use of all the literary styles and conventions known to his countrymen," its "dialect often becomes established as the national language," its author "takes his place as national poet or national classic," and it "becomes the focus of a large and persistent exegetic and textual industry comparable to the industry founded upon the Bible."[61] Thinking of *Infinite Jest* as an encyclopedic narrative helps to make sense not only of the book's after-life but also of such characteristics as its hybrid combination of realism with near-future science fiction, the spy thriller, and other "literary styles and conventions." But it also points to the larger-scale violations of good fictional form that parallel Wallace's sentence-level infelicities. While Stephen J. Burn has written extensively about the encyclopedic qualities of Wallace's fiction,[62] Letzler's argument is interesting because it grounds the novel's encyclopedic dimensions in what might be understood as bad writing: the excessive pointlessness of Wallace's pharmaceutical foot-notes which, crucially, echo "the pseudo-scientific cetology chapter of ... *Moby-Dick*."[63] This in turn points to the way in which *Moby-Dick*'s digressive qualities – appropriate, perhaps, in the work of an essayist like Thoreau – seem willfully to violate the rules of narrative momentum. Just as Melville has finally gotten Ishmael aboard the *Pequod*, and the *Pequod* out to sea – just as Ahab yells "Look sharp, all of ye! There are whales hereabouts"[64] – the "Cetology" chapter, with its pseudoscientific taxonomy of the ocean's whales, looms up like a rock on which the plot runs aground.

The encyclopedic narrative is not interested, that is, solely in narrative, and it is also willing to approach its goals through a grab bag of styles. Here Melville's setting of chapters of *Moby-Dick* in the form of dramatic dialogue anticipates Wallace's omnivorous absorption of past fictional forms, includ-ing but not limited to the very realism to which the romance tradition stands in opposition. While David Hering convincingly contends, for instance, that *Infinite Jest* and *Brief Interviews with Hideous Men* stage a "retreat into institutional space" and away from Wallace's earlier regionalism,[65] portions of the Gately sections of the novel read distinctly like regionalist realism in their commitment to describing Boston and its environs in the late 1980s and early 1990s:

> You can get on the Storrow 500 off Comm. Ave. below Kenmore via this long twiny overpass-shadowed road that cuts across the Fens. Basically the Storrow 500 is an urban express route that cuts along the bright-blue gloomy thunder-ing skies. Gately has decided to buy the newcomers' omelette [*sic*] stuff at Bread & Circus in Inman Square, Cambridge ... Bread & Circus is a socially hyper-responsible overpriced grocery full of Cambridge Green Party granola-crunchers, and everything's like microbiotic and fertilized only with organic genuine llama-shit, etc.[66]

Gately's narrative as a whole can read like one of Theodore Dreiser's stories of lower-class decline. Or again, *The Broom of the System* evokes, even as it ironizes, "the climax of [Frank Norris's 1899 novel] McTeague," with the title character "handcuffed to the corpse of his malevolent foe, Marcus Schouler, in the middle of a desert."[67] In this respect we might read *Infinite Jest*'s concluding sentence – "And when he came back to, he was flat on his back on the beach in the freezing sand, and it was raining out of a low sky, and the tide was way out"[68] – with its image of a human figure counterposed against an indifferent nature, as a less direct, but also less self-conscious, nod to Norris, Crane, and other naturalist writers.

Here we perhaps come full circle, to the importance of remembering that the romance tradition is not the opposite of realism per se but of a particular kind of realism. As O'Connor's opposition between "manners and customs," on the one hand, and living "characters," on the other, suggests, the post–World War II writers and critics who named and taxonomized the romance tradition emphasized asocial individuality for reasons of their own.[69] But Melville, as C. L. R. James among others realized early on, is as deeply committed to forms of collective social organization as he is suspicious of individualism.[70] McGurl makes a very similar point about Wallace, arguing, "whether it is a nursing home, a halfway house, Alcoholics Anonymous, a tennis academy, mammoth federal bureaucracy, or the university, the 'institution' in Wallace is first and foremost a communal antidote to atomism, a laboriously iterated wall against the nihilism attendant to solitude."[71] And Andrew Warren, in his thoughtful account of the relationship between different narrative models and the imagination of community in Wallace's fiction, notes that in the section of *Infinite Jest* on Boston AA, "the narrative voice weaves the speaker's words, Gately's thoughts and the more general mood of the Group into a kind of choral refrain, a call and response."[72]

As I argue above, *Infinite Jest*, like *Moby-Dick*, seeks to give weight to extreme versions of both individual anomie and collective social description. It is, in this regard, perhaps no accident that Wallace tends to associate realist writing with Don Gately, just as Melville associates his visions of collectivity with the *Pequod*'s ordinary working sailors. But Wallace's concerns with collective social organization in fact extend beyond the simple class hierarchy of Enfield Academy on its hilltop and Ennet House Drug and Alcohol Recovery House below. For both these places are institutions whose residents have made a paradoxical choice to commit themselves to a routine of involuntary discipline (tennis practice, the 12 Steps) that organize forms of social life around them and allow these forms to continue even when individuals like Hal may not. In this respect, we might understand both places as versions of the *Pequod* that don't sink.

Notes

1. David Foster Wallace, "A Supposedly Fun Thing I'll Never Do Again," in *A Supposedly Fun Thing I'll Never Do Again: Essays and Arguments* (Boston: Little, Brown, 1997), p. 261.
2. Ibid., p. 266, n. 13.
3. Ibid., p. 296.
4. Mark McGurl, "The Institution of Nothing: David Foster Wallace in the Program," *boundary* 2 41.3 (Fall 2014), p. 30.
5. Ibid., pp. 34–35.
6. Ibid., p. 35.
7. Ibid., p. 36.
8. For the classic account of Wallace's (highly mediated) relationship to the regionalist tradition, see Paul Quinn, "'Location's Location': Placing David Foster Wallace," in Marshall Boswell and Stephen J. Burn (eds.), *A Companion to David Foster Wallace Studies* (New York: Palgrave, 2013), pp. 87–106. David Hering begins his chapter on the relationship between Wallace's "'performative' regionalism" and his representation of institutions by noting that while Wallace was writing *The Pale King* he kept a notebook labeled "Midwesternisms" that "consist[ed] almost entirely of Midwestern colloquial phrases"; see *David Foster Wallace: Fiction and Form* (New York: Bloomsbury, 2016), pp. 41, 41–78. Hering sees in Wallace what he describes as a postmodern concern with "the loss of the authentic, non-mediated Midwest ... and its replacement with a culturally encoded 'Midwest,'" (p. 75), although as scholars of regionalism have long argued, this dynamic was central to its project from the outset. See, for instance, Richard Brodhead, *Cultures of Letters: Scenes of Reading and Writing in Nineteenth-Century America* (Chicago: University of Chicago Press, 1993), pp. 107–210; and (on the use of vernacular dialect) Michael North, *The Dialect of Modernism: Race, Language, and Twentieth-Century Literature* (New York: Oxford University Press, 1994), pp. 3–34.
9. Willa Cather, *My Ántonia* (1918; Mineola, NY: Dover, 1994), p. 17.
10. David Foster Wallace, "Getting Away from Already Pretty Much Being Away from It All," *A Supposedly Fun Thing*, pp. 91–92.
11. Ibid., p. 261.
12. Ibid., p. 262.
13. Ibid., p. 263.
14. Ibid., p. 265.
15. Herman Melville, *Moby-Dick*, Second Norton Critical Edition, ed. Hershel Parker and Harrison Hayford (1851; New York: Norton, 2002), pp. 321–322.
16. Ibid., p. 140.
17. Paul Giles, "All Swallowed Up: David Foster Wallace and American Literature," in Samuel Cohen and Lee Konstantinou (eds.), *The Legacy of David Foster Wallace* (Iowa City: University of Iowa Press, 2012), pp. 6, 3–22.
18. Ralph Waldo Emerson, "Nature," in *Nature and Other Essays* (Mineola, NY: Dover, 2009), p. 2.
19. Ibid., p. 3.

20. Charlie Rose interview with David Foster Wallace, March 27, 1997, https://charlierose.com/videos/23311, accessed February 19, 2017.

21. Henry David Thoreau, *Walden; or, Life in the Woods* (1854; Mineola, NY: Dover, 1995), p. 184.

22. Charlie Rose interview.

23. Melville, *Moby-Dick*, p. 135.

24. Ibid., p. 136.

25. David Foster Wallace, *Infinite Jest* (Boston: Little, Brown, 1996), p. 49.

26. Richard Chase, *The American Novel and Its Tradition* (1957; Baltimore, MD: Johns Hopkins University Press, 1980), p. 13.

27. Wallace, *Infinite Jest*, pp. 792–795.

28. Nathaniel Hawthorne, "The Minister's Black Veil," in Leland S. Person (ed.), *The Scarlet Letter and Other Writings* (New York: Norton, 2005), p. 198.

29. Ibid., p. 195.

30. Ibid., p. 196.

31. Wallace, *Infinite Jest*, p. 538.

32. Ibid., p. 940.

33. Ibid., p. 940.

34. Ibid., p. 939.

35. Ibid., p. 940.

36. Ibid., p. 788.

37. Ibid., p. 789.

38. Ibid., p. 850.

39. Ibid., p. 857.

40. Lee Konstantinou, *Cool Characters: Irony and American Fiction* (Cambridge: Harvard University Press, 2016), p. 193.

41. Laura Miller, "David Foster Wallace" (March 9, 1996), *Salon*, www.salon.com/1996/03/09/wallace_5/, accessed December 31, 2016.

42. Flannery O'Connor, "Some Aspects of the Grotesque in Southern Fiction," in *Collected Works* (New York: Library of America, 1988), p. 815.

43. David Foster Wallace, *Brief Interviews with Hideous Men* (Boston: Little, Brown, 1999), p. 70.

44. Ibid., p. 71.

45. Ibid., p. 72.

46. Ibid., p. 72.

47. Ibid., p. 74.

48. Ibid., p. 72.

49. Ibid., p. 72.

50. Ibid., p. 74.

51. Wallace, *Infinite Jest*, p. 795.

52. Ibid., p. 374.

53. I owe the idea that the Boston sequence functions as an articulation of Wallace's literary dicta to Halvor Aakhus, who was a student in my Fall 2016 graduate seminar on approaches to periodizing post-1960 US fiction.

54. Wallace, "E Unibus Pluram: Television and U.S. Fiction" in *Review of Contemporary Fiction* 13.2 (Summer 1993), pp. 169–171.

55. Stephen J. Burn, *Jonathan Franzen at the End of Postmodernism* (New York: Bloomsbury, 2008).

56. D. H. Lawrence, *Studies in Classic American Literature* (New Delhi: Atlantic Publishers and Distributors, 1995), pp. 157–158.

57. Andrew Hoberek, "The Novel after David Foster Wallace," in Boswell and Burn (eds.), *A Companion*, pp. 216–217.

58. Wallace, *Infinite Jest*, p. 39.

59. Ibid., p. 38.

60. David Letzler, "Encyclopedic Novels and the Cruft of Fiction: *Infinite Jest*'s Endnotes," in Boswell (ed.), *David Foster Wallace and "The Long Thing": New Essays on the Novels* (New York: Bloomsbury, 2014), pp. 168, 162–190.

61. Edward Mendelson, "Encyclopedic Narrative: From Dante to Pynchon," *Modern Language Notes* 91 (1976), p. 1268. Marshall Boswell, *Understanding David Foster Wallace* (Columbia: University of South Carolina Press, 2009), pp. 122–123 relates *Infinite Jest*'s encyclopedic character to its Pynchonian interpolation of various popular genres.

62. Stephen J. Burn, *David Foster Wallace's* Infinite Jest: *A Reader's Guide*, Second Ed. (New York: Continuum, 2012).

63. Letzler, p. 168.

64. Melville, *Moby-Dick*, p. 114.

65. Hering, *Fiction and Form*, p. 67.

66. Wallace, *Infinite Jest*, p. 478.

67. David Foster Wallace, *The Broom of the System* (New York: Penguin, 1987), pp. 440–441.

68. Wallace, *Infinite Jest*, p. 981.

69. See my *The Twilight of the Middle Class: Post–World War II American Fiction and White-Collar Work* (Princeton, NJ: Princeton University Press, 2005), pp. 95–112.

70. C. L. R. James, *Mariners, Renegades, and Castaways: The Story of Herman Melville and the World We Live In*, ed. Donald Pease (1953; Hanover: University Press of New England, 2001).

71. McGurl, "The Institution of Nothing," p. 38.

72. Andrew Warren, "Modeling Community and Narrative in *Infinite Jest* and *The Pale King*," in Boswell (ed.), *David Foster Wallace and "The Long Thing,"* pp. 76, 61–84.

3

LEE KONSTANTINOU

Wallace's "Bad" Influence

"We need this control thing made explicit. No more games. People tell
me what to do and think and say and call them, and I do it. It'll all be
simple."

– The Broom of the System

Almost a decade after his suicide, "David Foster Wallace" has become
a name to conjure with. Mostly, Wallace's name has conjured enthusiasm.
Journalists, scholars, and artists have discussed the author's legacy at great
and affectionate length. Appreciative allusions to his life and work have
appeared on television shows such as *The Simpsons, Parks and Recreation,
Weeds,* and *The Office.*[1] The indie rock band *The Decemberists* has filmed
a music video, directed by Michael Schur, that visually invokes the Eschaton
chapter of *Infinite Jest.*[2] Online groups such as Infinite Summer (2009) and
Infinite Winter (2016) have provided popular occasions to discuss Wallace's
writing, especially his 1996 magnum opus, *Infinite Jest.* And James
Ponsoldt's 2015 film, *The End of the Tour,* has painted a loving, arguably
idolizing portrait of the author. But after a decorous period, critiques of
Wallace's legacy have become increasingly common, even among his friends
and critics who otherwise champion his work.[3] Some complain that new
readers often only know the author through his 2005 Kenyon College
commencement speech, which was published after his death as a short
book called *This Is Water: Some Thoughts, Delivered on a Significant
Occasion, about Living a Compassionate Life* and was adapted into a much-
viewed online video by The Glossary, a multimedia design and production
company. Jonathan Russell Clarke wants to reclaim Wallace from the "lit-
bros" who have appropriated his legacy.[4] Christian Lorentzen has dispar-
aged the tendency to reduce Wallace to a "wisdom-dispensing sage" who
espoused a Pollyannaish view of life and literature.[5] Against the culture's
beatification of his dead friend, Jonathan Franzen has claimed that "the
people who knew David least well are most likely to speak of him in saintly
terms."[6] Those most inclined to celebrate Wallace, these commentators
worry, misunderstand Wallace's writing and ignore the less savory dimensions of his legacy. Wallace has been transformed into an empty literary
brand name, an author whose books are often purchased but rarely read.

Many have taken their criticism further. Some have sought out, with Mark McGurl, "the limits of [Wallace's] seductively fine mind," engaging in a collective "refusal, as readers, to enter into [his] project and finish it on his terms."[7] Others are more extreme in their refusal. In Amy Hungerford's view, Wallace's desire to "fuck the reader," a desire she insists is at once biographical and literary, should be adamantly resisted.[8] When Wallace tries to seduce us, we should tell him to fuck off. Unlike Clarke's, Lorentzen's, and Franzen's effort to differentiate Wallace from what might be called the Wallace Industry, critics such as McGurl and Hungerford suggest that the two might be the same, and that Wallace should be vigilantly resisted. This growing refusal might be viewed, on the one hand, as the inevitable backlash that arises against any cultural figure who draws any measure of attention (just another turn of the culture industry) or, on the other hand, as the normal, healthy operation of literary history, in which readers, critics, and writers debate the significance of this or that artist, preserving a handful, discarding almost everyone else. These are plausible hypotheses, but this chapter, which surveys Wallace's influence in the decade since his death, argues against both. As the vocabulary of fucking and fucking over readers suggests, critics who refuse Wallace in the strongest terms don't just argue that he is misunderstood or has serious limitations. They worry that his art seduces readers, and they suggest that even *to read* Wallace (critically or not) exposes one to his malign charms. Wallace is here figured as a master manipulator. The danger isn't that we might fail to read Wallace correctly, but that we might read his dangerously seductive writing just as he intended it.

Though these fears are, if taken in their most extreme form, wildly over-stated, they're not groundless. These were fears, after all, Wallace had about himself, fears he incorporated directly into his fiction. Wallace's reception is, I would therefore argue, an unavoidable question for scholars committed to understanding his writing – and to mapping its significance. That is, Wallace's reception isn't an extrinsic concern but, to the degree that Wallace's fiction is unusually concerned with anticipating its own reception, central to the work itself. Indeed, from the start of his career, Wallace created figurations of authors (and author-like figures) who manipulate readers (or reader-like figures). In his first novel, *The Broom of the System* (1987), Wallace depicts Rick Vigorous's nervous efforts to verbally control the novel's protagonist, Lenore Beadsman, through storytelling. Vigorous's manic desire to create a controlling language seems like a reaction to Lenore's grandmother's Wittgenstein-inspired claim that "any telling automatically becomes a kind of system, that controls everybody involved."[9] It is as if Vigorous hopes he can both talk himself out of the controlling system of language that he inhabits and replace that system with his own controlling language. This ambition, the desire to create new controlling languages, is again evident in James O. Incandenza's effort in *Infinite Jest* to create a film capable of overcoming his prodigious son Hal's robotic solipsism. Later in Wallace's oeuvre, these (usually male) author-figures increasingly manipulate the conditions of their own reception by seeming to level with the reader about their skill at manipulation, seduction, and control. *Brief Interviews with Hideous Men* (1999), for example, fixates on the sort of man who worries aloud that he "might be one of those guys who uses ... women," a hideous type whose confession that he's "a guy who's bad news" *is* the very act of manipulation that makes him bad news.[10] In these stories, an author-figure scripts the negative reception of his work *within* that work as a means of forestalling that negative reception. This prescripting can be viewed as the necessary result of what Clare Hayes-Brady has aptly called "an inescapable paradox in the relationship between author and reader," in which "the author depends on the reader's approval."[11] Wallace was obsessed with this paradox.

Sometimes, the author's approval-seeking anticipatory rhetoric triggers the very bad reception the author most wishes to avoid, as is the case with the protagonist of "The Depressed Person," whose self-conscious discussion of her emotional pain only increases her isolation, thereby amplifying her depression. At other times, anticipatory rhetoric is a sign of selfishness rather than sincerity, as with the collection's many hideous men. One incisive definition of Wallace's New Sincerity precisely emphasizes the paradoxes Wallace's anticipatory rhetoric creates. As Adam Kelly writes, New Sincerity connotes a situation in which "the anticipation of others' reception of one's outward behavior begins to take priority for the acting self, so that inner states lose their originating causal status and instead become effects of that anticipatory logic."[12] Wallace criticism has emphasized the danger that this anticipatory logic poses to an author's sense of agency. But anticipation doesn't only degrade the anticipator's autonomy. As Wallace shows in "Octet," the effort to evince "completely naked helpless pathetic sincerity" can very easily be mistaken for, and might not be so different from, "interhuman manipulation and bullshit gamesmanship."[13] The author's interlocutor – that is, the reader – therefore necessarily faces the possibility that her reaction to the artist, positive or negative, is itself merely the effect of manipulation. And Wallace himself, when describing his own reading and media-consumption habits, expressed a fear that he might himself be susceptible to such manipulation, speaking about his attempted "patricide" of the postmodern tradition embodied by Barth, Coover, Burroughs, Nabokov, and Pynchon precisely as an effort to transcend postmodern bullshit gamesmanship.[14] Considered in light of these fears, professions of Wallace's

New Sincerity or postirony raise unresolved questions of control and manipulation that complicate standard models of literary reception and influence. There has been much critical commentary on the way *Infinite Jest* invokes Harold Bloom's revisionary ratios from *The Anxiety of Influence*.[15] But relatively little scholarship has considered how Wallace's readers – both his critics and his fellow artists – have responded to Wallace's rhetorical prefiguration or anticipation of his own reception. If you aren't content to ignore Wallace, how do you overcome an author who has preemptively incorporated your reception of him into his art?

One response has sought to resist Wallace by identifying the author's work with his biographical presence – treating the two as if they were the same – and then resisting the work by criticizing the person. Person and persona, author and fiction, here merge. Mary Karr, who had a troubled relationship with Wallace, dramatizes this merger of person and persona in two poems she wrote after Wallace's suicide. "Suicide's Note: An Annual" speaks about the personal hurt Wallace's self-destruction caused her and those who knew him. "Despite / your best efforts," she writes, "you are every second / alive in a hard-gnawing way for all who breathed you deeply in."[16] And yet the poem equivocates on what it means for a person to have "breathed" Wallace in. The phrase "for all who breathed you deeply in" may, after all, speak about those who had a personal connection with Wallace or those who have only read his fiction, essays, or journalism. Karr herself has claimed that "the best parts of David Foster Wallace's fiction are nonfiction."[17] On this view, then, Wallace's suicide gets figured as a selfish "effort" whose intention is thwarted by the "hard-gnawing" life Wallace's writing evokes (where this writing is understood, at its best, to give nonfictional access to Wallace himself). Many readers have claimed, like Karr, to have inhaled Wallace's spirit from his writing. As Kathleen Fitzpatrick has suggested, Wallace wanted to forge "connections between reader, writer and text" that were "inescapably personal," and many readers have attested to feeling such a connection with the author.[18] From this perspective, the reader cannot help but feel disappointed when the writer with whom she has forged a personal connection destroys himself. Karr's other poem, "Read These," tempers the confidence with which "Suicide's Note" asserts that she (and the reader) can thwart Wallace's effort at self-annihilation by finding him again, still somehow alive, in his writing. In this poem, Karr suggests that Wallace's fans, his "worshipful subjects," are "no more / than instruments of his creation."[19] Wallace himself becomes "the King," a man who wants "the web browsers to ping / his name in literary mention everywhere on the world wide web." Wallace dominates his readers, "holding forth on the dullest / aspects of the human heart / with the sharpest possible wit. Unreadable / as Pound on usury or Aquinas on sex."[20] This poem, which again identifies Wallace with his writing, resists Wallace by insisting on his witty unreadability. Those who follow the King's dictates are obedient servants of his genius; those who find him unreadable, who recognize his venal desire for literary fame, grasp the true tragedy of his short life. Taken together, these two poems highlight the problem many have felt in following Wallace. On the one hand, Wallace inhabits everyone who breathes him in; on the other hand, those who have inhaled him become mere "instruments of his creation," little more than the products of his creative genius. Wallace threatens to destroy the person who comes into contact with him, absorbing that person into himself; yet again, persistent themes in Wallace's fiction are replicated in the lives of his readers, exactly as they are scripted within Wallace's fiction.

While Mary Karr's poems identify Wallace with his writing, quickly collapsing the distinction between fiction and nonfiction, another response to Wallace's legacy has been to separate Wallace's life from his art. It may seem indecorous to suggest that Wallace's widow, the visual artist and poet Karen Green, might be writing in opposition to her former husband's literary legacy, but her poetry volume, *Bough Down*, is best understood as an effort to differentiate Wallace as a person from Wallace as a writer, and in so doing to reclaim private grief from the public memorialization of her husband's death. As Green has suggested in an interview, she thought that public memorials that turn Wallace "into a celebrity writer dude" would "have made him wince, the good part of him. It has defined me too, and I'm really struggling with that."[21] The book that emerges from this struggle, a collection of prose poems and original collage images, recounts elements of their marriage. Figuring Wallace's dead body, Green worries that she "broke your kneecaps when I cut you down."[22] She writes, "I want him pissed off at politicians, ill at ease, trying to manipulate me into doing favors for him I would do anyway. I want him looking for his glasses, trying not to come, doing the dumb verb of journaling, getting spinach caught between canine and gum, berating my logorrhea, or my not staying mum."[23] These details – the sound of breaking kneecaps, the texture of spinach caught between teeth – figure Wallace as an individual person, not as an author. Unlike Karr's two poems, Green's book rigorously avoids linking Wallace to his writing, and yet *Bough Down* cannot entirely avoid the fact of Wallace's literary celebrity. Green writes:

Strangers feel free to email:

Nobody knew you before your husband took his life.
Nobody knew me, nobody knew me. I think this may be true.[24]

A stranger e-mails the poem's lyric speaker (whom I will call Karen), announcing to her, in italicized type (it is unclear whether the italicized text is the content of the e-mail or its implied message), that she had not attained public recognition before her husband's suicide. At the same time, this unsolicited communication becomes an occasion for true revelation. Karen accepts the judgment of the stranger: she was not known before her husband's death. By using poetry to make this point, Green finds a form best suited to express the paradox of this type of recognition. Karen's (and by extension Green's) ability to be known not only as a person but as an artist is, she fears, subordinated to the fact of Wallace's death, mediated through Wallace's artistic construction of a false sense of intimacy between himself and strangers. But the project of separating Wallace from his writing proves difficult even for those who were personally closest to him. Wallace can too easily become identified with his public image. Elsewhere in the book, Wallace's stylistic tics and quirks are replicated on the page. "I don't want to be Satan but will you join me [in smoking]," he tells her.[25] The fear that nobody knew Karen before her husband's suicide can therefore be read as the fundamental literary problem that *Bough Down* itself faces. Though the book aspires to be the meditation of an individual widow who has faced personal loss, it figures its own incorporation into a system of discourse that has emerged around the author's lost husband. The anxiety here is that in order to be known, Karen can only be recognized *through* the death of her husband. For her book of poems to be a private memorial, it must first traverse public spectacle. Green's identity, like the identity of Wallace's readers in Karr's poems, yet again becomes an effect of Wallace's art and fame. The book's title – *Bough Down* – itself dramatizes this situation. It figures Wallace's death as the falling of the branch of a tree in the garden that Green and Wallace together cultivated before his death, and it alludes to an act of supplication (bow down), the supplication Green's book itself is forced to make to the powerful literary influence whose aura cannot easily be overcome. The effort to separate Wallace's life from his writing confronts the paradox that, though Wallace's name itself doesn't appear within *Bough Down*, a poem about his life cannot help but enter into a literary-historical (rather than private) relationship with the deceased.

Taking for granted that Wallace and his writing or persona are inseparable, a third strategy for overcoming Wallace is to try to discredit, disavow, or overcome his characteristic literary style. The seeds of this critique are already visible in Franzen's claim that Wallace was "our strongest rhetorical writer."[26] What, after all, does the adjective "rhetorical" exclude? For Franzen, one thing it excludes or perhaps even inhibits is love. Wallace's characters, who stage elaborately crafted modes of rhetorical self-presentation and who manipulate the reader/listener, seem necessarily, by virtue of their rhetorical acumen, to be separated from "close loving relationships," which "have no standing in the Wallace fictional universe."[27] Wallace's rhetorical prowess is placed by Franzen into opposition with the possibility of a genuinely loving relationship between the reader and the writer. Similarly, it's Wallace's rhetorical style, his "slangy approachability," that Maud Newton blames or "pins" on Wallace.[28] The valence here is, as in Franzen's judgment, decidedly negative. Wallace's writing "prefigures many of the worst tendencies of the Internet," and "Wallace's moves have been adopted and further slackerized by a legion of opinion-mongers who not only lack his quick mind but seem not to have mastered the idea that to make an argument, you must, amid all the tap-dancing and hedging, actually lodge an argument."[29] Rejecting Wallace's rhetorical style, Newton concludes that "the best way to make an argument is to make it, straightforwardly, honestly, passionately, without regard to whether people will like you afterward."[30] James Wood critiques Wallace's style on slightly different grounds, arguing that Wallace enacts an "unidentified free indirect style," in which the characteristic voices of a community or society inflect the style of the third-person narrator.[31] Though he doesn't categorically condemn this technique in *How Fiction Works*, Wood's distaste for Wallace's "hideously ugly" and "rather painful" commercial idiom is apparent.[32] Wallace allegedly "prosecutes an intense argument about the decomposition of language in America," embracing a linguistic world that is "debased, vulgar, boring."[33] In all of these cases, Wallace's individual style is read as a rhetorical capaciousness, an ability to absorb the culture's voices and thereby replicate the culture's pathologies. And in all of these cases – Franzen, Newton, and Wood – we encounter an implied call to sincerity and directness that one might very well expect one of Wallace's own characters to give, perhaps after a lengthy rhetorical explanation of why it's so incredibly difficult to be straightforward and passionate. The difference is, of course, that these writers challenge the idea that such rhetorical excess is the necessary precursor to sincere and direct expression. Just say what you want to say, they seem to advise. Be direct. Speak well.

Taking up this challenge, many writers have refused Wallace's style. But to do so also seems to require dramatizing the process of resisting the temptation Wallace's style poses. Wallace's literary peers have therefore cast a critical eye on his legacy by writing him into their fiction. That is, they have written fictions that include Wallace-like figures as a strategy for motivating their own stylistic commitments (this is a variation of what I have elsewhere called storytelling neorealism).[34] Characters putatively based on Wallace have appeared in Jonathan Lethem's *Chronic City* (2009), Franzen's

Freedom (2010), Jennifer Egan's *A Visit from the Goon Squad* (2010), and most notably Jeffrey Eugenides's *The Marriage Plot* (2011). In *Chronic City*, Lethem invents an author named Ralph Warden Meeker who has written an incredibly boring "thousand-page prose poem" called *Obstinate Dust*, an obvious surrogate for *Infinite Jest*.[35] About this book, one character complains, "Next thing you know the characters' names will be X, Y, and Z," an allusion no doubt to Wallace's short story "Octet," in which characters are indeed named X and Y.[36] The accessible (if meandering) style of *Chronic City* takes on its meaning partly in relation to the inaccessibility of *Obstinate Dust*. Lethem's novel's interest in esoteric knowledge doesn't come wrapped in the form of a thousand-page prose poem. Lethem also arguably overcomes Wallace by plagiarizing him, incorporating Wallace's writing into his essay "The Ecstasy of Influence: A Plagiarism," a patchwork essay first published in 2007 in *Harper's* magazine that argues for the unavoidability and desirability of literary appropriation, cut-up, and collage.[37] Even so, Lethem's use of the term "influence" in the title of this essay is arguably misleading. Borrowing of Wallace's prose demotes Wallace's voice from influence to source.

Like *Chronic City*, Franzen's *Freedom* figures its own artistic project in opposition (again an affectionate or respectful opposition) to Wallace's alleged inability to move beyond his own rhetorical pyrotechnics. Franzen has reported that he was partly motivated to complete *Freedom* by his anger at Wallace's suicide. "I've got one advantage over you," he remembers thinking, "and that's that I'm still alive, and I'm going to show what I can do."[38] Some critics have argued that Franzen also incorporates Wallace into *Freedom* in the guise of Richard Katz, a charismatic, occasionally suicidal, aging punk.[39] After having an affair with Richard, the novel's protagonist Patty Berglund is ultimately reconciled with her estranged husband, Walter (Richard's former roommate). If we accept that Richard stands in for Wallace, Franzen would be figuring the power and charisma of Wallace's style in the form of *Freedom*'s love triangle, that is to say, a triangle in which Richard is incapable of loving Patty, and Walter (the proxy for Franzen himself) must learn to overcome his anger in order to allow himself to accept her love. The climax of the novel supports this view. After refusing to reconcile with Patty, who nearly freezes to death sitting on the porch of the cabin at the Nameless Lake where he is living, Walter finally "stopped looking at her eyes and started looking into them, returning their look before it was too late."[40] Franzen's riposte to Wallace manifests both as subject matter (Walter finally learns to allow himself to love) and style (*Freedom*, more even than *The Corrections*, epitomizes the reader-friendly "Contract Novel" Franzen dedicated himself to writing after he rejected postmodernism).[41] Franzen's anger motivates him to produce a work of fiction that makes room for the love he earlier claimed was missing from Wallace's fiction.

Jeffrey Eugenides confronts the legacy of Wallace in similar terms. A thinly disguised surrogate of Wallace – the character Leonard Bankhead, a mentally ill, bandana-wearing manipulator – appears in *The Marriage Plot*. As Marshall Boswell has convincingly argued, Eugenides's novel "stages an artistic battle between himself and Wallace that parodies Wallace's own self-conscious critiques of Harold Bloom's *The Anxiety of Influence*."[42] No mere passing mention of Wallace, Eugenides has written a novel that places his artistic confrontation with Wallace front and center. Mitchell Grammaticus, the character who stands in for Eugenides in this artistic battle, confronts Leonard, the Wallace surrogate, for the heart of Brown English-major Madeleine Hanna. When Leonard and Mitchell finally face each other at the end of the novel, Mitchell realizes that, "under other circumstances, he and Leonard Bankhead might have been the best of friends. He understood why Madeleine had fallen in love with him, and why she had married him."[43] Leonard finally quits the scene, leaving Mitchell with a free hand to win Madeleine's heart. But unlike *Freedom*, which affirms the power of Patty and Walter's love, *The Marriage Plot* doesn't end with a fulfilled love plot. Instead, Mitchell concludes that Madeleine has "more important things to do with her life" than get together with him.[44] The important thing that Madeleine has to do with her life is go to graduate school and join "a new class of academics" who "were talking about all the old [Victorian] books she loved, but in new ways."[45] That is, Madeleine is destined to become a "Victorianist."[46] This ending retroactively frames *The Marriage Plot* as a neo-Victorian novel. Eugenides means to distinguish the neo-Victorian realist novel not only from high postmodernism (the distinction that most critics of the novel have discussed) but also from contemporary rivals (that is, from the rhetorical maximalism of David Foster Wallace and his imitators).

Eugenides's literary conflict with Wallace suggests that Wallace's "slack-erized" style should not be identified with post-postmodernist fiction as such. If we recognize that Wallace's intentionally "debased, vulgar, and boring" prose is but one option among many that writers have developed after postmodernism, we would need to modify Andrew Hoberek's reading of Wallace's bad style. Wallace's "true literary legacy," Hoberek argues, is his "participation in this periodic revival of bad form."[47] Wallace "turns *to* postmodernism in reaction *against* minimalism," thereby facilitating a historical transition from minimalism to maximalism.[48] Hoberek takes the difference between Junot Díaz's *Drown* (1996) and his *The Brief Wondrous Life of Oscar Wao* (2007) as exemplary of this transition, claiming that "Wallace's elaboration of an intentional bad form starting at the level of the sentence and extending outward" should be the starting point to assess his impact on twenty-first-century American writing.[49] Hoberek emphasizes the intentionality of Wallace's bad form, suggesting that "bad form in the aesthetic sense merges with bad form in the social sense to connote sincerity."[50] For authors such as Díaz, Adam Levin, Dave Eggers, and others, a messy maximalism becomes a new, historically effective way to tell the truth. This is, I think, an accurate but partial reading of the contemporary literary field. Indeed, Díaz himself followed *Oscar Wao* with the much more conventional voice-driven short story collection, *This is How You Lose Her* (2012).

One might argue that the sort of formal badness Hoberek attributes to the whole literary field after the dominance of minimalism – a "badness" we might also attribute to the fiction of, say, William Vollmann or Donald Antrim – has by now become a David Foster Wallace trademark, a named object of reverence and critique. Support for this view can be found in comments made upon Wallace's death by the novelist and essayist Benjamin Kunkel. Kunkel writes that "Wallace showed that you could write in a colloquial and informal register – the register in which we sound to ourselves like the people we actually are – without thereby cordoning off any part of your vocabulary or experience."[51] Though he found Wallace's style seductive, Kunkel concludes that "Wallace's stylistic naturalism ... could end up subverting the honesty it proposed to serve." It could "become mannered, even baroque" and so he realizes "that relaxed diction could be a tremendous strain and artifice. Afterwards I understood that I wrote more naturally and honestly when more formally." In one sense, Kunkel arrives at a position not unlike that espoused by James Wood above. And it's surely important that Kunkel and the other founding editors of the literary journal *n+1* revered Wood's *New Republic* reviews as students at Harvard during the 1990s. But Kunkel sees Wallace's style as a stage to be worked through. In the formality of diction one finds in Kunkel's essays, and in the fiction one typically finds in the pages of *n+1* – the writing of, say, Sheila Heti, Helen DeWitt, or Nell Zink – one sees the outlines of an alternative aesthetic project, one that has parted ways with Wallace even as it recognizes him as a weighty figure in the literary field. I would suggest that Wallace himself came to agree with these criticisms of his style – he came to see himself as mannered and baroque – and at the end of his career struggled against the gravitational field generated by his own reputation. Evidence that Wallace sought to overcome his own bad form – as well as the project of taking bad form as synonymous with sincerity – is evident in his posthumously published novel *The Pale King* (2011). As D. T. Max and David Hering have shown, we should read this book at least in part as an effort on Wallace's part to overcome the power of his own achievement in *Infinite Jest*.[52] That is, like his readers, Wallace found it hard to escape his own persona, and the "Author Here" chapters of *The Pale King* can be fruitfully read as a parody of the author's own style.[53] Unlike other moments in which Wallace invokes a version of himself (in "Octet" or "Good Old Neon"), the David Wallace of *The Pale King* is not meant to be mistaken for the author. David's biography, his facial scarring, and his promised manipulation of cloyingly good Leonard Stecyk block easy identification between David and Wallace.[54]

In light of this disidentification, I would conclude by suggesting that the "Author Here" sections also signal Wallace's fear that he might not be up-to-date in the literary marketplace of the twenty-first century. For all the efforts to suggest that Wallace predicted dimensions of Internet culture, it might be most accurate to say, following Kunkel's argument, that Wallace was a figure who reached his peak influence in the late 1990s. The character David's effort in *The Pale King* to cash in on the market success of memoirs suggests that Wallace's main influence may be negative. The "reality hunger" fictions that David Shields has described (autofiction, experimental memoir, essays as fiction) that have flourished in the twenty-first century take Wallace's desire to speak 100-percent honestly seriously but, unlike Wallace, do not agonize over the mediating operations required to engage in such honesty. The autofictions and affective fictions of Heti, Tao Lin, Teju Cole, Ben Lerner, and Karl Ove Knausgård, among others, participate in Wallace's project without feeling any particular need, or at least feeling less need, to acrobatically describe the processes of mediation in minute detail.

The example of autofiction illustrates the possibility of a final strategy for following Wallace: the possibility of the nonanxious incorporation of Wallace into the contemporary novel. This nonanxious approach to following Wallace might also be best exemplified by the Wallace surrogate who appears in Egan's *A Visit from the Goon Squad*. In this novel, Egan includes a heavily footnoted chapter written by a journalist named Jules Jones, which in various ways invokes Wallace's style – making it the style of celebrity journalism as such – while putting this chapter on equal footing with a range of other chapters, each of which adopts a different perspective. This is what developing a healthy stance toward Wallace's writing might look like formally. That is, Egan's *Goon Squad* doesn't elevate Wallace to a demiurge or take him as a figure who must be eradicated, but understands his contribution to recent literary history as one of a variety of productive possibilities available for writers in the twenty-first century. Neither scourge nor hero, this version of Wallace would represent one strand of contemporary fiction. To be clear, when

I write that Wallace is "one strand of contemporary fiction" I do not mean to diminish the importance of Wallace's artistic achievement. Wallace represents, in my view, a monumentally important writer, one whose writing merits close attention and repays intense critical scrutiny. Nonetheless, what Egan's novel has done is find a way to fictionally recognize Wallace's formal power without being tyrannized by his legacy. I will end by suggesting Egan's example exemplifies a desirable aspiration for both critical and literary responses to Wallace. One might engage with him, find value in his project, argue with him, analyze him, debate his artistic success, putting aside once and for all the dick-waggling drama of Oedipal struggle his example has sometimes elicited. We might read him (or not) without being haunted by him.

Notes

1. For an overview of these references, see Chloe Schildhause, "The David Foster Wallace TV and Film References You May Have Missed," *UPROXX*, February 21, 2015, http://uproxx.com/tv/david-foster-wallace-pop-culture-references/.
2. For an account of the creation of this video, see Dave Itzkoff, "'Infinite Jest' Imbues Decemberists Video by Michael Schur," *The New York Times*, August 22, 2011, www.nytimes.com/2011/08/23/arts/music/michael-schur-directs-decemberists-video.html.
3. For relatively positive appraisals of Wallace's legacy, see Samuel Cohen and Lee Konstantinou (eds.), *The Legacy of David Foster Wallace* (Iowa City: University of Iowa Press, 2012). For an argument that analyzes Wallace's commitment to open or "failed" forms as well as a well-informed critique of Wallace's various intellectual and aesthetic failings, see Clare Hayes-Brady, *The Unspeakable Failures of David Foster Wallace: Language, Identity, and Resistance* (New York: Bloomsbury Academic, 2016). For an argument that critics shouldn't criticize Wallace's writing but refuse to read him altogether, see Amy Hungerford, *Making Literature Now* (Stanford, CA: Stanford University Press, 2016).
4. Jonathan Russell Clarke, "Reclaiming David Foster Wallace from the Lit-Bros," *Literary Hub*, August 20, 2015, http://lithub.com/reclaiming-david-foster-wallace-from-the-lit-bros/.
5. Christian Lorentzen, "The Rewriting of David Foster Wallace," *Vulture*, June 30, 2015, http://www.vulture.com/2015/06/rewriting-of-david-foster-wallace.html.
6. Jonathan Franzen, *Farther Away: Essays* (New York: Farrar, Straus, and Giroux, 2012), p. 39.
7. Mark McGurl, "The Institution of Nothing: David Foster Wallace in the Program," *boundary 2* 41.3 (Fall 2014), pp. 48–49.
8. Hungerford, *Making Literature Now*, p. 144.
9. David Foster Wallace, *The Broom of the System: A Novel* (New York: Penguin, 1987), p. 122.

10. David Foster Wallace, *Brief Interviews with Hideous Men* (Boston: Little, Brown, 1999), p. 91.

11. Hayes-Brady, *The Unspeakable Failures of David Foster Wallace*, p. 150.

12. Adam Kelly, "David Foster Wallace and the New Sincerity in American Fiction," in David Hering (ed.), *Consider David Foster Wallace: Critical Essays* (Los Angeles: SSMG, 2010), p. 136.

13. Wallace, *Brief Interviews with Hideous Men*, p. 154.

14. David Foster Wallace, "An Expanded Interview with David Foster Wallace," by Larry McCaffery in Stephen J. Burn (ed.), *Conversations With David Foster Wallace* (Jackson: University of Mississippi, 2012), p. 48.

15. The first discussion of Wallace's engagement with Bloom can be found in Marshall Boswell, *Understanding David Foster Wallace* (Columbia: University of South Carolina Press, 2003). See also the important essay by A. O. Scott, "The Panic of Influence," *New York Review of Books*, www.nybooks.com/articles/2000/02/10/the-panic-of-influence/, accessed January 20, 2017. For an argument that Wallace's "Westward the Course of Empire Takes Its Way" engages in "a self-aware misprision" of Barth's "Lost in the Funhouse," see Charles B. Harris, "The Anxiety of Influence: The John Barth/David Foster Wallace Connection," *Critique: Studies in Contemporary Fiction* 55.2 (2014): p. 122. See also Brian McHale, "The Pale King, Or, The White Visitation," in Marshall Boswell and Stephen J. Burn (eds.), *A Companion to David Foster Wallace Studies* (New York: Palgrave Macmillan, 2013), pp. 191–210. For a discussion of Wallace's relation to Bloom's *apophrades*, see David Hering, *David Foster Wallace: Fiction and Form* (New York: Bloomsbury Academic, 2016). For a discussion of Wallace's use of *tessera*, see Lucas Thompson, *Global Wallace: David Foster Wallace and World Literature* (New York: Bloomsbury Academic, 2016). Thompson argues that other than this one ratio, Wallace was "at sharp odds with the conception [of influence] set forth in *The Anxiety of Influence*," p. 40. Wallace told David Lipsky, however, that "I believe in Harold Bloom's theory of *misprision*." David Lipsky, *Although of Course You End Up Becoming Yourself: A Road Trip with David Foster Wallace* (New York: Broadway Books, 2010), p. 127.

16. Mary Karr, "Suicide's Note: An Annual," *Poetry*, September 1, 2012, www.poetryfoundation.org/poetrymagazine/poems/detail/55744.

17. Scott Timberg, "Mary Karr on the 'Loser, Outsider Weirdos' of Memoir and Skipping the David Foster Wallace Movie: 'The Whole St. David Thing … It's a Little Hard to Take,'" *Salon*, September 27, 2015, www.salon.com/2015/09/27/mary_karr_on_the_loser_outsider_weirdos_of_memoir_and_skipping_the_david_foster_wallace_movie_the_whole_st_david_thing_its_a_little_hard_to_take/.

18. Kathleen Fitzpatrick, "Infinite Summer: Reading, Empathy, and the Social Network," in Samuel Cohen and Lee Konstantinou (eds.), *The Legacy of David Foster Wallace* (Iowa City: University of Iowa Press, 2012), p. 184.

19. Mary Karr, "Read These," *Poetry*, September 1, 2012, www.poetryfoundation.org/poetrymagazine/poems/detail/55743.

20. Ibid.

21. Tim Adams, "Karen Green: 'David Foster Wallace's Suicide Turned Him into a 'Celebrity Writer Dude', Which Would Have Made Him Wince',"

The Guardian, April 9, 2011, sec. Books, www.theguardian.com/books/2011/apr/10/karen-green-david-foster-wallace-interview.

22. Karen Green, *Bough Down* (Los Angeles: Siglio, 2013), p. 29.
23. Ibid., p. 34.
24. Ibid., p. 74.
25. Ibid., p. 17.
26. Bruce Weber, "David Foster Wallace, Influential Writer, Dies at 46," *New York Times*, September 14, 2008, www.nytimes.com/2008/09/15/books/15wallace.html.
27. Franzen, *Farther Away*, p. 39.
28. Maud Newton, "Another Thing to Sort of Pin on David Foster Wallace," *New York Times*, August 19, 2011, www.nytimes.com/2011/08/21/magazine/another-thing-to-sort-of-pin-on-david-foster-wallace.html.
29. Ibid.
30. Ibid.
31. James Wood, *How Fiction Works* (New York: Farrar, Straus, and Giroux, 2008), p. 31.
32. Ibid., p. 32.
33. Ibid., p. 33.
34. Lee Konstantinou, "Neorealist Fiction," in Rachel Greenwald Smith (ed.), *American Literature in Transition: 2000–2010* (Cambridge: Cambridge University Press, 2017).
35. Jonathan Lethem, *Chronic City*, reprint edition (New York: Vintage, 2010), p. 102.
36. Ibid.
37. Jonathan Lethem, *The Ecstasy of Influence: Nonfictions, Etc.* (New York: Vintage, 2012).
38. Ed Pilkington, "Jonathan Franzen: 'I Must Be Near the End of My Career – People Are Starting to Approve,'" *The Guardian*, September 24, 2010, sec. Books, www.theguardian.com/books/2010/sep/25/jonathan-franzen-interview.
39. Keith Miller, "*Freedom* by Jonathan Franzen: Review," September 24, 2010, sec. Culture, www.telegraph.co.uk/culture/books/bookreviews/8020599/Freedom-by-Jonathan-Franzen-review.html. See also David Haglund and Matthew Dessem, "Yes, Jeffrey Eugenides Was Thinking of David Foster Wallace," *Slate*, October 10, 2011, www.slate.com/blogs/browbeat/2011/10/10/jeffrey_eugenides_david_foster_wallace_jonathan_franzen_and_the_.html.
40. Jonathan Franzen, *Freedom: A Novel* (New York: Farrar, Straus, and Giroux, 2010), p. 594.
41. Jonathan Franzen, "Mr. Difficult," in *How to Be Alone: Essays* (New York: Picador, 2003), pp. 238–69.
42. Marshall Boswell, "The Rival Lover: David Foster Wallace and the Anxiety of Influence in Jeffrey Eugenides's *The Marriage Plot*," *MFS Modern Fiction Studies* 62.3 (2016), p. 500.
43. Jeffrey Eugenides, *The Marriage Plot: A Novel* (Picador, 2012), p. 401.
44. Ibid., p. 406.
45. Ibid., p. 177.
46. Ibid., p. 180.

47. Andrew Hoberek, "The Novel after David Foster Wallace," in Marshall Boswell and Stephen J. Burn (eds.), *A Companion to David Foster Wallace Studies* (New York: Palgrave Macmillan, 2013), p. 217.

48. Ibid.

49. Ibid.

50. Ibid.

51. Benjamin Kunkel, "DFW," *n+1*, April 27, 2011, https://nplusonemag.com/online-only/online-only/dfw-1962–2008/.

52. See D. T. Max, *Every Love Story Is a Ghost Story: A Life of David Foster Wallace* (New York: Viking, 2012) and Hering, *Fiction and Form*.

53. Lee Konstantinou, "Unfinished Form," *Los Angeles Review of Books*, July 6, 2011, https://lareviewofbooks.org/article/unfinished-form/.

54. My reading parts ways from the interpretation of the David Wallace character offered by Hering, Miley, and Boswell. See Hering, *David Foster Wallace*. Mike Miley, " ... And Starring David Foster Wallace as Himself: Performance and Persona in *The Pale King*," *Critique* 57.2 (2016), pp. 191–207. Marshall Boswell, "Author Here: The Legal Fiction of David Foster Wallace's *The Pale King*," *English Studies* 95.1 (2014), pp. 25–39. In my view, the character of David Wallace in *The Pale King* partly becomes a figure of Wallace's prior style. Wallace's late-career effort to overcome his mid-career achievement mirrors Charles B. Harris's description of an earlier moment in Wallace's career, when he again confronted the "strong precursor" of his first novel. Harris, "The Anxiety of Influence," p. 120.

PART II

Early Works, Story Collections, and Nonfiction

4

MATTHEW LUTER

The Broom of the System and Girl with Curious Hair

It is easy to think of the two earliest published books of David Foster Wallace, the debut novel *The Broom of the System* (1987) and the story collection *Girl with Curious Hair* (1989), as Wallace's apprentice work, but this is not because these early books are somehow incomplete or insufficiently entertaining, or easily dismissed as juvenilia. Instead, both of these books are the work of a writer still figuring out what sort of writer he is going to be. Where *Infinite Jest* (1996), the later stories, and *The Pale King* (2011) are the work of a mature writer at the height of his power, *Broom* and *Girl* are more defined by their influences (both literary and philosophical) and Wallace's careful responses to them. At times, Wallace the apprentice is ecstatically in thrall to those influences, as is the case in his embrace of Thomas Pynchon and Ludwig Wittgenstein in *Broom*. In other moments, though, especially in some of the stories in *Girl*, he defines himself in direct opposition to influences like John Barth and contemporaries like Bret Easton Ellis, while also forging a more fruitful and genuinely communicative path forward for contemporary literary fiction.

Wallace wrote *The Broom of the System* as a thesis project while an undergraduate at Amherst. Wallace later dismissed *Broom* as immature, even adolescent work, recalling that, "there's a lot of stuff in that novel I'd like to reel back in and do better," since "I still thought in terms of distinct problems and univocal solutions."[1] D. T. Max, however, sees that comment as overly self-deprecating, arguing, "this adolescent is not just smart; he is attempting to communicate."[2] *Broom* is set in Cleveland, in the then near future of 1990, after the Ohio landscape has been altered by the construction of the artificial Great Ohio Desert (or G.O.D.), a black-sanded void that was built to lend gravitas to a space that, in the view of Ohio's onetime governor, was too comfortable and needed to become a site of spiritual extremity. The book's central character is Lenore Beadsman, a young woman whose great-grandmother, also named Lenore Beadsman, has just disappeared (along with a number of other residents) from a senior living facility.

The younger Lenore spends the book searching for the older Lenore while quietly despairing over the state of her relationship with her boyfriend, Rick Vigorous. Other important subplots involve Lenore's pet parrot becoming an unlikely popular sidekick on a televangelist's show and the corporate intrigue attached to the discovery of a new baby food ingredient that could help the language cortex of babies' brains grow with precocious speed (and might be responsible for the parrot's sudden loquaciousness). Like many digressive and ambitious first novels, *Broom* is full of stories within stories and tangents that sometimes lead nowhere, making it a book that is simultaneously single-minded in focus (where is Lenore Senior?) and maddeningly diffuse in potential strains of meaning.

This multivalence of meaning comes out of *Broom*'s obsession with what language can and cannot accomplish. In fact, Wallace has described the novel as essentially "a conversation between Derrida and Wittgenstein."[3] The work of Ludwig Wittgenstein is the primary philosophical source for the novel: Lenore Senior was a student of Wittgenstein's decades ago, and one of her prize possessions is a copy of Wittgenstein's *Philosophical Investigations*, a book whose personal and intellectual significance to Lenore few other characters seem to understand. Where Jacques Derrida and other deconstructionist linguists view language as inherently unstable to the point that language can hardly convey believable meaning whatsoever, Wittgenstein's linguistic theory allows that specific context can help define (and hence stabilize, even if for only a moment) the meaning of a particular utterance. A word may have dozens of potential uses and potential definitions, he allows, but successful communication can arise when speakers, writers, listeners, and readers consider the specific rhetorical situation in which an utterance takes place.[4]

In *Broom* communication acts often do not entirely succeed (more on this shortly), but not because, as Wallace's interpretation of Derrida would have it, language has been evacuated of its ability to transmit meaning.[5] When language fails in *Broom*, this takes place because the message, medium, or receiver is somehow inappropriate for the moment, as defined by the speaker's intent. As a result, *Broom* functions as a philosophical act, in which Wallace rejects the Derridean view of language and embraces Wittgenstein's thought. The latter view admits that language is unstable and sometimes self-contradictory but still holds out of the possibility that authentic communication can create genuine emotional and intellectual connections between people, including the reader–writer relationship. This is a crucial move in the development of the apprentice Wallace, as it indicates a desire to leave behind linguistic (and literary) gamesmanship that does not communicate truth and instead to seek ways for language (and fiction) to speak to listeners or readers with more sincere and genuine intent. Wallace's attempt at making this paradigm shift will come into clearest focus in *Girl with Curious Hair*'s final story, "Westward the Course of Empire Makes Its Way," but he initially gestures toward this shift in *Broom*.

If *Broom*'s primary philosophical source is Wittgenstein, then its primary literary source is the American postmodern novelist Thomas Pynchon. Wallace includes brief nods to some other postmodernist predecessors, most notably Vladimir Nabokov, as Rick Vigorous, when waxing lyrical about the beauty of Lenore, can sound reminiscent of *Lolita*'s Humbert Humbert at his most ecstatic.[6] And an often unheralded influence, Wallace says, is the Argentine novelist Manuel Puig, whose work Wallace has complimented on multiple occasions and which frequently includes, as does *Broom*, lengthy passages of narration-free dialogue.[7] But the single book that casts the longest shadow over *Broom* is no doubt Pynchon's second novel, *The Crying of Lot 49* (1965). Pynchon's protagonist, Oedipa Maas, who is roughly the same age as Lenore Beadsman, finds out in her novel's opening page that a recently deceased ex-boyfriend has named her the executor of his will. Her attempt to find out why she is in this position leads to a complex investigation that may unearth a shadowy conspiracy that dates back centuries. Wallace shares with Pynchon a weakness for funny names (in *Broom*, Biff Diggerence and Judith Prietht, to name just two; in Pynchon, Mucho Maas and Genghis Cohen, among others) and stoner humor, as in the college-set scenes in *Broom* that involve fraternity hijinks and drinking games. And compare the virtuoso opening sentence of *Lot 49* – which gestures toward the time, place, and milieu of our main character while introducing the central problem of the will, in an economical seven sentences – to the opening of section 3b of *Broom*: "Well, now, just imagine how you'd feel if your great-grandmother ... were just all of a sudden missing, altogether, and was for all you knew lying flat as a wet Saltine on some highway with a tire track in her forehead and her walker now a sort of large trivet, and you'll have an idea of how Lenore Beadsman felt."[8] Wallace's passage, without my truncation, runs over 21 lines, effectively out-Pynchoning Pynchon.

In *Lot 49* the complexity of the conspiracy that Oedipa Maas unearths eventually leads her to question what world she actually lives in altogether: she might either be the victim of a wildly elaborate hoax, simply hallucinating everything, entirely correct about how the world really works, or completely insane.[9] Similarly, Lenore Beadsman doubts her own reality throughout the novel. In the midst of a crucial scene of philosophical dialogue with his sister, Lenore's brother LaVache suggests that "Lenore [Senior] has you believing, with your complicity ... that you're not really real, or that you're only real insofar as you're told about, so that to the extent that you're real you're controlled, and thus not in control, so that you're more like a sort of character than a person, really."[10] Sensing that many in her life bear greater forces of will than she does, Lenore complains to her therapist that "everybody for some reason wants to *get* me out there," speaking both of her lack of desire to visit the Great Ohio Desert and, in an idiomatic sense, a belief that everyone is out to get her.[11] She admits later that her family "tends to see life as more or less a verbal phenomenon."[12] As Patrick O'Donnell puts it, where Pynchon is "semiotic," Wallace is more interested in "affective, environmental relations" between people than just treating plots as plots and characters as characters.[13] Put another way, for Pynchon, a character such as Lenore who thinks of herself as more fictional than human might be a fun literary opportunity, but for Wallace, such a fate is problematic to say the least.

Pynchon's gleefully frustrating ending to *Lot 49* closes the novel immediately before a final scene that would, the entire novel has implied, help put to rest many of the core plot's remaining open questions. Wallace's ending, conversely, does answer the core plot's open question indirectly. *Broom* establishes early on that Lenore Senior can only live in rooms kept at 98.6 degrees, so when the phone system repairman reveals that a tunnel beneath the phone console has been mysteriously set to the temperature of the human body, we discover than Lenore's great-grandmother has been literally under her nose for much of the novel. Even so, Wallace does not clarify fully why Lenore Senior has been there, for how long, or, most intriguingly, whether she is still alive. Where Pynchon deliberately defers closure of *Lot 49*'s primary plotline, Wallace appears to give the search for Lenore Senior closure – here she is/was! – but does not bother to explain any further questions raised by the limited closure he does provide.[14] Most prominently incomplete of all is *Broom*'s unfinished final sentence. Rick Vigorous promises Lenore, "I'm a man of my" as the book ends mid-sentence.[15] The missing word is quite obviously *word* – but in a book as obsessively focused on the limits of communication as this one, the truncated sentence also lets Wallace question how necessary any single word is to communication. If the word "word" is missing, yet readers are still able to grasp Rick's point, then language itself may not be as essential to communication (or to our best understandings of reality) as we might otherwise believe.[16] Read another way, the deletion of "word" implicitly rejects logocentrism.[17] In *The Broom of the System*, the G.O.D. is a desert, and the primary presence of traditional religion is a fatuous piece of televangelism that presents a parrot as a prophet, spouting language that has an audience but little communicative intent. By this reading, it is no wonder, then, that the book's final linguistic gesture can be read as a rejection of the logocentric.

Indeed, communication that does not entirely achieve successful transmission appears in *Broom* in abundance. The novel is full of language that does not reach its intended audience: a recurring gag in the book concerns the internal phone system at Lenore's workplace, where she works the switchboard. The unpredictable phone console occasionally lets the correct call through, but Lenore also finds herself fielding calls not only for her employer but also for a cheese shop, a towing service, a cafe, a pet groomer, and a dominatrix.[18]

Other attempts at communication in *Broom* get obscured before they reach their audiences. Lenore Senior, linguist in daily life too, helps Alzheimer's patients replace words they cannot remember with phrases designating objects' use values: "water" becomes "[what] we drink, without color," for instance.[19] Lenore's stoner brother LaVache decides to call his telephone a "lymph node" so that if his father, trying to reach him, asks if he has a phone, he can honestly reply that he doesn't.[20] And in the novel's final scene, some attempted communication has broken down altogether, as sender and receiver are obscured: the malfunctioning phone system has reached the point that when people answer a ringing phone, they hear "just static and tones."[21] Still other communicative acts are utterances with a clear audience, but sometimes these cannot truly be said to have communicative intent behind them. When Lenore's pet bird, Vlad the Impaler, unexpectedly finds a limited kind of stardom as a televangelist's sidekick on the Partners with God program, he sometimes spouts religiously-inflected language. In the novel's penultimate scene, though, his on-air utterances – such as "Satisfy me like never before" – mimic speakers in his orbit that aren't necessarily thinking about fundamentalist Christianity, to say the least.[22] And perhaps most important for Wallace's purposes are the multiple ways that *Broom* employs stories within stories as communicative acts. Rick Vigorous runs a literary magazine and presses Lenore into service helping screen fiction submissions, marking him as "a kind of pomo Scheherazade."[23] He also makes sure Lenore reads some of his own writing (without telling her), and it's clear that Rick sees this – particularly via a story titled simply "Love," which appears in the novel soon after Rick tries to get Lenore to utter the phrase "I love you" – as a quixotic act of courtship.[24]

The sophistication of Wallace's meditations on communication and narrative in *The Broom of the System* make it a novel that succeeds on its own terms and not merely a dress rehearsal for later work. That said, *Broom* also contains some elements that will recur later in *Infinite Jest*, suggestively prefiguring some aspects of the novel to come. Both *Broom* and *Infinite*

Jest are set in a near American future in which the landscape has been altered by the addition of a vast and uninhabitable void: the Great Ohio Desert in the earlier novel, the Great Concavity in the latter. Both texts explore theoretical ideas through the narrative form of the philosophical dialogue, as Adam Kelly has observed while extending this comparison of *Broom* and *Infinite Jest* to include *The Pale King*.[25] And Lenore's therapist, Dr. Jay, centers his form of questionable psychoanalysis on something he calls "hygiene anxiety," a neurosis that, writ large in *Infinite Jest*, will eventually lead to the rise of the Clean U.S. Party. Such yet-incomplete literary gestures make *Broom* even more the groundwork for a more mature, fully formed novel to come.

Well before the publication of *Infinite Jest*, however, comes Wallace's first book of short stories, *Girl with Curious Hair*, which also finds Wallace defining himself as a writer by negotiating his relationships with his influences and contemporaries. While *The Broom of the System* frequently addressed itself to Wittgenstein and Derrida, the existing texts on which *Girl with Curious Hair* comments are more narrative than philosophical. In multiple cases Wallace appropriates an existing writer or mode in order to turn its raw material to his purpose. Wallace wrote several of the stories in *Girl* for workshops in the MFA program at the University of Arizona, making him a part of what Mark McGurl has termed "the program era." In the collection Wallace frequently addresses trends in 1980s fiction or directly parodies successful writers, all in service to discovering what kind of writer Wallace is going to be (and not be) as well as what he will conclude regarding what the language of fiction itself does.[26] But where *Broom* focuses obsessively on what language can and cannot accomplish in the abstract, *Girl* focuses on attempts to communicate successfully within human relationships and within the frame of literary fiction. But before getting to Wallace's grandest attempt at such to date – the novella "Westward the Course of Empire Takes Its Way" – the shorter stories that comprise most of *Girl* deserve attention.

Taken together as a collection, *Girl with Curious Hair* can read as a miscellany, which Wallace intended even as he selected and ordered the stories deliberately. Boswell emphasizes that the collection's sequencing tends to alternate short and long stories, more serious stories with those lighter in tone.[27] Max reports that Wallace was frustrated with reviews of *Girl* that tended to weigh the merits of individual stories instead of considering how the book as a whole might "open the door to a new kind of fiction."[28] Toward that end, much of the collection works as a diagnosis of then current trends. The compressed "Everything Is Green" works as a brief homage to Raymond Carver's minimalist fiction, work that influenced the

American short story like perhaps none other of the time. Wallace's story dramatizes his view that minimalist writing undervalues the authorial voice in its facade of realist objectivity, but Wallace himself has called Carver "an artist, not a minimalist," contrasting him with the mere "crank-turners" who follow in his wake.[29] The collection's other overt piece of commentary on a trendy form is the title story, "Girl with Curious Hair," which takes scathing aim at Brat Pack fiction, just as Wallace's 1988 essay "Fictional Futures and the Conspicuously Young" had done. Narrated by Sick Puppy, a Young Republican who attends a Keith Jarrett concert with "his friends who are punkrockers," "Girl with Curious Hair" savages the fashionably nihilistic poses of Bret Easton Ellis, a contemporary of Wallace's who is equally interested as Wallace in media's influence on fiction but whose work Wallace dismisses.[30] Ellis's detractors often argue that Brat Pack fiction uses stray references to luxury brands as a lazy mode of characterization, one that tells readers about an affluent character's lifestyle but little about what he or she may feel or value. Sick Puppy introduces himself via five references to his cologne on the story's first page, positioning himself as more consumer than character: "I have the English Leather Cologne commercial taped on my new Toshiba VCR," he reports.[31] Wallace has characterized Ellis's work as "a mordant deadpan commentary on the badness of everything" that, although it might depict the vulgarity of contemporary American life, stops short of offering any meaningful corrective – Wallace's story makes his disdain crystal clear.[32]

Besides Wallace's scathing parodies, though, *Girl with Curious Hair* is rich in homage to significant influences as well. In "Say Never," Wallace effectively ventriloquizes a narrative voice in Jewish-American vernacular that reads as a hat tip to Philip Roth. And "John Billy" is, in its way, a pious tribute to a master as well. Though Boswell, like many readers, identifies "John Billy" as "mock Faulknerian" due to the narrator's exaggerated faux-Southern dialect, Max clarifies that the real source for the story's distinctive voice is William Gass's *Omensetter's Luck*, which Wallace would later place on a list of "direly under appreciated U.S. novels" since 1960 for *Salon*.[33]

Aside from those stories in *Girl* that function as sly metaliterary commentary, other key stories in the development of Wallace's entire artistic project comment directly on television. Wallace's essay "E Unibus Pluram: Television and U.S. Fiction" (1993) would not appear in the *Review of Contemporary Fiction* until years after *Girl* hit shelves, but Wallace clearly works with ideas from the essay in "Little Expressionless Animals" and "My Appearance," two stories in which television is central. In "E Unibus" Wallace explains that the ironic mode had once worked in American fiction as a necessary voice of protest, especially in the turbulent sixties, when

American narrative television largely trafficked in escapism, ignoring the conflicts of the decade while novelists did not. But as television gradually discovered and capitalized on the ironic mode – via *Saturday Night Live*, David Letterman, *The Simpsons*, and more – and as the amount of television the average American watched daily continued to grow, television took irony from the novelist's toolbox and made it a kind of default mode for contemporary American discourse. Where irony once succeeded as a rhetorical tool that could point to truth, in the postmodern age, irony has become snark, or as Wallace defines it, "the contemporary mood of jaded weltschmerz, self-mocking materialism, [and] blank indifference."[34] A possible way out, Wallace suggests, is to reject irony in favor of sincerity, as "the next real literary 'rebels'" might be those "who treat old untrendy human troubles and emotions in U.S. life with reverence and conviction."[35] The stories in *Girl* that comment on television attempt to both diagnose this ironic malaise and offer earnest communication as a corrective.

For this to happen, though, Wallace realizes, one must first cut through decades of pop mythology attached to television. In *Broom* Wallace occasionally reveled in this sort of nostalgia, as in the novel's scenes set at a *Gilligan's Island*-themed bar.[36] Wallace's first step toward cutting through such mythos in *Girl* comes from appropriating actual television performers and resituating them as fictional characters: game-show hosts in "Little Expressionless Animals," talk-show host David Letterman in "My Appearance," and *Hawaii Five-O* star Jack Lord in "Westward the Course." Such a move has its risks, as Wallace learned when *Playboy* discovered, prior to their publication of "My Appearance," that Wallace had lifted some dialogue verbatim from an actual Letterman interview and placed it in the mouth of his story's main character.[37] As a result, the usual legal boilerplate on *Girl*'s copyright page became a more theoretical and playful deconstruction of media myth-making instead: "Where the names of corporate, media, or political figures are used here, those names are meant only to denote figures, images, the stuff of collective dreams; they do not denote, or pretend to private information about, actual 3-D persons, living, dead, or otherwise."[38] The slightly flippant tone aside, the disclaimer afforded Wallace legal protection while also emphasizing that he was looking to television not just for basic subject matter but also for mythos.

These stories, like "E Unibus," seek to interrogate how popular media affects viewers – how it can colonize the mind and the artist's creative life alike. "Little Expressionless Animals" describes the backstage machinery of the game show *Jeopardy!*, as Julie Smith goes on a three-year winning streak while having a romantic relationship with Faye Goddard, the daughter of a producer at the show. The story's form is fragmentary and nonchronological, in imitation of channel surfing; some intrusive lists of *Jeopardy!* categories in the narration recall the triads of brand names that recur in Don DeLillo's *White Noise*, a novel Wallace praises in "E Unibus."[39] Meanwhile, the story remains full of troubled communication: *Jeopardy!* host Alex Trebek is depicted in therapy; Faye rehearses with Julie responses to imaginary queries regarding why she is a lesbian; and the program's producers rig the game to make sure Julie is defeated by her autistic, minimally communicative brother by filling the board with questions about animals, knowing that a childhood trauma has made zoology trivia her Achilles' heel. In cruelly using knowledge of Julie's personal life against her in such a visible fashion, the producers bring Julie's private and public faces into collision. The story obsesses over faces, both literally and figuratively: in a private moment, Julie's beauty is described in lyrical detail from Faye's perspective, but her face changes when on the *Jeopardy!* set. Upon winning games, Julie is "blank-faced," while her face is "loose and expressionless" before taping begins.[40] While dominating the game, however, "her face, on-screen, gives off an odd lambent UHF flicker; her expression, brightly serene, radiates a sort of oneness with the board's data."[41] Soon after, though, Julie bursts into tears while playing the game (still amazingly well), and her long winning streak turns her into a minor celebrity: "She turns down a *People* cover. Faye explains to the *People* people that Julie is basically a private person."[42] Wallace will later elaborate on the downside of fame via the relentless strivings of the ambitious young tennis hotshots of *Infinite Jest*, but his suggestion that fame creates more problems than it solves begins here.

The two television-focused stories in *Girl with Curious Hair* share a critique of television for being predictable and rule-bound. In "Little Expressionless Animals" Julie fearlessly breaks some implicit rules of the television game show: she corrects an Alex Trebek error on-air and even flips him a middle finger.[43] "My Appearance," the story most clearly reflective of the concerns of "E Unibus," also features a woman's resistance to how formulaic televised interaction must be. Edilyn, a well-known but decidedly B-list actress, appears on *Late Night with David Letterman*, a show whose 1980s heyday was defined by a gleeful baring of formulaic television's glaring artificiality, a smiling acknowledgment that everything viewers see is phony. Having just appeared in a hot-dog commercial and fearful of being made fun of for selling out, Edilyn receives coaching from her husband on how to appear on what he terms an "anti-show."[44] Edilyn's husband explains, "The whole thing feeds off *everybody's* ridiculousness. It's the way the audience can tell he *chooses* to ridicule himself that exempts the clever bastard from ridicule."[45] After Edilyn seems to short-circuit the irony circuit – or, significantly, appears to do so – by being honest – or appearing honest – in her interview, she questions the value of conversational illusion at story's end. "Because if no one is really the way we see them," she tells her husband, "that would include me. And you."[46] The story argues successfully that to accept the insincerity of overly ironic communication in popular media is only a first step to accepting insincere communication in one's own private life more broadly. Additionally, where troubled communication often occurred in *Broom* due to disconnects between speaker and audience, the most meaningful disconnect in "My Appearance" separates different *types* of communicators. Edilyn understands herself to be an open book, even as Wallace implies that Edilyn fibs to Letterman on-air when she says she did the hot-dog commercial for free. Edilyn's husband, however, chooses not to resist the emerging dominance of Letterman's ironic mode of conversation, which comes to strike Edilyn less as a difference of opinion and more as a character flaw.

The two TV-centered stories in *Girl* won notice and notoriety for treating real media figures as fictional characters. Wallace appropriates the life stories of another real person in "Lyndon," but in this story he rewrites history altogether. "Lyndon" has President Johnson die in office, cared for (possibly quite intimately) by Rene Duverger, a young gay man who is dying of a disease that, anachronistically, resembles AIDS. David Boyd, aide to Johnson and husband to Rene, narrates the story, which capitalizes on the popular image of Johnson as a consummate but unpolished politician – and then subverts the facts of his life while keeping his mythos intact. David Boyd starts as a mailboy in then Senator Johnson's office, eventually becoming one of the vice president's most trusted advisors, dutifully reminding citizens in a form letter following the Kennedy assassination that "no two consecutive presidents have ever died in office."[47] Wallace again attends to the distance between public and private faces of famous media figures: David helps keep Johnson's heart troubles secret, and he is present in the Dallas motorcade and its ensuing chaos, hearing Johnson admit to trepidation at taking "a job ain't mine by right or by the will of folks."[48] The story culminates with a conversation between David and Lady Bird Johnson in which the latter theorizes about the dying president's understanding of love: "his hatred of being alone is a consequence of what his memoir will call his great intellectual concept: the distance at which we see each other, arrange each other, love."[49] In other words, people naturally live disconnected lives; and even though Lady Bird speaks of the practical, political power of love and not its emotional force, love can, she explains, like "a federal highway," put "communities, that move and exist at great distance, in touch."[50] Here Wallace risks great sentimentality in order to suggest the power of genuine communication and single-entendre values to create real connection. Lady Bird's discourse on love also adumbrates the disarmingly direct final sentence of *Girl*'s final story.

Indeed, for all of its metacommentary about 1980s American fiction and pop-cultural mythology, Wallace's ultimate goal in *Girl* is to propose a way that literary fiction could communicate genuinely with an audience. In fact, in a 1993 interview, Wallace describes his intent as "writ[ing] a very traditionally moral book," in that he wants to transmit to readers a message he understands as vital and urgent.[51] But he also understands that as a then twenty-something writer in the age of irony, it's difficult to "endorse single-entendre values," as he puts it in "E Unibus."[52] What's more, a media landscape in which irony has become the default mode is a world in which millions are left wondering if anything is worth valuing: "I'm still writing about younger people trying to find themselves in the face not only of conform-or-die parents," Wallace explains, "but also this bright seductive electromagnetic system all around them that tells them that they don't have to."[53] As a result, Kasia Boddy sees a generation gap at work here in one of *Girl*'s recurring images, as multiple stories in the collection depict "the death of an old man observed, with detailed relish, by a young man."[54] In this collection, as in *Broom*, even the best attempts at authentic communication don't necessarily bridge the gaps between people. "Here and There," told entirely in dialogue, finds a lovesick young man attempting "fiction therapy" with an occasionally intrusive analyst. When he insists, "This kind of fiction doesn't interest me," he not only is a resistant patient (like both Lenore and Rick in *Broom*), but he also questions whether storytelling – at least in the context of therapy – will help him connect with others.[55] And "Luckily the Account Representative Knew CPR," as described by D. T. Max, is defined by "a passionate need for encounter telegraphed by sentences that seem ostentatiously to prohibit it."[56] This rhetorical trend toward self-complication of every imaginable communicative act will be taken to a logical extreme in the collection *Brief Interviews with Hideous Men* (1999), especially in hyper-self-aware stories like "The Depressed Person," "Octet," and the second story titled "The Devil Is a Busy Man."

Extremes of a different sort dominate the longest and most complex piece of *Girl*, the novella "Westward the Course of Empire Takes Its Way." An exceptionally high-concept piece of fiction, "Westward" follows a group of creative writing students who are on the way to a reunion of everyone who has ever appeared in a McDonald's commercial (where, of course, another ad, the McDonald's commercial to end all McDonald's commercials, will be filmed). Additionally, the story functions as Wallace's extended response to the metafictional mode of John Barth, the postmodern author best known for his groundbreaking story collection *Lost in the Funhouse* (1968). The story's central character, Mark Nechtr, a thinly veiled Wallace analogue, studies with a Professor Ambrose, author of "Lost in the Funhouse" and hence an even more thinly veiled analogue for Barth. "Westward," like "Lost in the Funhouse," contains authorial intrusions meant to remind readers that the story on the page is a textual construction, not an unmediated piece of pure narrative. Wallace's intrusions, though – including ones titled "A Really Blatant and Intrusive Interruption" and "I Lied: Three Reasons Why the Above Was Not Really an Interruption, Because This Isn't the Sort of Fiction That Can Be Interrupted, Because It's Not Fiction, But Real and True and *Right Now*" – cast explicit doubt on metafiction as a useful narrative mode.[57] Looking for something that replaces metafiction with something more genuinely communicative, Wallace also rejects as cop-outs any return to old-school realism that doesn't acknowledge the constructedness of all art.

But Wallace knows that metafiction easily becomes the snake that eats its own tail. As he has explained, "metafiction's real end has always been Armageddon," so "I wanted to get the Armageddon-explosion ... over with, and then out of the rubble reaffirm the idea of art being a living transaction between humans."[58] Toward that end, "Westward" never actually ends in a traditional sense; the majority of the story takes place on the way to the ad shoot, as late in the novella, Wallace abandons the road trip as Mark imagines a new story altogether. Or as Bradley Fest suggests, in refusing to lend "Westward" any traditional closure, "but rather to begin another narrative about the problems inherent in constructing a narrative, Wallace simultaneously acknowledges" the apparent strangeness of this overly self-aware narrative move while also asking why readers desire closure anyway.[59] Having abandoned both the core narrative and Mark's new story – and having concluded that "one of the things really great fiction-writers do ... is *give* the reader something," Wallace ends with a direct address to the reader: "You are loved."[60]

Even as "Westward" may not be as artistically successful as *Infinite Jest*, the statement of purpose here could not be clearer: while metafiction like "Lost in the Funhouse" may flatter readers who are pleased with the cleverness of Barth's inventiveness, the big-hearted but technically innovative and ethically centered fiction that Wallace aspires to create must do something more. It must challenge readers while not frustrating their efforts at understanding; it must entertain while not necessarily being fully reassuring; and it must be empathetic and fearless enough to attempt to speak truths both emotional and moral. To accomplish all of these would be an act of great love for one's readers, and the so-called apprentice fiction helps Wallace arrive at that new imperative, on full display in *Infinite Jest*.

Taken together, *The Broom of the System* and *Girl with Curious Hair* introduce some core themes that Wallace will continue to explore for the remainder of his career. Meanwhile, as a highly ambitious young writer, publishing his early work in a marketplace hungry for new voices, Wallace uses nods to his influences and contemporaries to signal what kind of writer he will become. *Broom* repeatedly depicts the difficulty of successful communication in terms both concrete and abstract, intimate and theoretical. *Girl* develops that concern further via its keen attention to an age in which many communicators seldom appear to say what they really mean. All the while, Wallace foregrounds the fictionality of his characters and situations (even when they borrow from real-life figures, as in several stories in *Girl*); doing so lets him celebrate the possibilities of literary creativity, as he plays around in the metafictional sandbox, while also questioning the limitations of metafiction's ability to connect with readers in genuinely emotional ways. Even as *Infinite Jest* remains the title most synonymous with Wallace's name (and for good reason), Wallace's first two books remain vital for readers interested in the roots of this writer's ambition, aesthetic, and ethical center.

Notes

1. David Foster Wallace, "An Expanded Interview with David Foster Wallace," by Larry McCaffery and Stephen J. Burn (ed.), *Conversations with David Foster Wallace* (Jackson: University of Mississippi, 2012), p. 32.
2. D. T. Max, *Every Love Story Is a Ghost Story: A Life of David Foster Wallace* (New York: Viking, 2012), p. 48.
3. David Lipsky, *Although of Course You End Up Becoming Yourself: A Road Trip with David Foster Wallace* (New York: Broadway Books, 2010), p. 35.
4. For a brief and accessible summary of Wittgenstein's theories on language and their relevance to *The Broom of the System*, see Marshall Boswell's *Understanding David Foster Wallace* (Columbia: University of South Carolina Press, 2009), pp. 23–27. See also Clare Hayes-Brady, *The Unspeakable Failures of David Foster Wallace* (New York: Bloomsbury, 2016), chap. 4.
5. Wallace's apparent characterization of Derrida's theories on the ultimate self-referentiality of all language is debatable but not uncommon. Again, Boswell's explanation of Derrida's work and its relevance to *Broom* is useful; see *Understanding*, pp. 28–31.
6. David Foster Wallace, *The Broom of the System* (New York: Penguin, 1987), p. 59.
7. Wallace in Burn (ed.), *Conversations*, pp. 10, 20, 35.
8. Ibid., p. 31.

9. Thomas Pynchon, *The Crying of Lot 49* (1965; New York: Harper Perennial, 2006), pp. 140–141.

10. Wallace, *The Broom of the System*, p. 249.

11. Ibid., p. 329.

12. Ibid., p. 398.

13. Patrick O'Donnell, "Almost a Novel: *The Broom of the System*," in David Hering (ed.), *Consider David Foster Wallace* (Los Angeles: SSMG, 2010), p. 2.

14. O'Donnell goes so far as to call the novel "an ode to incompletion" in "Almost a Novel," p. 6.

15. Wallace, *The Broom of the System*, p. 467.

16. See Adam Kelly, "Development through Dialogue," in Marshall Boswell (ed.) *David Foster Wallace and "The Long Thing": New Essays on the Novels* (New York: Bloomsbury, 2013). Kelly writes that "because there is no real ambiguity concerning the next word in the sentence, the reader's agency is in fact negated," suggesting that Wallace's gesture toward including readers in meaning-building actually fails, p. 271.

17. See Boswell, *Understanding*, pp. 34–35: the school of thought that regards language as an essentially accurate reflection of reality tends to equate language itself with ultimate reality (i.e., God), as in the Christian understanding of "the Word" in the opening of the Gospel of John.

18. Wallace, *The Broom of the System*, pp. 48–50. Furthermore, Lance Olsen views these phone-system troubles as "fitting images indeed for the novel itself which is one grand system of communication and which tells story after story … upsetting traditional narrative boundaries along the way" in "Termite Art, or Wallace's Wittgenstein," *Review of Contemporary Fiction* 13.2 (1993), pp. 210–211.

19. Wallace, *The Broom of the System*, p. 150.

20. Ibid., p. 214.

21. Ibid., p. 451.

22. Ibid., p. 464.

23. Olsen, "Termite Art," p. 210.

24. Wallace, *The Broom of the System*, pp. 285, 312–323.

25. See Adam Kelly's "Development through Dialogue," which traces Wallace's formal use of the philosophical dialogue from *Broom* through *The Pale King*.

26. For further discussion of Wallace in terms of the culture of the MFA workshop, see Mark McGurl's *The Program Era: Postwar Fiction and the Rise of Creative Writing* (Cambridge: Harvard University Press, 2009); and Kasia Boddy, "A Fiction of Response: *Girl with Curious Hair* in Context," in Marshall Boswell and Stephen J. Burn (eds.) *A Companion to David Foster Wallace Studies* (New York: Palgrave Macmillan, 2013), pp. 23–41.

27. Boswell, *Understanding*, p. 69.

28. Max, *Every Love Story*, p. 129.

29. Wallace, "Expanded Interview," in Burn (ed.), *Conversations*, p. 46.

30. Wallace, *Girl with Curious Hair*, p. 58.

31. Ibid., p. 55.

32. Wallace, "Expanded Interview," in Burn (ed.), *Conversations*, p. 26.

33. Boswell, *Understanding*, p. 85; Max, *Every Love Story*, p. 74; David Foster Wallace, *Both Flesh and Not: Essays* (New York: Little, Brown, 2012), p. 203.

34. David Foster Wallace, "E Unibus Pluram: Television and U.S. Fiction," *Review of Contemporary Fiction* 13.2 (Summer 1993), p. 181. Clare Hayes-Brady makes a convincing case that Wallace's rejection of what she calls "liberal ironism" does not begin with "My Appearance" or "E Unibus Pluram" but with the depiction of Lenore's brother LaVache in *Broom*. See Hayes-Brady, "The Book, the Broom, and the Ladder," in Hering, *Consider*, pp. 34–35.

35. Wallace, "E Unibus Pluram," pp. 192–193.

36. David Foster Wallace, *The Broom of the System* (New York: Penguin, 1987), p. 142.

37. Max, *Every Love Story*, pp. 106–109.

38. Wallace, *Girl with Curious Hair*, copyright page.

39. Wallace, "E Unibus Pluram," pp. 169–171.

40. Wallace, *Girl with Curious Hair*, pp. 12–13, 16, 17.

41. Ibid., p. 17.

42. Ibid., pp. 18, 29.

43. Ibid., pp. 19, 23.

44. Ibid., p. 198.

45. Ibid., p. 181.

46. Ibid., p. 200.

47. Ibid., p. 112.

48. Ibid., p. 102.

49. Ibid., p. 115.

50. Ibid.

51. Wallace, "Looking for a Garde of Which to Be Avant: An Interview with David Foster Wallace" by Hugh Kennedy and Geoffrey Polk, in Burn (ed.), *Conversations*, p. 18.

52. Wallace, "E Unibus Pluram," p. 192.

53. Wallace, "Looking for a Garde," in Burn (ed.), *Conversations*, p. 18.

54. Boddy, "A Fiction of Response," pp. 25–26. In addition to *Girl with Curious Hair*'s visible generation gaps, Boddy also emphasizes that four stories in the collection "end with a solitary voice calling out for a response," p. 38.

55. Wallace, *Girl with Curious Hair*, p. 153.

56. Max, *Every Love Story*, p. 78.

57. Wallace, *Girl with Curious Hair*, pp. 264, 334.

58. Wallace, "Expanded Interview," in Burn (ed.), *Conversations*, pp. 30, 41.

59. Bradley J. Fest, "'Then Out of the Rubble': David Foster Wallace's Early Fiction," in Boswell (ed.), *David Foster Wallace*, p. 298.

60. Wallace, "Expanded Interview," in Burn (ed.), *Conversations*, p. 50; *Girl with Curious Hair*, p. 373.

5

ADAM KELLY

Brief Interviews with Hideous Men

In "B.I. #28," one of the eighteen "Brief Interviews" that provide the backbone of David Foster Wallace's second collection of short fiction, two men offer their views on the sexual psychology of the contemporary woman. The names of these men are given only as K— and E —, and their interviewer is implicitly female, although – as in all the interviews – her questions to the men are not printed in the text and her conversational input is marked only by the letter Q. She listens, along with the reader, as K— expounds his theory that "the modern woman has an unprecedented amount of contradictory stuff laid on her about what it is she's supposed to want and how she's expected to conduct herself sexually."[1] E— agrees, and together they outline the "double bind" facing today's woman, deriving from a clash between "the old respectable-girl-versus-slut thing" and "the new feminist-slash-postfeminist expectation that women are sexual agents, too, just as men are."[2] Citing "evidence" from evolutionary biology, poststructuralist philosophy, psychoanalysis, and postmodern semiotics, the two men eventually agree that what women really want, underneath all their rhetoric of autonomy and liberation, is some way to escape this double bind. In other words, "they want to be rescued," and all a man needs to do is "to gallop in on your white charger and overwhelm them with passion, just as males have been doing since time immemorial."[3] This is not, according to the men, simply a reactionary reassertion of premodern gender norms. It is rather the result of a sophisticated and logical response by the contemporary male to the coded situation facing his female counterpart:

> K— : 'The only way not to get lost in the code is to approach the whole issue logically. What is she really saying?'
> E— : 'No doesn't mean yes, but it doesn't mean no, either.'[4]

There is, then, in the way Wallace presents this scene, a double silencing. Not only do we not hear from the only woman present – the interviewer – but we are told that anything a woman might contribute on this topic could not be taken at face value. What she would "really" be saying would not be anything she actually does say, but what the paradoxical logic of her situation indicates she must be saying. And according to this logic, what she says can only be radically ambiguous, radically undecidable: "*No* doesn't mean yes, but it doesn't mean no, either." In the end, the power to decide what she is saying, like the power to decode the paradox that governs her, lies with the man.

For all the palpable hideousness of this scenario, there is evidence that the man who wrote *Brief Interviews with Hideous Men* (1999) thought of his book's project as a feminist one. "A parody (a feminist parody) of feminism": this was how Wallace described the collection in a letter to a former teacher in April 1998.[5] Yet what should the reader make of this description of a set of stories that feature virtually no female voices amid a cacophony of misogynistic male ones? Does *Brief Interviews* represent a parody of feminism or a feminist parody of feminism, and what would the difference between these be? If we were tempted to follow Wallace in calling the collection a feminist text, what could we possibly mean *by* feminism? And what could the book's possible feminist categorization mean *for* feminism?

I am not the first to ask questions like these. It has long been recognized that *Brief Interviews* represents Wallace's most concerted attempt to address the conjoined themes of male–female relationships and of sex, themes that had featured in *The Broom of the System* (1987) and *Girl with Curious Hair* (1989) but had been relatively absent from his major novel *Infinite Jest* (1996). Scholars have addressed the collection in these terms and have sometimes found it wanting, most notably in Clare Hayes-Brady's claim that Wallace's "writing of both female characters and romantic relationships is patchy at best and enormously problematic at worst."[6] This deficiency stems, in her view, from the fact that "Wallace was overwhelmed by what he saw as the alterity of the female experience; that is to say, its total alienation from his experience of the world."[7] While acknowledging the validity of these concerns, this chapter nevertheless argues that whether or not we can legitimately call *Brief Interviews* a feminist text, the effort to understand it as such can allow us to say significant things about it. These include not only the ways the collection extends Wallace's earlier work but also how its author might have conceived it as responding and even contributing to the aims of contemporary feminism.

Contemporary feminism comes in many stripes, of course, and Wallace was undoubtedly familiar with a range of these.[8] Yet although Annette Kolodny, a widely read feminist scholar, was Dean of Humanities at the University of Arizona in the late 1980s when Wallace was studying there for his MFA, it was not her brand of Anglo-American feminism that most interested him. Rather, it was the so-called French feminists, highly influential in the US academy during the 1980s, that represented for him the vanguard of the field. These were theorists who combined training in the psychoanalysis of Jacques Lacan with an interest in the new poststructuralist approaches to language pioneered by Jacques Derrida, whose work Wallace had studied avidly at both Amherst and Arizona.[9] It was these theorists' interrogation of the question of the feminine – and particularly the question of how the feminine can and should be represented in writing – that provided vital inspiration for the imaginative landscape and storytelling techniques of *Brief Interviews*.

It is important to acknowledge that the term "French feminism" is a construct of the US academy, and that it conceals some significant differences between its three most celebrated figures, Julia Kristeva, Hélène Cixous, and Luce Irigaray. Kristeva, for instance, rejected the feminist label, although her key distinction between the *symbolic* and the *semiotic* has proven highly influential among feminists. The symbolic, in Kristeva, names the referential, rule-bound, systematic dimension of language; in psychoanalytic terms, she associates the symbolic with accession to the Oedipal stage and the "law of the father," Lacan's phrase for the social order. The semiotic, on the other hand, names the bodily drives and pre-Oedipal, maternal elements that underlie language but can only be known as a disruptive trace within the symbolic. Kristeva associates the semiotic with the fluidity of poetic language, particularly its rhythm and tone.[10] This connects the semiotic to the notion of *écriture feminine*, a multivocal practice of writing articulated by Cixous in opposition to "the language of men and their grammar."[11] Drawing on the female body and the insights of deconstruction, *écriture feminine* operates not by opposing patriarchal language directly but through a practice that Irigaray dubs "mimicry," where woman uses language "to try to recover the place of her exploitation by discourse, without allowing herself to be simply reduced to it."[12] According to this view, women can resist the oppressions of patriarchal discourse not by speaking out against those oppressions in the discourse's own terms but instead by disrupting the discourse. "The issue is not one of elaborating a new theory of which woman would be the *subject* or the *object*," Irigaray remarks, "but of jamming the theoretical machinery itself."[13]

Jamming the theoretical machinery is an evident aim of David Foster Wallace's fiction. But there remains a question as to whether, as a male author, Wallace's writing might justifiably be read as *écriture feminine* or whether the disruptive mimicry recommended by Irigaray is only available to those born as women. This question has been a source of heated debate within feminism, and the texts of Cixous and Irigaray seem to point in both directions at once. "Woman must write herself," Cixous avers at the opening of her manifesto, "The Laugh of the Medusa," yet she also credits figures like James Joyce and Jacques Derrida with the capacity to create *écriture feminine*.[14] This apparent contradiction – between the priority of the female body and the availability of feminine writing to male authors – is in fact welcomed by Cixous and Irigaray as a generative paradox, an example of the impossible logic that constitutes *écriture feminine* itself. For Kristeva things are both more straightforward and more controversial: her primary examples of the "revolution in poetic language" are male modernist writers like Mallarmé, Lautréamont, Joyce, and Artaud.[15] Kristeva privileges male writers because, as Kelly Oliver summarizes, "whereas in males an identification with the maternal semiotic is revolutionary because it breaks with traditional conceptions of sexual difference, for females an identification with the maternal does not break traditional conceptions of sexual difference."[16] As Elizabeth Grosz points out, this theoretical claim enables Kristeva "to position men, the avant-garde, in the best position to represent, to name or speak the feminine."[17]

In *Brief Interviews with Hideous Men*, Wallace wades into this contentious realm of feminist debate in a characteristically self-conscious manner. The first thing my admittedly brief outline of the concerns of the French feminists gives us is a way to interpret the text's fractured structure. This structure has been well described by Mary Holland, who notes that the collection "withhold[s] overarching closure and coherence by comprising pieces and series of pieces that signify gaps, incompletion, and disorder as much as meaningful presence."[18] This emphasis on incompletion and disorder can be read in the terms set by the French feminists, as a gesture toward a female principle that remains unrepresentable at the level of "firmly established form, figure, idea or concept," in the words of Irigaray.[19] "Feminine silence," notes Hayes-Brady of the female Q. in the interviews, "may be read as another way in which Wallace disrupts the circularity of patriarchal systems of narrative," and this insight can be extended to a reading of how the 23 pieces that make up the text do or do not fit together.[20] Although Marshall Boswell claims that the ordering of the collection "creates a dialectical pattern of thesis, antithesis, and synthesis," the dialectic at work here in fact seems closer to the dialectic between symbolic and semiotic in Kristeva.[21] In *Brief Interviews* the structuring principles of the symbolic – what Boswell identifies as Wallace's "contrapuntal method of alternating longer stories with short sketches and of placing thematically related pieces next to each other" – are pitted against the destructuring energies of the semiotic.[22]

These destructuring energies are perhaps most evident in the three vignettes labeled "Yet Another Example of the Porousness of Certain Borders."
These vignettes are numbered VI, XI, and XXIV, suggesting a long sequence
of which we are glimpsing only a few nodes. The fact that number 24 is the
23rd and last story in *Brief Interviews* and that "Yet Another Example of the
Porousness of Certain Borders (VIII)" was published separately to the collection suggests further that the bounded (and masculine) logic of "the book" is
here being overridden by the excessive (and feminine) logic of "writing."[23]
These vignettes likewise engage the drives of the semiotic through their
dreamlike quality. The first, numbered XI, begins as follows:

> As in all those other dreams, I'm with somebody I know but don't know how
> I know them, and now this person suddenly points out to me that I'm blind.
> As in literally blind, unsighted, etc. Or else it's in the presence of this person that
> I suddenly realize I'm blind.[24]

The characteristic ambiguity of the dreamscape, where we know things
without knowing how we know them, is immediately evoked here.
The opening allusion to "all those other dreams" suggests that this dream
is simply one in a repeating series, while the suddenness of the "now" shocks
the reader into the present dream, and the realization of blindness, simultaneously with the narrator. If the direct cause of this sudden realization is
unclear, the narrator's reaction is nonetheless stark: "I get sad. It makes me
incredibly sad that I'm blind."[25] This reaction emphasizes the unmediated
quality of the dream state, its propensity for naked and childlike emotion.
When the narrator wakes from the dream he is crying, and throughout
his day at work he finds himself "incredibly conscious of my eyesight and
my eyes" and unable to stop meditating on all "those blind people I see on the
subway."[26] This consciousness and newfound empathy prove "tiring as
hell," and the narrator leaves work early, goes back to bed, and enters the
blindness of sleep, only for the cycle, we assume, to begin again.[27]

For Freud, dreams were the "royal road to the unconscious." Their manifest
content – that which the dreamer remembers – was to be read for its latent
content, the unconscious thoughts, drives, and desires that are being repressed
by the subject who dreams. Kristeva, preoccupied with "a practice – the *text* –
which is only of secondary interest to psychoanalysis," developed from
Freud's distinction an opposition between the phenotext (corresponding to
the manifest content) and the genotext (corresponding to the latent content).[28]
Where the phenotext "obeys rules of communication and presupposes
a subject of enunciation and an addressee," the genotext is "a process; it
moves through zones that have relative and transitory borders and constitutes
a path that is not restricted to the two poles of univocal information between

two full-fledged subjects."[29] These "transitory borders" can be compared to the "porous" ones in Wallace's text, and the challenge these porous borders present to the transmission of "univocal information between two full-fledged subjects" complicates many of Wallace's early, celebrated statements about literature, such as the claim that "writing is an act of communication between one human being and another."[30] In dreams, as in the thought of the French feminists, human beings do not preexist their articulation as the subjects of discourse in this way; the text (and its texture) comes first.

The layered and dreamlike texture of much of *Brief Interviews* therefore marks an important development from Wallace's earlier work. Stories like "Think," "Signifying Nothing," and "Church Not Made with Hands," along with the vignettes described above, all add a new, uncanny, unsettling dimension to the logical game-playing and self-conscious parody of prior literary styles that characterized his fiction from *The Broom of the System* to *Infinite Jest*.[31] This turn in Wallace's aesthetic practice was no doubt inspired in part by the expressionist art of Franz Kafka and David Lynch, both of whom he wrote about during the gestation period of the collection. But that there is also a feminist underpinning to this development becomes more evident when we turn to one of the most acclaimed stories in *Brief Interviews*, "Forever Overhead." Written in the second-person singular, this story addresses a boy on his thirteenth birthday, "your first really public day."[32] The narration emphasizes the connection between the boy's discovery of a public self – a self "for people to recognize" – and his internalization of this outside gaze into an interior division between "I" and "you."[33] This grammatical marker of the boy's growing self-consciousness is supplemented by physical markers: the sprouting of body hair, the deepening of the voice, the oiliness of the skin. And then there are the dreams:

> For months there have been dreams like nothing before: moist and busy and distant, full of yielding curves, frantic pistons, warmth and a great falling; and you have awakened through fluttering lids to a rush and a gush and a toe-curling scalp-snapping jolt of feeling from an inside deeper than you knew you had, spasms of a deep sweet hurt[34]

The language here is lyrical, the imagery resonant, the passage itself reminiscent of the famous opening of Joyce's *Portrait of the Artist as a Young Man*. Moreover, the physical result of the boy's dreams – "a clean sweet smell you can't believe comes from anything you made inside you" – finds expressionist analogy with the smell of the swimming pool, where the story is set: "a bleached sweet salt, a flower with chemical petals."[35] The triply repeated "sweet," allied with the complex metaphor of "a flower with chemical petals" (we are told a few lines later that the water "connects with a chemical haze inside you," once again blurring the border between inside and outside) conveys both the poetic energies of the semiotic and the burgeoning power of the young male subject to describe the world in language.[36] As in John Barth's story "Lost in the Funhouse," wherein the narrator Ambrose discovers the mirror of writing at the same time as he sees himself in the reflection of a funhouse mirror, Wallace's unnamed adolescent is here discovering the self who can access the world in a lyrical language of metaphor and simile, rendering it complexly aestheticized both for himself and for the reader.[37]

Responding to these aesthetic qualities, Holland reads "Forever Overhead" as "one of few pieces in this collection that is more realist than metafictional," the story that "provides the *bildungs-roman* heart of this narratively and structurally antirealist collection."[38] Yet the way Wallace frames this realism is worth examining. The link between the young boy's coming-to-consciousness and the story's lyrical style is suggested in particular by its fifth paragraph:

> Around the deck of this old public pool on the western edge of Tucson is a Cyclone fence the color of pewter, decorated with a bright tangle of locked bicycles. Beyond this a hot black parking lot full of white lines and glittering cars. A dull field of dry grass and hard wheels, old dandelions' downy heads exploding and snowing up in a rising wind. And past all this, reddened by a round slow September sun, are mountains, jagged, their tops' sharp angles darkening into definition against a deep red tired light. Against the red their sharp connected tops form a spiked line, an EKG of the dying day.[39]

The description of these concentric circles – from deck to fence to parking lot to field to mountains to sky – places the male observing subject at the radiating center of the world, as the suitably rippling source of these sensuous descriptions. The realism of such prose is shown to depend crucially upon the centrality of this subject, and the subject's temporary lack of internal division – notably, this paragraph features no you–I split – is associated with his visual mastery of the external landscape. Unlike the blindness experienced by the dreaming subject in the "porous borders" vignette above, here the subject displays visual prowess, and this lends power and certainty to his language. Indeed, for Zadie Smith, this story embodies nothing less than "a dream of language: that words might become things, that there would exist no false gap between the verbal representation of something and the something itself."[40]

But where does language come from, and what is its fundamental character? For Kristeva, the accession to language takes place through a process she dubs *abjection*, which involves the expulsion of anything that retards the clear separation of subject and object: namely, anything associated with the (mother's) body, including blood, mucous, and excrement.[41] Kristeva argues that this process is easier for the male than the female to undergo, and we see its nascent stages in "Forever Overhead," where the emergence of subjectivity from embodiment happens not only through the abjection of bodily fluids and visual mastery of the exterior world but also through the objectification of familial relations. For instance, when the protagonist first comes to the pool, he notices his sister playing "It" in a game called Marco Polo. She must swim after the other players with her eyes closed, chasing their echoes, which brings her "halfway to tears, too long to be It."[42] Lack of visual power here renders his sister an object rather than a subject, while at the same time this objectification supports the boy's emerging individuality: having "asked to come to the pool," he discovers that he "wanted to come alone," conscious of his newfound subjective separateness.[43] This separateness accentuates as the story progresses, and in its complex conclusion the boy's dive from the high board – his entry into the water – mirrors the entry into language, where the formerly undifferentiated self becomes simultaneously subject and object. Indeed, the story ends with the archetypal interpellation of the subject as object, the call to which one can only respond: "Hello."[44]

If "Forever Overhead" subtly probes language as emerging from the fundamental separation of subject and object, we see in many of the "Brief Interviews" some worrying consequences of this separation. Here adult male speakers often treat their own behavior as an external object, but only in order to treat women as objects, insidiously returning power to themselves as subjects. A good example is "B.I. #2," in which the speaker tells his girlfriend – again, the silent Q. – about his past history of abruptly ending relationships at the very moment he appears to have committed to them fully and entirely. The speaker repeats the phrase "to be honest" throughout the interview, making a fetish of his wish for openness and honesty in the face of what he calls his "record": "So, to be honest, this is my record with this sort of thing, and as far as I can tell it seems to indicate a guy who's bad news for women, which concerns me. A lot."[45] At the same time as the man claims to be confessing to his partner, he evades responsibility for his behavior, instead describing these scenes of breakup as happening "both fast and slow, like a car crash, where it's almost more like you're watching it happen than that you're actually involved in it."[46] In professing realism about his behavior, the speaker manages to objectify it as something to be observed rather than lived. He tells his partner that he has repeated the same behavior "forty, forty-five times, maybe. To be honest, possibly more," making it into a compulsive addiction, impossible to take responsibility for and cease.[47] Here we have an apparent reversal of "B.I. #28," the story with which

I began, where the female is silenced because anything she says can only be radically undecidable, owing to the contradictory "codes" that govern her. In "B.I. #2," by contrast, the female is offered the power of decision, yet it is a poisoned chalice: the reasonable thing to do is clearly for the woman to leave the man, but that is what he wants. His "confession" is therefore inseparable from its performative context: this is a conversation that repeats the exact structure that is being described within it, where the man pulls away from his relationship by talking about his record of pulling away from relationships. And the speaker can do this all while successfully embodying the 1990s media archetype of the "new man" – honest about his own limitations, caring about his partner's expectations, respectful of her autonomy, putting the decision in her hands.

This employment of a discourse of "honesty," drawn from media representations of modern "relationships," displays Wallace's fascination with the insidious ideologies that underlie apparently neutral language use.[48] Even more striking examples of this fascination come in pieces like "Datum Centurio," "Pop Quiz 6(A)" (in "Octet"), and "The Depressed Person," where unbearably long sentences of merciless precision – a kind of parody of an overbearing masculine style – serve to exhibit Wallace's belief "that words are worlds, that no language is neutral."[49] But the crucial question that shadows *Brief Interviews with Hideous Men* more generally is whether the system of language *as a whole* might be no more than a non-neutral expression of patriarchal dominance. For Cixous and Irigaray, language should be understood as a "phallocentric system," a system that from the Greeks onward has been conceived on the metaphysical (and male) priority of sameness.[50] They focus particularly on Freud, who "defines sexual difference by giving *a priori* value to Sameness, shoring up his demonstration by falling back upon time-honored devices such as analogy, comparison, symmetry, dichotomous oppositions, and so on."[51] This kind of phallocentric language, the language of reason itself, is forged through the abjected body of the mother and the occlusion of sexual difference. In Irigaray's view, such language reduces difference to a sameness that "would leave room neither for women's sexuality, nor for women's imaginary, nor for women's language to take (their) place."[52]

With this French feminist critique of sameness in mind, the centrality of sameness to *Brief Interviews* becomes newly visible and interpretable. This centrality is evident as early as the collection's opening story – in which an unnamed man and woman, both "hoping to be liked," end up driving home alone, "with the very same twist to their faces" – and as late as the closing story, which focuses on "the gross and pitiless *sameness*" of a pair of twins.[53] But sameness becomes particularly important at certain heightened moments in the collection, for instance in "B.I. #20," the last and longest of the interviews. Here the male speaker tells Q. of seducing a young woman who went on to make an enormous impact on his life when she recounted to him "the story of the unbelievably horrifying incident in which she was brutally accosted and held captive and very nearly killed."[54] Through the early part of the interview, the speaker emphasizes that the woman conforms closely to a type he calls "a quote Granola Cruncher, or post-Hippie, New Ager, what have you," a type for whom he admits scorn even as this "prototypical Cruncher" comes to prove unexpectedly different.[55] Indeed, the dialectic of sameness and difference is at the heart of the story: "It never even occurs to them their certainty that they are different is what makes them the same," claims the man of the "Cruncher genus" early in the interview, but late on it is the woman's difference that comes to matter to him.[56] Moreover, it is her most recognized marker of singularity, her name, that becomes crucial; when her story has ended, "I kept saying her name and she would ask What? and I'd say her name again."[57] As Hayes-Brady points out, in this episode "the power of naming is clearly visible" as "the narrator seeks to claim the girl by repeating her name."[58] Nevertheless, the reader does not learn the girl's name, so that even while the speaker's power to name is reinforced, the text's power to name is withheld. This is a complicated move: while, on the one hand, the difference of the individual name opposes the reductive sameness of the type, on the other hand, naming has its own cultural logic, which has since Genesis been associated with the Adamic male power to render the world knowable through language. At the conclusion of "B.I. #20," the male speaker combines the name and the type in an explosive outburst against his interlocutor: "I know your type and I know what you're bound to ask.... Judge me, you chilly cunt. You dyke, you bitch, cooze, cunt, slut, gash."[59] While ostensibly offering his female listener the power of judgment, the speaker preempts that judgment as simply the emanation of her "type." The male capacity to reduce difference to sameness here seems complete. The speaker's claim that "I knew she could. I knew I loved. End of story," rings hollow in the face of the lack of love for the Q. figure on display in this interview and in the many others that have preceded it.[60]

So can the female ever speak back in a language so dominated by this reduction of difference to phallocentric sameness? This question is framed most clearly in "Octet," which sits right at the heart of *Brief Interviews* and has tended to be read as Wallace's primary fictional statement on his aims as a writer and the relationship he tries to establish with his reader.[61] Ostensibly conceived as "a cycle of very short belletristic pieces," the proposed "octet" is presented in a broken-down state.[62] The various mini-narratives have failed to cohere into the planned unifying form, and only four of these pieces –

Pop Quiz 4, 6, 7, and 6(A) – appear in the text. Pop Quiz 9, outside the original octet and addressed to a "you" who is "unfortunately, a fiction writer," has then been added so that the writer-narrator can explain the failure of the original structure.[63] The pieces, he claims, are "supposed to compose a certain sort of '*interrogation*' of the person reading them, some-how"; they have been conceived as parabolic vehicles for the writer to "palpate" (or "demonstrate" or "transmit" or "evoke" or "limn") an affec-tive state in the reader.[64] Near the end of this final "quiz," the writer summarizes the affective goal of these parables:

> the surviving semiworkable pieces all seem to be trying to demonstrate some sort of weird ambient *sameness* in different kinds of human relationships, some nameless but inescapable "*price*" that all human beings are faced with having to pay at some point if they ever want truly "to be with" another person instead of just using that person somehow … The fact that there could be (you feel) such an overwhelming and elemental *sameness* to such totally different situa-tions and *mise en scenes* and conundra – that is, that these apparently different and formally (admit it) kind of stilted and coy-looking "Pop Quizzes" could all finally reduce to the same question (whatever exactly that question is) – seems to you urgent, truly urgent, something almost worth shimmying up chimneys and shouting from roofs about.[65]

This invocation of a "weird univocal urgency" that is meant to bind together the pieces of the octet has proven compelling to critics, yet it is difficult to miss the centrality of sameness – twice italicized in this passage – to this vision of the narrator-writer's aesthetic project.[66] This heavy emphasis on sameness becomes more notable when we recall that in Wallace's fiction, as well as in his voluminous nonfiction and interviews, the reader is always characterized as female: the reader is always a She. So when, directly after the quoted passage above, the narrator writes, "And then you'll have to ask the reader straight out whether she feels it, too, this queer nameless ambient urgent interhuman sameness," what we have is an implicitly cross-gendered encounter, where the question of sameness is being put by a male writer to a female reader, *as a question*.[67] But the complications go deeper than this, because whether the reader can even be asked this question has itself become a question for the "you" of the text to decide upon – the final line of the story is "So decide."[68] The person called to decide, here, seems simultaneously and undecidably to be both the narrator-writer and (given the conventions of literary address) the reader of *Brief Interviews*. If this reader is female, then it can only be she who decides whether sameness can ever be a virtue, whether univocality should be acclaimed or resisted, whether language itself can be something other than a mode of patriarchal oppression.

If in "B.I. #28" the power of decision is unquestionably male, and "B.I. #2" and "B.I. #20" feature only a false and manipulative transfer of the power of judgment and decision to the female, then "Octet" proposes asking the female reader directly to decide whether language is only and everywhere a vessel of patriarchal sameness or whether sameness can signify something else. This can itself be a manipulative gesture, of course, and the fiction writer of "Octet" can as easily be read as the counterpart of Wallace's hideous men as their bene-volent other. Indeed, as I have tried to show in this chapter, even a story as apparently ingenuous as "Forever Overhead" can sustain a suspicious reading along feminist lines. But it is this very courting of suspicion, this willingness not to make light of the problem of language – and particularly language as employed by a male writer – that accounts for the interest *Brief Interviews* possesses as a potentially feminist text.[69] Rather than an expression of mis-ogyny on its author's part, we can see in *Brief Interviews* an experimental answer to the central question of French feminism, as posed by Laura Mulvey: "how to fight the unconscious structured like a language (formed critically at the moment of arrival of language) while still caught within the language of the patriarchy?"[70] For Mulvey, the answer was to "begin to make a break by examining patriarchy with the tools it provides,"[71] and Wallace's collection of stories offers an unusual contribution to this project. There is an inevitable darkness to the world of *Brief Interviews*, a world in which one sex can speak while the other remains silenced. But if the book does not make for pretty reading, its continued capacity to provoke its readers – both male and female – seems unlikely to diminish until the equality through difference of the sexes is finally achieved.

Notes

1. David Foster Wallace, *Brief Interviews with Hideous Men* (Boston: Little, Brown, 1999), p. 226.
2. Ibid., p. 227.
3. Ibid., pp. 233–234.
4. Ibid., p. 234.
5. D. T. Max, *Every Love Story Is a Ghost Story: A Life of David Foster Wallace* (New York: Viking, 2012), p. 247.
6. Clare Hayes-Brady, *The Unspeakable Failures of David Foster Wallace* (New York: Bloomsbury, 2016), p. 167.
7. Ibid., p. 171. Hayes-Brady is here describing Wallace's fiction in general, but her particular assessment of *Brief Interviews* is in line with her broader claims, such as when she describes the figure of Q. in the brief interviews as "deeply problematic" (ibid., p. 176). Nevertheless, Hayes-Brady is also sensitive to the feminist concerns Wallace is engaging and is generous to his intentions in many of the individual readings she offers.

8. This familiarity is on display in Wallace's most extensive nonfiction engagement with feminist concerns, his 1990 review-essay of a novel by David Markson. See David Foster Wallace, "The Empty Plenum: David Markson's *Wittgenstein's Mistress*," in *Both Flesh and Not: Essays* (New York: Little, Brown, 2012), pp. 73–116.

9. On Wallace's interest in Derrida, see Max, *Every Love Story Is a Ghost Story*, p. 38, 56. For a reading of Wallace's engagement with Lacan, see Marshall Boswell, *Understanding David Foster Wallace* (Columbia: University of South Carolina Press, 2003), pp. 128–33, 151–60.

10. Julia Kristeva, *Revolution in Poetic Language*, (ed. and trans.) Margaret Waller (New York: Columbia University Press, 1984), pp. 19–106.

11. Hélène Cixous, "The Laugh of the Medusa," (trans.) Keith Cohen and Paula Cohen, *Signs* 1.4 (1976), p. 887.

12. Luce Irigaray, *This Sex Which Is Not One*, (trans.) Catherine Porter with Carolyn Burke (Ithaca, NY: Cornell University Press, 1985), p. 76.

13. Ibid., p. 78.

14. Cixous, "The Laugh of the Medusa," p. 875.

15. Kristeva, *Revolution in Poetic Language*, p. 15.

16. Kelly Oliver, "Julia Kristeva's Feminist Revolutions," *Hypatia* 8.3 (1993), p. 97.

17. Elizabeth Grosz, *Sexual Subversions* (Boston: Allen and Unwin, 1989), p. 95.

18. Mary K. Holland, "Mediated Immediacy in *Brief Interviews with Hideous Men*," in Marshall Boswell and Stephen J. Burn (eds.), *A Companion to David Foster Wallace Studies* (Basingstoke: Palgrave, 2014), p. 109.

19. Irigaray, *This Sex Which Is Not One*, p. 79.

20. Hayes-Brady, *Unspeakable Failures*, p. 178.

21. Boswell, *Understanding David Foster Wallace*, p. 182.

22. Ibid.

23. See Jacques Derrida, "The End of the Book and the Beginning of Writing," in *Of Grammatology*, (trans.) Gayatri Chakravorty Spivak (Baltimore: Johns Hopkins University Press, 1976), pp. 6–26.

24. Wallace, *Brief Interviews*, p. 35.

25. Ibid.

26. Ibid., pp. 35–36.

27. Ibid., p. 36.

28. Kristeva, *Revolution in Poetic Language*, 87.

29. Ibid.

30. Wallace, "Greatly Exaggerated," in *A Supposedly Fun Thing I'll Never Do Again: Essays and Arguments* (Boston: Little, Brown, 1997), p. 144.

31. Wallace's earlier fictions do contain some quite blatantly Freudian dreams, but those dreams are usually less uncanny or quietly disconcerting than either parodic, as with Rick Vigorous's phallic dreaming in *Broom*, or horrific, as in Hal's "face in the floor" dream in *Jest*.

32. Wallace, *Brief Interviews*, p. 5.

33. Ibid.

34. Ibid.

35. Ibid., p. 6.

36. Ibid.

37. For further comparisons between Barth's story and Wallace's, see David Coughlan, "'Sappy or no, it's true': Affect and Expression in *Brief Interviews with Hideous Men*," in Philip Coleman (ed.), *Critical Insights: David Foster Wallace* (Ipswich, MA: Salem Press, 2015), pp. 166–168.

38. Holland, "Mediated Immediacy," p. 112.

39. Wallace, *Brief Interviews*, p. 6.

40. Zadie Smith, "*Brief Interviews with Hideous Men*: The Difficult Gifts of David Foster Wallace," in *Changing My Mind: Occasional Essays* (London: Penguin, 2009), p. 262.

41. Julia Kristeva, *Powers of Horror: An Essay on Abjection*, (trans.) Leon S. Roudiez (New York: Columbia University Press, 1982).

42. Wallace, *Brief Interviews*, p. 8.

43. Ibid., p. 6.

44. Ibid., p. 16.

45. Ibid., p. 93.

46. Ibid., p. 95.

47. Ibid., p. 96.

48. "Relationship" is described as a "near-nauseous term in contemporary usage" in the story "Octet." Wallace, *Brief Interviews*, p. 132, n. 8.

49. Smith, "Difficult Gifts," p. 288.

50. Cixous, "The Laugh of the Medusa," p. 883.

51. Irigaray, *This Sex Which Is Not One*, p. 72.

52. Ibid., 33.

53. Wallace, *Brief Interviews*, pp. 0, 320.

54. Ibid., p. 287.

55. Ibid., p. 288.

56. Ibid., pp. 290, 289.

57. Ibid., p. 317.

58. Hayes-Brady, *Unspeakable Failures*, p. 173.

59. Wallace, *Brief Interviews*, p. 318.

60. Ibid. The force and intricacy of "B.I. #20" has seen it receive a particularly high number of involved readings by critics. See, for instance: Christoforos Diakoulakis, "'Quote Unquote Love... a Type of Scotopia': David Foster Wallace's *Brief Interviews with Hideous Men*," in David Hering (ed.), *Consider David Foster: Critical Essays* (Los Angeles: Sideshow Media Group Press, 2010), 147–155; David P. Rando, "David Foster Wallace and Lovelessness," *Twentieth-Century Literature* 59.4 (2013), pp. 575–595; and Rachel Haley Himmelheber, "'I Believed She Could Save Me': Rape Culture in David Foster Wallace's 'Brief Interviews with Hideous Men #20,'" *Critique* 55 (2014), pp. 522–535.

61. See the discussions by Boswell, Coughlan, Hayes-Brady, Holland, and Smith, op. cit., as well as Lee Konstantinou, "No Bull: David Foster Wallace and Postironic Belief," in Samuel Cohen and Lee Konstantinou (eds.), *The Legacy of David Foster Wallace* (Iowa City: University of Iowa Press, 2012), pp. 83–112; and Iain Williams, "(New) Sincerity in David Foster Wallace's 'Octet,'" *Critique* 56 (2015), pp. 299–314.

62. Wallace, *Brief Interviews*, 145. This broken quality is one way in which the story can be said to mirror the collection as a whole.

63. Ibid.
64. Ibid., pp. 145, 155, n. 7.
65. Ibid., pp. 155–156.
66. Ibid., p. 150. As Smith points out in her comments on this passage, sameness functions in Wallace's work as both an apparent ethical principle – whereby one consciousness can find commonality with another through a shared language – and an aesthetic feature: "There is a weird ambient sameness to Wallace's work." Smith, "Difficult Gifts," p. 291.
67. Wallace, *Brief Interviews*, p. 157.
68. Ibid., p. 160.
69. It seems important to emphasize this potential because it has recently become possible for prominent critics to argue that, on the basis of details found in his biography, Wallace's fiction can be dismissed as a priori misogynistic before it is even read. See Amy Hungerford, "On Not Reading DFW," in *Making Literature Now* (Stanford, CA: Stanford University Press, 2016), pp. 141–166.
70. Laura Mulvey, "Visual Pleasure and Narrative Cinema," *Screen* 16.3 (1975), p. 7.
71. Ibid.

6

DAVID HERING

Oblivion

Why did David Foster Wallace title his 2004 short story collection *Oblivion*? A reader of Wallace's earlier fiction might presume that the title refers to the pursuit of willed numbness. After all, many characters in these works are marked by their desire to block out the world via alcohol, drugs, or some other form of addictive behavior. In the title story of *Girl with Curious Hair* (1989), Sick Puppy lives in a state of willed dissociation and numbness from his environment, only able to "feel" when he is burned with a lighter, while Don Gately, the recovering addict in *Infinite Jest* (1996), participates in a multiday drug binge with his friend Fackelmann, "numb from the scalp on down and climbing."[1] *Oblivion*, conversely, is not characterized by substance abuse – indeed, the soberness of its protagonists is marked. However, it retains those motifs of physical constraint, suffering, endurance, and embodiment evident in much of Wallace's earlier fiction, contrasting them repeatedly with states of *disembodiment*. In the collection, this state of disembodied oblivion is positioned against a sense of embodied suffering, which presents itself in extremes of physical agony and relentless emotional distress. The stories also stage a series of ethical and philosophical questions that draw upon and develop motifs of consciousness and communication explored in the earlier fiction. These questions interrogate how and why one seeks oblivion from suffering, how the body suffers, whether one can will oneself beyond a state of suffering, and what the condition of suffering says about the subject.

Consciousness Is Nature's Nightmare

The stories in *Oblivion* draw repeatedly upon a connection between consciousness, suffering, and environment. This is crystallized in the corporate motto, "Consciousness Is Nature's Nightmare," of O Verily Productions, which is responsible for developing the Suffering Channel, a cable network that broadcasts images of human pain in the story of the same name.[2] This maxim is, in fact, a direct and unacknowledged quote from *Tears and Saints* (1937), a work by the Romanian philosopher E. M. Cioran that is concerned with religious mysticism and is a source text of some significance for *Oblivion*. Cioran's gnomic book, which in its aphoristic style and preoccupation with the human "will to power" is both reminiscent of and responsive to Friedrich Nietzsche's *Beyond Good and Evil* (1886), locates consciousness as born of human "freedom and laziness":

> Animals may well have evolved to the rank of men when they started to walk upright, but *consciousness* was born in moments of freedom and laziness. As you lie stretched out on the ground, your eyes staring at the sky above, the separation between you and the world opens up like a gap – without which consciousness is not possible.[3]

Cioran posits a symbiotic relationship between consciousness and suffering, whereby consciousness, which is "*not* nature," is "a symptom of estrangement from life caused by illness,"[4] before suggesting, quoting Dostoevsky's *Notes from the Underground,* that "suffering is the cause of consciousness."[5] For Cioran, then, human consciousness is a reflective moment of estrangement from nature that provokes, and is provoked by, suffering.

In *Oblivion* Wallace torques Cioran's concept of "freedom and laziness" to incorporate the physical and psychological stasis engendered by late twentieth-century work and living environments. The stories are generally located within airless clinical or corporate spaces (airplane cabins, boardrooms, sleep therapy chambers) and feature characters trapped within cycles of behavior or patterns of obsessive thought that are often specifically triggered by these locations. The enforced, unnaturally hermetic *stillness* of these spaces restricts physicality and provokes thought, leading to a painful, involuted consciousness that manifests as extended reveries on troubling elements of the protagonists' lives. For Terry Schmidt, hapless product tester for the Reesemeyer Shannon Belt corporation in "Mister Squishy," the conference room is a space of duplicity and alienation, where he muses on his romantic failure with coworker Darlene Lilley and entertains disturbing thoughts of product tampering and chemical terrorism. The room's features exacerbate its separation from nature, with "a thick tinted window" that creates "a more or less natural-lit environment,"[6] its depth cutting the noises outside "to almost nothing."[7] Similarly, the narrator of "The Soul Is Not a Smithy," seated in a classroom, attempts to escape from his environment by daydreaming a story that takes place within the wire mesh of the school's windows, which have been designed to make the view "less diverting and to minimize the chances that a pupil could become distracted or lost in contemplation of the scene outside."[8] The enclosed flight cabin in "Another

Pioneer" initiates the telling of a recursive series of nested stories, while in "Philosophy and the Mirror of Nature" a mother and son's lengthy ride inside a bus with a "flesh-colored" interior prompts a series of reflections on failed litigation and personal, vengeful, unhappiness.[9] In the collection's climactic novella, "The Suffering Channel," Wallace returns to the board-room setting of "Mister Squishy," juxtaposing it with an equally claustro-phobic Midwestern duplex, the home of the suffering artist Brint Moltke, who produces perfectly detailed fecal sculptures directly from his colon.

These unnatural environments provoke consciousness as an evasive response to the physical constraint or boredom they generate. However, more often than not, and following Cioran's model of consciousness, that very act of evasion is a fallacy that simply provokes a greater degree of suffering. Terry Schmidt's reveries only deepen his existing frustrations, while the narrator's wire-mesh fantasies in "The Soul Is Not a Smithy" place him in physical danger from his substitute teacher, who is suffering from a violent psychological breakdown. This fallacy can be better under-stood by considering the concept of "oblivion" outlined by Friedrich Nietzsche, Cioran's intellectual predecessor. Nietzsche's *On the Genealogy of Morals* (1887) provides a useful model through which to view these scenarios and to understand Wallace's approach to consciousness and suffer-ing in *Oblivion*. Nietzsche defines oblivion (sometimes referred to in other translations as "forgetfulness") as "an active ... inhibiting capacity," a closing of the doors of consciousness and a shutting away of external disturbance.[10] On Nietzsche's view, oblivion is an essential quality, as the quietude it affords acts as a necessary precursor to "the superior functions and functionaries – those of governing, anticipating, planning ahead"[11] that are characteristic of the strong individual. Nietzsche sees a lack of oblivion as a mark of weakness, "an active *will* not to let go."[12] However, the characters in *Oblivion* often appear to be caught within a double bind: they try to forget, to shut their consciousness away from their environments, but those very attempts at forgetfulness relocate them into a fallacious version of Nietzsche's oblivion, one which only deepens their suffering.[13]

Why, then, do the characters in *Oblivion* seem to be resistant to that restorative inner silence? It would be reductive to suggest, *qua* Nietzsche, that this is simply a sign of weak will. Instead, it would be more productive to think of these characters as involuntarily *internalizing* that external distur-bance against which oblivion should act as a bulwark. On Wallace's view, this environmental disquiet is markedly harder to avoid in a culture char-acterized by what he defines as "Total Noise, the seething static of every particular thing and experience, and one's total freedom of infinite choice about what to choose to attend to and represent and connect, and how, and why, etc."[14] As this definition suggests, Total Noise should not necessarily be understood as something that can be shut away with the closing of a door, or indeed the hermetic sealing of a work environment. It is, instead, a kind of default psychological state in late twentieth-century American culture, one that works *in tandem* with those static locations depicted by Wallace in *Oblivion* and that problematizes the removal of oneself from the external world. In this model, Nietzsche's external disturbance migrates permanently inward and causes the conscious subject, already constrained within these circumscribed environments, to suffer further. This inseparability is not simply a matter of individual will in Wallace's fiction. Instead, it is an environmental fact, one that is only exacerbated by attempts to nullify the pain through quick-fix approaches, as Wallace has remarked in interview:

> In most other cultures, if you hurt, if you have a symptom that's causing you to suffer, they view this as basically healthy and natural, a sign that your nervous system knows something's wrong . . . if you just look at the number of ways that we try like hell to alleviate mere symptoms in this country . . . you can see an almost compulsive tendency to regard pain itself as the problem.[15]

Wallace's fiction is littered with these flawed attempts to mollify suffering. In *The Broom of the System* (1987), Rick Vigorous attempts to redirect his feelings of inadequacy by composing self-justifying metafictional stories, while Hal Incandenza in *Infinite Jest* uses drugs and alcohol to treat his anxiety and depression without discovering its root cause, with disastrous consequences. However, in *Oblivion* there is a marked lack of an ameliorating substance: the characters seem, by and large, to be alone with their pain and unable to treat it and, in accordance with Cioran's model, the stasis of their environments only provokes further awareness of their suffering.

Dreams and Disembodiment

Is there any escape, then, from this purgatorial state of conscious suffering? A possible solution presented in several stories in *Oblivion* is a more dramatic kind of literal disembodiment, an escape from the body itself as a liberation from suffering. However, this strategy is enacted by characters with only varying degrees of success. In "Oblivion," Randall, a rather obnoxious husband and stepfather, recounts at exhaustive length a series of marital disagreements being caused by sleep: Randall's wife Hope complains about his snoring, but he maintains that he was awake on the nights in question. The narrative takes on a more sinister bent with a number of implicit suggestions, which erupt occasionally throughout the story, that Randall may be sexually abusing his stepdaughter, Audrey. The putative climax of "Oblivion," where Randall and Hope attend a sleep clinic in order to resolve their argument, is upended when the narrative suddenly breaks down.

> "up. Wake up, for the love of."
> "God. My God I was having."
> "Wake up."
> "Having the worst dream."[16]

The preceding story appears to have been a bad dream experienced by Randall's wife, who has sublimated her unspoken waking suspicions about Randall into this nightmare. "Oblivion," therefore, grimly suggests that the fallacious version of Nietzschean oblivion that characterizes the collection extends even further, to *unconsciousness*. Hope's sleeping mind attempts to shut out and recontextualize the waking horror of her complicity in the abuse, but the dream ultimately becomes a nightmare inflected by the conditions of her waking state. Furthermore, while the plot of "Oblivion" could be read as a fairly anodyne example of psychological displacement, a more developed reading might consider how Wallace partially dramatizes Cioran's critique of Schopenhauer in *Tears and Saints*, which ends with the quote Wallace uses in "The Suffering Channel":

> Schopenhauer is right to maintain that life is a dream. But he is wrong to condemn illusions instead of cultivating them, for he thereby implies that there might be something better beyond them ... Life would be unbearable if it were real. As a dream, it is a mixture of charm and terror to which we gladly abandon ourselves. Consciousness is nature's nightmare.[17]

Cioran accepts Schopenhauer's dictum, following Kant, that the world is epistemologically constructed as a reflection of the human mind (a "dream"), but, in a paradoxical piece of rhetoric, defines consciousness *itself* as nightmare. In "Oblivion," this situation is literalized: Hope's dream, an attempt to psychologically divert the abuse taking place in the waking world, cannot sustain itself, and she is doomed to wake from the disrupted dream into the "nightmare" of consciousness. In this story Wallace appears to suggest, pessimistically, that the suffering consciousness of the waking mind resists even the disembodiment of the dreamscape. There is no escape from this pain, even when unconscious.

In "Incarnations of Burned Children," a baby, scalded on the genitals in a household accident, responds to his pain and disfigurement by learning "to leave himself and watch the whole rest unfold from a point overhead, and whatever was lost never thenceforth mattered."[18] This particular disembodiment appears figurative rather than literal, as "the child's body expanded and walked about and drew pay and lived its life untenanted, a thing among things."[19] Here the response to bodily suffering, which due to the wound's location might also involve the inability to perform sexually and reproduce, involves a process of willed disembodiment that leads to an accelerated sense of social detachment. The "untenanted" subject watches from "a point overhead," but while it becomes "a thing among things," it is not able to achieve true objecthood: it exists as a lonely consciousness apart from the world itself, in a state somewhere between embodiment and disembodiment, where true "oblivion" is unattainable.

The collection ends with "The Suffering Channel," a novella that strongly reemphasizes embodiment and physical suffering. Brint Moltke's bizarre talent comes from a bodily movement (peristalsis) that creates highly crafted sculptures from his own excrement. His morbidly obese wife, Amber, is "less a person than a vista."[20] R. Vaughn Corliss, creator of the Suffering Channel, which displays images of human anguish, dreams of a channel devoted wholly to "images of celebrities shitting," and interns at *Style* magazine spend their lunch hours discussing toilet design.[21] Skip Atwater, a *Style* journalist who is writing a story on the Moltkes for his lurid column "What in the World," experiences a strange bodily sensation when undergoing pain:

> When anything painful or unpleasant happened to his body, Skip Atwater often got the queer sense that he was in fact not a body that occupied space but rather just a bodyshaped area of space itself, impenetrable but empty, with a certain vacuous roaring sensation we tend to associate with empty space.[22]

In an amendment to the examples of disembodiment in "Oblivion" and "Incarnations of Burned Children," Atwater's response to physical suffering is to experience his body as empty rather than absent (though his consciousness remains), while the reference to vacuity also indicates a veiled loathing of the tawdry journalistic environment in which he works. Furthermore, Atwater's sensation is set against the relentlessly embodied suffering of Brint Moltke, whose gift is inextricable from his body and who seems unable to escape his predicament. In a particularly grim episode, Moltke writes a surreptitious note to the journalist in his own feces that reads "HELP ME," without realizing that the similarly unhappy Atwater's magazine column depends upon the exploitation of his talent.[23] Strikingly, Atwater and Moltke are not even afforded the fallacious attempts at oblivion experienced by the narrators of "The Soul Is Not a Smithy" and "Oblivion." They remain steadfast, embodied, suffering. The implied apocalyptic event that haunts the novella, much of which takes place in the World Trade Center in the weeks before 9/11, seems to foreclose on the possibility of reconciliation.

Suffering and Saintliness

The relentless focus on suffering in *Oblivion* lends the collection a despairing atmosphere: Marshall Boswell has referred to it as the "bleakest" of Wallace's books.[24] However, the depiction of suffering in the collection also goes beyond the aforementioned diagnosis and description of environmental and social malaise and into a critique of the act of suffering itself. An attentive reading of Cioran's approach to suffering in *Tears and Saints*, and an understanding of the complexity of Wallace's composition process around the turn of the twenty-first century, gives a more developed picture of the approach to suffering, embodiment, and consciousness in *Oblivion*.

As a number of critics have argued, the composition of *Oblivion* between 1999 and 2004 is often inextricable from that of Wallace's third novel project, which would eventually be published, unfinished, as *The Pale King*.[25] A number of the stories, including "Incarnations of Burned Children," "The Soul Is Not a Smithy," and "Mister Squishy," were composed as parts of the third novel before being placed instead in *Oblivion*. With such a strong process of cross-composition, it is inevitable that several motifs from *Oblivion* are also present in that novel. For example, Lane Dean Jr.'s work environment at the IRS in *The Pale King* is characterized by extreme boredom and stasis ("the more you looked at the clock the slower time went")[26] while Chris Fogle is informed that in his career in the tax service he will "experience . . . a type of death."[27] Furthermore, chapter 36 of the novel, which depicts a young boy attempting to kiss every inch of his own body, overlaps significantly with the subject matter of *Oblivion*. The boy's actions are intercut with a series of digressions on saints and mysticism, one of which includes a reference to the same work from which Wallace took "consciousness is nature's nightmare" for *Oblivion*:

> Hands lack the anatomical mass required to support the weight of an adult human . . . Classical crucifixion required nails to be driven through the subject's wrists, not his hands. Hence the, quote, "necessarily simultaneous *truth* and *falsity* of the stigmata" that existential theologian E. M. Cioran explicates in his 1937 *Lacrimi si sfinti*.[28]

The invocation of *Tears and Saints* in *The Pale King* suggests a strong thematic connection with the ideas of endurance and suffering explored in *Oblivion*. The boy's achievements, which involve much endurance and often suffering (one contortion provokes "pain beyond naming")[29] and which appear to precipitate to some degree his father's isolation and a breakdown in communication between father and son (he "[keeps] his feelings to himself" sitting alone outside the boy's room)³⁰ have, I will suggest, a strong connection to Cioran's reading of sainthood in *Tears and Saints.*

The inscrutability or loathsomeness of children are common tropes in Wallace's later work. The injured baby in "Incarnations of Burned Children" suffers because he cannot make himself understood to his parents, while the child-seer in "Another Pioneer" inspires both devotion and rage. "Everyone hates" young Leonard Stecyk,³¹ whose relentless acts of kindness in *The Pale King* remind them of their own empathetic failings, while the "fierce" infant from chapter 35 of the same novel,³² who may later be used by Merrill Lehrl to vet candidates for promotion, is viewed with both horror and suspicion.³³ These examples are, of course, a development of certain earlier scenarios of parent-child miscommunication in *The Broom of the System* and *Infinite Jest*, but in the later work the *mystery* of the supernatural-seeming child, a figure who comes to assume some considerable power over adults, is a site for the dramatization of certain ideas about saintliness and suffering. I want to suggest that these ideas are responsive to Cioran's argument in *Tears and Saints* about suffering, embodiment, and the power of will.

In *Tears and Saints*, Cioran uses the term "saint" interchangeably with the word "mystic." Christian mysticism is defined here by Cioran as the pursuit of a state of intense self-directed contemplation and endurance in order to achieve a state of ecstatic union with God: examples used in *Tears and Saints* include St. Teresa and St. Catherine of Siena.³⁴ Cioran, heavily influenced by Nietzsche, critiques these mystics by positioning their pursuit of suffering and endurance as an example of the "will to power." For Cioran, as for Nietzsche, God is dead (and described in *Tears and Saints* as a "universal Absentee"),³⁵ so the mystic's suffering is a hollow enterprise, a vacuum filled only by a self-aggrandizing will. "Saintliness interests me for the delirium of self-aggrandizement hidden beneath its meekness," states Cioran, "its will to power masked by goodness."³⁶ Suffering, for Cioran, merely begets more suffering: saintliness "cannot exist without the voluptuousness of pain and a perverse refinement of suffering."³⁷ Wallace makes an early reference to mysticism in *Infinite Jest*, where the juxtaposition of Bernini's sculpture *The Ecstasy of St. Teresa* with Joelle Van Dyne's drug overdose suggests a correlation between the mystic pursuit of ecstasy and the disembodied state of oblivion sought by the addict.³⁸ However, in *Oblivion* (and in *The Pale King*) Wallace's invocation of Cioran goes, at times, beyond the description of suffering as symptomatic of environment and culture and actively problematizes the act of suffering itself.

Why is Wallace interested in Cioran's figure of the self-aggrandizing, suffering mystic, and how is this enacted in *Oblivion*? A useful example can be found in the story "Another Pioneer," where a narrator overhears a story about a mysterious child, an "extraordinarily highly-powered, supernaturally advanced human" born into an isolated rainforest village. The child's powers are described by the storyteller, who may be a "corporate or academic scientist," in terms of "cognitive ability, raw IQ" rather than "messianic."[39] The child, who is "fully capable of answering all manner of both trivial and also profoundly non-trivial questions" soon becomes a holy figure, consulted on "religious-grade questions" by the villagers.[40] However, a shaman from a neighboring settlement, determined to undermine the child's considerable power, succeeds in asking a question that destabilizes his influence. The question is approximately reported as follows:

> You, child, who are so gifted and sagacious and wise: Is it possible that you have not realized the extent to which these primitive villagers have exaggerated your gifts, have transformed you into something you know too well you are not? Surely you have seen that they so revere you precisely because they themselves are too unwise to see your limitations? How long before they, too, see what you have seen when gazing deep inside yourself? Surely it has occurred to you.[41]

The shaman performs an amended version of the critique of the mystic described by Cioran in *Tears and Saints* but does so directly to the individual in question, suggesting that the child's supposedly mystic status masks a desire for power and mastery, and a self-awareness of the fraudulence of this enterprise. The child's vindictive, unheard answer to this question "instantly destroys" the shaman's "higher faculties or spirit or soul," leading the villagers to fear and eventually abandon the child and the village.[42] In the description of this abandonment, Wallace invokes Cioran's critique of saintly self-aggrandizement:

> The child simply endures the catastrophe of the queues' and offerings' end and of his own utter isolation and in effect perverse banishment at the precise center of a village whose center everyone now goes way far out of their way to avoid, the child here enduring alone on the dais for months and months ... here evidently echoing the way certain medieval hagiographies depict their own extraordinarily high-powered, supernaturally advanced subjects as being capable of fasting for months and even years without discomfort.[43]

The pointed alignment of mystic "hagiography" with the capacity for isolation suggests the strong sense of ambivalence with which Wallace approaches suffering and endurance in *Oblivion*. "Another Pioneer," then, presents an amended version of the fallacious approaches to oblivious "forgetting" elsewhere in the collection: the attempt to transcend or remove oneself through endurance or suffering alleviates nothing and instead self-indulgently celebrates, after Cioran, its own "voluptuousness." This can also be seen in the behavior of Leonard Stecyk in *The Pale King*: Wallace suggests in notes for the novel that Stecyk's apparently selfless behavior does in fact *cause* suffering and is "actually sadistic, pathological, selfish."[44] Furthermore, the self-kissing boy in chapter 36, in his feats of endurance and patience bent toward an absent goal (as Cioran sees the mystic's endurance as futile in the absence of God), isolates his father, his attempts at transcendence amounting to a form of negligence of social and familial communication.

Conjoined Consciousness

In the midst of these scenarios of failed oblivion and self-aggrandizing suffering, Wallace offers a model of consciousness that seeks to overcome the pain caused by stasis of environment and embodiment, and the self-indulgence that might lie within it. "Good Old Neon" is narrated by Neal, a creative associate who suffers from a compulsion to "create a certain impression of me in other people."[45] This results in a hollow kind of success: Neal is liked and respected but cannot escape his own feelings of fraudulence. In one sequence, Neal participates in a meditation class where "through sheer force of will I'd always force myself to remain totally still" until "my knees and lower back were on fire and I had what felt like swarms of insects crawling all over my arms and shooting out of the top of my head."[46] Later, his instructor refers to him as "the statue," which Neal takes as a "subtle rebuke" of his fraudulence.[47] In this sequence, Wallace presents a slightly different example of a failed attempt at Nietzschean "oblivion." Meditation, which is supposed to free the mind and body, here only accentuates the physicality of the suffering body. The instructor's reference to "the statue" both compounds Neal's suffering and aligns him with the static, seated child in "Another Pioneer" as a fraudulent, self-indulgent sufferer.

However, Neal makes a reference early in the story that reframes the entire narrative:

> I know this part is boring and probably boring you, by the way, but it gets a lot more interesting when I get to the part where I kill myself and discover what happens immediately after a person dies.[48]

It becomes evident that "Good Old Neon" is being narrated by Neal after his death. Neal's "ghost" explains that a postdeath state of consciousness affords an unprecedented degree of communication and spatiotemporal flexibility, and a reprieve from the embodied suffering of his life:

> You already know the difference between the size and speed of everything that flashes through you and the tiny inadequate bit of it all you can ever let anyone know. As though inside you is this enormous room full of what seems like everything in the whole universe at one time or another and yet the only parts that get out have to somehow squeeze out through one of those tiny keyholes you see under the knob in older doors ...
>
> But it does have a knob, the door can open ... Think for a second – what if all the infinitely dense and shifting worlds of stuff inside you every moment of your life turned out now to be somehow fully open and expressible afterward, after what you think of as you has died, because what if afterward now each moment itself is an infinite sea or span or passage of time in which to express it or convey it.[49]

Initially, "Good Old Neon" might seem to offer the most pessimistic vision of all the stories in *Oblivion*, suggesting that only death can offer a reprieve from the embodied suffering of consciousness. The story is, thankfully, more complex than a glib advocation of suicide as liberating disembodiment. Instead, the appearance of a certain "David Wallace" at the end of the story, who is thinking about Neal's suicide and trying "through the tiny keyhole of himself" to imagine "what all must have happened to lead up to my death," ultimately shifts the focus of the narrative away from Neal and toward another's attempt to understand his suffering.[50] "Good Old Neon" therefore climaxes with a dialogic moment of shared communication: Neal describing Wallace trying to imagine Neal, with the metafictional inflection of David Wallace's appearance reminding the reader of Wallace's own position in relation to the narrative.

Neal's postdeath narration and Wallace's authorial presence in "Good Old Neon" thus posits a communicative model of shared consciousness that Wallace offers as a rebuttal to, rather than a dramatization of, Cioran's "nightmare" of suffering consciousness. This model recalls the question posed by Jean-François Lyotard in *The Inhuman*: "can thought go on without a body?"[51] Lyotard, considering the future possibility of disembodied thought, suggests that our options are either to "remain in the life of the mind and in earthly phenomenality" or to concern ourselves with "the job of simulating conditions of life and thought to make thinking remain materially possible after the change in the condition of matter."[52] "Good Old Neon" dramatizes this "job," with Wallace imagining a move from "earthly phenomenality" to an unbound, disembodied consciousness. One might, of course, plausibly critique Wallace's presence in the story as the collapse of everything into a single embodied consciousness (the writer himself), but through his metafictional appearance within this scenario, Wallace suggests that literature *itself* might create the conditions for such a sharing of consciousnesses. Those embodied subjects elsewhere in the collection, in their enclosed unnatural environments, are then set against the liberation and dialogue of the interpenetrating consciousnesses of the "enormous room" that Neal describes.

On this view, the model of shared consciousness in "Good Old Neon" attempts a transcendence of isolated suffering and endurance. Neal's disembodied dialogue after death offers a movement away from the kind of environmental stasis that provokes suffering, and the metaleptic alignment with the narrating voice of "David Wallace" ameliorates his earlier condition of suffering as a self-aggrandizing exercise. The association in "Good Old Neon" between Neal and "David Wallace" also illustrates how the motif of the disguised, self-interested saint can be mapped on to certain models of authorship found in the fiction: Wallace employs the figure of the implied author in "Good Old Neon" and "Octet" from *Brief Interviews with Hideous Men* in an attempt to interrogate this very problem. The implied Wallace figure of the "fiction writer" in "Octet," who tries to be "more like a reader . . . down here quivering in the mud of the trench with the rest of us," rather than "clean and dry and radiant of command presence and unwavering conviction as he coordinates the whole campaign from back at some gleaming abstract Olympian HQ," is later dramatized and embedded into the story world of "Good Old Neon," desanctified, in an attempt to communicate collectively "in the mud of the trench" with the consciousnesses of his characters.[53]

In his commencement address at Kenyon College in 2005, given shortly after the publication of *Oblivion* and later published as *This Is Water* (2009), Wallace offers his most prescriptive account of how the problems of suffering and consciousness that are explored in that collection might be addressed:

> In the day-to-day trenches of adult life, there is actually no such thing as atheism. There is no such thing as not worshipping. Everybody worships. The only choice we get is what to worship.[54]

The implied absence of a unitary God in this model of being accords, of course, with Nietzsche and Cioran. Wallace indicates that rather than seeking transcendence by suffering alone, one should instead choose an object of worship. In *Oblivion*, this implicit object of worship is the kind of dialogic partner suggested by the climax of "Good Old Neon." From this vantage point, we see that many of the characters in *Oblivion* suffer because they have failed to identify an object of worship other than the "voluptuousness" of their own suffering, a tortured consciousness from which they are unable to pervasively free themselves. In "Good Old Neon," Wallace describes a model whereby suffering might be alleviated, and disembodied consciousnesses twinned, the better to escape from this nightmare.

Notes

1. David Foster Wallace, *Infinite Jest* (Boston: Little, Brown, 1996), p. 975.
2. David Foster Wallace, *Oblivion: Stories* (New York: Little, Brown, 2004), p. 282.
3. E. M. Cioran, *Tears and Saints*, (trans.) Ilinca Zarifopol-Johnston (Chicago: University of Chicago Press, 1995), p. 31.
4. Ibid., p. 95.
5. Ibid., p. 100.
6. Wallace, *Oblivion*, p. 3.
7. Ibid., p. 17.
8. Ibid., p. 71.
9. Ibid., p. 186.
10. Friedrich Nietzsche, *On the Genealogy of Morals*, (trans.) Douglas Smith (Oxford: Oxford World's Classics, 1996), p. 39.
11. Ibid.
12. In "Getting Away from It All: The Literary Journalism of David Foster Wallace and Nietzsche's Concept of Oblivion," in Sam Cohen and Lee Konstantinou (eds.), *The Legacy of David Foster Wallace* (Iowa City: University of Iowa Press, 2012), pp. 25–52, Josh Roiland analyzes the Nietzschean concept of oblivion in relation to Wallace's journalism, rather than his fiction. Roiland argues that Wallace's hyperdetailed journalistic style displays his extreme consciousness in the recording of detail from the external world.
13. In "The Constant Monologue Inside Your Head: Oblivion and the Nightmare of Consciousness," in Marshall Boswell and Stephen J. Burn (eds.), *A Companion to David Foster Wallace Studies* (New York: Palgrave Macmillan, 2013), p. 152, Marshall Boswell's observation that a number of stories in *Oblivion* "open up an outer layer of interiority into which the story's principal layer has been nesting all along" posits the existence of this false exteriority that appears to lie beyond the external environment.
14. David Foster Wallace, "Deciderization 2007 – a Special Report," in David Foster Wallace (ed.), *The Best American Essays 2007* (Boston: Houghton Mifflin, 2007), p. xiv.
15. David Foster Wallace, "An Expanded Interview with David Foster Wallace," by Larry McCaffery in Stephen J. Burn (ed.), *Conversations with David Foster Wallace* (Jackson: University of Mississippi Press, 2012), p. 23.
16. Wallace, *Oblivion*, p. 237.
17. Cioran, *Tears and Saints*, p. 102.
18. Wallace, *Oblivion*, p. 116.
19. Ibid.
20. Ibid., p. 250.
21. Ibid., p. 295.

22. Ibid., p. 313.
23. Ibid., p. 314.
24. Boswell, "The Constant Monologue Inside Your Head," p. 151.
25. The composition process is analyzed in detail by Tim Groenland in "A King of Shreds and Patches: Assembling Wallace's Final Novel," in Philip Coleman (ed.), *Critical Insights: David Foster Wallace* (Amenia, NY: Grey House/Salem Press, 2015), pp. 221–237; by David Hering in *David Foster Wallace: Fiction and Form* (New York: Bloomsbury, 2016); and by Toon Staes, "Work in Process: A Genesis for *The Pale King*," *English Studies* 95.1 (2014), pp. 70–84.
26. David Foster Wallace, *The Pale King* (New York: Little, Brown, 2011), p. 377.
27. Ibid., p. 228.
28. Ibid., p. 399.
29. Ibid., p. 395.
30. Ibid., p. 398.
31. Ibid., p. 32.
32. Ibid., p. 387.
33. Ibid., p. 534.
34. Cioran, *Tears and Saints*, pp. 4–6.
35. Ibid., p. 72.
36. Ibid., p. 57.
37. Ibid., p. 59.
38. Wallace, *Infinite Jest*, p. 238.
39. Wallace, *Oblivion*, p. 119.
40. Ibid., p. 120.
41. Ibid., p. 138.
42. Ibid., p. 137.
43. Ibid., pp. 138–9.
44. Wallace, *The Pale King*, p. 542.
45. Wallace, *Oblivion*, p. 141.
46. Ibid., p. 159.
47. Ibid., p. 160.
48. Ibid., p. 143.
49. Ibid., p. 178.
50. Ibid., p. 180.
51. Jean-Francois Lyotard, *The Inhuman: Reflections on Time*, (trans.) Geoffrey Bennington and Rachel Bowlby (Cambridge: Polity, 1991), p. 8.
52. Ibid., pp. 11–12.
53. David Foster Wallace, *Brief Interviews with Hideous Men* (Boston: Little, Brown, 1999), p. 160.
54. David Foster Wallace, *This Is Water: Some Thoughts, Delivered on a Significant Occasion, about Living a Compassionate Life* (New York: Little, Brown, 2009), pp. 98–101.

7

JEFFREY SEVERS

Wallace's Nonfiction

In summer 1993, with the first full draft of *Infinite Jest* still about six months from completion, *Harper's* magazine asked David Foster Wallace to report on the Illinois State Fair in Springfield, near Bloomington, where he would begin teaching at Illinois State University that fall. While he had published several essays already, "Wallace hesitated," D. T. Max writes. "He worried that he had never done reporting," but he "was intrigued too" and "eager to make some money."[1] *Harper's* had first asked him, in 1990, to write a thousand words on television – a piece that never came to fruition but formed the basis for the far longer "E Unibus Pluram: Television and U.S. Fiction," published in the *Review of Contemporary Fiction* in 1993.[2] The state fair essay, though, titled "Ticket to the Fair," would launch a major new phase of Wallace's career, in which he was an in-demand reporter on varied subjects for popular magazines, from *Harper's* and *Rolling Stone* to *Premiere, Esquire,* and *Gourmet.* Along with "Shipping Out," the celebrated Caribbean cruise piece that would be republished as the title essay of his first nonfiction collection, *A Supposedly Fun Thing I'll Never Do Again,* in 1997, Wallace's *Harper's* writing introduced a writer who had found a new, more direct means than his fiction for documenting the folly of American excess – frequently in gargantuan essays that, appropriately, far exceeded journalistic word limits.

Here I offer an anatomy of Wallace's nonfiction corpus, focusing primarily on the transformation in his approach and subject matter between *Supposedly Fun Thing* and the second essay collection he assembled in his lifetime, *Consider the Lobster* (2005), with some attention as well to the essays from throughout his career collected posthumously as *Both Flesh and Not* (2012). Several other Wallace works could be included among his nonfiction – his books *Signifying Rappers* and *Everything and More,* his undergraduate philosophy thesis, and *This Is Water* – but I leave those aside in favor of attention to the essay form, which, as I suggest, meshed well with Wallace's impulse toward

experimental and interrogative modes. After noting their often incongruous material contexts, I divide the essays into three basic categories: first,
book reviews and aesthetic analyses, which come throughout his
career; second, accounts of consumer spectacle, largely concentrated in
Supposedly Fun Thing; and third, pieces at the intersection of ethics and
politics, largely concentrated in *Consider the Lobster*. While there are no
bright lines separating tactics, genres, or periods in Wallace's nonfiction
oeuvre, with each arm in this triad comes a distinct agenda. When
Wallace writes about others' books, artworks, and pop-cultural artifacts,
he (to a greater degree than usual for a novelist) implicitly ruminates on
his own artistic impulses and future fictional projects. When he tackles
decadent late-capitalist environments, such as a supposedly fun cruise, he
engages his gift for embodied narrative and portrays a sickness over
a systematized surfeit of consumer pleasures. And when he turns fully in
the twenty-first century to more explicitly political and civic themes, he
refines his abiding method of sensory saturation and minutely focused
attention to create a less aggressively comedic genre he calls the "service
essay," marked by an epistemic humility and, as a consequence, an ethic
of doubt.

For most purposes, the essays in their book forms comprise the "canon" of
Wallace's nonfiction. But no story of Wallace the nonfiction writer is complete without tales of his battles with magazine editors as he violated, often to
a comical degree, contracted word limits. The magazines put his originals
"through meat grinders," Wallace says in a 1998 interview, and the books
were a "chance to do kind of a director's cut." "Shipping Out" was originally
"about 110 pages," once editors made him double-space the original draft,
which he had craftily submitted (as was his custom) "single-spaced, in eight-
point font." We know the long version from its book form, but *Harper's* cut
it "just about in half."[3] "Authority and American Usage" was first published
in *Harper's*, with major cuts, as "Tense Present: Democracy, English, and the
Wars over Usage," after being rejected by several other magazines for being
far too long to run. His John McCain piece exists in even more iterations: it
first appeared as a 12,000-word article titled "The Weasel, Twelve Monkeys,
and the Shrub" in the April 2000 issue of *Rolling Stone* before being republished at its original, 27,000-word length in three forms: as an e-book by
Little, Brown in 2000; as "Up, Simba: Seven Days on the Trail of an
Anticandidate" in *Consider the Lobster* (with the e-book preface included
as an "OPTIONAL FOREWORD"); and as the 124-page paperback
McCain's Promise (2008, coinciding with McCain's next presidential
run).[4] Studying the pieces' various iterations side by side can help scholars
explore the self-conscious rhetorical stances the essays strike in relation to

their expected audiences – producing tensions that, Wallace told Michael Silverblatt in 2006, were ironically most present once he had restored expurgated mentions of the magazines in the post-magazine incarnations.[5]

Wallace once said of his relationship to his audience, "I like stuff that sounds intimate to me, and that sounds like almost there's somebody talkin' in my ear."[6] His fiction provides numerous scenes of dialogue and interview that engage the reader's ear and first-person monologues like Chris Fogle's that possess a confessional tone. But it is his essays that provide the most extensive examples of direct address to readers, largely without the fiction's tendency to treat reader relations as a philosophical paradox. Building up their sense of connection, his essays strategically offer coyly self-deprecating reminders of who their "I" is – sent on a $3,000 cruise by *Harper's* editors before they have seen "pithy sensuous description one," fumblingly unaware of how professional journalists should act.[7] But Wallace's sentences simultaneously construct a profile for "you" that offers steady solace about just how difficult a caring, unselfish life in postmodern America has become, while also insisting on moral challenges. Lines from his account of McCain being offered early release in Vietnam provide an incisive example: "Try to imagine it was you. Imagine how loudly your most basic, primal self-interest would cry out to you in that moment . . . Would you have refused the offer? *Could* you have? You can't know for sure. None of us can."[8] Paul Giles finds a "hortatory idiom" reminiscent of sermonizing in *This Is Water* and other Wallace, but Giles is attuned to Wallace's more frequently modest positioning when, using the state fair essay as an example, he claims that Wallace's writing "operate[s] allegorically as an attempt to make connections with a world outside of himself," probing "how an isolated self enters into dialogue . . . with a wider community."[9]

The first community Wallace found in his nonfiction venues was that of fellow readers (and film and TV viewers). Before *Harper's* came calling for his investigative work, he largely supplemented his income from fiction-writing and teaching work with book reviews. Wallace's reviews (most from the early 1990s and uncollected) include writing on J. G. Ballard, Kathy Acker, Clive Barker, and Paul Auster for the *Philadelphia Inquirer*, the *New York Times*, and other venues. When he has more room to stretch out as a critic in scholarly journals, as in "The Empty Plenum" and "E Unibus Pluram," Wallace – always attuned to competition with both contemporaries and predecessors, and a somewhat narcissistic critic – mounts aesthetic analyses that involve more gazing in the mirror than assessment of a wholly external object, resulting in the much-discussed manifesto mode of the latter essay and formulations ripe for quoting by interpreters of his fiction. Whether the ostensible subject was minimalist peers, David

Markson's *Wittgenstein's Mistress*, Joseph Frank's biography of Dostoevsky, or the oblique humor in Kafka, Wallace's true subject was often his own work, past and future. As Lucas Thompson suggests about his readings of foreign writers, specific historical and cultural contexts generally mattered less to Wallace than sometimes-simplified analogies to his own contemporary United States.[10] Wallace's reviews of H. L. Hix's *Morte d'Author* ("Greatly Exaggerated") and Edwin Williamson's *Borges: A Life* ("Borges on the Couch") are as much statements about how autobiography figures in his own fictions as they are objective takes on the theorist or biographer. Even in his take-down pieces, such as his pan of John Updike or "Rhetoric and the Math Melodrama," a keen reader, with hindsight, can see Wallace's own fiction being mapped out in negative: Updike's apocalyptic impotence may be ridiculous, but how is it improved upon in the thwarted masculinism of Terry Schmidt in "Mister Squishy" or Skip Atwater in "The Suffering Channel"? If novels about mathematicians tend to misjudge their audience, how will a novel about tax accounting reach its own?

Wallace's more frequent goal in the art and review essays is to understand what precisely makes an artist so appealing or disturbing to him – and worthy of imitation. Thus "David Lynch Keeps His Head" fits this first category. The essay can be read for its premonitions of the odd contortions of the horror genre in fiction that was soon to come: "The Granola-Cruncher," much of *Oblivion*, and the Toni Ware section of *The Pale King*. As in Wallace's reading of Kafka, Lynch's art becomes so valuable by withholding all "reassurance" and leaving the receiver's self undone, dissected, or just unbearably present.[11] "It's little wonder that I find Lynch's movie 'sick,'" Wallace writes, for "nothing sickens me like seeing on-screen some of the very parts of myself I've gone to the movies to try to forget."[12] "*CONTRARIA SUNT COMPLEMENTA*," as the Latin motto in (the Lynch-influenced?) *Blood Sister* goes. "We Are What We Revile."[13]

Making US society face its constitutive sickness was the imperative behind the second major category of essay (and most common gateway to fandom for beginning readers), his tours of outlandish consumer spectacle. Wallace explains his aversion to the fair rides in "Getting Away from Already Being Pretty Much Away from It All" (the retitled "Ticket to the Fair") in lines encapsulating the sensibility of *Supposedly Fun Thing*: he has long been "extremely sensitive: carsick, airsick, heightsick; my sister likes to say I'm 'lifesick.'"[14] The consumer-spectacle essays suggest that "lifesick" is an appropriate response to the late-capitalist United States and its insatiable appetites. Illness, loss of bodily control, and death are the keynotes of these essays, which do not reach a narrative or argumentative climax but trail off into scenes of impotence and dread. "I've put off a real survey of the Near-

Death Experiences until my last hour," Wallace writes punningly as night begins to fall and he investigates the harrowing rides midway in the final segment of "Getting Away."[15] Premonitions of his sickness unto near-death have appeared throughout the preceding pages: what begins as a funny misrecognition of Wallace's employer (supposedly) as *Harper's Bazaar* leads to an ellipsized scene of massive dessert consumption (to go along with ample attention to the junk food for sale) and then a series of surrogate vomiting scenes, with a ten-year-old Golden Gloves boxer, after getting pummeled in the ring, throwing up. Wallace has a nightmarish vision of "those great literalizers of all metaphor, little kids – boxers and fudge-gluttons, sunstroke casualties … the rural Midwesterners of tomorrow, all throwing up," and moments later a "thick coil of vomit" arcs from the shaken car of a ride.[16] One of Wallace's first projected nonfiction topics was the porn industry, as Max recounts (the *Playboy* editor who in 1989 offered to help with his research for a novel about porn was hoping he would also "write a novelist-visits-a-porn-set piece" for the magazine).[17] Wallace would partially fulfill this impulse in 1998 by writing in *Premiere* about the Adult Video Awards in an essay titled "Big Red Son," a piece from *Consider the Lobster* that belongs in this category of consumer spectacle. But much less obscene settings in *Supposedly Fun Thing* also have the feel of the orgiastic, with capitalism's always-promised pleasure repeated to the point that it has become (like porn stars' faces during the act) "cold, dead, mechanical."[18]

Wallace was a systems thinker through and through, and in the decadent zones he surveys, he fastens onto the labor that makes these worlds go (waitstaff, vendors, and maids merit much attention) as well as the plumbing and waste beneath the sparkling surfaces. To amplify the sense in "Getting Away" that the entire capitalist pleasure system is hopelessly ill, not just individual bodies, Wallace converts the fair itself into a giant digestive system: "The Main Gate's maw admits us, slow tight-packed masses move peristaltically along complex systems of branching paths … and are finally … expelled out of exits designed for heavy flow."[19] The hidden, inverted system of the Illinois State Fair is one whereby attendees, there to witness prize cattle, are themselves the livestock being fattened for slaughter. Thus the essay moves from a visit to the literal livestock pens to noticing the "bovine and herdlike quality of the crowd" of fairgoers, engaged in a "Bataan March of docile consumption," and ends with an amusement that makes a dangling man "look like livestock in a sling" from afar.[20] Onboard the *Nadir*, mighty acts of gluttony must be equaled by the most powerful of waste-disposal systems, Wallace knows, and so he makes a central metaphor out of his cabin's "*vacuum toilet*," with "a concussive suction so awesomely powerful" that it seems to render waste "an abstraction" – "a kind of existential-level sewage treatment" and a succinct preview of Empire Waste Displacement in *Infinite Jest*.[21]

Josh Roiland, one of very few critics to focus on Wallace as literary journalist, argues that his essay persona is able to cultivate an oblivion (inspired by Nietzsche) as an antidote to the depicted environments overloading his consciousness; but these consumerist essays portray a body that has already in some sense burst, with the mind effectively following suit.[22] Wallace ends "Supposedly Fun Thing" as a patient in his bed: there he dreams of the *Nadir* floating along at night looking "majestic and terrible ... to any poor soul ... alone in a dinghy, or ... simply and terribly floating, a man overboard, treading water, out of sight of all land." Awake, he undergoes a "trance [that] ... lasted all through the next day and night, which period I spent entirely in Cabin 1009, in bed, mostly looking out the spotless porthole [and eating fruit], ... feeling maybe a little bit glass-eyed but mostly good – good to be on the *Nadir* and good soon to be off, good that I had survived (in a way) being pampered to death (in a way)."[23] That repeated "good" is highly suspect, and this deathly ending owes something to *Moby-Dick* and the fate of the black boy Pip, who is abandoned to open sea by his shipmates, has terrifying visions, and goes mad before he is rescued. The *Nadir*, "so clean and so white it looked boiled," may be Wallace's postmodern white whale, heaped with new American sins and destroying itself.[24] Wallace thus pulls out a grand literary allusion to reinforce the point that excessive consumerism leads toward death-in-life, sickness, or madness for the ship of state – essentially the thesis of *Infinite Jest* as well.

As the use of Melville's outsized idioms hints, especially in *Supposedly Fun Thing*, there is much fiction in Wallace's nonfiction, much mythmaking. Wallace's best friend, Jonathan Franzen, told David Remnick in 2011 that Wallace did indeed make up scenes in his essays: "Those things didn't actually happen," Franzen says of dialogue in the cruise ship essay, without specifying further what other "things" might not have been fact-checked.[25] Readers of Wallace's too-hilarious-to-be-true skeet-shooting, chum-tossing, and baton-twirling scenes cannot be totally surprised. "He put a layer of myth over his experience," Max says of "Getting Away," which "grew increasingly Boschian" in the hands of a writer "not particularly worried by veracity."[26] While the gigantism of *Infinite Jest* is one parallel for the essays contemporaneous with it, the trend toward fiction-laced fact may have been set with Wallace's very first piece for *Harper's*, the 1992 memoir essay "Tennis, Trigonometry, Tornadoes," later republished as "Derivative Sport in Tornado Alley" to open *Supposedly Fun Thing*. Wallace's junior tennis career and the Illinois landscape take on mythic proportions: weather and "grotesquely fertile soil" in his hometown Philo have a tall-tale quality; the author is "a medicine boy of wind and heat"; and he survives a trial by epic tornado, ironically (as in any good myth) the wind that was once his special tennis power.[27] Charles B. Harris, Wallace's friend and colleague at Illinois State, published a postscript to his 2010 career overview in which he noted that Wallace's parents had corrected his biographical claims: David had never lived in Philo, Illinois, and there had been no tornado.[28] Such fiction-laced autobiography later migrates into *The Pale King*, most notably in the "Author's Foreword," where the authorial persona claims to be writing a "nonfiction memoir" and again names Philo, Illinois, as his hometown.[29] Despite my essay's purview, then, for a writer so enamored of the liar's paradox, fiction cannot ever be fully separated from non-, even if Wallace's provocations are often more subtle and less pervasive than those of, say, Philip Roth or John Edgar Wideman.

Tennis led to mythos in another sense, too. The speed and power of world-class tennis players offered ready proof of something Wallace said more philosophically in "E Unibus Pluram": apprehending the world through a screen flattens perception. His 1995 *Esquire* piece on 79th-in-the-world Michael Joyce aims to capture "the untelevised realities" of top-level tennis, for "you really have no idea at all" how fast the game moves until watching it up close.[30] Wallace's tennis essays – on Joyce, Roger Federer, and the 1995 US Open (the latter two in *Both Flesh and Not*) – form a subset of the consumer-spectacle pieces because they too focus on and contend with the money mechanisms that make high-level sports go, from athletes' celebrity to ad-plastered, consumption-friendly stadiums. These essays clarify why the pro tennis circuit in *Infinite Jest* is called the Show. In "Democracy and Commerce at the U.S. Open," Wallace meticulously describes both concessions and the endless tournament sponsorship deals that bring to mind the college bowl games that inspire Subsidized Time in *Infinite Jest*.

But distinguishing these sports essays from the other spectacle pieces, so often about profane appetites, is a countervailing narrative of transcendence when Wallace analyzes the athletes' dedication and achievements. The Joyce essay calls its subject not only "a transcendent practitioner of an art" but an "ascetic," one of "our culture's holy men."[31] The Federer essay, most distant from the *Supposedly Fun Thing* era and largely dispensing with analysis of tennis as commodity, depicts a worshipful Wallace "down on one knee" over a Federer winner seen on TV, mere preliminary to the "near-religious experience" of seeing the planet's greatest live at Wimbledon.[32] The essay's essential subjects are divinity and grace. Even Tracy Austin, despite her disappointing autobiography, is an example of "*techne*, that state in which

Austin's mastery of craft facilitated a communion with the gods themselves."[33] Wallace sees in athletes' genius and their clichéd pronouncements a paradox of embodiment, the question of whether humans in general can both *do* and *know* at the same time – or if, as Alcoholics Anonymous counsels throughout *Infinite Jest*, the latter is best sacrificed in favor of the former.

When asked, Wallace unified *Supposedly Fun Thing* around the relationship to the audience that he cultivated, no distant god but still highly attuned to sublimity and scale. "I ... set myself up as the sort of companion ... the reader could tell might be somewhat annoying but ... was not going to adopt a certain kind of posture where I'm up here and the reader's down there," he said. He acted as a "tour-guide who was very observant but was also every bit as bound up and Americanized and self-conscious and insecure as the reader."[34] His image in a 1998 interview was more visceral: "I will slice open my head for you."[35] To Charlie Rose, Wallace described himself in some of the essays of *Supposedly Fun Thing* as "basically an enormous eyeball floating around something, reporting what it sees."[36] If a TV-driven world has created a populace devoted to obsessively "ogling" others' pretty exteriors, as "E Unibus Pluram" argues, the other essays in *Supposedly Fun Thing* would, paragraph by paragraph, propound a more capacious vision of the mundane and thus a thinking more faithful to open minds (Wallace's and the reader's) in dynamic conversation.[37]

American glut and saturation, as seen by an incredibly acute observer, continued to be the connective theme of Wallace's journalism, but in the later essays, those of my third and final category, the glut is more often explicitly mental, an indication of Wallace's increasing interest in theories of human information processing and neuroscience (documented by Stephen J. Burn)[38] and of a new mode of epistemic humility. Perhaps all his experience shortening *Infinite Jest* and his early essays played a role in his heightened emphasis on the mind's need to filter the available data. In "Deciderization 2007 – A Special Report," his editorial introduction to *The Best American Essays* and republished in *Both Flesh and Not*, Wallace praises the journalists in the volume who have written "service essays," who (giving human form to the computerized processing that determines so much of contemporary life) have "arranged an immense quantity of fact, opinion, confirmation, testimony, and on-site experience."[39] He also used the phrase "service essays" to characterize much of *Consider the Lobster* for Silverblatt in 2006.[40] The idea of a service essayist nuances the tropes of the companion and enormous eyeball, bringing a more deeply political and ethical dimension to cultural critiques that, earlier, offered only a mocking or helpless witnessing of awful American bloat. There is a subliminal connection here, as

118

well, to "the Service," as accountants in *The Pale King* often call the IRS, which in Wallace's hands is one of the largest information-sifting systems that a well-governed polity needs.[41]

A gross imbalance between contemporary knowledge and the capacity to care about it – and the ethical implications of that imbalance – is what the later essays are largely about. "As usual, . . . there's more to know than most of us care about," Wallace writes in "Consider the Lobster," the 2004 exploration of the Maine Lobster Festival and animal rights that throws into relief Wallace's transition to new concerns.[42] This essay leads with the disbelief over what most Americans find sumptuous that pervaded *Supposedly Fun Thing*, with Wallace cataloging the many ways lobsters are served, lamenting "loud, hot, crowded tourist venues," and even calling the festival "a midlevel county fair with a culinary hook."[43] In fact, "Getting Away" offers a distant precedent for the lobster piece's PETA-sympathies by empathizing with livestock, especially pigs, a contradiction abruptly resolved when Wallace is seen downing a corn dog mere hours later. In the second half of "Lobster," though, Wallace minimizes his earlier narrative-oriented mode that ratchets up humor in absurd situations, instead adopting a more detached, scientific perspective that goes deep into animal anatomy and a thorny issue of very specific consumption: lobsters, boiled alive. Where the ending of "Supposedly Fun Thing" winked at its reader with hollow claims about feeling mostly good inside the capitalist pleasure dome, here Wallace concludes with a barrage of stark "queries" for *Gourmet* readers, culminating with one "about what the adjective in a phrase like 'The Magazine of Good Living' is really supposed to mean."[44]

Wallace told Silverblatt that the long pieces in *Consider the Lobster* were "about ideology," and this newly ascendant term (analyzed in depth in "Host") underscores how much more versatile the later essays can be as they guide the reader toward new perspectives.[45] The earlier pieces warned of mindless consumption, but the later ones grant that there are many more dimensions to mindful living, especially in a precarious democracy. Inevitably we will line the two essay collections up with Wallace's two big novels: the burlesques of Johnny Gentle and O.N.A.N., dealing with massive waste, correlate with the limited, economy-driven politics of *Supposedly Fun Thing*, while Glendenning's and others' thoughts on Tocqueville, Reagan, and fundamental beliefs get at the dynamic course in American Studies that Wallace's later fiction and nonfiction open up. A trio of 2000–2005 essays forming the backbone of *Consider the Lobster* all concern themselves with forms of communication within supposed democracies: the usage essay claims politics and language are inseparable; the McCain profile wonders whether modern stump speeches can ever be sincere; and "Host," about conservative radio personality John Ziegler, questions whether mass-media discourse can again "serve the public interest" or will remain another polarizing product of the neoliberal marketplace.[46] While one can arguably see Wallace's nonfiction engaging directly with political questions as far back as *Signifying Rappers* in 1990, *Consider the Lobster* condenses his late-career effort to place civic questions at the front of the reader's mind.

Wallace's more mature persona also proves a different sort of alienated participant in *Consider the Lobster*. In the consumer-spectacle pieces, even as he remains a reader companion, identifies with the appetites of fairgoers, passengers, and porn viewers, and dons a tuxedo T-shirt at dinner, Wallace is merciless in his portraits of his subjects and even willing to wield such troubling socioeconomic categories as "Kmart People," who are "overweight, polyestered," and seen "slapping their kids."[47] How much more honest and sinuous a point emerges when Wallace explores more bourgeois and supposedly refined desires and asks tough questions about vegetarianism, doing so while admitting that his desire to keep eating meat must mean "that I believe animals are less morally important than human beings."[48] In "The View from Mrs. Thompson's" and the context of 9/11, the construction-paper flag he makes when unable to find one to buy casts him again as a comical, naïve child, but similar effects in "Getting Away" seem in retrospect much more of a staged trick. There is also simply more at stake in fitting his dual East Coast and Midwest identities into this rural Illinois community in "Mrs. Thompson's," where "a feeling of alienation from these good people" and their innocence "builds in [Wallace] all throughout" the televised "Horror."[49]

The key turning point in Wallace's nonfiction career was a 2000 piece sympathetic to a Republican politician, but the question of just how conservative Wallace was has the most power when we remove it from strictly electoral decisions and see his efforts to place a seemingly incongruous term alongside democracy: authority. The term arises in the new title he gave "Tense Present," "Authority and American Usage," an argument that ultimately endorses grammarian Bryan Garner's "technocratic authority,"[50] which aids the service essay and is, as I have argued elsewhere, the destination of Wallace's career-long search for a viable form of postmodern moral values.[51] For Wallace, McCain's POW experience "gives him the moral authority both to utter lines about causes beyond self-interest and to expect us ... to believe he means them."[52] In this context, the scathing Updike review belongs here because *Consider the Lobster* is Wallace's most coordinated attempt to pursue a thesis about his country's post-1960s maturation that arose fitfully throughout his early career and exists in utero in the incomplete *Pale King*: Updike's "evection of the libidinous self" from the 1960s forward may have struck a blow to "hypocritical conformity and repression" but has,

by the complicated fin de siècle, grown tired and immature.[53] So an instinc-
tually conservative Wallace, apparently unbothered by questions of racial and
gender privilege, turns to what he sees as adult authorities for the present age:
Garner, who opposes descriptivists with "their ideological roots firmly in the
US Sixties," and McCain, who rescues from the Vietnam War era a gravitas
that somehow survives as well the image-obsessed 1980s and 1990s.[54]

In the last lines of "Host" and of the whole collection, Wallace writes of
Ziegler: "What a bleak and merciless world this host lives in – believes, nay,
knows for an absolute *fact* he lives in. I'll take doubt."[55] *Consider the Lobster*
claims that US democracy could use a strong dose of doubt, important (along
with fact sifting) to the service essayist's defeat of "reflexive dogma."[56]
On abortion rights in "Authority and American Usage," Wallace's middle
way – of somehow being "both Pro-Life *and* Pro-Choice" – descends from
acknowledging the role of "irresolvable doubt" on both sides.[57] Religious
doubt is of radical importance in Dostoevsky's work, and perhaps this is why
"Joseph Frank's Dostoevsky," first published in 1996 and included in review
copies of *Supposedly Fun Thing* before being pulled, is included here.
The bundles of questions that punctuate that review are vehicles of doubt, as
are the many questions that conclude "Lobster." Doubt is also a rhetorical
strategy in the pivotal scene of "Up, Simba," where McCain's podium
response to Donna Duren's story prompts a wave of questions about political
fakery and cynicism. "WHO CARES" is this essay's first heading – a question
that, taking no question mark, marks the defeat of the ethically curious mind
by widespread apathy.[58] Better to find new questions and be, as Wallace says
about his lobster queries, "genuinely curious" – which, as authentic and
democratic stances go, may end up more durable than trying to remain
sincere.[59] Wallace was – as the title says in his very last magazine piece, one
rife with questions on the dogma-riddled issue of terrorism – "Just Asking."

Wallace the reporter often eschewed the Q-and-A format of interviews,
and he once built an entire character around the erasure of the Q's in
deconstructed interviews. His essays become so long, meandering, and
prone to doubts because, even when he has someone to profile, he seeks all
the questions beneath the surface that cannot be volleyed back by a subject,
per rigid media logic. Whatever his genre, he tends toward what Catherine
Belsey, elucidating the disruptive effects of poststructuralism on reading,
calls "the interrogative text."[60] Wallace reminds us that the essay – whether
a "service" one drawing together disparate material or not – is from the Old
French *essai*, a trial, an attempt. Thus it makes sense to call Wallace in his
various nonfiction modes – reviews, reported journalism, memoirs – fundamentally an essayist. As he lays one paragraph atop another, Wallace knows
he is making a mockery of conventional argumentative strategies – and in

that is a performance, not a flaw. Nearly 30 pages into "E Unibus Pluram" comes the heading "I Do Have a Thesis."[61] "Host" takes Wallace's patented footnotes (already a joke about the possibility of scholarly explanation) and turns them into a mad flowchart. Questions of grammar and usage are "ones whose answers have to be literally *worked out* instead of merely found."[62] What such working out meant varied with context, but the process seems deeply connected to the trial-driven nature of the essay as Wallace practiced it. Reviewing *Supposedly Fun Thing*, Richard Stern quotes the great popularizer of the *essai* as a literary form, Michel de Montaigne (also noted in Wallace's "Deciderization" essay): "I go out of my way, but by license not carelessness ... I want the material to make its own divisions ... without my interlacing them with words, with links and seams put in for the benefit of ... inattentive readers."[63] The nod to a sixteenth-century figure suggests that, as post-postmodern as they may seem, Wallace's essays belong in a very long tradition of undermining thetic sureties that has been incubated in the essay form, so heterogeneous as to escape easy definition (but still, as with obscenity, "we feel we pretty much know an essay when we see one").[64]

For not a small number of readers, Wallace's appeal begins and ends with the nonfiction: for them, the fiction is forbiddingly long and dense, whereas the essays offer humor and insight without all the work Wallace expected of his fiction's readers. Instead, the essays served the populace, in ways that, extrapolated, benefited democracy. Fleeing addiction, Wallace had gone away from the world to get back to writing fiction in earnest, holing up in his small Syracuse apartment between 1991 and 1993 to finish *Infinite Jest*. But his magazine work took him out into the world, in ways that undoubtedly influenced his turn toward political themes in the second half of his career. Writing my own humble service essay about essays, I have offered a way of ordering the huge number of stances and ideas Wallace poured into works that, accreting over two decades, have become central to his reputation and influence. In them, we ride around in a floating eyeball, touring satire and ambiguities, as Wallace speaks truths, punctuated by question marks, into our ear. I know there are many moments when they slice my head open too.

Notes

1. D. T. Max, *Every Love Story Is a Ghost Story: A Life of David Foster Wallace* (New York: Viking, 2012), p. 184.
2. Ibid., p. 148.
3. David Foster Wallace, "David Foster Wallace," by Tom Scocca in Stephen J. Burn (ed.), *Conversations with David Foster Wallace* (Jackson: University of Mississippi, 2012), p. 84.

4. This last reissue includes a foreword by *Slate* columnist Jacob Weisberg. David Foster Wallace, *McCain's Promise: Aboard the Straight Talk Express with John McCain and a Whole Bunch of Actual Reporters, Thinking About Hope* (New York: Back Bay, 2008).

5. "David Foster Wallace (Consider the Lobster)," interview by Michael Silverblatt, Bookworm, KCRW, March 2, 2006.

6. *David Foster Wallace: The Last Interview and Other Conversations* (Brooklyn, NY: Melville House, 2012), p. 41.

7. David Foster Wallace, *A Supposedly Fun Thing I'll Never Do Again: Essays and Arguments* (Boston: Little, Brown, 1997), p. 256.

8. David Foster Wallace, *Consider the Lobster and Other Essays* (New York: Little, Brown, 2005), p. 165.

9. Paul Giles, "All Swallowed Up: David Foster Wallace and American Literature" in Samuel Cohen and Lee Konstantinou (eds.), *The Legacy of David Foster Wallace* (Iowa City: University of Iowa Press, 2012), pp. 6, 10.

10. Lucas Thompson, *Global Wallace: David Foster Wallace and World Literature* (New York: Bloomsbury, 2016), p. 155.

11. Wallace, *Consider*, p. 64.

12. Wallace, *Supposedly*, p. 167.

13. David Foster Wallace, *Infinite Jest* (Boston: Little, Brown, 1996), pp. 713, 1054, n. 298.

14. Wallace, *Supposedly*, p. 99.

15. Ibid., p. 132.

16. Ibid., p. 131–132.

17. Max, *Every Love Story*, p. 125.

18. Wallace, *Consider*, p. 17, n. 14. Richard Godden and Michael Szalay tie Wallace's writing about pornography and bodily fluids to anxiety-provoking financial liquidity under capitalism. See "The Bodies in the Bubble: David Foster Wallace's *The Pale King*," *Textual Practice* 28.7 (2014), pp. 1311–1314.

19. Wallace, *Supposedly*, p. 131.

20. Ibid., pp. 104, 137.

21. Ibid., p. 305.

22. Josh Roiland, "Getting Away from It All: The Literary Journalism of David Foster Wallace and Nietzsche's Concept of Oblivion," in Cohen and Konstantinou (eds.), *Legacy*, pp. 25–52.

23. Wallace, *Supposedly*, p. 352.

24. Ibid., p. 260.

25. For a transcript of the exchange, see Michelle Dean, "A Supposedly True Thing Jonathan Franzen Said about David Foster Wallace," *The Awl*, October 11, 2011.

26. Max, *Every Love Story*, 185. Josh Roiland ("David Foster Wallace and the Nature of Fact," *Literary Journalism Studies* 5.2 [Fall 2013], p. 148), documenting Wallace's various diversions from fact in the essays while also criticizing Max for suggesting unproven discrepancies, argues that Wallace saw himself as not a journalist but "a novelist who write[s] nonfiction" and thought he thus might operate according to "a different set of rules" than conventional journalists.

27. Wallace, *Supposedly*, pp. 4, 11.

28. Charles B. Harris, "David Foster Wallace's Hometown: A Correction," *Critique* 51.3 (Spring 2010), pp. 185–86.
29. David Foster Wallace, *The Pale King* (New York: Little, Brown, 2011) pp. 77, 80.
30. Ibid., pp. 241, 236.
31. Ibid., pp. 254, 237.
32. David Foster Wallace, *Both Flesh and Not: Essays* (New York: Little, Brown, 2012), pp. 6, 7.
33. Wallace, *Consider*, p. 254.
34. "David Foster Wallace (*A Supposedly Fun Thing I'll Never Do Again*)," interview by Michael Silverblatt, Bookworm, KCRW, May 15, 1997.
35. Wallace, "David Foster Wallace," in Burn (ed.), *Conversations*, p. 86.
36. "David Foster Wallace," interview by Charlie Rose, PBS, March 27, 1997.
37. Ibid., p. 21.
38. Stephen J. Burn, "'A Paradigm for the Life of Consciousness': *The Pale King*," in Marshall Boswell (ed.), *David Foster Wallace and "The Long Thing": New Essays on the Novels* (New York: Bloomsbury, 2014), pp. 149–168.
39. Wallace, *Both Flesh*, p. 315.
40. "David Foster Wallace (*Consider the Lobster*)," interview by Michael Silverblatt.
41. Wallace, *Pale King*, p. 14.
42. Wallace, *Consider*, p. 236.
43. Ibid., p. 240.
44. Ibid., p. 254.
45. "David Foster Wallace (*Consider the Lobster*)," interview by Michael Silverblatt.
46. Wallace, *Consider*, p. 313.
47. Wallace, *Supposedly*, p. 120.
48. Wallace, *Consider*, p. 253.
49. Ibid., p. 139.
50. Ibid., 123.
51. Jeffrey Severs, *David Foster Wallace's Balancing Books: Fictions of Value* (New York: Columbia University Press, 2017), pp. 247–249.
52. Wallace, *Consider*, p. 166.
53. Ibid., p. 54.
54. Ibid., p. 80.
55. Ibid., pp. 334, 343.
56. Wallace, *Both Flesh*, p. 316.
57. Wallace, *Consider*, p. 82.
58. Ibid., p. 160.
59. Ibid., p. 254.
60. Catherine Belsey, *Critical Practice*, 2nd ed. (New York: Routledge, 2002), pp. 70–84.
61. Wallace, *Supposedly*, p. 49.
62. Wallace, *Consider*, p. 72.
63. Richard Stern, "Verbal Pyrotechnics," *Chicago Tribune*, March 9, 1997. Wallace, *Both Flesh*, p. 301.
64. Wallace, *Both Flesh*, p. 300.

PART III

The Major Novels

8

MARY K. HOLLAND

Infinite Jest

When *Infinite Jest* appeared on February 1, 1996, David Foster Wallace was an up-and-coming young writer whose potential talent had received more recognition than had his published fiction, and postmodernism was a literary and cultural mode that had already received the most breathless accolades and bitter disdain it was ever going to generate. At the nexus of this explosion of Wallace and deflation of postmodernism, *Jest* stands as the most accomplished single product of Wallace's career, and one of the most influential works of fiction of the past 50 years. Wallace wrote most of the book from 1991 to 1993, when he was also delivering the interview and TV essay that would appear in the 1993 *Review of Contemporary Fiction*, in which he criticized recent fiction for reproducing ground-clearing postmodern technique but without meaning or purpose, and envisioned "new literary 'rebels'" who were "willing to risk ... accusations of sentimentality, melodrama. Credulity."[1] Accordingly, one important and common way to read *Jest* is as a pivotal text in Wallace's oeuvre, in which he turned away from the madcap Pynchonian and estranging Barthian postmodernism that shaped his first two works (*The Broom of the System* [1987] and *Girl with Curious Hair* [1989]) and developed new methods for writing fiction that turned postmodernism's primary dangers – irony, image, language, and self-reflexivity – into tools for generating empathy and sincerity. This endeavor would define his writing for the remainder of his life.

Meanwhile, criticism of the past decade argues that the 1990s mark the end of exactly the blankly ironic postmodernism that Wallace criticized in interview and essay, as fiction began to chart new ways of recuperating much of what seemed to have been lost in that era, including history, belief, and human connection.[2] Thus *Infinite Jest* is simultaneously a defining achievement and the beginning of a new literary project for Wallace, and a transition out of postmodern exhaustion for both Wallace's work and American literature in general. But however momentous, *Jest* was not contained in a single moment: Wallace wrote pieces of it a decade or more before the novel was published and was drafting at least one section of the novel that would be published 15 years after it (the posthumous *The Pale King*) while he was writing *Jest*.[3] At once pinnacle, pivot point, and through line, *Infinite Jest* expresses in grand style the complex potential of its author and its period to reimagine the future of America, and of American letters.

Jest's Connections and Recursions

Many of the major themes that *Jest* develops were originally explored by Wallace in earlier works. The novel's critique of media- and entertainment-dominated America, which is governed by a celebrity president, sponsored by corporations that name and own years and monuments alike, and populated by people so addicted to passive entertainment that they choose to be entertained to death, is presaged by *Broom*'s televangelical parrot and a *Jeopardy!* contestant's strange intimacy with the TV audience in "Little Expressionless Animals." The dangerous continuity between irony and sincerity depicted by an actress's nearly unreadable performance of both for David Letterman in "My Appearance" becomes an overt concern in the world of *Jest*, where irony is so pervasive – like the air we breathe, or, more accurately, the water fish breathe[4] – that it is impossible to communicate without it. Those who attempt bald earnestness are freaks: malformed Mario, sweat-licking Lyle, legless Marathe. And the utter self-enclosure that is the result of Bruce's disaffected narcissism in "Here and There" becomes the fate that every character in *Jest* struggles, and perhaps fails, to avoid, as each is driven by infantile need that goes unsatisfied in its world of abandoning and self-obsessed parents.[5]

This desire to transcend the empty, suffering self results in a culture of addiction that takes many forms: drugs, tennis, fame, sex, love, and, of course, entertainment – the last containing all the rest, as every attempt to escape solipsism by way of connection transforms the other into another tool for self-satisfaction. In fact, everything posited by the novel as a potential cure for the ills generated by American culture – programs (AA and NA), institutions (Enfield Tennis Academy and Ennet House), religion and belief, even language, art, and the novel itself – can be and has been read as also reproducing the disaffection, solipsism, or infantile narcissism that fuels the addiction.[6] Such looping recursivity is the thematic and structural engine of the novel, and a literal engine of its futuristic world: just as O.N.A.N. uses annular fusion to export the waste that powers the fusion, the characters' attempts to escape solipsism and addiction move the plot along by spawning more of the same, ending in a narrative moment that thrusts us back to the structural beginning that is the chronological end. The obscurity of both endings sends us back into the perpetual loop.[7]

Jest repeats this and other innovative structural elements used earlier in *Broom* and *Girl* – fracturing the narrative into nonsequential fragments, leading to an open ending, even insinuating missing plot points – but raises them to a considerably more complex level by deploying them over the course of a 1,079-page encyclopedic novel. Like its postmodern predecessors, William Gaddis's *The Recognitions* (1955), John Barth's *The Sot-Weed Factor* (1960), and Thomas Pynchon's *Gravity's Rainbow* (1973), its size alone implies a totality of information and containment, while its deft interweaving of seemingly discontinuous plotlines (junior tennis players' pursuit of a powerful new drug; terrorist activities of wheelchair-clad Quebecois separatists; the sufferings and uneven recoveries of drug and alcohol addicts) via blink-and-you'll-miss-them clues strewn throughout its sprawl insists that every line is crucial, and everything may be connected. Late in the writing process, while Wallace was editing the completed draft, he introduced another structural element meant to exacerbate these encyclopedic aspects: end notes, which, according to a letter to his editor Michael Pietsch, Wallace hoped would allow the book to "mimic the information-flood and data-triage I expect'd be an even bigger part of US life 15 years hence" and "have a lot more technical/medical verisimilitude."[8] *Jest* also aims for verisimilitude – if we take the word of the wraith Incandenza, and equate his agenda for film with Wallace's for fiction, as many critics do[9] – by unfurling a parade of voices, constructed through various, multilayered, and shifting points of view. At times characters seem to speak directly to us using second-person address, in a novelistic version of dramatic monologue, or a reproduction of the intimate speeches at an AA meeting. The only sustained first-person point of view, Hal's, for the most part dissolves at the end of the book's first section, and other characters who take it, however major (like Incandenza[10]) or minor (like yrstruly[11]) do not hold it for long. More often, characters communicate their interior thoughts via free indirect discourse, so that focalization floats among them, from Ken Erdedy's insectile paralysis to Don Gately's heroic resistance to drugs at novel's end, as if cast by a democratic spotlight.

Like the practical solutions offered by the novel, each of these structural innovations both exacerbates and helps cure the recursive cycles of addiction and solipsism the novel has diagnosed as its and our culture's central problems. In this way, the novel indicates a discrepancy between Wallace's proclaimed faith that art can once again be "nourishing, redemptive,"[12] and his artist-character Incandenza's more qualified demonstration, through films like *Pre-nuptial*, that "the self-forgetting of alcohol [is] inferior to that of religion/art."[13] But Incandenza – and Wallace – work hard at their ameliorative art. The proliferation of voices, perspectives, and points of view makes the novel clearly dialogic, rather than monologic,[14] and thus an example of Incandenza's theorized "radical realism," in which everyone has a speaking role. The variety of jargons employed by these voices, and the intimate knowledge suggested by this floating perspective, exemplified by the wraith's freeindirect access to hospitalized Gately's thoughts, weaves these disparate voices into relationships and communities in which the reader participates.[15] Likewise, the novel's narrative fragmentation and incompleteness motivate the reader to rearrange and connect pieces, fill in gaps, and follow leaps in time and perspective, causing her to empathize with a variety of characters and with the author who handed us the puzzle to figure out, or perhaps even to create the missing chapter that enables her to escape the recursive loop in which all of its characters are bound.[16]

But to read the fragmentation and partiality of the novel as pointing toward a whole that the reader must pursue implies a kind of totality, or teleology, that is exactly the opposite of the "anti-eschatology" and "anti-teleology" for which Wallace's work has been celebrated,[17] while also identifying the novel's addictive qualities. And for all its dialogic refusal to dominate its characters with a single omniscient point of view, and its self-awareness of the duplicity of language, the novel's explosion of voices and of jargon also threatens to collapse under the weight of its collective uselessness (how do we distinguish the pointless jargon of tennis and drugs from the similarly capitalized terms and clichés of AA, for example?) or to atomize into a wash of white noise. Tellingly, it is Incandenza who both theorizes the "real egalitarian babble of figurantless crowds" and creates the infantile babble of the *Infinite Jest* film that he intends to awaken his son but which instead induces death by solipsism.[18] The inherent treachery of using language to restore whole selves is also at work in the novel's encyclopedicness, its thousand pages of stories and hundred pages of disruptive, expanding endnotes in part generated by the narrative's inability or refusal to pinpoint exactly what it is trying so earnestly to say. Certainly its massive allusiveness is on its own purposeful, rendering the novel "not as an isolated object, but as a node in a connectionist network,"[19] and its recursive structure teaches the crucial posthumanist truth of the "illusion of autonomy and the fact of recursivity."[20] But *Jest*'s hyperconnected encyclopedicness also perpetuates the paranoia of Pynchon's *Gravity's Rainbow* and *The Crying of Lot 49* (1965) and Don DeLillo's *Libra* (1988), so that it recapitulates and exaggerates the postmodernism its recursive engines aim to abandon, its procession of earnest monologues threatening to blur into a chorus of mewling, Concavity-born Infants.

The Wraith in the Machine

Jest's endnotes draw attention to another technical aspect that is quietly but crucially at odds with the novel's overt claims about and structural gestures toward "radical realism" and the characters' abilities to get outside of their own heads, and of the author's controlling head. Many of the endnotes distinguish characters/speakers from a consciousness that is narrating them, by correcting or otherwise altering the words or information they narrate. For example, endnotes 140 and 141 give slang or racist terms used by Gately, which the narrative in the main text elides, while endnote 315 points out a mishearing by Mario that the narrative has absorbed, and endnote 381 corrects a date given by Hal's first-person description of a *Metropolis* poster. Endnote 123, which Pemulis dictates to Hal, dramatizes this character/ implied-author relationship, as we see Hal's authorial corrections intruding on Pemulis's first-person narrative. As Richard Stock points out, nothing in the note explains its inclusion in the narrative as a whole, which then implies the existence of a separate author beyond Hal or Pemulis who has inserted it.[21] This implied author seems to intrude into the notes themselves in endnote 278, in which a first-person narrator raises questions about Pemulis's brother that seem to be beyond the knowledge of the narrator in the main text. Then, as Toon Staes notes in his reading of the "Coatlicue Complex," endnote 216 ("No clue") separates this implied author from the real author (who certainly is aware that the Coatlicue Complex concerns incest and fearful dependence on the mother, both of which characterize Avril's relationships with her children).[22] Taken together, these endnotes imply a higher-level narrator, who is not David Foster Wallace, but whose knowledge exceeds that of the characters and who has the power to arrange and edit their words at will. Phrases repeat without reason across unconnected characters (for example, "sank without bubbles," used by Hal to describe Lyle and by Gately when remembering his youth;[23] and "eliminate your map," throughout), reinforcing this sense of a controlling narrator, whose omniscience is also established by classic organizing devices of sudden connection and sustained revelation: Gately's car throwing a cup that hits the storefront of Antitoi Entertainment, carrying the narrative focalization with it;[24] the unfolding in minute detail of Gately's shooting as if viewed in slow motion.[25] These implications of controlling knowledge, diction, and vision seem even, in moments, to be packaged in a unifying time line when our narrator points to "this past July" or "tonight."[26] However ownerless, fragmented, and unresolvable the narrative may feel to its readers, *Jest* implies throughout a consciousness that knows and manages its disparate pieces.[27]

Wallace admitted as much to Pietsch, when he explained his desire to use the endnotes to allow "a discursive, authorial-intrusive style."[28] That intrusion of the author into the reader's experience of the novel, and into the novel's otherwise antifigurant "radical realism," is akin to the wraith's intrusion into helpless Don Gately's head: the wraith can rhapsodize about artistic egalitarianism and his desperate desire to empathize with his son all he wants, but doing it by way of beaming himself and his foreign vocabulary uninvited into a suffering man's mind is "lexical rape," not empathy, and is emblematic of the dominating narrative devices of a traditional realism that is in no way "radical."[29] Indeed, Timothy Jacobs has posited that *Jest* "mimes what is arguably the first realist novel, [Stendhal's] *The Red and the Black*," and Andrew Hoberek argues that we should read *Jest* not as experimental fiction but as a return to premodernist realism through a "renewed maximalism" whose attempt to represent the social realities of our sprawling contemporary culture results in the novel's excesses.[30] These characterizations of *Jest* are in line with Wallace's own. In interviews spanning 13 years, he described himself as a realist several times, never identified with metafiction (whose "real end" he famously described as "Armageddon"), and spoke often about devising a new kind of realism that would expose both the mediated, information-permeated world we live in and the truth of fiction – that it is an illusion.[31] This paradoxical need to write self-reflexively in order to write realistically is one way of understanding *Jest*'s own paradoxes of structure and literary mode. It simultaneously offers a traditionally realist depiction of the sweep of contemporary life, resists realism's domination of that life's distinct details and voices by singular and/or omniscient point of view, and reintroduces the ghost of that dominating higher narrator in its effort to expose its constructedness, or the wraith in the machine.

Such ambiguous structural elements of inclusion/omission, totality/insufficiency, egalitarianism/domination not only define *Jest*; they signal the novel's connection forward to future work in which Wallace developed them. One prominent example is the use of "Q" to signify omitted questions, which simultaneously empowers the reader, who is invited to imagine the missing questions, while silencing one half (notably the female half) of a conversation. This technique permeates *Brief Interviews* but first appeared in *Jest*, in transcripts (and one letter) of agent "Helen" Steeply's interviews of Orin.[32] The connection between the ambivalent intimacy and dominance of the "Q" structure and Orin's fraught need to dominate women – essentially his mother – by turning them into "subjects" through sexual intimacy becomes clear in Lorin Stein's interview of Wallace in 1999. There, Wallace expressed a desire to revisit both the "q&a form" and "other unfinished business" from the novel that had not satisfied him, specifically

Orin's sex addiction, which led to his writing the interviews of his next short story collection: Orin was the original hideous man.[33]

The implied author that emerges from the complicated layering of points of view and focalizing in *Jest* is also a precursor to further experiments in perspective in *Oblivion* and *The Pale King*. The nearly hidden (and often overlooked) first-person narrator in "Mister Squishy," who lurks in a late footnote, ultimately asserts total control over the seemingly free-indirect-discourse–empowered Schmidt, in an intensification of Wallace's endnote technique in *Jest*, while "Good Old Neon" replaces one narrative trick with another: it's weird enough to discover that our first-person narrator is dead and empathizing with his live self, but by the end we are asked to conceive of a dead narrator empathizing with "David Wallace's" attempt to empathize with *him*. Who is this David Wallace? How is he related to our author, David Foster Wallace, who in his real life also did not use his middle name? Is that David Wallace the same as the one narrating, in first person, *The Pale King*?

The implied author of *Jest* becomes increasingly visible over the course of Wallace's fiction, at times intensely identified with Wallace himself and at times distinguished from him, but often there, hovering around the edges of his fiction, like Gately's wraith or the ghostly companions to *The Pale King*'s scribblers. In this way, Wallace's fiction belies the self-birthing theory of texts posited by Barthes and Foucault as the "death of the author" (a shift Wallace also asserted in his essay "Greatly Exaggerated"). This signaled authorial presence also contributes to the new realism he developed from *Jest* on. However much his massive cast of characters, geographies, and dialects reprises aspects of "big-R Realism," *Jest*'s realism is also truly radical: it applies old mimetic intention to the "information-flood and data-triage" of the late twentieth-century world, while representing not just the look and feel of the world but also the mechanisms of representation itself. Thus it spawns this panoply of new techniques including end notes, multiplied narrators, and shifting point of view, making Wallace not just a "novelist of ideas"[34] but also a novelist of techniques that developed over the course of his writing life.

Infinite Jest as Historical Novel

As its publication recedes into the past, *Jest* increasingly becomes less a contemporary or futuristic American novel and more a historical one. The bulk of its action takes place in the Year of the Depend Adult Undergarment, which events allow us to date as 2009; it ends the next year, in 2010.[35] When Wallace was writing the novel, those dates lay nearly two decades in the future, and the sci-fi projections he invented to mark the distance, including videophony, the death of broadcast television, the ascension of a vapid celebrity to the presidency, and America's colonization by waste and subsequent domination of Canada via exporting that waste, were reasonable exaggerations of the cultural threats and technological developments of the 1990s. (Indeed, as we witness the Trump administration in action, President Gentle seems downright prescient). Twenty years later, however, the novel feels quaint.

The entertainment world Wallace imagined as futuristic and fundamentally responsible for the downfall of culture, self, and community is now the reality we live unremarkably in. The philosophical core of the novel, so important to Wallace that he refused to cut it, despite repeated requests by Pietsch,[36] is the Marathe-Steeply debate about the relationship among freedom, choice, and responsibility problematized by nearly limitless choice in passive entertainment – a pleasure/danger that greets us today from a multitude of devices *Jest* did not imagine. And, more significantly, this ubiquity of simulacra-spewing media is no longer seen as primarily a threat in our popular culture. Consider the film *Inception* (2010), in which virtual reality is merely a tool used by good and bad guys alike and is ultimately offered as a legitimate, perhaps superior alternative to the pain of real life; or films such as *Her* (2013) and *Ex Machina* (2015), in which AI seems more human than the humans, and deserving of our respect and love. Such reliance on, even habitation in, the seamless spectrum of real and virtual is a far cry from the deadly film *Infinite Jest*, with which even a moment's encounter means death. Instead, the film, an unlabeled cartridge that moves mysteriously around the country, pulling chains of people into its deadly maw, is much more akin to the deadly videotape in the 1999 horror film *The Ring*. *Jest*'s anxiety about media's ability to colonize the human, to turn the viewer into a paralyzed, dehumanized, un-selfed statue – like the viewer-characters in Incandenza's *The Medusa v. the Odalisque*, or even, metaphorically, in *The Joke* – is literalized by *The Ring*'s staticky girl, who steps out of a film to suck the soul out of her stupefied viewer's mouth, a terror of technology and mediation that motivates many other popular films of the period as well, from the people-eating TVs in *Poltergeist* (1982) and *Videodrome* (1983) to two *Terminator* films (1984, 1991) and *The Matrix* (1999).[37]

The book's central, horrifying image of individuals glued to their chairs in dark rooms, TV images flickering on their faces, alone and dying in their own excrement, becomes strange, even comical, for readers who are likely to have spent more time in conversation with others on headsets while playing massively multiplayer online games, or running around town in phone-wielding pursuit of Pokemon, than they do sitting alone and silent in front of a TV. That is to say, for all of its open-endedness, ambiguity of structure, theme, and language, and strategies of endless recursivity, *Infinite Jest* is grounded in a technological materialism that shapes the novel as more of an artifact of the 1990s than a harbinger of the digital age. The materiality of those cartridges, and the need to physically possess them in order to use, disseminate, or copy them (and the need for specific hardware to play and reproduce master copies), motivates much of the action and movement in the book. It brings members of the A.F.R. and F.L.Q. from Canada down into America, to Boston and Tucson, to interview Incandenza family members and track down master copies, meanwhile causing most major plot elements, most directly, the shooting of Gately by an F.L.Q. member. It is 60s Bob's trade of material goods with the Antitoi brothers (his moldy unlabeled cartridges and DMZ for their lava lamps) that links them to the A.F.R. (causing Lucien's torturous death by broom, a horrible perversion of the beloved material object), links the A.F.R. back to Don Gately (from whom 60s Bob acquired the tapes, which Gately stole from Du Plessis), and ferries Kite's mind-destroying DMZ from Gately to the Antitois, who sell it to Pemulis, who then, we assume, gives it to Hal, possibly leaving him in the incoherent state in which we meet him. None of these deadly fencings would have been possible if the film *Infinite Jest* were streamable. If we assume that Gately gets the "crusty old mossy boot-and-leg Read-Only cartridges" from Incandenza's grave (*IJ* 482), where Gately and Hal meet in an unnarrated moment to dig up the head of Incandenza (*IJ* 17), then the physicality of the medium causes (and also stands in for) this crucial, catalyzing meeting of narrative lines as well.

The causal materiality of the film *Infinite Jest*, and of all the novel's imagined technology (even the videophone causes retro evolution, first to high-def masks and then to pre-video phones), so characteristic of the decades in which the book was written, reflects the insistent materiality of *Infinite Jest* the book. With its arrival in the midst of the electronic literature explosion – Shelley Jackson's defining hypertext *Patchwork Girl* was published in 1995 – it's tempting to read the nonlinear, networked structure of *Jest*, and its requirement of reader participation and multiple encounters, as hypertextual, and perhaps influenced by the literary experimentations with digital media and the Internet (which became public in 1991) that also define the 1990s. But Wallace rejected this reading absolutely, writing to Pietsch: "I pray this is nothing like hypertext."[38] (Wallace also stated in interviews in 1996 and 1998 that he had "never been on the internet."[39]) Instead, Wallace wanted reading the book to be a laborious, embodied endeavor that would "make the reader go literally physically 'back and forth' in a way that perhaps cutely mimics some of the story's thematic concerns,"[40] thereby accomplishing through its physical burden part of the agenda he set out in the McCaffery interview, to make the reader "fight *through* the mediated voice presenting the material," preventing exactly the kind of absorption that was to him the direst threat of passive (and electronic) entertainment.[41]

So it is ironic that one of the legacies of *Jest* seems to be the development of techniques used by the print medium to mimic hypertextual, electronic fiction. In just the decade or so after Wallace's hundred pages of fragmenting/networking endnotes appeared, and as printing technologies expanded alongside digital technology, writers began experimenting in diverse ways with paratextual devices that radically altered what fiction looks like and how it works, mixing documents and textual registers, incorporating colors, fonts, and images, adding footnotes, endnotes, and side notes, to multiply authors, worlds, and realities far beyond the complications begun by *Infinite Jest*.[42] But while Wallace continued to use the note as a paratextual element to multiply narrative perspectives and narrators throughout his career (more sparsely in *Oblivion*, but extensively in *Brief Interviews* and *The Pale King*), his fiction never aspired to leap off the page, instead confining the reader's relationship and adventure to the textual realm. In this way *Jest* might be seen as a kind of bridge between the encyclopedic print novels of its time, including Gass's *The Tunnel* (1995) and DeLillo's *Underworld* (1998), and these virtual-reality–producing print hypertexts of today.

Infinite Jest: A Failed Entertainment

However much its hybridity resembles the novel's own, 20 years of criticism on *Infinite Jest* turns out not to be terribly contentious. It tends to refine, expand, and reassert, occasionally adding a new limb to the hybrid beast – with one significant exception. Perpetually at issue in our analyses of this shapeshifter is how we read its end and beginning (which is really the story's end), and so, in the largest terms, whether or not we read the novel as providing working solutions to the cultural problems it diagnoses. The ultimate fates of Hal and Gately, which, like the plot's resolution, occur according to Wallace "sort of outside the right-frame of the picture,"[43] have generated significant critical disagreement. Most readers agree that Hal, who ends up trapped in his own mind, unable to communicate, and appearing deranged enough to anticipate exiting the story bound to a stretcher, exemplifies the inability to escape the damage of the cycles of addiction and solipsism created by the cultures of his nation and family.[44] Still, so strong is our desire to save this book from its irresolution and its central characters from the horrifying fates that befall so many around them that some critics have strained textual credulity to read Hal's end as redemptive: Catherine Nichols uses a Lacanian framework to argue that Hal's inability to speak is an escape from the symbolic realm that delineates the novel's problems, and Allard den Dulk suggests that Hal's seeming insanity is actually sincerity as viewed by a culture unable to comprehend it.[45] More indeterminate is Gately's end, and the plot's end, which is metrically soothing, aurally lovely, and imagistically rich, but narratively elusive: "And when he came back to, he was flat on his back on the beach in the freezing sand, and it was raining out of a low sky, and the tide was way out."[46] Perhaps most revealing is that two critics could use quite similar frameworks for reading the novel, Lacan and Freud, and yet end up with opposing readings of the ending: whereas Boswell reads Gately as "reborn from the womb of his addiction,"[47] thus allowing the novel to signal a way out of its recursive cycles, I read Gately regressing to the infantile narcissism that is one of the novel's most present forms of addiction and causes of solipsism, so that no major character escapes the traps of irony and narcissism set by the novel.[48]

It is a tribute to the passion of Wallace's readers, and the intense intimacy with the book and its author inspired by *Jest*, that I have been asked to rethink that reading many times over the last 10 years, by readers and critics at conferences, in emails, and via published argument.[49] In writing again on this novel, after several subsequent readings of the book, I find that I still read more frustrated struggle than successful escape, for a host of new textual readings that could comprise their own essay. However else we read the entire novel and its ambiguous final scene, it is undeniable that Wallace leaves us in utter frustration, with both main characters unable to express themselves intelligently, trapped inside the storms of their isolated minds. Tellingly, this is exactly how Wallace described himself as he was finishing the draft of *Infinite Jest*: "I have never felt so much a failure, or so mute when it comes to articulating what I see as the way out of the loop."[50] A year later, as the novel was being edited for publication, Wallace tried to convince Pietsch to subtitle the book "A Failed Entertainment," an idea he dropped once Pietsch pointed out its potential impact on sales.[51] To point out the ways in which the novel thematically and structurally reproduces the problems it sets out to solve, and to note Wallace's own awareness that the novel articulates its loop more clearly than it imagines a way out, is not to say that the novel is a failure but that it is what Wallace wanted it to be, a "failed entertainment." Failing to satisfy, resolve, or lie still, requiring our intervention and commitment, offering in the end ambiguity, ambivalence, and multiple contradictory readings, *Infinite Jest* fails to deliver the passive, packaged pleasure of stupefaction – that, we can all agree on. But it also fails to reassure even those who pour their critical faculties into it that everything will be all right, that art will save us. Like its namesake film, *Infinite Jest* diagnoses and disturbs more powerfully than it cures. But in so doing, it generates an endless conversation that moves us out of our homes and into classrooms, conference halls, and reading groups, searching for that resolution that happens just outside of the frame, and participating in the dialogue that Wallace hoped would only "seem like it just stops," when really "it's supposed to stop and then kind of hum and project."[52]

Notes

1. David Foster Wallace, "E Unibus Pluram: Television and U.S. Fiction," in *Review of Contemporary Fiction* 13.2 (Summer 1993), pp. 192, 193.
2. Stephen J. Burn cogently presents this argument about the 1990s as transitional in chapter 1 of *Jonathan Franzen at the End of Postmodernism* (New York: Continuum, 2011). For an overview of criticism on the topic, see the "Introduction" of my *Succeeding Postmodernism: Language and Humanism in Contemporary American Literature* (New York: Bloomsbury, 2013).
3. A typed draft of the Wardine/Roy Tony section of *Jest* bearing his University of Arizona return address is included in correspondence between Wallace and his longtime agent, Bonnie Nadell, at the Harry Ransom Center; Wallace was in the MFA program at Arizona from 1985–1987. A handwritten draft titled "Freewriting" and "fierce infant" contained with a folder of early *Infinite Jest* drafts at the HRC records a story later included in *The Pale King*.
4. David Foster Wallace, *Infinite Jest* (Boston: Little, Brown, 1996), p. 445.
5. See my "'The Art's Heart's Purpose': Braving the Narcissistic Loop of David Foster Wallace's *Infinite Jest*," in *Critique* 47.3 (2006), pp. 225–228.
6. On AA as solution, see Petrus van Ewijk, "'I' and the 'Other': The Relevance of Wittgenstein, Buber and Levinas for an Understanding of AA's Recovery Program in David Foster Wallace's *Infinite Jest*," *English Text Construction* 2.1, pp. 134–135; and Allard den Dulk, "Good Faith and Sincerity: Sartrean Virtues of Self-Becoming in David Foster Wallace's *Infinite Jest*," in Robert K. Bolger and Scott Korb (eds.), *Gesturing Toward Reality: David Foster Wallace and Philosophy* (New York: Bloomsbury, 2014), pp. 214–215; on AA as addictive, see Holland, "'The Art's Heart's Purpose'," pp. 233–234; and Elizabeth Freudenthal, "Anti-Interiority: Compulsiveness, Objectification, and Identity in *Infinite Jest*," *New Literary History* 41.1 (2010), pp. 201–202. On the duality of institutions, see Mark McGurl, "The Institution of Nothing: David Foster Wallace in the Program," in *boundary 2* 41.3 (2014), pp. 38–43. On the novel's addictiveness, see Frank Louis Cioffi, "'An Anguish Become Thing': Narrative as Performance in David Foster Wallace's *Infinite Jest*," *Narrative* 8.2 (2000), p. 170; and Timothy Aubry, "Selfless Cravings: Addiction and Recovery in David Foster Wallace's *Infinite Jest*," in Jay Prosser (ed.), *American Fiction of the 1990s: Reflections of History and Culture* (London: Routledge, 2008), p. 208.
7. On the centrality of recursivity in the novel, see N. Katherine Hayles, "The Illusion of Autonomy and the Fact of Recursivity: Virtual Ecologies, Entertainment, and *Infinite Jest*," *New Literary History* 30.3 (1999), pp. 675–697.

8. D. T. Max, *Every Love Story Is a Ghost Story: A Life of David Foster Wallace* (New York: Viking, 2012), p. 195.
9. See, for example, Tom LeClair, "The Prodigious Fiction of Richard Powers, William Vollmann, and David Foster Wallace," *Critique* 38.1 (1996), p. 32.
10. Wallace, *Infinite Jest*, p. 491.
11. Ibid., p. 128.
12. Wallace, "Expanded Interview," in Burn (ed.), *Conversations*, p. 22.
13. Wallace, *Infinite Jest*, p. 742.
14. In Bakhtin's terms; see Cioffi, "'An Anguish Become Thing'," p. 169.
15. Andrew Warren, "Modeling Community and Narrative in *Infinite Jest* and *The Pale King*," in Marshall Boswell (ed.), *David Foster Wallace and "The Long Thing": New Essays on the Novels* (New York: Bloomsbury, 2014), pp. 65–71.
16. Toon Staes, "Rewriting the Author: A Narrative Approach to Empathy in *The Pale King* and *Infinite Jest*," *Studies in the Novel* 44.4 (2012), pp. 409–427 and Iannis Goerlandt, "'Put the Book Down and Slowly Walk Away': Irony and David Foster Wallace's *Infinite Jest*," in *Critique* 47.3 (2006), p. 324.
17. Bradley J. Fest, "The Inverted Nuke in the Garden: Archival Emergence and Anti-Eschatology in David Foster Wallace's *Infinite Jest*," *boundary* 2 39.3 (2012), p. 129; Stephen J. Burn, "'Webs of Nerves Pulsing and Firing': *Infinite Jest* and the Science of Mind," in Marshall Boswell and Stephen J. Burn (eds.), *A Companion to David Foster Wallace Studies* (New York: Palgrave Macmillan, 2013), p. 61.
18. Wallace, *Infinite Jest*, pp. 835–836.
19. Stephen J. Burn, *David Foster Wallace's* Infinite Jest: *A Reader's Guide* (New York: Continuum, 2003), p. 74.
20. Hayles, "The Illusion of Autonomy," p. 677.
21. Richard Stock, "Beyond Narratology: David Foster Wallace's *Infinite Jest*," *Prague Journal of English Studies* 2.1, p. 47.
22. Toon Staes, "The Coatlicue Complex in David Foster Wallace's *Infinite Jest*," *Explicator* 72.1 (2014), pp. 67, 69.
23. Wallace, *Infinite Jest*, pp. 128, 447.
24. Ibid., p. 480.
25. Ibid., pp. 608–611.
26. Ibid., pp. 442, 475.
27. David Hering proposes that Wallace appears as a "revenant author" throughout his work, demonstrating his discomfort with the post-structural "death of the author," in chapter 1 of *David Foster Wallace: Fiction and Form* (New York: Bloomsbury, 2016). While he identifies this "revenant author" specifically with the wraith character in *Jest*, whose domination of the narrative and of Gately he considers "ambivalent," I am arguing here that the novel as a whole, via structure (endnotes) and technique (point of view), conjures a wraith beyond this particular wraith, an author-figure that functions outside or above the novel's many other voices rather than democratically, or even dialogically, alongside them.
28. Max, *Every Love Story Is a Ghost Story*, p. 195.
29. Wallace, *Infinite Jest*, p. 832.

30. Jacobs, "Wallace's *Infinite Jest*," *Explicator* 58.3 (2000), p. 174; Andrew Hoberek, "The Novel after David Foster Wallace," in Boswell and Burn (eds.), *A Companion*, p. 224. Such a reading is quite at odds with James Wood's criticism of *Jest* as an example of "hysterical realism," which he believes describes recent novels whose excesses are anything but realistic.

31. Wallace, "Expanded Interview," in Burn (ed.), *Conversations*, p. 30. See my "David Foster Wallace and the Future of (Meta)Fiction" for an overview of Wallace's ideas about realism and metafiction.

32. See, Wallace *Infinite Jest*, pp. 665; 938; 1026, n. 145; 1038, n. 234.

33. Wallace, "David Foster Wallace: In the Company of Creeps," by Lorin Stein, in Burn (ed.), *Conversations,* pp. 90, 91. For examination of the gender critique in *Brief Interviews* that also originates in *Jest*, see my "'By Hirsute Author': Gender and Communication in the Work and Study of David Foster Wallace," *Critique* 58.1 (2016), pp. 65–78; and Clare Hayes-Brady's "' . . . ': Language, Gender, and Modes of Power in the Work of David Foster Wallace," in Boswell and Burn (eds.), *A Companion*, pp. 131–150. For elaboration of the structure of *Brief Interviews*, see my "Mediated Immediacy in *Brief Interviews with Hideous Men*" in Boswell and Burn (eds.), *A Companion*, pp. 107–130.

34. Adam Kelly, "Development Through Dialogue: David Foster Wallace and the Novel of Ideas," *Studies in the Novel* 44.3 (2012), pp. 267–283.

35. Burn, *Reader's Guide*, p. 35.

36. Max, *Every Love Story Is a Ghost Story*, p. 200.

37. Wallace "revered" the *Terminator* movies, reading them "as a metaphor for all literary art after Roland Barthes," and analogizing Cyberdyne's murderous self-awareness with postmodern literary self-referentiality. See Wallace, "Expanded Interview," in Burn (ed.), *Conversations*, pp. 30, 33.

38. Max, *Every Love Story Is a Ghost Story*, p. 196.

39. Wallace in Burn (ed.), *Conversations*, pp. 57, 88.

40. Max, *Every Love Story Is a Ghost Story*, pp. 195–196.

41. Wallace, "Expanded Interview," in Burn (ed.), *Conversations*, p. 33.

42. See, for example, Lee Siegel's *Love in a Dead Language* (1999), Mark Danielewski's *House of Leaves* (2000), Steve Tomasula's *VAS: An Opera in Flatland* (2002), and Debra DiBlasi's *The Jiri Chronicles and Other Fictions* (2007).

43. Wallace, "The Connection: David Foster Wallace" by Michael Goldfarb, in Burn (ed.), *Conversations*, p. 145.

44. For readings of this opening scene as depicting the downfall of Hal for a variety of reasons, see Darling, "David Foster Wallace and the Athlete's War with the Self"; Freudenthal, "Anti-Interiority"; Holland, "'The Art's Heart's Purpose'"; Burn, "'Webs of Nerves Pulsing and Firing'"; and McGurl, "The Institution of Nothing," though McGurl's reading of the impact of institutions is more ambivalent than wholly negative.

45. Nichols, "Dialogizing Postmodern Carnival in *Infinite Jest*"; den Dulk, "Sartrean Self-Becoming in *Infinite Jest*."

46. Wallace, *Infinite Jest*, p. 981.

47. Marshall Boswell, *Understanding David Foster Wallace* (Columbia: University of South Carolina Press, 2003) p. 179.

48. Holland, "'The Art's Heart's Purpose'," pp. 236–239.

49. See Allard den Dulk, "Beyond Endless 'Aesthetic' Irony: A Comparison of the Irony Critique of Søren Kierkegaard and David Foster Wallace's *Infinite Jest*," *Studies in the Novel* 44.3 (2012), pp. 342–343, n. 6.
50. Max, *Every Love Story Is a Ghost Story*, p. 91.
51. Ibid., p. 200.
52. Wallace, "David Foster Wallace Winces at the Suggestion That His New Book is Sloppy in Any Sense," by Anne Marie Donahue in Burn (ed.), *Conversations*, p. 72.

9

CLARE HAYES-BRADY

"Palely Loitering": On Not Finishing (in) *The Pale King*

The Pale King (2011), Wallace's final work, opens on a scene of eerie stillness, the eye at the heart of a storm. The novel was planned as a narrative with no climax: "a series of set-ups for stuff to happen, but nothing actually happens."[1] Indeed, as Marshall Boswell notes, while the manuscript's development was undeniably interrupted by its author's death, the novel's editor Michael Pietsch has said that the central story does not have a clear ending and that "although *The Pale King* never reaches a conclusion per se, it is clear that Wallace always intended to deny his readers any such satisfying sense of closure in any case."[2] Certainly the work is unwieldy, running in different directions without approaching a clear structure, but as I will argue over the following pages, *The Pale King* is not alone in Wallace's corpus in this respect. In fact, the final novel represents simultaneously a continuation of and a turn away from his earlier concerns. *The Pale King* can been seen both as a reply of sorts to *Infinite Jest* (1996), its similarly ungovernable predecessor, and as a movement past the fundamentally adolescent concerns of *Jest* and the earlier works,[3] articulating a less extreme vision of life, engaging with the realities of adulthood and the challenges of navigating what he called the "day-to-day trenches" of the real world in its naked, tangible tedium. Published posthumously in 2011, the incompleteness of *The Pale King* is partially accounted for by being actually unfinished at the time of Wallace's death; Pietsch was ultimately responsible for the shape the publication took. Nevertheless, it has become a strong focus of Wallace scholarship, in part because it is visible as a work in progress. The 2014 collection of essays, *David Foster Wallace and "The Long Thing": New Essays on the Novels*, offers readings of the novel that engage with consciousness, posthumanism, solipsism, and affect, all themes that recurred throughout Wallace's career. The introduction of boredom as a key theme, related to consciousness and affect, is one of the major innovations of *The Pale King*, as both Burn and Clare have observed in detail. Boswell positions *The Pale King* as a development of Wallace's long preoccupation with systems, reading it as a novel deeply engaged with thoughtful citizenship and maturity, a theme taken up by other critics including Darien Shanske, who offers an engaging, if not altogether successful, legal perspective on the work. Toon Staes and Tim Groenland have offered astute genetic readings of the work's "shreds and patches," and Jorge Araya uses the novel's unfinished state to assess Wallace's often problematic engagement with race.[4] Indeed, the fact of being unfinished appears to have helped, rather than hampered, critical attention to Wallace's final novel, proving it rich in possibility and endlessly open to speculation.

While criticism is liberated by this incompletion, in real terms it is of course fruitless to speculate how *The Pale King* might ultimately have developed. Yet in its published form the novel engages with the incomplete in a number of ways, both structurally and narratively. This essay explores the novel's title, offering as a source John Keats's 1819 poem "La Belle Dame sans Merci." Taking Keats as a structuring principle, I offer a reading of Wallace's final work that pays particular attention to ideas of engagement and different modes of heroism. Approaching Keats by way of the late postmodernist discourse with which Wallace was engaged, it becomes clear that the heroism in *The Pale King* combines the figure of the romantic hero with that of the ironic hero, ultimately figuring the kind of reflective romanticism Wallace advocated across the board in his writing. Indeed, it is commonly noted that *The Pale King* is one of Wallace's more uplifting works, notwithstanding its well-established themes of ennui and disconnection. The heroism Wallace depicts and seeks in *The Pale King* is a psychological heroism, at its heart linked to romantic and poetic heroism in the Keatsian vein. This kind of heroism is necessarily incomplete, a process of attention rather than its product. *The Pale King*, an incomplete novel in itself, also encodes the persistent resistance to closure that marked all of Wallace's work. A quest narrative with no denouement, a realist novel teeming with ghosts, a narrative concerned with the endless tedium of adult life, *The Pale King* is all about noncompletion. Completion, for Wallace, entailed perfection and stasis, often death. *The Pale King* offers reversal and renewal, struggle and continuation.

The Pale King, then, may be read not only as a continuation of Wallace's own concerns regarding connection, attention, and postmodern irony but as a strengthening of his engagement with literature beyond the postmodern. In particular, *The Pale King* works as a reinscription of nineteenth-century literary conventions. It is also worth noting that possible title sources for much of Wallace's work reflect a strong pattern of engagement with texts that often move far beyond the commonly referenced postmodern canon visible in his work. "Westward the Course of Empire Takes Its Way" refers to George Berkeley, who is mentioned in *Everything and More*, by way of the famous frieze of the same name in the US House of Representatives. *Infinite Jest*, of course, evokes *Hamlet*, and *The Broom of the System* (1987) obliquely references the works of Ludwig Wittgenstein, while traces of Joyce and Beckett are visible in "The Soul Is Not a Smithy" (in *Oblivion*, 2004) and "Consider the Lobster" (2004), among numerous others. Indeed, as Konstantinou has argued, Wallace was a globally indebted writer in general, engaged in a kind of failed cosmopolitanism, calling on Russian, British, Irish, and other literatures.[5]

Reading Romantically

The prevailing mood of *The Pale King* is one of stillness – not of peace, but of intense concentration. It is this "tornadic" quality that most links the novel atmospherically with Keats's poem, "La Belle Dame sans Merci," in which the action is recollected at a distance, if not wholly imagined. Keats's poem opens with the image of a knight who refuses to leave the side of a lake. Haggard, feverish, and confused, the knight is obviously unwell. The knight recounts his encounter with "a maiden in the meads, / Full beautiful, a faery's child," and outlines his obsession with her. He talks of her lulling him to sleep and recalls waking alone "here / On the cold hill's side." The unidentified interlocutor (the poetic subject) speaks only in the first stanza, prompting the narrative, and is thereafter silent (a structure Wallace used to great effect in *Brief Interviews with Hideous Men*). Like *The Pale King*, the poem is a plot without a denouement, written as it is in an interstitial period between action and foreboding; the knight's encounter with the maiden is over, but he is now effectively waiting to die. This sense of betweenness is mirrored in the "series of set-ups" Wallace talked about as a guiding principle for *The Pale King*. Besides the common mood and structure, there are also distinct points of textual contact between the two texts. First, and most obviously, there is the phrase itself, a clear echo of stanza 10 of the poem, which opens "I saw pale kings and princes too." However, what differentiates the Keats source from other possible sources are the references to British poetry in Irrelevant Chris Fogle's monologue in §22. Fogle mentions his father quoting "Ozymandias" and then, rather ostentatiously, fails to name the British poet in question – Percy Shelley – and incorrectly credits him with writing "the original Frankenstein," which was of course written by Mary Wollstonecraft Shelley. All three works concern death, decay, and the supernatural and were published within a year of each other.[6]

A reading of *The Pale King* that takes "La Belle Dame sans Merci" as an organizing structure is dominated by the nature of heroism, but also engages questions of reality and perception. Keats's vision of heroism in the poem is key to comprehending Wallace's heroism of attention in the novel. Furthermore, we can see echoes of Keats's preoccupation with mind–body dualism in *The Pale King*'s recurrent imaginings of illness, pain, and death. The novel's preponderance of oddly tedious supernatural happenings – the psychics, levitators, and especially the ghosts that pepper the novel – are also central in a Keatsian reading. Meredith Rand presents a plausible figure for La Belle Dame sans Merci herself, with possible knight figures surrounding her, including her husband and Drinion (both associated with death and the supernatural) to say nothing of the many colleagues presented as being in thrall to Meredith. Secondly, the central supernatural effect in this scene, Drinion's levitation, is associated with sympathy and with concentration, two characteristics that are key to Wallace's ethics of attention and the form of heroism under discussion here.[7] Turnbull, among others, has argued that Wallace's work comes freighted with the "vital moral importance of the questions of what we choose to attend to, and how we choose to conceptualise things."[8] The ethical dimension of engagement, as this confluence of sympathy and concentration is commonly termed, provides a lens through which to articulate a comparison of Keats's hero with Wallace's. Keats's "knight-at-arms" offers a character for whom vocation equals self-sacrifice (literally unto death), but also a delirium of bliss on the other side of the confusion and horror of intense focus. Finally, the figure of the (British) romantic hero offers a valuable mode of comparison to the representation of heroism in *The Pale King*. Wallace's vision of contemporary heroism in fact draws heavily on the persona of the romantic hero in general, and the Keatsian hero in particular, in uneasy but fruitful juxtaposition with the Kierkegaardian ironic hero, whose commitment to his vocation and unwillingness to conform to normative practices offers a contemporary reevaluation of heroism itself. Both Boswell and, more expansively, Allard den Dulk explore Wallace's encounters with Kierkegaard, who is particularly useful to an understanding of his uses of irony.[9]

The poem's title is a phrase commonly used to personify the illness tuberculosis, which of course killed Keats, and which had become symptomatic the summer he wrote the poem. Besides its vernacular usage, the title is appropriated from the fifteenth-century French poem of the same name by Alain Chartier, a courtly love poem. The two titles combine to connect love with suffering (not an unusual juxtaposition), but with the added dimension that in this case the suffering is an explicit illness rather than the malaise of disappointed love. I do not suggest that the poem is a simple metaphor for

Keats's illness, but given the clear allusions, the conjunction of love with illness and pain provides an interesting perspective on the present question of heroism and attention in Wallace's novel. *The Pale King* is full of instances of illness of various kinds, from Cusk's excessive sweating to Meredith's stint in the hospital, along with the violence and disease that follow Leonard Stecyk. More abstract illness and pain occur in the shapes of the discomfort and ultimate deformity of the child who contorts his body to kiss every part of it, and whose story segment contains a meditation on pain, as well as in the violence of Toni Ware's childhood, which of course leads to her learning to play dead. The novel is full of bodies, most of them somehow in distress. Significantly, the novel's final subsection is itself a meditation on the body, the fact of corporeality and the peculiar discomfort of embodiment.

"She looked at me": The Romantic Body as Object

The physical travails discussed in the novel are various in effect, but awareness of the physical self is often presented as a response to the gaze of some powerfully subjective other, whose mere observation of the self traumatically decenters it. Cusk's sweating arrives with puberty, when, as observed in a footnote, "psychodynamically, he was, as a subject, coming to a late and therefore traumatic understanding of himself as also an object."[10] Cusk's sweating problem is related to his awareness of his self, not just as a self but as an other. It becomes particularly pronounced when he is aware/afraid of the gaze of other subjects: relinquishing his subjectivity and becoming object has made him lose control of his body. In this, Cusk may be said to echo Keats's knight, whose illness comes upon him after he meets the belle dame of the title, who he says "looked at me as she did love," in other words, when he is subjected to a woman's gaze. Here, then, the masculine subject is problematized by the awareness of the possibility that it may not *only* be a subject.

The question of bodies in Wallace's writing generally is something of a vexed one. Gregory Phipps has offered a meditation on the ideal athlete in *Infinite Jest,* and Wallace's own interest in sport would seem to invite readings of the body throughout his work. As the figurative body of criticism on Wallace expands, perhaps the literal body will become more prominent. The question of embodiment, as I argue elsewhere, is critical to a reading of Wallace's gender politics. Wallace's treatment of bodies tends to conform to the physical, active male and the ethereal, passive female, a divide that persists in *The Pale King,* where the subjectivity of the masculine characters is emphasized, while the objectivity of the feminine is also highlighted. The decentered self, of course, is not a specifically masculine experience, though it is here literalized in the masculine body. Wallace persistently returned to the necessity of sacrificial interaction throughout his career, depicting interactions with the other in which something of the self is offered, a rupturing of the boundaries between self and other.[11]

This goal is enacted in *The Pale King* in the ethical exaltation of engagement, but the physical ramifications of such engagement, including the necessity of recognizing the agency of another and so the fundamental alterity of the self, occasion complex literalizations of the resulting discomfort, like the knight of Keats's poem, rendered helpless by the gaze of a powerful female subject. This discomfort hints at Wallace's engagement with the age-old problem of dualism. Schopenhauer's challenge to Fichte's all-encompassing We offers some comfort to Wallace's fear of solipsism by reason of the objecthood of the body of the knowing subject, and his engagement with the literal body throughout his writing speaks to a post-Kantian desire to locate the self both in opposition to and in cooperation with the unknowable other. In other words, the very fact that the subject can be decentered by the agency of another subject serves to legitimize the very possibility of true subjective agency in both self and other. Wallace's engagement with the body, then, aligns with the dualism of the body posited by Schopenhauer, which is at once idea and object. The decentering of the self is profoundly, even physically, uncomfortable, but it is a necessary step in dismissing the specter of solipsistic entrapment. In his intense engagement with the problematic body, Wallace very much continues a theme from his earlier works, becoming even more directly concerned with the body as the object of another gaze than before.

Another subject/object conflict echoing Keats's knight emerges in the boy who seeks to kiss his extremities, a clear instance of the deforming intrusion of full self-consciousness. His ambition of making contact with all of himself arrives early, aged six, when he "came to understand that unimaginable challenges lay ahead of him."[12] The injuries sustained by the child in his pursuit of this ambition begin with "a flat pop in the upper part of his back and then pain beyond naming,"[13] later named as the "traumatic T3 subluxation" that leads him to his first encounter with Doctor Kathy,[14] the chiropractor who serves as his "formal introduction both to incremental stretching and to the adult idea of quiet daily discipline and progress towards a long-term goal" (a clear echo of the Jesuit's definition of heroism).[15] This long-term goal of self-delineation functions as a basic literalization of the drive toward full self-awareness: physically outlining the object that is his body enacts the othering of his self by linking the inner consciousness with the outer physicality, echoing the literally sickening self-awareness that comes upon Keats's knight after he sees himself being seen. The boy's motivation – or lack of it – is flagged by the narrator. It is suggested that the boy wants to become physically accessible to himself, to "pierce that evil of inaccessibility – to be, in some childish way, self-contained and – sufficient."[16] However, it is further suggested that this motivation is unknown to him, being "just a little boy," ironically implying that while he may be physically self-accessible, he is still psychically inaccessible in his motivation for this, further reinforcing the idea that full, transcendent self-awareness is both extremely painful and probably impossible.

By contrast with the traumatic decentering of the self experienced by Cusk and Keats's knight, and to a lesser degree numerous other characters in *The Pale King*, the voluntary displacement of subjectivity is presented in the narrative of Toni Ware as a possible (though extreme) defence against hostile objectification. Toni is one of the most complex characters in *The Pale King*, and one of the most disturbing in Wallace's whole body of work. Toni's childhood of flight and feigned death contains perhaps the most visceral instance of violent discomfort and self-awareness, in which she is so focused that she can literally disconnect her eye contact, playing a convincing corpse as her mother is murdered beside her. Toni's response to threat, this game of "play dead," contrasts in its focus with the boy's self-delineation but has essentially a similar result, to a higher degree. Toni absolutely objectifies herself, to the point of rejecting selfhood in order to save it, a characteristic she shares with the Granola Cruncher in "Brief Interview 20." Toni's capacity for literal self-denial is in fact the strongest affirmation of her self-sufficiency, her feigned death the mark of her absolute life. With regard to the idea outlined in the case of other characters of the gaze of the other as a final mark of selfhood, Toni arguably transcends the nauseating othering of another subject's active gaze, by instead actively abjecting her agency, by making herself the ultimate other – that is to say, a final object, totally passive in death.

"Not the same as real ghosts": The Supernaturally Boring and the Boringly Supernatural

Keats's poetic landscape is haunted by images of death. The lake is described in terms of infertility, decay, and atrophy, and the knight's fevered imagination is dominated by looming, screaming ghosts. The stillness of the scenery contrasts sharply with the horrific activity of the dead, in a striking reversal of order between nature and death. In *The Pale King*, a similar connection of death with agency in Toni's narrative provides a point of contact between the treatment of bodies and the representation of un-passive death. While Wallace considered his work realist,[17] it is perhaps surprising to reflect upon just how frequently the *super*natural – or at least the potentially supernatural – occurs in Wallace's writing, from "John Billy" in *Girl with Curious Hair* and the cold-blooded Lenore Sr. from *The Broom of the System* through to a weirdly archetypal prophet-child and imagined afterlife monologue in "Another Pioneer" and "Good Old Neon," respectively, as well as the infamous cartridge, about which there is something decidedly unnatural, if not strictly supernatural, in *Infinite Jest*, itself a reference to a play riven with hauntings. *Brief Interviews with Hideous Men* (1999) invokes the possibility, albeit at a remove, of connections between souls, and a number of that collection's titles explicitly reference things associated with death and the supernatural. In fact, while Wallace's fidelity to lived experience has long been a point of critical attention, it is also notable that in recent scholarship some attention has indeed been paid to the hauntology of his writing, on the blog project *Poor Yoricks' Summer* and most assiduously by David Hering in his masterly *David Foster Wallace: Fiction and Form*, where Hering addresses the "non-realist story event" as a feature of Wallace's writing.[18] While the Wraith in *Infinite Jest* is a common feature of critical writing, it is more usually treated as a kind of linguistic hallucination rather than a specter in any traditional sense. But, as Hering notes, there is a common "disavowal of reality" in Wallace's work that is not specifically fantastical but that rather emerges from the "modernist association of the dead and the creative imagination" and functions as a way of "disrupting narrative authority."[19] In this respect, then, the nonrealist occurrences in the novel work in the same way as the fictional-but-human Dave Wallace, himself a specter of sorts, erupting through the narrative's prosaic surface to remind the reader that we are in a teeming, mediated, largely hidden world.

Spectral and supernatural activity is as common in *The Pale King* as in Wallace's earlier works, and the supernatural in the novel, as a rule, functions as a pointer to items of importance, not unlike the ghosts as harbingers of danger in "Le Belle Dame sans Merci." One of the novel's more memorable features is the intrusion, in §26, of the phantoms. The section opens by saying that "Phantom refers to a particular kind of hallucination that can afflict rote examiners at a certain threshold of concentrated boredom."[20] Such hallucinations are presented not as instances of the supernatural but as comfortingly comprehensible "irruptions" of the darker side of an intensely concentrated psyche. The so-called phantoms are reassuringly ascribed to human projection (again, here there seems to be a clear link with Keats's feverish knight). Almost immediately, however, the tables are turned by the matter-of-fact declaration that, notwithstanding the fact that most of the examiners do not believe in ghosts, there are "two actual, non-hallucinatory ghosts haunting Post 047's wiggle room."[21] This is perhaps the most interesting thing about the ghosts, who are otherwise represented – and that only briefly – as simply facts of the IRS. Partly because of the mundanity of their appearance, they become the proverbial ghosts in the machine, another example, comic if it were not so dull, of Wallace's tendency to literalize concepts that interest him. The function of the ghosts in the novel is unclear, except insofar as they firmly establish the novel's irrealist plot space. Interestingly, the "true ghosts" are presented as much more reassuring than the hallucinations, which are deeply disturbing and frightening. It may be that this representation presents a perspective whereby nothing, in the world or out of it, can compare to the capacity of the concentrated mind to horrify and, by extension, also to uplift.

Reading the ghosts and phantoms through the structure of "La Belle Dame sans Merci" supports this theory: the "pale kings and princes too" that Keats's knight-at-arms encounters are creatures of his own mind, much more threatening in their aspect than the faery's child who has entranced him. Perhaps, then, the ghosts work as a counterintuitively comforting suggestion that only our minds have the power to truly horrify, a concept that obliquely touches on Wallace's overarching concern with the terror of solipsism. Besides this, the ghosts embody the sense of the IRS center's work as bigger than its operatives, highlighting the fundamental incompleteness, the *ongoingness* of the tax system, itself a synecdoche of bureaucratic civilization. Ghosts are, by their nature, a representative of the unfinished; in his pale phantoms, Wallace engages at a narrative level with the unfinished, even as the novel engages with it at a structural level.

The ghosts, of course, are far from the only instance of what might be termed supernatural activity in the novel, but as with the ghosts, all such instances are decisively, almost affectedly, mundane. Sylvanshine, the fact-psychic, is represented as profoundly uninterested in, and even irritated by, the intrusions of knowledge that punctuate his days. The notes to the novel suggest in places that Sylvanshine's gift, if it can be called such, is known and exploited by Lehrl, who, it is also suggested, is responsible for bringing examiners with unusual or special abilities into the Peoria center. Lehrl, it is noted, believes in the occult. In other words, he is able to exploit a gift he is conscious of only because he believes in things unseen. Chris Fogle's connection to the supernatural is hinted at in the notes rather than explained in the novel: it is suggested that he is in possession of a sequence of numbers that provide him with the power of total concentration. Drinion possesses this naturally, and of all the characters, he is the only one described as happy (in the notes). Meredith Rand, whose exchange with Drinion involves Drinion's levitation (a side effect of his intense concentration) is the closest parallel in the novel to the "faery child" of Keats's poem. She is associated with illness in almost every way, given that she is herself a victim of mental illness. We see her, via her narrative, in the hospital, and her relationships are couched in the terms of her illness. Meredith is a fleshed out version of the Depressed Person from *Brief Interviews with Hideous Men*, "a yammerer of the most dire kind."[22] Her beauty is entrancing, but she is decisively other, a person whose entrance into a conversation alters its dynamic instantly. The men in her vicinity change palpably, responding to her beauty in uncontrollable and wholly predictable ways, evoking the pale princes of the poem, in thrall to La Belle Dame sans Merci.

Knights, Errant

By contrast with the other men around Meredith, Drinion is unperturbed by her beauty. He is "in thrall" to her only in the sense that he is wholly concentrated on her story as shown by the levitation that results from his concentration. Drinion's close focus on Meredith's story does not appear to be matched by any particular understanding of or engagement with her as an individual, in a troubling echo of the narrator of "Brief Interview #20," but his moral rectitude or turpitude is not as significant here as his *presentness*. Where Keats's knight is told in his dream that he is in thrall to the lady, by the time his interlocutor comes on the scene, he has awoken. As such, he is not lost to the possibility of recovery: there is no real end or denouement to the poem. Structurally, too, the poem returns to its beginning. It circularity mirrors the unfinished, unfinishable nature of the knight's quest; it is always only of the present. Returning to *The Pale King* with this in mind, it is clear that Drinion embodies the primary traits that Wallace describes as heroic or admirable. He offers a combination of intense presentness and ironic detachment. His capacity to concentrate intently gives him a kind of transcendent consciousness, the kind of "bliss" Wallace describes in the notes to *The Pale King* as being on the other side of intense boredom, symbolized in the novel by Drinion's tendency to levitation. Drinion's endless capacity to suffer boredom – literally, his endless patience – is at the root of his heroism. But Drinion does not seem particularly heroic. He is pale, boring, and antisocial, and he works day in and day out on a thankless task as a tax official, which could not easily be termed swashbuckling. That said, the fact remains that Drinion *is* presented as a hero. He is the focus of one of the pivotal scenes, the man to whom the beautiful woman in distress turns for comfort.

Could it be time to reexamine our ideas of what constitutes a hero? In *This Is Water*, Wallace explicitly connects the compassionate observation of and engagement with the more mundane aspects of life with freedom, and in *The Pale King*, he explicitly connects the exercise of that freedom with heroism. Indeed, he engages with heroism more in this novel than anywhere else, dismissing classical visions of heroism – "the grand gesture, the moment of choice, the mortal danger, the external foe, the climactic battle whose outcome resolves all" – as "theater."[23] "There is no audience," the Jesuit professor tells a spellbound Chris Fogle. "True heroism is *a priori* incompatible with audience or applause or even the bare notice of the common run of man."[24] Heroism is tedious, repetitive, always incomplete, always unacknowledged. "True heroism is minutes, hours, weeks, year upon year of the quiet, precise, judicious exercise of probity and care – with no one there to see or cheer. This is the world."[25] For Wallace, then, heroism is inextricably connected with the direction of attention, and it is always, necessarily unfinished, a process rather than a product, redolent of the lone cowboy, another decidedly American incarnation of the romantic hero, plying his trade unwitnessed under big skies. Indeed, the Jesuit invokes the figure of the cowboy several times in his speech, positioning accountants as frontier wranglers: "In today's world, boundaries are fixed, and most significant facts have been generated. Gentlemen, the heroic frontier now lies in the ordering and deployment of those facts ... You have wondered, perhaps, why all real accountants wear hats? They are today's cowboys."[26]

The character of heroism was of keen interest to Keats, too, who considered man a creature of circumstance and heroism a collection of reactions. In a journal letter from April 1819, just months before he wrote the poem, Keats wrote a letter considering the formation of character. Observing that man was formed by circumstances, which he saw as tests of the soul, Keats asks, "And what was his soul before it came into the world ... ? An intelligence without identity – and how is this identity to be made? Through the medium of the heart? And how is the heart to become this medium, but in a world of circumstances."[27] In other words, it is only by engaging with his surroundings and the daily workings of the world – what Keats called "these provings and alterations and perfectionings" – that the identity can be formed. The hero's identity is contingent upon his reaction to – and so his engagement with – circumstance. By contrast with the Byronic hero of action and disruption, the Keatsian hero is one of reaction and process – a poet, for example. The knight in "La Belle Dame sans Merci" is not a hero of brave exploits but of engagement with another soul, albeit a supernatural one. In fact, observing the pertinence of British romanticism in *The Pale King* and Wallace's work more broadly offers a lens through which to tie his vision of patient heroism with the work's animating resistance to closure. Christie suggests that "under the influence of Romantic notions of the creative imagination and of genius, the Romantic artist-as-hero was seen to undertake the psychic equivalent of the traditional heroic (or chivalric) pilgrimage."[28] Even in its partial state, the novel does seem to revolve around the quest for "immersives" like Drinion. The notes refer, also, to the series of numbers that, it seems, will allow a subject to somehow *become* an immersive; perhaps this is the novel's Grail. Of course, this being a Wallace novel, we never fully identify, never mind approach, the Grail; to end is too much like taking authorial control, too much like solipsistic self-indulgence. Instead, the sacredness of immersion, of the eternal present, is foregrounded, thus doing away with the very possibility of achievement: Drinion's levitation, the mark of his heroic attention, ends the moment he becomes aware of it, redirecting his attention to himself. I have written elsewhere of Wallace's use of the quest structure in *Broom* and *Jest*,[29] and *The Pale King* mirrors that tendency. While the earlier two novels involve the *failure* of their central quests, however, *The Pale King* marks a real departure in the sense that the quest is one that *cannot* be completed. If the central feature of Wallace's writing is a resistance to closure, *The Pale King* marks (rather ironically) the apotheosis of this resistance, and Shane Drinion its unstudied hero.

The heroism of Drinion's ability to focus is that he allows his subjectivity to be displaced by the agency of another subject. In this respect, Drinion enacts Keats's vision of the poet-hero, as a man with no identity: he is not actually without identity, but his subjectivity is controlled, enabling him to act as a mirror rather than a foil. According to a letter he wrote to Richard Woodhouse, Keats viewed the poet as "the most unpoetical of anything in existence, because he has no identity, he is continually in for – and filling – some other body."[30] Like Keats's poet, acting as a perfect sounding board, a perfect reflector, Drinion is able to put aside his agency, thus conversely confirming its absolute coherence. In other words, Drinion's heroism is literally passive (patient), since it inheres in his capacity of abject agency. The heroism of self-abjection/abnegation appears in varying degrees throughout Wallace's work: violently in "Brief Interview #20," abstractly in the figure of Lenore Sr. in *The Broom of the System*, and supernaturally here, among others. Abjection, or the voluntary decentering of the self, is presented as a heroic act. As we displace ourselves from the throne of self-regard, we free up our attention to be directed as it should, so actualizing the world around us, and paradoxically reinforcing our own subjective agency. Such a vision ties in well with Wallace's exploration of heroism in general, which he showed as occurring in the most mundane places, not despite but because of their ordinariness, involving both detachment and engagement. In *The Pale King*, then, Wallace presents us with a recontextualization of romantic heroism; in Shane Drinion, a knight-errant for the bureaucratic age. The final novel, then, is both new and old. It dramatizes a revolutionary resistance to ending and makes heroic the proper direction of attention (away from the self), while also embedding itself firmly in old, old narratives of virtue, courage, and self-denial. Even – especially – in its haunted, haunting, forever-incomplete state, *The Pale King*, like the best of Wallace's work, is both a hearkening back and a striking out.

Notes

1. David Foster Wallace, *The Pale King* (New York: Little, Brown, 2011), pp. 201, 546.
2. Marshall Boswell, "Introduction: David Foster Wallace's *The Pale King*," *Studies in the Novel* 44.4 (Winter 2012), pp. 367–370, 369.
3. The term adolescent here refers to the plots of *Infinite Jest* (Boston: Little, Brown, 1996) and *The Broom of the System* (New York: Penguin, 1987), which are concerned with entertainment, recreation, games, and, even more fundamentally, actual adolescence and adolescents, rather than suggesting that *Jest* forms part of Wallace's juvenilia, although *Broom* certainly does.
4. See among others Darien Shanske, "The Philosophy of Tax: A Review of David Foster Wallace's *The Pale King*," *Law, Culture and the Humanities* 12.2 (2016), pp. 401–418; Toon Staes, "Work in Process: A Genesis for *The Pale King*," *English Studies* 95.1 (2014), pp. 70–84; and Tim Groenland's "A King of Shreds and Patches: Assembling Wallace's Final Novel" and Jorge Araya's "Why the Whiteness?: Race in *The Pale King*" in Philip Coleman (ed.), *Critical Insights: David Foster Wallace* (Ipswich: Salem Press, 2015), pp. 221–237 and 238–252.
5. Lee Konstantinou, "The World of David Foster Wallace," *boundary 2* 40.3 (2013), pp. 59–86, 77.
6. Several other possible title sources have been mooted. Wyatt Mason's suggestion of Edward Bulwer Lytton's "King Arthur" offers a similar schema within which the novel might be read – heroism, British romanticism, and the supernatural; see Wyatt Mason, "Three Kings," *Harper's*, March 2009, http://harpers.org/archive/2009/03/hbc-90004512.
7. See, in particular, Tom Tracey, "David Foster Wallace: American Literature after Postmodernism" (PhD diss., Oxford University, 2011 [unpublished]); Daniel Turnbull, "*This Is Water* and the Ethics of Attention: Wallace, Murdoch, and Nussbaum," in David Hering (ed.), *Consider David Foster Wallace* (California: SSMG, 2010), pp. 209–217; and Leland de la Durantaye, "How to be Happy," *Boston Review*, March 2011, http://bostonreview.net/BR36.2/leland_de_la_durantaye_david_foster_wallace.php. For a discussion of Wallace's ethics, see Marshall Boswell, "Trickle-Down Citizenship: Taxes and Civic Responsibility in David Foster Wallace's *The Pale King*," *Studies in the Novel* 44.4 (winter 2012), pp. 464–479.
8. Turnbull, "*This Is Water*," p. 211.
9. See Marshall Boswell, *Understanding David Foster Wallace* (Columbia: University of South Carolina Press, 2003), pp. 137–140; and Allard den Dulk, *Existential Engagement in Wallace, Eggers, and Foer* (New York: Bloomsbury, 2015), pp. 60–85.
10. Wallace, *The Pale King*, p. 92, n. 1.

11. Clare Hayes-Brady, "'[. . .]': Language, Gender, and Modes of Power in the Work of David Foster Wallace," in Marshall Boswell and Stephen J. Burn (eds.), *A Companion to David Foster Wallace Studies* (New York: Palgrave Macmillan, 2013), pp. 131–150.

12. Wallace, *The Pale King*, p. 394.

13. Ibid., p. 395.

14. Ibid,. p. 404.

15. Ibid., p. 396.

16. Ibid., p. 401.

17. Wallace referred to his work as realist in interviews with both Larry McCaffery and Laura Miller. See Larry McCaffery, "An Interview With David Foster Wallace," *Review of Contemporary Fiction* 13.2 (Summer 1993), pp. 127–151; and Laura Miller, "The Salon Interview: David Foster Wallace," *Salon* 9 (March 1996), www.salon.com/09/features/wallace1.html.

18. David Hering, *David Foster Wallace: Fiction and Form* (New York: Bloomsbury, 2016), p. 15.

19. Ibid., p. 16.

20. Wallace, *The Pale King*, p. 314.

21. Ibid., p. 315.

22. Ibid., p. 546.

23. Ibid., p. 231.

24. Ibid., p. 232.

25. Ibid., p. 230.

26. Ibid., pp. 234–235.

27. John Keats, "Journal Letter to George and Georgina Keats, 14 February to 13 May 1819 (extracts)"; quoted in Duncan Wu (ed.), *Romanticism, An Anthology*, 2nd ed. (Oxford: Blackwell, 1998), pp. 1053–1054.

28. William Christie, "Hero," in Christopher John Murray (ed.), *Encyclopedia of the Romantic Era* (New York: Fitzroy Dearborn, 2004), p. 497.

29. Clare Hayes-Brady, *The Unspeakable Failures of David Foster Wallace* (New York: Bloomsbury, 2016), pp. 86–7.

30. Keats in Wu, *Romanticism*, p. 1042.

PART IV

Themes and Topics

IO

ROBERT L. MCLAUGHLIN

Wallace's Aesthetic

To begin thinking about David Foster Wallace's aesthetic, I find myself drawn back to one of his comments in his interview with Larry McCaffery: "I've found the really tricky discipline to writing is trying to play without getting overcome by insecurity or vanity or ego. Showing the reader that you're smart or funny or talented or whatever, trying to be liked, integrity issues aside, this stuff just doesn't have enough motivational calories in it to carry you over the long haul. You've got to discipline yourself to talk out of the part of you that loves the thing, loves what you're working on. Maybe that just plain loves. (I think we might need woodwinds for this part, L.M.)"[1] This quotation touches on four points that make Wallace's aesthetic so complicated. One is the demand to write out of the part of you that loves, that seeks a connection with the reader over a shared idea or feeling. A second point is the danger of writing to be liked, to let the desire to be clever or funny so as to impress the reader overwhelm the desire to connect with the reader. Third, after warning of the danger of writing to be liked and making his most sincere statement about writing from love, Wallace appends his parenthetical aside, "I think we might need woodwinds for this part." The joke undercuts the sincerity, announces how funny and clever Wallace is, and provides protection from the reactions of oh-so-cool-and-jaded readers. The final point is the most confusing. By referring to McCaffery as "L.M.," not as "Larry" or "Professor McCaffery" or even "Mac," Wallace calls our attention to a convention of the interview format wherein who's speaking, interviewer or interviewee, is indicated by initials. With this self-referential nudge, he reminds us of the textuality of what we're reading, the mediation of discourse between the author and reader. The tensions implied among these four points – tensions between the call for sincerity and the staying power of irony, between the need for empathetic connection and the writer's practice of manipulating readers, between the desire to return to an innocent language and the inability to forget the post-structural problematization of language and representation – are central to Wallace's aesthetic and his fiction.

For Wallace, the role of fiction is to address the fundamental problem of turn-of-the-twentieth-century America: loneliness, or, as he puts in it *Infinite Jest*, "excluded encagement in the self."[2] Elsewhere he says, "I think all good writing somehow addresses the concern of and acts as an anodyne against loneliness. We're all terribly, terribly lonely. And there's a way, at least in prose fiction, that can allow you to be intimate with the world and with a mind and with characters that you just can't be in the real world. . . . I think what I would like my stuff to do is make people feel less lonely."[3] Wallace thus emphasizes the relationship established by the fiction text, the relationship between the author and the reader and the potentially dynamic, empathetic, and human connection that it makes. Good examples of stories that seem overtly to seek such a relationship are "Octet" and "Good Old Neon," but any reader who has become captivated by the main narrative voice in *Infinite Jest* will understand what Wallace means.

This emphasis on the author–reader relationship also helps us understand Wallace's critique of both popular, commercial fiction and postmodern, experimental fiction. Commercial fiction and popular culture in general allow us to enjoy their pleasures passively and demand nothing from us. That's their appeal and that's their problem. In "E Unibus Pluram," popularly known as the TV essay, Wallace uses television as his main example of the pleasurable and the problematic. He argues that television happily offers us the illusion of human relationships, wherein we can interact with the people on the screen – come to know them, get involved in their lives, judge them – all while comfortably ensconced in our Barcaloungers and all without our having to give anything of ourselves. Wallace writes, "Television's greatest minute-by-minute appeal is that it engages without demanding. One can rest while undergoing stimulation. Receive without giving. In this respect, television resembles certain other things one might call Special Treats (e.g. candy, liquor), i.e. treats that are basically fine and fun in small amounts but bad for us in large amounts and *really* bad for us if consumed in the massive regular amounts reserved for nutritive staples."[4] The really bad result is that these palliative things (television, candy, liquor) we come desperately to rely on to assuage our loneliness serve only to make us more alone.

The critique of what Wallace pretty much interchangeably calls metafiction, postmodern fiction, and experimental fiction is twofold.[5] First, and the opposite of his critique of popular fiction, such fiction can make the reader work too hard for what she is likely to get out of it. Often, the author–reader relationship is compromised by the author's desire to be perceived as smart, clever, and daring, what a character in "Westward the Course of Empire Takes Its Way" describes as "a sort of look-Dad-no-hands quality."[6] The author's focus is on projecting an image of himself and not on establishing a relationship with the reader. The reader becomes a faceless thing whose purpose is to be an appreciative audience for the author's clever tricks. The second critique of postmodern fiction focuses on the ways its cultural functions have transformed from its 1960s heyday to the end of the century. In "E Unibus Pluram" Wallace argues that postmodernism's iconoclasm, expressed primarily though its use of double-coded language, or irony, was once vitally important to expose the lingering hypocrisies of the conformist, commodified 1950s. However, by the 1990s, postmodern irony has done its job too well: its precepts have trickled down into the popular culture, and irony has become a generation's lingua franca, with deleterious results. Postmodern irony becomes just another part of popular culture, just another medium of exchange between us and the world, just another way to sell us something. Moreover, the cultural dominance of irony leads to an ideological stasis as the ease with which we can tear things down results in a condition in which nothing can be built up.[7] Wallace writes, "Anyone with the heretical gall to ask an ironist what he actually stands for ends up looking like an hysteric or a prig. And herein lies the oppressiveness of institutionalized irony, the too-successful rebel: the ability to interdict the *question* without attending to its *subject* is, when exercised, tyranny."[8]

So given the commodification of popular culture, the soul-killing bequest of postmodern irony, the ideological inertia and pervasive loneliness of late-twentieth-century America, what does Wallace see as the function of his fiction? It can be summed up in two words: relieve and redeem. Fiction can relieve loneliness by engaging the reader and providing the opportunity to spend time experiencing the world through the consciousnesses of others. This is not the kind of fiction one can absorb passively: "in order for it to be anything like a full real human relationship, [the reader is] going to have to put in her share of the linguistic work."[9] And this work complicates and even disrupts the author–reader relationship by emphasizing the mediation through which the reader experiences the story and characters, mediation effected by the narrative voice. While Wallace bemoans postmodern irony, he makes significant use of the self-referentiality associated with postmodern fiction as a way to make the reader aware of the mediated nature of the reading experience and to remind her that the mediating voice is not a neutral agent but one with an agenda. Fiction can redeem by helping us to remember that the reality that is represented for us through the mechanisms of popular culture – TV, the Internet, the advertisements overt and covert that are flung our way by the hundreds every day – is not the only or even the best form reality can take. Wallace revises Shklovsky's concept of defamiliarization: instead of making the familiar strange, Wallace would return strangeness to the world, reminding us that the world that has become familiar to us values us in only limited, objectifying ways, encourages us to objectify others, and ought to be intolerable.[10]

The more we study Wallace's aesthetic, the more we see the relationship between the author and reader being compared to actual human relationships. In writing and in life, Wallace sees the need for dynamic relationships, relationships that involve reciprocal taking and giving, that involve work, that recognize the humanness of each person, that relieve and redeem loneliness. As we see so frequently in his fiction, fin-de-siècle relationships are built around what one party can get from the other – attention, amusement, pleasure, sex. To so use another person, to turn her into an object for our own gratification, is to dehumanize her and thus to increase her loneliness and our own. These ideas are central to "B.I. #20," the ultimate brief interview in Wallace's *Brief Interviews with Hideous Men*. The interviewee, possibly a graduate student or a young business professional, resentful of privilege, savvy and cynical about language, sums up the story he is about to tell the female interviewer in his second answer to her queries: "In bed together, in response to some sort of prompt or association, she related an anecdote about hitchhiking and once being picked up by what turned out to be a psychotic serial sex offender who then drove her to a secluded area and raped her and would almost surely have murdered her had she not been able to think effectively on her feet under enormous fear and stress."[11] In his previous response, the first of the interview, the man reveals the climax of the story: he fell in love with the woman about whom he's talking. Wallace signals immediately that plot isn't the point here, allowing readers to focus their attention on the storytelling, the double narrations of the hitchhiker to the interviewee and the interviewee to the interviewer, really the same story told twice.

The inner story, narrated by the unnamed woman whom the interviewee dismissively and contemptuously refers to as the Granola Cruncher, elaborates on the events summarized at the beginning of the interview. Although the interviewee (let's call him the Hideous Man) follows the plot of narrative, his attention is equally focused on the manner of the narration and his responses to it. At first he mocks the Granola Cruncher's naïveté about language, at one point complaining that she uses "the quote L-word itself several times without irony or even any evident awareness that the word has through tactical over-deployment become trite and requires invisible quotes around it now."[12] As the story goes on, however, he finds himself appreciating the sincerity and the unselfconsciousness of her discourse. He says,

"It was tribute to the – her odd affectless sincerity that I found myself hearing expressions like *fear gripping her soul*, unquote, as less as televisual clichés or melodrama but as sincere if not particularly artful attempts simply to describe what it must have felt like."[13] Later, he admits, "canned clichés such as *fear seized me* or *this is something that only happens to other people* or even *moment of truth* now take on a horrendous neural resonance and vitality."[14] As the Granola Cruncher describes a double consciousness – her intensely focused attempt to make a soul connection with the psychopath combined with a compassion for the effect this connection is having on him – the Hideous Man moves from judging and dismissing her to empathizing with her; her story and her manner of telling it have made a true emotional connection. This empathy propels the Hideous Man into the realization that he has "never loved anyone"[15] and the desperate admission that he loves her, an admission she, demonstrating depths he hadn't perceived, refuses to take seriously.

The outer story, the story of the Hideous Man telling the interviewer about his picking up the Granola Cruncher and listening to her narration of her rape and near murder, suffers from postmodern exhaustion. The Hideous Man is aware that language is tired, overused, clichéd, in quotation marks, and he knows that his listener (and reader) is aware of that too. Connected with this attitude toward language is the Hideous Man's refusal to connect with the uniqueness of experience, because that experience is related through clichéd, been-there-done-that discourse. The Hideous Man subsumes the Granola Cruncher's story of the serial killer into the amorphous discourse of the popular press: "you're always reading *secluded area* in all the accounts of quote *brutal sex slayings* and *grisly discoveries* of *unidentified remains* by a scout troop or amateur botanist, et cetera."[16] Further, he demonstrates his inability to use language sincerely. All his statements that purport to be honest, candid, and sincere are in fact cynical attempts to manipulate his listener. We see this manipulation in his account of picking up the Granola Cruncher, and we see it in his attempts to influence the responses of the interviewer: "And yes and don't worry I'm aware of how all this sounds and can well imagine the judgments you're forming from the way I'm characterizing what drew me to her but if I'm really to explain this to you as requested then I have no choice but to be brutally candid rather than observing the pseudosensitive niceties of euphemism."[17] As part of this cynical candor, the Hideous Man anticipates that the interviewer will connect his comments about the serial killer's need to reduce others to desire-satisfying objects and his fear of making a real connection with another to himself and his relation with the Granola Cruncher, but his anticipation doesn't make it untrue. The Granola

Cruncher makes a real human connection with him in telling her story, just as she had with the serial killer, but the Hideous Man fails to make an empathic connection with the interviewer, his listener, because he still relies on habitual cynical candor in lieu of sincerity and honesty.

The tension between the inner and outer narratives illustrates the complexity and difficulty in Wallace's aesthetic. The kind of author he argues we need, one willing to create a human, dynamic, and loving relationship with the reader so as to relieve her loneliness, remind her what it means to be a human being in a culture that seeks to dehumanize her, is represented by the inner narrative and the remarkable, language-redeeming, empathetic Granola Cruncher. The kind of author who has inherited the dead ends of postmodern irony is represented by the ironic, cynical, and lonely Hideous Man, who is stuck with the self-referential awareness of language, its clichéd exhaustion, and can't find a way out of it. The story, I think, dramatizes Wallace's own struggles as an author who knows what fin-de-siècle fiction needs to do to move on from what he thinks of as the postmodern cul-de-sac and reclaim a vital purpose in the culture but who can't fight his way out of the self-consciousness of language he has inherited to achieve his goal of the sincere connection with the reader.

In the story "Octet" Wallace takes another approach, making the writer's desire to establish a relationship with the reader and to allow the reader empathetic connection to another through his words the subject of the fiction. The story's form is a series of pop quizzes (not eight as the title suggests, because the narrator has thrown out five of them and then added a ninth) each describing a situation that challenges the characters' "other-directedness" and exploring the "nameless but inescapable 'price' that all human beings are faced with having to pay at some point if they ever want truly 'to be with' another person instead of just using that person somehow."[18] The ninth quiz departs from the style of the others so that the narrator can directly address the reader, admit the failure of the foregoing quizzes, spell out exactly what he's trying to accomplish, and ask the reader how to accomplish it. The result is a fascinating balancing act wherein the narrator acknowledges the danger of his method seeming like "the now-tired S.O.P 'meta'-stuff"[19] and the danger of failing in his attempt to embrace sincerity. Of the former danger, the narrator says, "The disadvantage of flirting with metafictional self-reference ... which in the late 1990s, when even Wes Craven is cashing in on metafictional self-reference, might come off as lame and tired and facile, and also runs the risk of compromising the queer *urgency* about whatever it is you feel you want the pieces to interrogate in whoever's reading them."[20] The latter danger is subtler. While, on the one hand, the narrator proffers sincerity – a sincere relationship between author and reader – as a solution, on the other hand, he continually problematizes the distinction between the sincere and the appearance of the sincere. At one point he critiques metafiction's supposed honesty in admitting that what the reader is reading is indeed a fiction, something that's being manipulated by the author, who, in a show of sincerity, now steps from behind the curtain to reveal himself. The narrator writes that such a process "more than anything seems to resemble the type of real-world person who tries to manipulate you into liking him by making a big deal of how open and honest and unmanipulative he's being ... not interrogating you or have any sort of interchange or even really *talking* to you but rather just *performing* in some highly self-conscious and manipulative way."[21] As readers, we recognize that this disconnect between performed sincerity and inner truth is at the heart of the previous pop quiz, 6(A), and we can't help but realize that sham honesty used to manipulate others is a continuing theme throughout the collection, especially in the Brief Interviews, and is indeed one way in which characters objectify and dehumanize others. Some readers might then become suspicious of the narrator's repeated claims of "100% candor"[22] and wonder whether we are being invited into a human relationship with the narrator or manipulated to respond to the narrator, to admire or like him, to be, in the end, used.[23]

This problem of sincerity being undercut by the possibility of mock-sincerity is explored more deeply in *Infinite Jest*, particularly in the 8 November Interdependence Day chapter focusing on the White Flag Alcoholics Anonymous meeting. This is a complexly structured chapter, narrated from the hybrid focalization of Don Gately and the narrator and using the setting of the White Flag weekly meeting to discuss the practical workings of an AA meeting and further characterizing the denizens of Ennet House. Most important for my purposes are the addiction stories offered by the members of the Advanced Basics Group, the White Flaggers' guests for the evening. The novel positions the successful narratives as representative of the discourse of sincerity. Explaining what makes a successful narrative at an AA meeting, the narrator says, "The thing is it has to be the truth to really go over, here. It can't be a calculated crowd-pleaser, and it has to be the truth unslanted, unfortified. And maximally unironic. An ironist in a Boston AA meeting is a witch in church. Irony-free zone. Same with sly disingenuous manipulative pseudo-sincerity."[24] The goal is empathy, an emotional connection made between speaker and audience. The audience must participate in achieving this connection. The narrator says, "Everybody in the audience is aiming for total empathy with the speaker; that way they'll be able to receive the AA message he's here to carry. Empathy, in Boston AA, is called Identification."[25]

However, the AA stories are set into an interesting tension both with the narrative structure of the novel and its thematic development. Structurally, the AA narratives are heavily mediated. The narration of this chapter over-lays Gately's consciousness and sometimes his language with the voice, discourse, style, and intellectual preoccupations of the main narrator. Thus each of the narratives is refracted through Gately's consciousness and then more radically through the narrator's. Both Gately and the narrator critique the speakers, especially the Advanced Basics speaker whom they perceive as "dying to be liked up there" and who uses irony to "deprecate the Program rather than the Self"[26] as well as the speaker with the disturbed adoptive parents with the disabled natural daughter, whose harrowing story is received with judgment by Gately and the narrator:

> As she's telling what she sees as etiological truth, even though the monologue seems sincere and unaffected and at least a B+ on the overall AA-story lucidity-scale, faces in the hall are averted and heads clutched and postures uneasily shifted in empathetic distress at the look-what-happened-to-poor-me invitation implicit in the tale, the talk's tone of self-pity itself less offensive (even though plenty of these White Flaggers, Gately knows, had personal childhoods that made this girl's look like a day at Six Flags Over the Poconos) than the subcurrent of explanation, an appeal to exterior *Cause* that can slide, in the addictive mind, so insidiously into *Excuse* that any causal attribution is in Boston AA feared, shunned, punished by empathetic distress.[27]

The narrator also slyly passes judgment by mentioning another 12-step group the speaker belongs to: Wounded, Hurting, Inadequately Nurtured but Ever-Recovering Survivors, with the Pynchonesque acronym of WHINERS.[28] As a result, the various narrative levels mediating between the AA stories and us work against Identification or empathetic connection between storyteller and auditor; Wallace's narrational style not only creates a critical distance between the storyteller and the reader but also invites the reader to join the narrative voice in critiquing and judging the story.

Connected to disruption of the connection between speaker and listener is the narrator's presentation of the fundamental structure of the AA narrative. In introducing the first Advanced Basics speaker, John L., the narrator says, "Identifying, unless you've got a stake in Comparing, isn't very hard to do, here. Because if you sit up front and listen hard, all the speakers' stories of decline and fall and surrender are basically alike, and like your own."[29] The narrator then proceeds to alternate para-graphs, first a direct quotation from John L.'s narrative, then the narra-tor's presentation of the common elements of the addiction story, narrated in the second person. For example:

"Lost my damn job," [John L.] says. "I mean to say I still knew where it was and whatnot. I just went in as usual one day and there was some other fellow doing it," which gets another laugh.

– then more Losses, with the Substance seeming like the only consolation against the pain of mounting Losses, and of course you're in Denial about it being the Substance that's causing the very Losses it's consoling you about – [30]

This juxtaposition between the particular and the general does two things. First, it establishes an addiction master narrative, the fundamental structure, discourse, characters, and narrative attitude that are common to an addiction narrative. It's this common structure that makes Identification possible. As Gately tries to explain to Joelle and Erdedy, "*hearing* the speaker means like all of a sudden hearing how fucking similar the way he felt and the way I felt were, Out There, at the Bottom, before we each Came In."[31] Second, it establishes a model for successful addiction narratives. The subsequent stories are all judged by how well they adhere to the master narrative. Those that don't – like the fellow who uses irony to deprecate the program and the woman who uses her story to explain the cause of her addiction – are judged to have failed. Empathy or Identification between auditor and storyteller is dependent both on a shared experience of addiction and on a shared understanding of the conventions of the addiction story. The first speaker, whose narrative goes over so successfully, is surely performing – with practiced laugh lines and calculated pathos – as much as the program-denigrating speaker, but the former's performance works within the conventions of the AA master narrative and thus seems sincere to his auditors.

This shared understanding of the conventions of the addiction story, including the discourse through which it is narrated, further complicates the supposed sincerity of the stories. The narrator, after explaining the importance of sincerity for these stories, how they must be unironic and not calculated performances, adds this amendment:

This doesn't mean you can't pay empty or hypocritical lip-service, however. Paradoxically enough. The desperate, newly sober White Flaggers are always encouraged to invoke and pay empty lip-service to slogans they don't yet understand or believe – e.g. "Easy Does It!" and "Turn It Over!" and "One Day at a Time!" It's called "Fake It Till You Make It," itself an oft-invoked slogan. Everybody on a Commitment who gets up publicly to speak starts out saying he's an alcoholic, says it whether he believes he is yet or not; then everybody up there says how Grateful he is to be sober today and how great it is to be Active and out on a Commitment with his Group, even if he's not grateful or pleased about it at all. You're encouraged to keep saying stuff like this until you start to believe it.[32]

This kind of discourse adoption – using, often enthusiastically, the discourse of a group with which one wishes to affiliate – is common among newcomers to groups from religions to graduate programs. Its significance here is that it warns us that, by faking the discourse and adopting the conventions of the AA master narrative, a speaker could possibly deliver a most successful AA narrative – one that adheres to the conventions by which Gately and the narrator judge them – without being in the least sincere, by in effect faking sincerity. Similarly, listeners can fake their Identification with the speakers. The narrator notes of Gately: "He likes that Erdedy, sitting, looks right up at him and cocks his head slightly to let Gately know he's got his full attention. Gately doesn't know that this is a requisite for a white-collar job where you have to show you're attending fully to clients who are paying major sums and get to expect an overt display of full attention."[33]

By introducing this "Fake It Till You Make It" element of the AA narrative, the narrator connects these stories to the novel's larger concern with sincerity as a method of manipulation and with the difficulty in discerning between genuine sincerity and what the narrator had previously called "sly disingenuous manipulative pseudo-sincerity."[34] Manipulative sincerity at its worst can be seen in Orin Incandenza's seduction strategies, wherein he assumes the pose of absolute honesty to achieve a calculated response from his female "Subjects." This mock-sincerity both dehumanizes Orin and objectifies the women he pursues. A more complex example occurs in Barry Loach's story. Trying to prove to his brother that "the basic human character wasn't as unempathetic and necrotic as the brother's present depressed condition was leading him to think," Barry agrees to stand outside a Boston T-station, appearing to be homeless, and ask more affluent passersby to touch him, "extend some basic human warmth and contact."[35] He doesn't get anyone to touch him, but he does rake in a significant amount of change and small bills. As a result, "some of the T-station's other disreputable stem-artists became intrigued by Barry's pitch – to say nothing of his net receipts – and started themselves to take up the cry of 'Touch me, please, please, someone!,' which of course further compromised Barry Loach's chances of getting some citizen to interpret his request literally and lay hands on him in a compassionate and human way."[36] The other homeless beggars' mock-sincerity is indistinguishable from Barry's sincere-sincerity (just as Barry's mock-homelessness becomes indistinguishable from actual homelessness) and is interpreted by the audience (the more affluent passersby, experienced in the ways of T-station beggars) as just another come-on, which, in every case but Barry's, it is.

The fiction's conflation of sincere, empathetic, relationship-building narration and mock-sincere, manipulative, and dehumanizing narration might seem to undercut the aesthetic Wallace articulated in his interviews and essays, but I think it is seminal to it, in two ways. First, part of his ongoing struggles with the legacy of postmodernism is that he is unwilling to pretend that postmodernism, with its attention to and critique of language, with its intertextuality and self-referentiality, and, yes, with its irony, never happened. The postmodern era has made it impossible simply to return to good old-fashioned storytelling with clear narrative strategies, familiar, relatable characters, and transparent narrational style. Much of Wallace's fiction, especially *Infinite Jest*, in its structure and its style, seeks to represent postmodern irony's centrality to our culture and that centrality's deleterious effects on our relationships and our ability to be human. Discussing the fear of aloneness of Hal Incandenza's generation, the narrator says,

> The U.S. arts are our guide to inclusion. A how-to. We are shown how to fashion masks of ennui and jaded irony at a young age where the face is fictile enough to assume the shape of whatever it wears. And then it's stuck there, the weary cynicism that saves us from gooey sentiment and unsophisticated naïveté. ... Hal, who's empty but not dumb, theorizes privately that what passes for hip cynical transcendence of sentiment is really some kind of fear of being really human.[37]

Infinite Jest adopts double-coded, multilayered language so as to facilitate a critique of it. The main narrative style of the novel makes its own attention to language one of the things it seeks to be about. On the one hand, it emphasizes the overfamiliarity of everyday language by condensing it. When the narrator says things like, "24/7/365" or "Kitchens and Heat,"[38] he knows that the language is familiar enough, clichéd enough, for the reader to fill in the rest without thinking. On the other hand, and more typically, the narrative style is overly abundant, extravagant, expansive, trying impossibly as it rushes through time to lasso, capture, and represent a complex reality more and more exactly and always failing. The best examples of this are too long to include here, but we can see indications of this narrative impulse in endnotes 117 and 119 where the narrator admits he "overshot" the places where something should have been mentioned.[39] The form and style of the novel provide a constant awareness of the languages through which we experience the characters and plot and in this sense mirrors the characters' experiences of their world through layers and layers of language.

My second answer is something of the reverse of the first. Wallace knows that his audience is not the White Flag audience, straining to hear each speaker and to make that empathetic Identification. The contemporary reader, tempered by the postmodern novel, is like the narrator: maintaining a critical distance between herself and the storyteller; distrusting of authorial authority; wary of being manipulated into sentimental responses; aware, maybe hyperaware, of language and what it can and can't do. Wallace's challenge, how to write fiction that can connect with such a reader, resembles James Incandenza's goal for his last film, as his wraith explains to the hospitalized Gately:

> To concoct something the gifted boy [Hal] couldn't simply master and move on from to a new plateau. Something the boy would love enough to induce him to open his mouth and come *out* – even if was only to ask for more. ... Make something so bloody compelling it would reverse thrust on a young self's fall into the womb of solipsism, anhedonia, death in life. A magically entertaining toy to dangle at the infant still somewhere alive in the boy, to make its eyes light and toothless mouth open unconsciously, to laugh.[40]

Such a work must be made with an awareness of the discourse-and-irony-sodden culture in which both the writer and reader reside, an awareness that complicates and perhaps cripples the attempted sincerity. To return to the AA narrative, we might think of irony, standing for double-coded language and self-referential discourse, as both the Substance to which we've become addicted *and* the critical mechanism we use to resist Identification, the empathetic connection that might save us from our aloneness.

If these conclusions help us understand Wallace's aesthetic as it's enacted in his fiction, they might also help us understand the curious claim Wallace made in his interview with Laura Miller that he is a "realist."[41] He developed an aesthetic that would help him represent late twentieth-century America as he experienced it. If, as he put it, "fiction's about what it is to be a fucking *human being*,"[42] then he is driven in his fiction to depict the difficult challenge of choosing to be human in a highly mediated, irony-infused, commercially driven culture that seeks to dehumanize us, objectify us into consumers, passive audiences, or providers of other people's pleasure. Wallace's fiction is hard because being human and treating others as human is hard. His fiction helps us toward this goal and consoles us in our failures.

Notes

1. David Foster Wallace, "An Expanded Interview with David Foster Wallace," by Larry McCaffery in Stephen J. Burn (ed.), *Conversations with David Foster Wallace* (Jackson: University of Mississippi Press, 2012), p. 50.
2. David Foster Wallace, *Infinite Jest* (Boston: Little, Brown, 1996), p. 694.
3. Wallace, "Looking for a Garde of Which to Be Avant: An Interview with David Foster Wallace" by Hugh Kennedy and Geoffrey Polk, in Burn (ed.), *Conversations*, p. 16.

4. David Foster Wallace, "E Unibus Pluram: Television and U.S. Fiction," in *A Supposedly Fun Thing I'll Never Do Again: Essays and Arguments* (Boston: Little, Brown, 1997), p. 37.

5. For discussions of Wallace's critique of postmodernism, see chapter 1 of Marshall Boswell's *Understanding David Foster Wallace* (Columbia: University of South Carolina Press, 2003) and my "Post-Postmodern Discontent: Contemporary Fiction and the Social World," *symplokē* 12.1–2 (2004), pp. 53–68. For broader studies of Wallace's generation of writers' break from postmodernism, see chapter 1 of Stephen J. Burn's *Jonathan Franzen at the End of Postmodernism* (New York: Continuum, 2011); Jeremy Green's *Late Postmodernism: American Fiction at the Millennium* (New York: Palgrave Macmillan, 2005); Mary K. Holland's *Succeeding Postmodernism: Language and Humanism in Contemporary American Literature* (New York: Bloomsbury, 2013); part 2 of Lee Konstantiou's *Cool Characters: Irony and American Fiction* (Cambridge, MA: Harvard University Press, 2016); and my "After the Revolution: US Postmodernism in the Twenty-First Century," *Narrative* 21.3 (2013), pp. 284–295.

6. Wallace, "Westward the Course of Empire," in *Girl With Curious Hair* (New York: Norton, 1989), p. 329.

7. Many critics have explored Wallace's understanding of and use of irony in his fiction. See, for example, Boswell, *Understanding David Foster Wallace*, pp. 13–20; Allard den Dulk, "Boredom, Irony, and Anxiety: Wallace and the Kierkegaardian View of the Self," in Marshall Boswell (ed.), *David Foster Wallace and "The Long Thing": New Essays on the Novels* (New York: Bloomsbury, 2014), pp. 43–60; Lee Konstantinou, *Cool Characters: Irony and American Fiction* (Cambridge, MA: Harvard University Press, 2016).

8. Wallace, "E Unibus Pluram," p. 68.

9. Wallace, "Expanded Interview," in Burn (ed.), *Conversations*, p. 34.

10. See chapter 1 of Victor Shklovsky's *Theory of Prose*, (trans.) Benjamin Sher (Normal, IL: Dalkey Archive, 1991).

11. David Foster Wallace, *Brief Interviews with Hideous Men* (Boston: Little, Brown, 1999), p. 287.

12. Ibid., p. 293.

13. Ibid., p. 297.

14. Ibid., p. 298.

15. Ibid., p. 313.

16. Ibid., pp. 293–294.

17. Ibid., p. 289.

18. Ibid., pp. 138, 155.

19. Ibid., p. 147.

20. Ibid., pp. 146–147.

21. Ibid., p. 147.

22. Ibid., p. 148.

23. The extent to which Wallace aspires to and/or achieves a literature of sincerity is a lively topic of debate among scholars. See Clare Hayes-Brady, *The Unspeakable Failures of David Foster Wallace: Language, Identity, and Resistance* (New York: Bloomsbury, 2016); part 3 of Stefan Hirt's *The Iron Bars of Freedom: David Foster Wallace and the Postmodern Self* (Stuttgart: ibidem, 2008); Mary K. Holland,

"Mediated Immediacy in *Brief Interviews with Hideous Men*," in Marshall Boswell and Stephen J. Burn (eds.), *A Companion to David Foster Wallace Studies* (New York: Palgrave Macmillan, 2013), pp. 107–130; Adam Kelly, "David Foster Wallace and the New Sincerity in American Fiction," in David Hering (ed.), *Consider David Foster Wallace* (Los Angeles: Sideshow, 2010), pp. 131–146; Konstantinou, *Cool Characters*; Toon Staes, "Wallace and Empathy: A Narrative Approach," in Boswell (ed.), *David Foster Wallace and "The Long Thing,"* pp. 23–42; and Iain Williams, "(New) Sincerity in David Foster Wallace's 'Octet'," *Critique* 56.3 (2015), pp. 299–314.

24. Wallace, *Infinite Jest*, p. 369.
25. Ibid., p. 345.
26. Ibid., p. 367.
27. Ibid., p. 374.
28. Ibid., p. 372.
29. Ibid., p. 345.
30. Ibid., p. 346.
31. Ibid., p. 365.
32. Ibid., p. 369.
33. Ibid., p. 362. For other critics' discussions of AA discourse in the novel, see Timothy Aubry, "Selfless Cravings: Addiction and Recovery in David Foster Wallace's *Infinite Jest*," in Jay Prosser (ed.), *American Fiction of the 1990s: Reflections of History and Culture* (London: Routledge, 2008), pp. 206–219; Hirt, *Iron Bars of Freedom*, pp. 131–134; and Holland, *Succeeding Postmodernism*, esp. pp. 59–63 and 77–81.
34. Ibid., p. 369.
35. Ibid., p. 969.
36. Ibid., p. 970.
37. Ibid., pp. 694–695.
38. Ibid., p. 997.
39. Ibid., p. 1022.
40. Ibid., pp. 838–839.
41. David Foster Wallace, "The Salon Interview: David Foster Wallace," by Laura Miller, in Burn (ed.), *Conversations*, p. 60.
42. Wallace, "Expanded Interview," in Burn (ed.), *Conversations*, p. 26.

II

ANDREW WARREN

Wallace and Politics

When you say "Put on your sweater", the child learns what commands are and what authority is, and if giving orders is something that creates anxiety for you, then authorities are anxious, authority itself uncertain.

Stanley Cavell, *The Claim of Reason*[1]

The bureaucracy of the state is the imaginary state alongside the real state – the spiritualism of the state ... Authority is the basis of its knowledge, and the deification of authority is its conviction.

Marx, "Contributions to the Critique of Hegel's *Philosophy of Right*"[2]

A Political Wallace, or Apolitical Wallace?

When David Foster Wallace got to Amherst in 1981 he toyed with the idea of entering politics, eventually. In his freshman fall he took an introduction to political science, and soon after American Diplomatic History II and European Politics. In 1982 he withdrew from college, and on his return noted to his friend Mark Costello that "no one's going to vote for someone who's been in a nuthouse."[3] He wrote a Lockean op-ed to the Amherst College newspaper on the topic of "loudness-as-inalienable-right," in response to an "inconsiderate schmuck"'s opinion that requests to turn down his AC/DC infringed on his "freedom."[4] Before graduating, Wallace and his friends went to Maine, ate lobster, and talked about Reaganomics.[5] He voted, at some point, for Reagan.

At Harvard he enrolled in a class on Marx, alongside a course with Stanley Cavell, where he read "Contributions to the Critique of Hegel's *Philosophy of Right*." He also began a first-year colloquium with the leading theorist of liberalism, John Rawls, whose readings he found "impossibly dense."[6] During this period he cowrote a book on hip hop which contended that "the best rappers both exemplify and ridicule the contradictions inherent in '80's conservatism, in mixed images of political democracy and economic

Hobbesianism."[7] He voted, apparently, for independent candidate Ross Perot.

In 2000 he wrote a puzzlingly obsessive article on John McCain's first Republican primary bid, despite voting for Democrat Bill Bradley. Chatting with Dave Eggers in 2003, Wallace said that while writing the McCain piece he witnessed things "about our current president, his inner circle, and the primary campaign" that made him, "at present, partisan," that he planned "to knock on doors and stuff envelopes. Maybe even to wear a button. To try to accrete with others into a demographically significant mass. To try extra hard to exercise patience, politeness, and imagination on those with whom I disagree. Also to floss more."[8] In 2007 Brian Garner arranged a lunch between Wallace and Antonin Scalia. Wallace reported being "astonished at and slightly confused by how much he liked Justice Scalia – despite their political differences."[9]

In one of his last pieces, from November 2007, he wondered aloud whether, in the absence of a real discussion of national security and what it means, we can "trust our elected leaders to value and protect the American idea as they act to secure the homeland?":

> What are the effects on the American idea of Guantánamo, Abu Ghraib, PATRIOT Acts I and II, warrantless surveillance, Executive Order 13233, corporate contractors performing military functions, the Military Commissions Act, NSPD 51, etc., etc.? Assume for a moment that some of these measures really have helped make our persons and property safer – are they worth it? Where and when was the public debate on whether they're worth it? Was there no such debate because we're not capable of having or demanding one? Why not? Have we actually become so selfish and scared that we don't even want to *consider* whether some things trump safety?[10]

His email address, Ocapmycap@ca.rr.com, referenced Whitman's elegy of Lincoln, who had left America rudderless in the Civil War's wake: "My Captain does not answer, his lips are pale and still."[11] Wallace's unfinished *The Pale King* was about boredom, civics, and a sense of waning authority. Just before he died Wallace was considering, quite seriously, offering his speechwriting services to a young politician named Barack Obama.[12] He did not live long enough to vote for him.

Wallace and Politics' Other Scene

Against narratives claiming that Wallace was apolitical, or became political only late in life, this chapter makes the case that Wallace was interested – often intensely interested – in politics' ideals, foundations, and often disappointing or bewildering practice. His sole case study was America, either because he thought it exceptional or exemplary, or simply because it was all that he knew well enough to write about.[13] In 2007 he pleaded with readers to agree on a working definition of the American idea – "an open society, consent of the governed, enumerated powers, *Federalist* 10, pluralism, due process, transparency . . . the whole democratic roil."[14] This is fairly standard American-style liberalism of the sort Wallace promoted across his life. It is perhaps most robustly exemplified by Rawls's notion of *justice as fairness* and his *liberal principle of legitimacy*: (1) that social inequality is justified only if changing that inequality would visit *more* inequality on the least advantaged, and (2) that politics must proceed from what a society holds in common and its citizens can reasonably agree upon.[15] Democracy demands both the maximum degree of equality and a transparent political culture rooted in a publicly stated constitution.

Although Wallace was deeply and publicly invested in that American idea, and advocated for it, his work, particularly his fiction, frequently engaged politics more obliquely or on a different plane. Following Étienne Balibar, the political thinker I find most in line with Wallace's myriad approaches, I am calling that plane *politics' other scene*. Politics' other scene is both "*the scene of the other,* where the visible-incomprehensible victims and enemies are located at the level of fantasy" and the so-called "'real-scene' of economic processes, the development of capitalism and class struggle." It is "the *moment* where it becomes *manifest* that politics is not 'rational,'" nor purely "irrational," either. The other scene likewise inhabits a space between ideology's imaginary and economics' real social function, disrupting and interfering with one another. Individual subjects and citizens are formed from those struggles between fantasy and economic production.[16] The other scene's interferences and disruptions are the very stuff of *Infinite Jest* and *The Pale King*, where large-scale structures, threats, and fears are run through each individual character, whether they're elite and prodigious solipsists, addicts, or IRS workers. Wallace rarely addresses class inequality head on. He typically channels it through divisions in education (a not untrue marker of class) and, less frequently and perhaps less persuasively, through race.[17]

Balibar, more than Rawls, believes that politics' deep foundation is composed of irreconcilable differences that are economic, social, and racial but also imagined and theoretical. Changes to political systems are generated by our necessarily insufficient and often violent attempts to align those differences. Economics and ideology are at odds, but so are our modern ideas of equality and liberty. *Equaliberty* is Balibar's name for the hidden contradiction in the demand to create social or economic equality while also granting everyone the political or juridical liberty to act as they please. This antinomy or double bind comes from the other scene, a social and imagined site that, I argue, Wallace's work strives to access and describe.

Practically speaking, citizens are guaranteed freedom only at the cost of giving some of it up; our freedom, for instance, must suffer the imposition of laws and taxes to create a more egalitarian society. This is equaliberty's conundrum, perhaps most legible in *Infinite Jest*'s debates between Steeply, an American secret agent, and Marathe, a French-Canadian terrorist named after a radical French revolutionary, Marat. One of *Infinite Jest*'s clear models[18] is Peter Weiss's 1964 experimental play-within-a-play, *Marat/ Sade,* which represents "the conflict of an individualism carried to an extreme and the idea of a political and social upheaval."[19] Steeply, privileging freedom (like Rawls, and Sade), hopes that America has solved equaliberty's aporia: "each American seeking to pursue his maximum good results in maximizing *everyone's* good ... This is what lets us steer clear of oppression and tyranny. Even your Greekly democratic howling-mob-type tyranny. The United States: a community of sacred individuals which reveres the sacredness of the individual choice."[20] When Marathe brings up resource scarcity – what if there is only one can of pea soup and two people desire it? – Steeply lectures him on America's learned flexibility. Markets can trade or divide soup, and Americans have been educated to respect others' interests, even foreigners', and to delay gratification: "not to teach what to desire. To teach how to be free." Of course, "the system isn't perfect. There is greed, there is crime, there are drugs and cruelty and ruin and infidelity and divorce and suicide. Murder ... But this is just the price. This is the price of the free pursuit."[21] Steeply's discourse scrambles private desire, public policy, and the free market in the same way that ideological fantasy and economics are entangled in politics' other scene. Marathe's role, in a sense, is to push that scene to its crisis by introducing the *Infinite Jest* tape, a lethal entertainment that someone "freely" chooses to watch.[22] American citizens' lofty ideals, troubled lives, and political realities, *Infinite Jest* suggests, are born from the contradictions of such imagined scenes, which are, like dreams, both rational and irrational. One of Wallace's political interventions is to use fiction to show them to us. *Infinite Jest*'s bent reality, for instance, can depict the aleatory, lurid, and yet very real effects of improbable environmental disaster.[23]

At the heart of nearly all Wallace's other scenes lies a broken authority. Wallace's America lacks strong and flexible leadership, its families are anxious or authoritarian, and its citizens fail to govern their desires. *Girl with Curious Hair*'s title story, for instance, is about a sociopathic Young Republican who runs with a crew of nihilist punks. These two wildly disparate groups – nihilist punks and Young Free Market Reaganite

Republicans – are linked by a reactionary violence endemic to the alienating insincerity and irreality of a generation without solid models of authority. And "Lyndon," about LBJ's protracted (fictional!) affair with his chief of staff's gay, black, Haitian, HIV-infected lover, set literally against the backdrop of youth protests against Vietnam, maps 1980s multicultural politics onto 1960s-era radicalism. Its narrative spirals around a hypermasculine, charismatic, and warlike president – a figure who screams authority, perhaps literally – to reveal a centripetal vulnerability.

This question of authority – what it is, who has it, who grants it, and how – is the most consistent flash point in Wallace's political thinking. It is explicitly and repeatedly addressed in 2006's *Consider the Lobster*, my first case study and Wallace's easiest and most straightforward engagement with political issues. I end with *The Pale King*, the daunting and ultimately unfinished task he set himself for more than a decade: writing a book about *boredom* and *civics*. In between I tarry with a number of overt and covert liaisons between Wallace and politics, especially *Infinite Jest*'s many "other scenes," which so often intersect with other discourses or modes of life, such as religion, philosophy, economics, and psychology.

"Authority and American Usage," "Up, Simba," and "Host" – "Victory for the Forces of Democratic Freedom!"

Wallace's most explicit nonfiction discussion of politics' origin, impulse, and basic template comes in "Authority and American Usage." Its subtitle, "'Politics and the English Language' Is Redundant," is a point repeated throughout the piece. Dictionaries are often either "notoriously liberal" or "notoriously conservative" and debates about them and their historical context stir up "a veritable hurricane of controversies from technical linguistics and public education to political ideology."[24] At stake is "interhuman life itself" – that is, language which is "everything and everywhere ... what lets us have anything to do with one another."[25] Even Wittgenstein's abstract early philosophy of language has "politico-ethical implications."[26] Language is what gives us access to, or prevents us from accessing, what Wallace calls "ideology" – "a state of mind and a set of sensibilities"[27] that Carl Schmitt hailed as the foundation of the political: the sorting of Friend from Enemy, Us from Them.[28] Wallace's example is a young SNOOTlet unable to adapt his Standard White English to the playground's discourse community.

Wallace's larger goals are to explain English usage's basic political nature, to map the stormy controversies surrounding and defining it, and to advocate for what he calls a "Democratic Spirit." Such a spirit "combines rigor and humility, i.e., passionate conviction plus a sedulous respect for the convictions of others" and believes that answers must be worked out rather than dogmatically decreed or miraculously discovered.[29] Language is a good test case for this Democratic Spirit because English usage, after all, is enmeshed in "the very weird and complicated relationship between Authority and Democracy" that structures so much of American life.[30]

Another way to put all this is that debates over English usage – and, by implication, politics and interhuman life itself – are inherently rhetorical. Which, of course, they are. But Wallace's point is that they should be explicitly and self-consciously so. It is, further, in Wallace's words, *politically redemptive*.[31] The progressive Left's problem isn't, for him, "conceptual or ideological but spiritual and rhetorical." The Left's argument for wealth distribution obscures its true goals and intentions: viz., "that we who are well off should be willing to share more of what we have with poor people not for the poor people's sake but for our own; i.e., we should share what we have in order to become less narrow and frightened and lonely and self-centered people."[32] In good liberal fashion Wallace believes that clear communication facilitates healthy, public debate. It does not eliminate difficulties or complexities so much as bring them to light, a hallmark of Wallace's fiction. Laying bare the conditions under which one works and produces art, and laying bare the conditions under which someone else receives it, by no means simplifies that process and relationship. It typically exacerbates it, but in a way that, Wallace hopes, strengthens and or deepens it. There is an unrelenting drive for such transparency in Wallace, even as he realizes its impossibility. It leads him to describe what small-*a* (healthy, flexible) versus Large-*A* (ideological, authoritarian) authority might look like, both in writing and in political life.

If "Authority and American Usage" is about the structural foundations of "the political," as they are or as they might someday be, "Up, Simba" is about its actual practice, the ways that our hope and cynicism engender it in the real world. "Up, Simba" develops out of a tension between, on the one hand, the skepticism invoked in a "post-Watergate-post-Iran-Contra-post-Whitewater-post-Lewinski era ... in which politicians' statements of principle or vision are understood as self-serving ad copy and judged not for their truth or ability to inspire but for their tactical shrewdness, their marketability" and, on the other, the hope that a politician might actually be honest, or genuine, or committed to something beyond their own brand, image, and self-preservation.[33] Call it the dialectic of hype and realness. McCain, in 2000, sent Wallace, like many Americans, spinning through those seemingly incompatible options. What Wallace gives us, however, isn't a simple endorsement of realness over hype but, again, a dialectic shuttling between the two.

An authentic authority would tell us, above all, what is authentic – a fantasy. In typical Wallacian fashion, the piece ends by turning away from its ostensible subject (McCain's alleged hype or realness) and toward the reader's own ambivalent stance – a prescient conclusion given how much our own times' politics is shaped by a rage for authenticity.[34]

"Host," about a conservative talk-radio host, Jim Ziegler, also ends with a turn away from its subject, but this time Wallace gives us a positive program for combatting political spin: a commitment to doubt and empathy. Ziegler's decade-long hobbyhorse is the O. J. Simpson trial, and when one of the producers says he hopes O. J.'s children believe he's innocent, Ziegler snorts, "They know, and he knows they know, that he did it." "To which," Wallace considers, "the best response would probably be compassion, empathy. Because one can almost feel it: what a bleak and merciless world this host lives in – believes, nay, knows for an absolute *fact* he lives in. I'll take doubt."[35] Of course, that capacity for empathy is what allows Wallace to draw such an excoriating picture of Ziegler. Nevertheless, Wallace is clear that the rise of the radical Right through the likes of Fox News and talk radio didn't happen via Pynchonesque conspiracy but through market forces. Such venues enact change because they are profitable and entertaining,[36] and the forces behind them feed off of personalities like Ziegler's, as much as he feeds into them – hence the title, "Host."

Perhaps Wallace's most extended example of doubt and empathy's intertwining in these political essays comes when he asks why "the real energy in [Bush-era] US political life," its true "fun," comes from conservatism. He imagines US culture moving hard to the right after Reagan, and then considers the opposite possibility: what if "the US has moved so far and so fast toward cultural permissiveness that we've reached a kind of apsidal point?" Wallace then takes the perspective of "a God-fearing hard-working rural-Midwestern military vet," and asks why the Left – whose basic positions he does not question – has spent so little energy empathizing with him.[37] Even if cultural, moral, ideological, and even philosophical relativism is perhaps good for dialogue, it nevertheless causes a kind of vertigo in average citizens. There are simply too many sources of information to sort through,[38] the "Total Noise" that Wallace elsewhere associates with the problem of writing nonfiction.[39] The infinite choice we face is not just about the bits of data that flood our every waking moment, but also the connections we can make between them and the ethical choices that float up in their wake. We are "host" to them.

Wallace's essay is, visually, a scatter of boxes within boxes mimetic of our impossible task of taking in and framing everything there is. Of course, clearly framing the terms of a debate doesn't make it any easier, per se, to work through them. Difficulty, complexity, and their attendant frustrations and boredom are simply part of modern political life, a point made in "Up, Simba"[40] and *Pale King*.

Let me transition to Wallace's fiction by looking at the play between his explicit politics and what I'm calling politics' other scene. My example is the trope or image of boxes that recurs throughout "Up, Simba," an essay which opens with a brutal description of the time McCain spent in a "special closet-sized box called a 'punishment cell'."[41] The box quickly becomes a metaphor for the closest point we can get to in McCain's experience of the incarceration and torture that he chose, in the name of brotherly military codes, to endure: "with McCain it feels like we know, for a proven fact, that he is capable of devotion to something other, more, than his own self-interest."[42] We don't know how he felt, but we do know what he did, what he chose to do. We know about the box. The closed box's gripping and marketable fantasy depends upon our wanting to get inside it even as we fear it, what Alain Badiou has called our limitless "passion for the real."[43] Its kernel is an aspect of politics' other scene. "It helps," Wallace says, "to conceive a campaign week's events in terms of [mediating and mediated] boxes, boxes inside other boxes," beginning with the US electorate, and national and local press. The cascading frames end at a vision of McCain, the "anticandidate, someone who's open and accessible and 'thinks outside the box,' but who is in fact the campaign's Chinese boxes' central and inscrutable core box, and whose own intracranial thoughts on all these boxes and layers and lenses and on whether this new kind of enclosure is anything like Hoa Lo's dark box are pretty much anyone in the media's guess, since all he'll talk about is politics."[44] The Straight Talk Express is a box, too, and Wallace is later horrified by how the high-speed video feed warps McCain's face into "a physiognomic Rubik's Cube's constituent squares and boxes ... never quite resolving into a face."[45] These three boxes – the campaign's cascade of protective frames, the digital boxes disseminating McCain and his message, and the Hao Lin prison – coalesce in the piece's last paragraph, when Wallace tries to figure out who, for the hundredth time, this "real McCain" might be. He pulls the figure inside out: "the paradox here is that this box that makes McCain 'real' is, by definition, locked ... Whether he's truly 'for real' now depends less on what is in his heart than on what might be in yours."[46] This sequenced framing of a fantasy is a crucial example of politics' other scene, something that Wallace's fiction, with its never-ending play of frames and fantasies, interrogates even more nimbly.

Infinite Jest: The Whole Democratic Roil

Perhaps the most bizarre plotline in the many-plotted and exceedingly bizarre *Infinite Jest* deals with the so-called Great Concavity – a large swath of toxic, hypertrophic land the United States has "experialized" to Canada. America's annexation pastiches how characters sacrifice pieces of themselves to their addictions (drugs, entertainment, sex, secrecy, achievement) to guard and purify another aspect of themselves. Katherine Hayles has noted how the novel's politics was modeled in its recursive account of pleasure and the self, a fact some have argued has always been a crucial aspect of politics as such.[47] States, like individuals, must regulate and secure their necessarily porous borders, often at their own peril.[48] This is the double bind that 2007's "Just Asking" described as the open threats that "a democratic republic cannot 100-percent protect itself from without subverting the very principles that make it worth protecting."[49] *Infinite Jest* describes a world of overregulated borders – between domestic and foreign, self and other, pleasure and restraint. States and individuals alike are unwilling to risk their well-being for something greater than themselves, and thereby disrupt themselves and the environments they inhabit. With its relentless catalog of bodies maimed, distorted, and stunted by toxins, *Infinite Jest* ties rapacious environmental policy to political violence.

Steeply, and O.N.A.N. and the United States, cannot understand the A.F.R. as a "political body" because it and its members do not have "positive political goals," "desires for self" or self-preservation.[50] Being wholly negative, like Wallace's depiction of irony as a "ground-clearing ... Third World rebel" group,[51] it doesn't participate in the nation-state politics that the United States has mastered. Refusing "desire," it has no "business" that Steeply can manage.[52] Marathe's repeated reply to Steeply is that the existential threat posed by the A.F.R. and the Entertainment should make the United States reflect upon itself. Despite its emphasis on freedom, suggests Marathe, America has forgotten how to choose while other nations "will die for something larger."[53] In emphasizing "freedom from constraint and forced duress" Americans have neglected *positive* freedom: "What of freedom-*to*. How for the person to freely choose? How to choose any but a child's greedy choices if there is no loving-filled father to guide, inform, teach the person how to choose?"[54] Again, the problem of equaliberty, the demand for both unfettered freedom and instituted equality. Steeply will defend American free markets and the self's desires,[55] and Marathe will claim that true freedom necessitates authority and sacrifice.

Sacrifice becomes central to Wallace's mature political and ethical thinking, an aspect that puts him in vexed dialogue with religion. Recall Steeply's definition of the United States as "a community of sacred individuals which reveres the sacredness of the individual choice."[56] Wallace has described addiction as a "distortion of ... a religious impulse," seeking "something you're willing to give yourself away to."[57] In the logic of the novel, Gerhard

Schtitt, ETA's athletic director, provides the more-sensible positive response to Marathe's negative provocations, and he does so from within a European (and "Kanto-Hegelian") context. He grew up believing in "Old World patriarchal stuff like honor and discipline and fidelity to some larger unit" and thought that "the needs, the desires, the fears, the multiform cravings of the individual appetitive will" must be sacrificed "to the larger imperatives of a team (OK, the State) and a set of delimiting rules (OK, the Law)."[58] The problem is that the American state is a "sloppy intersection of desires and fears" rather than coherent whole. "The selfish end in its actualization," says Hegel, "establishes a system of all-round *interdependence*, so that the subsistence and welfare of the individual and his rightful existence are interwoven with, and grounded on, the subsistence, welfare, and rights of all, and have actuality and security only in this context."[59] This is, in a nutshell, Steeply's vision of O.N.A.N. (America, Mexico, and Canada), whose (inter) national holiday is called, painfully, Interdependence Day.

The problem with such a state is that it is premised on the individual's easily unbounded desires and appetites. "I believe, with Hegel, that transcendence is absorption," says Hal Incandenza, who is "by all appearances addicted to everything that is not tied down, cannot outrun him, and is fittable in the mouth."[60] Hal is aware that his addictions, like many others' in the novel, are an attempt to fill an emptiness, and he "theorizes privately that what passes for hip cynical transcendence of sentiment is really some kind of fear of being really human" because humans are vulnerable and dependent.[61] Judith Shklar, in a book Wallace may have known, reads Hegel's politics through the self's relationship to irony, sincerity, and community: "Irony exists to protect the self against community and the burdens of purposive action. Because it can make every objective value naught and vain [through ridicule and cool distance], Hegel assumed that eventually it must feel its own vanity and emptiness."[62]

This emptying out of "values, motivating principles, spiritual principles" creates a "hunger" that feeds into what is perhaps the novel's most primal "other scene": the gruesome image of brothers banding together to kill and devour the father, which Wallace borrows, perhaps via Žižek, from Freud's *Totem and Taboo*. Freud's scene of broken-down authority is also "the beginning of so many things – of social organization, of moral restrictions, of religion." For him, that primal scene still structures how we live today – in fact, "the dead father became stronger than the living one had been," a fair description of both *Infinite Jest* and its prime intertext, *Hamlet*.[63] Hal is, perhaps like Hamlet, a hysteric.[64] He obsessively undermines authority figures' knowledge even as he craves that authority, as when he (allegedly) outsmarts the grief therapist and breaks into "hysterical mirth"[65] *not* over the trauma of his father's death but because of the man's tiny hands.[66] Each is an instance of castrated authority, and Hal's reported mirth is an early expression of his later "hysterics."[67] Hal, whose first thought before discovering his father's exploded head in a microwave was *"That something smelled delicious!,"*[68] and his brother Orin, who perhaps distributed the lethal Entertainment as filial revenge for his mother's infidelities, both operate in the vacuum left by their father's death. Their appetites are synecdochical of America's and, like many other characters in the book, Hal and Orin seek alternative institutions and communities to curb them.[69]

Elsewhere I have argued that Wallace's fiction models itself within itself and that it does so in order to model different kinds of community – political communities, surely, but also language communities and communities and contracts between readers and authors.[70] The most extreme version approaches what Jean-Luc Nancy has called *une communauté désoeuvrée*, an inoperative or unworked community. Such a community is not comprised of precomposed singularities, citizens or individuals who share or buy into a common bond; an inoperative community, rather, is parasitic upon such traditional forms of community. It unworks them. What is shared in them is merely finitude, and exposure to threat, what *The Disavowed Community* calls "a sharing of unshareable solitudes." There Nancy cites "our age's preoccupation with the common character of our existence, in which we are not first and foremost distinct atoms but rather we exist with the relation, ensemble, and sharing [*partage*] in which discrete entities (individuals, persons) serve only as facets or punctuations."[71] Wallace, it seems, yearns for this common character, the idea that another consciousness feels the way he does, that he feels unalone – a quality he finds, occasionally, miraculously, in reading.[72]

Brief Interviews has many different names for it, such as "Octet"'s "a weird ambient sameness" (155), "overwhelming and elemental sameness" (156), "this queer nameless ambient urgent interhuman sameness" (157), "entropic homeostasis of nakedly self-obsessed sameness" (158); he, an unfortunate fiction writer, worries about "transmitting any felt 'sameness'" (159); in "Forever Overhead," that sameness becomes the tanning splotches of skin at the end of a diving board that the narrator invites you to step and disappear into (14), just as you are invited to step into the skins of the collection's hideous men.[73] This isn't pleasant; the sameness is both comforting and horrifying. We won't fully avow that affinity, even as we crave it. Similarly, tragedy in Cavell's reading of *Hamlet* – an essay Wallace surely contemplated while composing *Infinite Jest* – is defined as the burden of a knowledge, often an inherited knowledge, that one can't acknowledge.[74] Wallace's mature fiction, I suggest, oscillates between a desire for sharing these unshareable solitudes and a desire to escape from them. It both holds out hope and expresses disgust for that queer ambient sameness, another case where "a political experience has moved back out from the mind onto the skin and into the senses."[75] Cavell suggests history forces that movement from mentation to sensation, but so too can fiction.

The Pale King – "I Think It Goes Beyond Politics"

The Pale King is an intensely political novel. It takes place at an IRS regional office in Peoria, and one of its central scenes involves an extended debate, in a broken-down elevator, over the role of taxes in American life, "civics and selfishness":

> Americans are in a way crazy. We infantilize ourselves. We don't think of ourselves as citizens – parts of something larger to which we have profound responsibilities. We think of ourselves as citizens when it comes to our rights and privileges, but not our responsibilities. We abdicate our civic responsibilities to the government and expect the government, in effect, to legislate morality.[76]

Scenes like this undergird Pale King just as Marathe and Steeply's discussions of citizenship and duty structure Infinite Jest. But what in Jest is a state of ecstatic emergency becomes in Wallace's last work the crushing, crushing boredom of the modern bureaucratic state. Pale King is less about "elegant complexity" than "irrelevant complexity."[77] Because so much strong work has been done on the novel's treatments of boredom and politics,[78] I will limit myself to connecting its explicitly political discussions to its "other scenes" – according to Marx, bureaucracies are, after all, "imaginary" states operating alongside "real" states.

Submitting oneself to bureaucratic boredom and irrelevance demands a sacrifice to what Infinite Jest calls "something larger."[79] In Pale King, for instance, an evangelical IRS agent (a "substitute Jesuit")[80] preaches about "Effacement. Sacrifice. Service." in the face of "Routine, repetition, tedium, monotony, ephemeracy, inconsequence, abstraction, disorder, boredom, angst, ennui."[81] Pale King, like Infinite Jest,[82] contrasts this old-fashioned and resilient duty to Americans' self-infantilization.

That contrast is made explicitly in the elevator civics lesson, above, but also, implicitly, in one of the novel's uncanny other scenes, originally published as "The Compliance Branch": "My audit group's Group Manager and his wife have an infant I can describe only as fierce. Its expression is fierce; its demeanor is fierce; its gaze over bottle or pacifier or finger – fierce, intimidating, aggressive ... When it feeds or sleeps, its pale face reddens, which makes it look all the fiercer."[83] The narrator babysits this terrifying infant that, defying its defining characteristic (*in-fans*, "without speech"), speaks. The infant is uncanny – literally *unheimlich* or unhomely there in the IRS's audit offices. The fragment ends: "I came to see that I deferred to the infant, respected it, granted it full authority, and therefore waited, abiding, both of us in that small and shadowless father's office, in the knowledge that I was, thenceforth, this tiny white frightening thing's to command, its instrument or tool."[84] This, Wallace suggests, is our inherited world: a father's empty office, a ventriloquizing voice, and an infrastructure ruled by an infant – a pale king and fearful compliance. Here and elsewhere Wallace's politics should be read as a dialogue between his explicit political statements and the images glimpsed, or nearly glimpsed, in his fiction's and nonfiction's other scenes.

"Inequality works," says Jacques Rancière, "to the extent that one 'believes' it, that one goes on using one's arms, eyes, and brains" as one always has. "This is what consensus means. And this is the way domination works."[85] Art is only redemptive to the extent that it changes how we live by changing what we can think, sense, and say. It is, in other words, essentially political. So too, in this way, is Wallace's art. His writing strives to access the core conditions under which we speak, sense, and think and to create new possibilities for speaking and sensing and thinking and relating to one another.[86] He does so through explicit argument and at the level of style, but also by rendering our shared other scenes – those semiconscious, peripheral, shaping fears and fantasies – tangible. Those scenes, and that style, is what can draw political experience back out of thought and onto the skin and into the senses. This means that Wallace didn't, and perhaps couldn't, have "a politics." Rather, Wallace's politics, perhaps like any topic in his work, asks to be read between its explicit and implicit incarnations, the fiction and the nonfiction, the clearly stated and the merely sensed.

Notes

1. Stanley Cavell, *The Claim of Reason: Wittgenstein, Skepticism, Morality, Tragedy* (New York: Oxford University Press, 1999), pp. 176–177.
2. Karl Marx, "Contributions to the Critique of Hegel's *Philosophy of Right*," in Robert C. Tucker (ed.), *The Marx-Engels Reader* (New York: Norton, 1978), p. 24.
3. D. T. Max, *Every Love Story Is a Ghost Story: A Life of David Foster Wallace* (New York: Viking, 2012), p. 25.
4. Gavon Laessig, "David Foster Wallace's Hilarious Letter to His College Newspaper," www.buzzfeed.com/gavon/david-foster-wallaces-hilarious-letter-to-his-col/, accessed February 10, 2017.

5. Adam Plunkett, "King of the Ghosts," https://nplusonemag.com/online-only/book-review/king-of-the-ghosts/, accessed February 10, 2017.

6. Max, *Every Love Story*, p. 133.

7. David Foster Wallace and Mark Costello, *Signifying Rappers* (New York: Back Bay Books, 2013), p. 133.

8. "David Foster Wallace," *Believer*, November 2003, www.believermag.com/issues/200311/?read=interview_wallace, accessed February 10, 2017.

9. David Foster Wallace and Brian A. Garner, *Quack This Way: David Foster Wallace and Bryan A. Garner Talk Language and Writing* (New York: RosePen Books, 2013), p. 15.

10. David Foster Wallace, "Just Asking," in *Both Flesh and Not: Essays* (New York: Little, Brown, 2012), pp. 322–323.

11. Walt Whitman, "O Captain! My Captain!" in Justin Kaplan (ed.), *Poetry and Prose* (Washington, DC: Library of America, 1982), l. 17.

12. Max, *Every Love Story*, p. 299.

13. Self-consciously so; see Lee Konstantinou, "The World of David Foster Wallace," in *boundary 2* (2013), p. 68.

14. Wallace, "Just Asking," p. 321.

15. See John Rawls, *A Theory of Justice* (Cambridge: Harvard Belknap, 1999), pp. 12–13; and *Political Liberalism: Expanded Edition* (New York: Columbia University Press, 2005), pp. 13–15.

16. Étienne Balibar, *Politics and the Other Scene*, (trans.) Christine Jones, James Swenson, and Chris Turner (New York: Verso, 2002), pp. xiii-xiv.

17. See, e.g., David Foster Wallace, *Infinite Jest* (Boston: Little, Brown, 1996), p. 37.

18. Ibid., p. 993, n. 24.

19. Peter Weiss, *The Persecution and Assassination of Jean-Paul Marat as Performed by the Inmates of the Asylum of Charenton Under the Direction of the Marquis de Sade*, (trans.) Geoffrey Skelton (New York: Atheneum, 1984), p. 107.

20. Wallace, *Infinite Jest*, p. 424.

21. Ibid., p. 429. Elsewhere during this time Wallace posited that equality can only come at the price of unbridled capitalism, as the wrenched allegory of democracy, commerce, and authoritarianism in his US Open piece suggests. Wallace, "Democracy and Commerce at the U.S. Open," in *Both Flesh and Not*, pp. 133, 146.

22. Wallace, *Infinite Jest*, p. 430.

23. Something perhaps foreclosed by the realist novel's emphasis on mundane probability and believability; see Amitav Ghosh, *The Great Derangement: Climate Change and the Unthinkable* (Chicago: University of Chicago Press, 2016), pp. 7–24.

24. David Foster Wallace, "Authority and American Usage," in *Consider the Lobster* (New York: Little, Brown, 2005), pp. 67, 69.

25. Ibid., p. 70.

26. Wallace, *Both Flesh and Not*, p. 78.

27. Ibid.

28. Carl Schmitt, *The Concept of the Political*, (trans.) George Schwab (Chicago: University of Chicago Press, 2007), p. 38.

29. Wallace, "Authority and American Usage," p. 72.

30. Ibid., p. 73.

31. Ibid., p. 78.
32. Ibid., pp. 113–114.
33. David Foster Wallace, "Up, Simba," in *Consider the Lobster*, p. 161.
34. On liberalism and sincerity, see Adam Kelly, "Dialectic of Sincerity: Lionel Trilling and David Foster Wallace," *Post45*, October 17, 2014.
35. David Foster Wallace, "Host," in *Consider the Lobster*, p. 343.
36. Ibid., p. 290.
37. Ibid., pp. 287–288.
38. Ibid., p. 284.
39. Wallace, "Deciderization," in David Foster Wallace (ed.), *The Best American Essays 2007* (New York: Houghton Mifflin, 2007), p. xiv.
40. Wallace, "Up, Simba," p. 186.
41. Ibid., p. 164.
42. Ibid.
43. Badiou's term for the twentieth century's impossible desire to touch or abstractly frame something's horrifying reality; see Alain Badiou, *The Century*, (trans.) Alberto Toscano (London: Polity, 2007).
44. Ibid., p. 174.
45. Ibid., p. 186.
46. Ibid., p. 234.
47. See N. Katherine Hayles, "The Illusion of Autonomy and the Fact of Recursivity: Virtual Ecologies, Entertainment, and *Infinite Jest*," *New Literary History* 30.3 (Summer 1999), p. 692.
48. See Jacques Derrida, *Rogues: Two Essays on Reason*, (trans.) Pascale-Anne Brault and Michael Naas (Stanford: Stanford University Press, 2005), pp. 13–15.
49. Wallace, "Just Asking," p. 22.
50. Wallace, *Infinite Jest*, pp. 421–422.
51. David Foster Wallace, "E Unibus Pluram: Television and U.S. Fiction," in *A Supposedly Fun Thing I'll Never Do Again: Essays and Arguments* (Boston: Little, Brown, 1997), p. 67.
52. Wallace, *Infinite Jest*, p. 422.
53. Ibid., p. 318.
54. See, too, Adam Kelly, "David Foster Wallace and the Novel of Ideas," in Marshall Boswell (ed.), *David Foster Wallace and "The Long Thing": New Essays on the Novels* (New York: Bloomsbury, 2013), pp. 11–17.
55. Wallace, *Infinite Jest*, p. 421.
56. Ibid., p. 424.
57. Wallace, "Interview with Michael Silverblatt," KCRW, 1996.
58. Wallace, *Infinite Jest*, pp. 82–83.
59. G. W. F. Hegel, *Philosophy of Right*, (trans.) Allen W. Wood (Cambridge: Cambridge University Press, 1991), p. 221; my emphasis.
60. Wallace, *Infinite Jest*, pp. 12; 1074, n. 322.
61. Ibid., p. 694.
62. Judith N. Shklar, *Freedom and Independence: A Study of the Political Ideas of Hegel's Phenomenology of Mind* (Cambridge: Cambridge University Press, 1976), pp. 131–132.

63. Sigmund Freud, *Totem and Taboo*, (trans.) James Strachey (New York: Norton, 1990), pp. 176–178.
64. For Hamlet's hysteria see Sigmund Freud, *Writings on Art and Literature* (Stanford: Stanford University Press, 1997), p. xii; the matter is somewhat less straightforward in Lacan.
65. Wallace, *Infinite Jest*, p. 256.
66. "The hysteric pushes the master … to the point where he or she can find the master's knowledge lacking." See Bruce Fink, *The Lacanian Subject: Between Language and Jouissance* (Princeton: Princeton University Press, 1996), p. 134; and Jacques Lacan, *The Other Side of Psychoanalysis, Seminar XVII*, (trans.) Russell Grigg (New York: Norton, 2007), p. 127. Relatedly: "The problem for the hysteric is how to distinguish what he or she is (his true desire) from what others see and desire in him or her"; see Slavoj Žižek, *How to Read Lacan* (New York: Norton, 2007), p. 36 – about which, see, e.g., "His Moms Avril hears her own echoes inside him and thinks what she hears is him" in Wallace, *Infinite Jest*, p. 694.
67. Ibid., pp. 906, 807.
68. Ibid., p. 256.
69. See Mark McGurl, "The Institution of Nothing: David Foster Wallace in the Program," *boundary2* 41.3 (Fall 2014), pp. 35–36.
70. Andrew Warren, "Modeling Community and Narrative in *Infinite Jest* and *The Pale King*," in Boswell (ed.), *David Foster Wallace*, esp. pp. 65–71.
71. Jean-Luc Nancy, *The Disavowed Community*, (trans.) Philip Armstrong (New York: Fordham University Press, 2016), pp. 60, 61.
72. Laura Miller, "Interview with David Foster Wallace," *Salon.com*, March 9, 1996, www.salon.com/1996/03/09/wallace_5/.
73. David Foster Wallace, *Brief Interviews with Hideous Men* (Boston: Little, Brown, 1999), pp. 155, 156, 157, 158, 159, 14.
74. Stanley Cavell, *Disowning Knowledge in Seven Plays of Shakespeare* (Cambridge: Cambridge University Press, 2003), p. 179.
75. Ibid., p. xii. Cavell's example is feminism, which is, with loneliness, *Brief Interviews'* chief theme.
76. David Foster Wallace, *The Pale King* (New York: Little, Brown, 2011), p. 130.
77. Wallace, *Infinite Jest*, p. 322; *Pale King*, p. 85.
78. See particularly David Herring, *David Foster Wallace: Fiction and Form* (London: Bloomsbury, 2016); and Stephen J. Burn's "'A Paradigm for the Life of Consciousness': *The Pale King*," Ralph Clare's "The Politics of Boredom and the Boredom of Politics in *The Pale King*," and Marshall Boswell's "Trickle-Down Citizenship: Taxes and Civic Responsibility in *The Pale King*," all in Boswell (ed.), *David Foster Wallace and "The Long Thing."*
79. Wallace, *Infinite Jest*, p. 318.
80. Wallace, *Pale King*, p. 178; "The bureaucrat must … deal with the actual state jesuitically" – Marx, p. 24.
81. Wallace, *Pale King*, p. 231.
82. Wallace, *Infinite Jest*, pp. 694, 800–808.
83. Wallace, *Pale King*, p. 389.
84. Ibid., p. 395.

85. Rancière and Honneth in Katia Genel and Jean-Philippe Deranty (eds.), *Recognition or Disagreement: A Critical Encounter on the Politics of Freedom, Equality, and Identity* (New York: Columbia University Press, 2016), p. 137.
86. One of Wallace's basic axioms, that everybody thinks and is equally capable of thought, is on this reading a thoroughly political stance (*IJ*, p. 203; "The Next Big Thing: Can a Downstate Author Withstand the Sensation of his 1,079-Page Novel?" by Mark Caro in Stephen J. Burn (ed.), *Conversations with David Foster Wallace*, (Jackson: University of Mississippi, 2012), p. 56; and *This Is Water*.

12

MATTHEW MULLINS

Wallace, Spirituality, and Religion

There are three stories in David Foster Wallace's collection *Brief Interviews with Hideous Men* in which characters experience what Zadie Smith calls "quasi-mystical moments, portraits of extreme focus and total relinquishment." She goes on to say that while many of us might be most comfortable describing these moments as meditation, "the right word is in fact *prayer*."[1] Why does prayer create more discomfort than meditation? Why would we prefer to think of Wallace as seeing promise in some vague form of spirituality rather than in a more traditionally religious ritual? Throughout his interviews, essays, and fiction, Wallace is preoccupied with our need to transcend the limits of our individual consciousness to combat loneliness, to empathize with others, and to avoid the various traps of solipsism. The church has historically been the locus of such transcendence. It has served not only as the site of theological instruction but also as the hub of communities where the many gather together as one, where self and neighbor meet. In his overview of the clashes between church and culture since the Enlightenment, Terry Eagleton recounts how we have sought to replace religion with everything from science to nationalism.[2] We have, it seems, looked elsewhere for the community and transcendence once assumed to be found in religion. Smith argues that "Wallace understood better than most that for the secular among us, art has become our best last hope of undergoing this experience."[3] She also insists, however, that his characters are not meditating but praying. Is Wallace merely looking for transcendence wherever he can find it, or is there something special about prayers said with knees bent and heads bowed?

In his well-known commencement address to Kenyon College graduates in 2005, later entitled *This Is Water*, Wallace argues that we all default to selfishness and that religion can be valuable because it can give us something to worship that is bigger than ourselves. "There is no such thing as not worshipping," he insists; "The only choice we get is *what* to worship. And an outstanding reason for choosing some sort of god or spiritual-type thing to worship – be it J. C. or Allah, be it Yahweh or the Wiccan mother-goddess or the Four Noble Truths or some infrangible set of ethical principles – is that pretty much anything else you worship will eat you alive."[4] It is clear throughout his work that Wallace saw some form of spirituality as desirable, but does this mean that he was a champion of religion or even a specific religious tradition? Is his writing religious? Is he a proponent or critic of the ambiguous "Higher Power" of the variety associated with Alcoholics Anonymous throughout *Infinite Jest*? Or is he invested in a generalized belief, faith, or transcendence? What is Wallace's view of spirituality?

The first step toward answering these questions is to clarify the terms spirituality, belief, faith, and religion. For the sake of this essay, I have tried to use these terms in ways Wallace uses them most consistently in his work. Spirituality, belief, and faith seem to go together. These three terms generally denote a kind of vague transcendence beyond the physical or commitment to such a transcendence. Religion, on the other hand, typically denotes something more specific, usually a particular, historical, organized tradition:

> If you're about 30, believing in something bigger than you is not a choice. You either do or you're a walking dead man, just going through the motions. Concepts like duty and fidelity may sound quaint but we've inherited the best and the worst, and we've got to make it up as we go along. I absolutely believe in something, even though I don't know what it is. And those friends of mine who are religious . . . I envy them because they don't have to think about it. You want to sleep with somebody who's not your wife? It's a sin and that's the end of it.[5]

There is a clear difference in this example between Wallace's idea of a generalized belief in "something bigger" and his notion of religion, which entails a recognizable tradition with a codified set of doctrines and moral guidelines. I make this distinction because it has significant implications for the prevailing scholarly understandings of his concern with spiritual things.

Scholars have typically described Wallace's relationship to faith and/or religion in one of three ways. First, some argue that Wallace's work is either resistant to or simply uninterested in the subject. Hubert Dreyfus and Sean Dorrance Kelly, for instance, claim that Wallace's writing has no serious spiritual vision.[6] D. T. Max, Wallace's biographer, is dismissive of spiritual concerns in the writer's life and writing. Max says of one of Wallace's many failed attempts to adopt religion that "Wallace's real religion was always language anyway. It alone could shape and hold multitudes; by comparison God's power was spindly."[7] However, these views are in the minority. The philosopher and theologian James K. A. Smith counters Dreyfus and Kelly by arguing that they "confuse

[Wallace's] postmodern playfulness and reflexivity with an amoral stance of cynicism or even nihilism,"[8] and he points out that "some have faulted Max for not taking Wallace's own religious seeking seriously."[9] Like Smith, most scholars maintain that there is more to Wallace's spirituality than apathy or nihilism.

Martin Brick and Michael J. O'Connell represent a second approach that treats Wallace as overtly religious. For his part, Brick claims that while Wallace's work steadily progresses "toward a Christian outlook" over time, it also bears the marks of an abiding spirituality from the beginning.[10] O'Connell goes even further, not only placing Wallace "alongside the long tradition of Christian, specifically Catholic literature," but also contending "that it makes sense to think of him as a Christian writer."[11] As with the first view, only a few Wallace scholars take this position. For the majority, Wallace is neither nihilist nor Christian. Instead, most read him as undoubtedly committed to faith, but not to the orthodoxies of any particular religion. For instance, when Zadie Smith analyzes a prayer in one of Wallace's stories, she notes that the prayer is "unmoored, without its usual object, God."[12] Prayer itself is more important than its object; the form of religion supersedes the content. As Marshall Boswell puts it: "Wallace approaches the concept of God, or rather of gods in general, pragmatically."[13] Channeling Wallace himself in *The Pale King*, Boswell traces this notion of pragmatic belief back to William James, as do others.[14] In this assessment, what is important is not the specific content of belief but rather the outcomes produced by that belief. In other words, belief itself is what counts.

Scholars have revived the notion of belief as an end in itself as a way of talking about religion in the works of postmodern writers. In her book *Postmodern Belief*, Amy Hungerford argues that the kind of belief without theological content that was popularized by nineteenth-century figures like Matthew Arnold and Ralph Waldo Emerson becomes, in the late twentieth century, "both a way to maintain religious belief rather than critique its institutions and a way to buttress the authority of the literature that seeks to imagine such belief. Belief without content becomes ... a hedge against the inescapable fact of pluralism."[15] Hungerford's analysis builds on John McClure's notion of "partial faiths," which positions some writers as affirming "the urgent need for a turn toward the religious even as they reject (in most instances) the familiar dream of a full return to an authoritative faith. The paths they chart do not, for the most part, lead back into the domain of conventional religious dwelling, where life unfolds under a sacred canopy of ontological givens, moral codes, and organized community."[16] For McClure and Hungerford, writers like Wallace belong not to the literary legacy of

Christianity, but to a long line of thinkers who recognize the pragmatic or cultural value of religion in general.

In short, those who reject or dismiss Wallace's spiritual convictions underread him, and those who would argue that he is a Christian writer overread him. He more properly belongs to the tradition of belief for belief's sake in which most scholars have located him. However, the traditions and practices of particular religions, especially Christianity, are so endemic to Wallace's cultural context and personal journey that they necessarily play a more significant part in framing his views of faith and spirituality than some scholars acknowledge. When Wallace turns to religious practice as an antidote for cultural malaise, it's worth noting that the most accessible traditions around him were almost always branches or offshoots of Christianity. Consequently, Wallace's faith in faith itself can best be outlined in three themes shaped largely by Christian practices voided of their particular meaning: conversion, worship, and community. The brief analyses that follow explore these themes and consider their implications for Wallace's vision of spirituality and religion for our everyday lives.

Conversion

D. T. Max recounts a few times in Wallace's life when he considered converting to Catholicism. On one occasion, after going through an initiation class, he was on the doorstep of conversion but simply could not move from an intellectual understanding of religion to a spiritual belief. "Faith was something he could admire in others but never quite countenance for himself," Max explains.[17] In this case, the generalized terms "belief" and "faith" denote belief or faith in the tenets of Catholicism. Wallace's struggle with conversion raises a number of important questions about belief that he wrestles with throughout his work. Is belief a purely intellectual endeavor, or does it involve something else, something like the heart? Can one understand something without believing it or believe something without understanding it? Does belief precede practice, or does practice produce belief? Wallace wanted desperately to believe but struggled with the idea of conversion, or moving from unbelief to belief. It seems he eventually came to think of conversion not as an inciting incident that one can unilaterally choose but as an outcome of practices and attitudes developed over time, an event that can only be seen in hindsight.

Wallace's frustration with conversion is apparent not only in his life as told by Max but also in his writing about others' lives, as in his review of Joseph Frank's magisterial biography of Dostoevsky. The review does what most reviews do, but it also contains a series of existential authorial interruptions presumably brought on by the themes of Dostoevsky's life and work. For instance, only a few paragraphs in, Wallace writes:

> **Am I a good person? Deep down, do I even really want to be a good person, or do I only want to *seem* like a good person so that people (including myself) will approve of me? Is there a difference? How do I ever actually know whether I'm bullshitting myself, morally speaking?**[18]

In various religious traditions, such questions are intended to demonstrate human inadequacy and drive the questioner to see the need for intervention from a higher power. These interruptions seem to follow this path as they turn toward Christianity: "What exactly does 'faith' mean? As in 'religious faith,' 'faith in God,' etc." And later, "Does this guy Jesus Christ's life have something to teach me even if I don't, or can't, believe he was divine? What am I supposed to make of the claim that someone who was God's relative, and so could have turned the cross into a planter or something with just a word, still voluntarily let them nail him up there, and died?"[19] A near-death experience in Dostoevsky's life gives the Russian writer the necessary motivation to convert to Christianity, albeit his own idiosyncratic form, as Wallace notes. But as Max tells us, Wallace seems to have been unable to convert.

Rather than abandoning conversion, however, Wallace revises it by cutting away the particulars of religious orthodoxy and rewriting it as a transformation from unthinking self-centeredness to thoughtful empathy. This revised doctrine of conversion is perhaps clearest in *This Is Water*, where the kind of conversion to thoughtfulness that a liberal arts education is supposed to incite can change one's life:

> If you've really learned how to think, how to pay attention, then you will know you have other options. It will actually be within your power to experience a crowded, hot, slow, consumer-hell-type situation as not only meaningful, but sacred, on fire with the same force that lit the stars – compassion, love, the subsurface unity of all things.[20]

Such power is only possible for those who have converted from default selfishness to hard-won empathy. Robert K. Bolger describes conversion in *This Is Water* by arguing that "Wallace ... presents a sort of tripartite theology that begins with an account of the innate problem of human selfishness (an interpretation of the 'sinful' human condition), presents a practical way to begin to overcome this 'fallen state' (an interpretation of 'conversion'), and finally offers suggestions on how we can begin to see the divine presence in the mundane stuff of the world."[21] Thus, Wallace's idea of conversion is fundamentally Christian in form. However, it is not so in content. Dying to self is a central orthodoxy of Christianity, but conversion in the Christian tradition entails belief in the sacrifice of Jesus Christ as the only atonement for sins like selfishness. Such exclusivity is absent from Wallace's vision of conversion.

Chris Fogle's conversion from self-proclaimed "wastoid" to aspiring IRS agent in the posthumously published novel *The Pale King* illustrates both the revised form of Christian conversion and the notion that conversion is less a conscious intellectual choice and more the product of circumstances, practices, and habits. Fogle experiences something like a conversion when he accidentally wanders into the wrong classroom during an exam review in college. Narrating the story years later, Fogle juxtaposes his own life-changing event with that of his roommate's girlfriend's conversion to evangelical Christianity but admits in hindsight that "it was ultimately much more like the evangelist girlfriend with the boots' own experience than I could have ever admitted at the time."[22] Although Fogle is converted from his wastoid nihilism to a life of motivation, hard work, and gainful employment, there is no need for him to embrace any particular religious orthodoxy. The conversion itself is enough. The language and form of Christian conversion gives Fogle (and Wallace) a way of talking about this experience, but the content of Christianity is something he avoids. Fogle's conversion produces a feeling in him that changes his attitude and actions, and although he acknowledges that his experience seems just as unlikely-divine as the roommate's girlfriend's, he explains that "a feeling is a feeling, nor can you argue with results."[23] As Boswell points out, Fogle's conversion recalls Williams James's pragmatic view of religion because it values the results of belief more than the particular content.[24] But he also goes on to note that Fogle's conversion "is not instantaneous." Fogle's conversion, along with Wallace's exhortations at Kenyon College and his fascination with Dostoevsky's faith, suggests that Wallace did not reject conversion as such but that he rejected the view of conversion as a singular moment in which one simply changes one's mind.

For Wallace, conversion is not merely an intellectual phenomenon. We do not change our minds and consequently change our behaviors and habits. Instead, conversion is equal parts epiphanic transformation and daily ritual. He examines this paradox most famously through Don Gately's long battle with belief in a "higher power" in *Infinite Jest*:

> How can you pray to a "God" you believe only morons believe in, still? – but the old guys say it doesn't yet matter what you believe or don't believe, Just Do It they say, and like a shock-trained organism without any kind of inde-pendent human will you do exactly like you're told, you keep coming and

coming, nightly, and now you take pains not to get booted out of the squalid halfway house you'd at first tried so hard to get discharged from, you Hang In and Hang In, meeting after meeting ... and at this point you've started to have an almost classic sort of Blind Faith in the older guys ... and now if the older guys say Jump you ask them to hold their hand at the desired height, and now they've got you, and you're free.[25]

Wallace's spiritual vision values practice, or what theologians would call liturgy. Liturgy is the public ritual that forms one's personal belief. To understand how Wallace treats spirituality in his work, we must pay attention not only to doctrines, beliefs, and principles that appeal to the mind but also to the liturgies that appeal to the body. Most spiritual traditions would call these liturgies forms of worship.

Worship

Wallace's work helps us understand worship in two different senses. First, worship is something we give. It is attention or time we ascribe to something. Second, worship can be conscious and unconscious. We not only give our attention and time but also give it constantly regardless of how aware we are of our own liturgies. Nowhere in Wallace's writing is this clearer than in the bodies of various white-collar workers that populate *The Pale King*. Everywhere they go they appear, as Chris Fogle describes his father, "slightly bent forward at the waist, at a slight angle, which added to the sense of tension or always walking into some kind of wind."[26] Or, as IRS agents are described in chapter 25, "Most sit up straight but lean forward at the waist, which reduces neck fatigue."[27] Even the ghost of a former examiner retains this posture: "The man moved slightly back and forth like his waist was hinged."[28] These characters do not walk into their jobs on the first day and decide to bow to their work. On the contrary, their work requires that they bow, and this posture becomes an integral part of who they are over time. Wallace focuses on how our rituals, the habits we engage in on a daily basis, form us in fundamental ways. They make us into certain kinds of people. There is no value judgment in any of these scenes. The point is that regardless of what our habits are, they will become our rituals, and rituals become liturgies – worship practices – that form who we are.

Wallace seems to have known and practiced aesthetically what philosopher and theologian James K. A. Smith maintains: that we are *embodied creatures*.[29] To understand how our affective, noncognitive practices and desires shape us as humans, we must shift "the center of gravity of human identity from the head (or more specifically, a disembodied mind) to the heart, which is more closely tethered to our sensible, affective nature. ... We feel our way around our world more than we think our way through it."[30] In a very serious sense, you become what you worship, what you desire. Smith would say, "You are what you love." In the philosophical tradition, this phenomenon is often studied under the rubric of habit. In *Nichomachean Ethics*, for instance, Aristotle claims that "an individual is responsible for being unjust, because he has cheated, and for being intemperate, because he has passed his time in drinking and the like; for each type of activity produces the corresponding sort of person."[31] Our habits form us. We become what we do, or, what our worship practices make us to be. And we are all worshipers. For Wallace, spirituality is not simply a matter of choosing to believe or worship but becoming aware of how our daily habits have shaped us into certain kinds of worshipers.

This view of worship can be frustrating for those who want to see faith exclusively as a set of principles or doctrines, or those who want to reduce religion to a system that a person can either choose or refuse to believe. Such frustrations play out constantly in *Infinite Jest* as the various members of the Ennet House recovery program wrestle with the Higher Power they hear about at Alcoholics Anonymous. Geoffrey Day, a professor, is the perfect example of an intellectual who wants to reduce the spiritual dimension of recovery to downloading a set of beliefs into his mind. As James K. A. Smith argues, "What's most maddening for [Day] is that his supposedly superior intellect is not prized in this environment, because the intellect isn't the primary site of (trans)formation. ... Day thinks the meetings are a means of dispensing the requisite information, a site of some propositional revelation; he misses the fact that what's redemptive is *the going*, not what he *gets*."[32] It is the practice, the habit, the ritual of going to the meetings, of Gately hitting his knees and asking for help every morning and evening, "whether he believes he's talking to Anything/body or not" that enables him to "somehow get ... through that day clean."[33] Faith, for Wallace, is irreducible to conscious belief in a system of doctrine because it is also fundamentally about how our daily practices form us into worshipers with access to dimensions of ourselves that we did not know we had.

The white-collar workers of *The Pale King* do not become the kind of people who can bend at the waist with intense focus by deciding to do so. It is their work, and the daily habits that their work requires, that forms them into such people. Wallace describes even such mundane practices as transcendent. One especially focused examiner, Shane Drinion, achieves a gravity-defying level of focus even beyond the walls of the office. Deep in conversation with the beautiful Meredith Rand at a bar, we see how Drinion's professional posture shapes his social interactions as well. The narrator tells us that

"Shane Drinion is leaning slightly forward. His bottom is now almost 1.75 inches off the chair seat; his work shoes' gumlike soles, darkened at the perimeter by the same process that darkens pencils' erasers, swing slightly just above the tile floor."[34] Drinion bears the trademark bodily posture of his discipline, he's bent forward at the waist, and he has achieved such a level of focus that he is levitating. Drinion does not make a conscious decision to become the kind of person who can focus to the point of levitating. He becomes this kind of person as the result of long hours and years of intense focus.

There is some resonance with Buddhism on this point. The notion that it is our practices and not our consciousness that drives our spiritual selves is a somewhat reductive way of characterizing Zen Buddhism, a subject that Max tells us interested Wallace for a time. When Wallace sought a reading list on Zen Buddhism from a young reader named Christopher Hamacher, Hamacher "told him don't read, just do: 'It's absolutely wonderful that you don't "know" anything about zen.'" Wallace himself seems to have struggled with this advice much as Geoffrey Day struggles with AA: "It was hard for Wallace to understand that Buddhism wasn't a course you tried to ace."[35] Such struggles reveal the need for the support that can only be found in community. When we suffer, when we need encouragement, when we need to see beyond our own problems and victories, only a community can give us what we need. Wallace needed Hamacher to tell him to stop trying to figure out how to meditate and just do it. But it's also the necessity of community that carries Wallace's view of faith away from a religious tradition like Buddhism. True spirituality, for Wallace, is not a matter of going deep inside oneself and transcending this mortal coil into the blissful beyond. Spirituality is a matter of transcending the self to imagine its interconnectivity with others. We cannot worship without the support of community.

Community

Wallace wrote and spoke a great deal about empathy. In his interviews, essays, and fiction, he maintains that his goal is to get us to think outside our own heads, to imagine the experiences of others. Perhaps this is why his spiritual sensibility is so attuned to, well, our senses. After all, how can we imagine the experiences of others if we do not understand our own experiences? How can we develop a desire not to hurt others if we do not know the experience of hurt ourselves? This kind of spiritual growth cannot happen in isolation. Community is necessary. Community is especially important to Wallace's spiritual vision in two ways. First, community seems indispensable to the cultivation of faith. Second, community seems to keep faith alive in times of trial. *Infinite Jest* provides helpful examples of both of these aspects.

In the world of *Infinite Jest*, isolation almost invariably leads to trouble. It is when the characters in recovery at Ennet House sneak off on their own that they are most tempted to relapse. It is Hal's lone hours in the tunnels beneath Enfield Tennis Academy that drive him deeper into the recesses of his own psyche until he is trapped alone in his own head even in a room full of people. O'Connell contrasts Gately's recovery with Hal's to demonstrate how Gately's communalism leads to greater success than Hal's isolationism. "Gately only comes to ask the God he doesn't believe in to help him because other, more experienced members of AA encourage him to do so," O'Connell argues; "No one gets there alone."[36] This reading resonates both with Wallace's view of worship and with Katherine Hayles's insistence on the importance of community in the novel. Hayles points out that, for Gately, "the AA routines seem magically to have the power to release him from his addiction; he is more surprised than anyone when days and then weeks pass without him even thinking about his Substance of choice."[37] For Hayles, such conversions are not only the results of routines-turned-rituals and not only reserved for those in recovery. Arriving at belief, truth, or what she terms "authenticity," is a broader theme of the book in its examination of our desire for distraction through entertainment: "Authenticity in this vision is not about escaping from the realm of the social, but rather about recognizing the profound interconnections that bind us all together, human actors and nonhuman life forms, intelligent machines and intelligent people. We escape from Entertainment not by going to the woods but by recognizing our responsibilities to one another."[38] Without community, conversion and worship seem unlikely if not impossible.

Community also helps keep the fire of belief burning in arctic weather. Nowhere is this clearer in Wallace's work than in another famous scene from *Infinite Jest* in which we learn the backstory of Barry Loach, head trainer at Enfield Tennis Academy. Barry's mother had wanted one of her children to enter the Roman Catholic clergy, but they all take other paths or tragically pass away until only Barry and one brother remain. Fortunately for Barry, his brother, "brimming over with abstract love and an innate faith in the indwelling goodness of all men's souls," decides to enter the church. But after a sharp spiritual decline "had killed whatever spark of inspired faith he'd had in the higher possibilities and perfectibility of man," it seems the lot will fall to Barry. In an effort to persuade his brother not to give up, Barry accepts a challenge to not shower and play the part of a homeless person standing outside the Park Street T-station near Boston Common asking, not for spare change, but for passersby to touch him. When no one reaches out,

Barry's own faith flickers; he "was dangerously close to disappearing forever into the fringes and dregs of metro Boston street life." But along comes a 14-year-old Mario Incandenza, who shakes Barry's "own fuliginous hand, which led through a convoluted but kind of heartwarming and faith-reaffirming series of circumstances to B. Loach."[39] It is the reaching across space, the human touch, the connection between the two people that begins to restore Barry's faith and ultimately brings him into the community of E.T.A. Faith, it seems, dies in a vacuum but flourishes in the interdependence of community.

Wallace warns against and attempts to redress the consequences of solipsism throughout his work. Many of his most important themes are somehow connected to solipsism: loneliness, entertainment, drug use, mundanity, and suicide are only a few examples. His interest in religion is also related to solipsism, and not only because of his emphasis on community. Wallace seems to have feared solipsism for two basic reasons. First, it prevents us from imagining the experiences of others and thus makes us more likely to hurt them. Second, it strands us on the islands of our individual minds and leaves us lonely. These fears were certainly personal. Jeffrey Severs and D. T. Max have both shown how important Wallace's AA group was in supporting him, giving him the opportunity to support others, and providing a good example of community against which to critique more instrumental models.[40] Wallace himself gives us glimpses into his own communities in essays such as "The View from Mrs. Thompson's" and "A Supposedly Fun Thing I'll Never Do Again." In the latter piece, he builds alliances with total strangers around daily meals on a cruise ship. This impromptu community offers respite from the loneliness of his cabin, where it would be easy to lie in bed all day and watch movies. Instead, he more often than not joins his new friends around the table and narrates his best attempts to empathize with those whom he dislikes. He does this not only because he feels the need to perform some amazing act of will but also because he is lonely, a word David Lipsky remarks that Wallace will "use a lot" throughout their own weekend together at the end of the *Infinite Jest* book tour.[41]

Community brings us back to the claim that Wallace's faith is not concerned with a particular set of doctrines but with a generalized belief in something larger than oneself. The "something larger" in this case is community itself. If the ragtag cast of *Infinite Jest* teaches us anything, it's that community will not necessarily save you, but it also seems to suggest that it's virtually impossible to be saved without community. The question of salvation, as we have seen with Wallace, does not have to be a question about the eternal state of one's soul. What does it mean to be "saved"? Saved from what? Saved for what? In Wallace's spiritual vision we are not saved from sin but from solipsism. We are not saved from licentiousness but from loneliness, self-absorption, and, ultimately, even self-destruction as worshipping the wrong things will "eat you alive."[42] We are saved, not for our own sake, but for others, for the sake of a community in which we are each a piece rather than the point. What does this mean for our everyday lives? For Wallace, the salvation offered to each of us through our own communities comes via the golden rule: trying to imagine the experiences and to regard the pain of others before we judge, speak, and act. He wants us to consider the complexity of our own lives as an indicator of the nuanced and complicated lives of others. He wants us to touch the untouchable, to worship something other than ourselves. He wants us to do unto others as we would have them do unto us. How fitting that at the heart of Wallace's spirituality we find a principle that is both unquestionably moral and historically religious.

Notes

1. Zadie Smith, *Changing My Mind: Occasional Essays* (New York: Penguin, 2009), p. 295.
2. Terry Eagleton, *Culture and the Death of God* (New Haven, CT: Yale University Press, 2014).
3. Smith, *Changing My Mind*, p. 295.
4. David Foster Wallace, *This Is Water: Some Thoughts, Delivered on a Significant Occasion, about Living a Compassionate Life* (New York: Little, Brown, 2009), pp. 99, 101–102.
5. David Foster Wallace, "1458 Words," *Speak Magazine* 2 (Spring 1996), p. 42.
6. Hubert Dreyfus and Sean Dorrance Kelly, *All Things Shining: Reading the Western Classics to Find Meaning in a Secular Age* (New York: Free Press, 2011), p. 57.
7. D. T. Max, *Every Love Story Is a Ghost Story: A Life of David Foster Wallace* (New York: Viking, 2012), p. 166.
8. James K. A. Smith, "David Foster Wallace to the Rescue," *First Things* (March 2013), p. 26.
9. Ibid., p. 29.
10. Martin Brick, "A Postmodernist's Progress: Thoughts on Spirituality across the David Foster Wallace Canon," *Christianity and Literature* 64. 1 (Autumn 2014), p. 71.
11. Michael J. O'Connell, "'Your Temple Is Self and Sentiment': David Foster Wallace's Diagnostic Novels," *Christianity and Literature* 64. 3 (June 2015), p. 267.
12. Smith, *Changing My Mind*, p. 295.
13. Marshall Boswell, *Understanding David Foster Wallace* (Columbia: University of South Carolina Press, 2003), p. 146.
14. Because Wallace has an essay by William James projected on a screen in the class in which Chris Fogle has his epiphanic conversion experience, Boswell, along with others, has persuasively argued that Wallace can be helpfully

compared to James, who saw religion as "a positive function in human life," even if specific traditions or orthodoxies themselves are beyond reason. Marshall Boswell, "Trickle-Down Citizenship: Taxes and Civic Responsibility in David Foster Wallace's *The Pale King*," *Studies in the Novel* 44.4 (Winter 2012), p. 474; David Foster Wallace, *The Pale King* (New York: Little, Brown, 2011), pp. 211–222; Robert K. Bolger, "A Less 'Bullshitty' Way to Live: The Pragmatic Spirituality of David Foster Wallace," in Robert K. Bolger and Scott Korb (eds.), *Gesturing Toward Reality: David Foster Wallace and Philosophy* (New York: Bloomsbury, 2014), p. 33; Robert C. Hamilton, "'Constant Bliss in Every Atom': Tedium and Transcendence in David Foster Wallace's *The Pale King*," *Arizona Quarterly* 70.4 (Winter 2014), pp. 171–173.

15. Amy Hungerford, *Postmodern Belief: American Literature and Religion since 1960* (Princeton, NJ: Princeton University Press, 2010), p. xiv.
16. John McClure, *Partial Faiths: Postsecular Fiction in the Age of Pynchon and Morrison* (Athens,: University of Georgia Press, 2007), p. 6.
17. Max, *Every Love Story*, p. 251.
18. David Foster Wallace, *Consider the Lobster* (New York: Little, Brown, 2006), p. 257.
19. Ibid., pp. 259, 269–270.
20. Wallace, *This Is Water*, pp. 91–93.
21. Bolger, "A Less 'Bullshitty' Way to Live," p. 33.
22. David Foster Wallace, *The Pale King* (New York: Little, Brown, 2011), p. 222.
23. Ibid., p. 232.
24. Boswell, "Trickle-Down Citizenship," p. 474.
25. David Foster Wallace, *Infinite Jest* (Boston: Little, Brown, 1996), pp. 350–351.
26. Wallace, *The Pale King*, p. 177.
27. Ibid., p. 314. Ralph Clare has compared these characters from *The Pale King* to the early Christian monks known as the Desert Fathers in "The Politics of Boredom and the Boredom of Politics in David Foster Wallace's *The Pale King*," *Studies in the Novel* 44.4 (Winter 2012).
28. Ibid., p. 385.
29. James K. A. Smith, *Desiring the Kingdom: Worship, Worldview, and Cultural Formation* (Grand Rapids, MI: Baker Academic, 2009), p. 57.
30. Ibid.
31. Aristotle, *Nichomachean Ethics*, 2nd ed., (trans.) Terence Erwin (Indianapolis, IN: Hackett, 1999), p. 38.
32. James K. A. Smith, *Imagining the Kingdom: How Worship Works* (Grand Rapids, MI: Baker Academic, 2013), p. 25.
33. Wallace, *Infinite Jest*, p. 443.
34. Wallace, *The Pale King*, pp. 499–500.
35. Max, *Every Love Story*, p. 291. Perhaps this is why so many of the characters in *Infinite Jest* struggle to understand and embrace the advice of the guru Lyle, who sits perched atop the weight-room towel dispenser waiting for opportunities to share his "fitness-guru wisdom." Wallace, *Infinite Jest*, p. 129.
36. O'Connell, "'Your Temple,'" p. 277.

37. N. Katherine Hayles, "The Illusion of Autonomy and the Fact of Recursivity: Virtual Ecologies, Entertainment, and *Infinite Jest*," *New Literary History* 30.3 (Summer 1999), p. 693.

38. Ibid., p. 696.

39. Wallace, *Infinite Jest*, pp. 967–971.

40. Jeffrey Severs, "Collision, Illinois: David Foster Wallace and the Value of Insurance," *MFS: Modern Fiction Studies* 62.1 (Spring 2016), pp. 140–141; Max, *Every Love Story Is a Ghost Story*, p. 263.

41. David Lipsky, *Although of Course You End Up Becoming Yourself* (New York: Broadway, 2010), p. 12.

42. Wallace, *This Is Water*, p. 102.

13

LUCAS THOMPSON

Wallace and Race

In recent years, representations of race throughout Wallace's work have come under increased scrutiny. Indeed, a consensus has slowly built up around Wallace's flaws on this issue, with many critics taking him to task over various problematic portrayals and asides in his fiction and literary journalism. Samuel Cohen, for instance, has written about "feeling ... a little let down" (239) over Wallace's dismissal of political correctness, Mark McGurl has drawn attention to Wallace's troubling "investment in the symbolic value of ordinary whiteness" (49), and Clare Hayes-Brady has argued that "issues of diversity are one of the major weaknesses of his writing" (168).[1] In 2014 Tara Morrissey and I also addressed some of "the undeniably problematic outcomes of [Wallace's] investment in race throughout *Signifying Rappers*," in an argument about the role of whiteness and the way the text fits within Wallace's larger literary project.[2] In short, the critical consensus is that though Wallace was highly self-aware about his own racial identity – referring to himself in one essay, for instance, as "resoundingly and in all ways white" – this self-awareness was not enough to prompt him to rethink the role of race in his work.[3] In fact, since so much of Wallace's work dramatizes the limitations of self-awareness, this particular failure might be viewed as an unintentional vindication of his own principle.

The claim that Wallace had serious blind spots and failings when addressing matters of race is now a critical commonplace, since several of his texts do indeed perpetuate racist tropes or at the very least betoken a problematic approach to racial difference. The Wardine section of *Infinite Jest*, for instance, has been read by many critics as a disconcerting portrayal of identity, as have many of the other more explicitly racialized portrayals through the novel, including the characterizations of Clenette Henderson, Alfonso Parias-Carbo, Audern Tallat-Kelpsa, Ruth van Cleve, and Yolanda Willis. For McGurl, the "dialect sections of *Infinite Jest*," in which such characters are placed, "have difficulty differentiating themselves from the long tradition of disrespectful racial mimicry in US culture."[4] Beyond the

Wardine section, Wallace uses similarly broad brushstrokes in depicting other non-American or non-white characters throughout the novel, including Middle Easterners, Hispanics, Europeans, and Africans. Indeed, the representations of non-white identity throughout the novel often cohere with Toni Morrison's observation on white novelists' tendency to invoke black characters in ways that are "sometimes sinister, frequently lazy, [and with] almost always predictable employment of racially informed and determined chains."[5] *Infinite Jest* has little interest in portraying people of color in any real depth. Many black characters, for instance, do not move beyond the ontological status of Mario's incongruous, and totally unexplained, doo-wopping black puppets in his film of Johnny Gentle's rise to power. (Mario chooses to "represent President Gentle's cabinet as made up mostly of tall-coiffured black-girl puppets in shiny imbricate-sequin dresses."[6]) In fact, the near absence of developed non-white characters in *Infinite Jest* could be seen as a failure to live up to James Incandenza's emphasis on what he calls "figurants" – those peripheral figures who hover around the edges of mainstream films like so much "human furniture."[7]

Yet in the rare instances in which Wallace's non-white characters move beyond figurant status, the results can be even more troubling. This is certainly the case for *The Pale King*'s Chahla Neti-Neti, whom the character David Wallace speculates is either "upper-caste Indian or Pakistani," but who is later revealed to be "Persian" (287).[8] The novel's physical description of this "ethnic lady" (290) conforms with pejorative pop-culture representations. Neti-Neti has "a creamily dark Persian woman's complexion," for instance, that appears "dark grey" in her IRS badge photo, which David Wallace associates with the appearance of an animal. Her complexion, he tells us, "exaggerated the wide-setness of her eyes so that in the ID photo she looked almost like a puma or some other strange kind of feline predator" (288–289). Neti-Neti is also portrayed as having a subservient stance toward Western men: Wallace describes her "initial greeting" as "verbally effusive and deferential" (289). Wallace also has no qualms about invoking cross-cultural "gender codes, which I knew were especially rigid in the Middle East," or with portraying Neti-Neti as sexually promiscuous, noting that "she seemed to emerge from a different wiggler's housing unit almost every morning during the month of August 1985" (296). And since she later performs fellatio on David Wallace, mistaking him for a higher-ranking IRS agent, the portrayal here brazenly perpetuates various Orientalist tropes, participating in what Edward Said describes as the "remarkably persistent . . . association between the Orient and sex." Indeed, the characterization of Neti-Neti reveals the ongoing relevance of Said's observation about pop-culture representations of "the Arab," as being "associated either with lechery or bloodthirsty dishonesty" (286). While Brian McHale has read this latter scene as a reimagined *"displacement"* of an encounter in Thomas Pynchon's *Gravity's Rainbow*, attempting to defuse some of Wallace's racial insensitivity, it is nonetheless a deeply offensive portrayal.[9] Wallace's depiction seems particularly misguided in a post-9/11 political climate wherein the representation of Middle Eastern, Islamic characters by a white American novelist already has such high stakes, let alone when the representation is such a pejorative one.

Although some of these examples may appear to be fairly clear-cut failures, showing an odd indifference to causing offense, the way that we interpret these failures in light of Wallace's wider body of work has not yet been thought through. In fact, many readers seem unsure of what to make of them. Do we give Wallace the benefit of the doubt, suggesting that he unwittingly offended due to certain points of blindness around representations of race? Is our first impulse to excuse some of these more obvious failures by seeing him as the product of a certain cultural moment, in which such portrayals could go unnoticed and thus unquestioned? Or do we instead take a harder line, wondering why Wallace, who had such sensitive and nuanced perspectives on other identity positions – regional identity, for instance, along with ideological and generational affinities – never seemed to devote a great deal of thought to the racial politics of contemporary US culture? My point is that we are still coming to terms with the racial content of Wallace's work. As such, many readers and critics are unsure of precisely how to frame his approach to race in relation to his broader artistic project.

While McGurl has made a productive gesture in this direction by situating Wallace's perspective on race in relation to his "embrace of institutional authority," there are several other preoccupations and recurring techniques that need to be brought into the critical discussion. This chapter opens up a new critical framework by exploring how various strategies of racial self-examination play out within Wallace's work and showing how his writing often shifts the interpretive demands relating to issues of race onto the reader. It also shows how various strategies of racial provocation play out in his fiction and literary journalism, and picks up on a persistent attempt at eliding racial difference, inspired in part by a long engagement with the work of Joseph Campbell. My strategy throughout is to take the long view, looking at broader issues that are explored across Wallace's artistic project, rather than focusing solely on isolated instances of failure or insensitivity. This approach thus folds some of the more problematic portrayals and asides that other critics have picked up on into a larger perspective on Wallace's work. My ultimate aim is not to try to rescue Wallace from accusations of racial insensitivity, or sideline those who have made such accusations, but instead to complicate the critical conversation concerning Wallace's approach to race.

Racial Self-Examinations

One way of reframing Wallace's writing on race is to read it as an attempt to represent and provoke moments of intense self-examination. There is an important section in "A Supposedly Fun Thing," for instance, where Wallace notices how "a lot of the people waiting – Caribbeanish clothing notwithstanding – look Jewish to me, and I'm ashamed to catch myself thinking that I can determine Jewishness from people's appearance."[10] Here, Wallace watches his own stream of consciousness as it moves in an unflattering direction, catching a racist mechanism in flagrante delicto. His sense of mortification is palpable, but to his credit, Wallace doesn't shy away from reporting such shortcomings to readers, despite the negative light it sheds on his journalistic persona. He later reinforces the point by reflecting on how being made aware of his own Americanness mirrors those unwelcome moments in which his whiteness is made visible:

> I've barely been out of the U.S.A. before, and never as part of a high-income herd, and in port – even up here above it all on Deck 12, just watching – I'm newly and unpleasantly conscious of being an American, the same way I'm always suddenly conscious of being white every time I'm around nonwhite people.[11]

The analogy here implies that the sudden awareness of one's racial identity is a deeply unpleasant one – an unwelcome intrusion that punctures one form of structural privilege. Such passages go some way toward explaining Wallace's reluctance to think at length about questions of race. If even acknowledging the fact of one's whiteness is an unpleasant act, then reflecting on its implications is hardly going to be more enjoyable. The footnote appended to this sentence reinforces the point, with Wallace noting that his realization on the cruise replicates a more general cognitive process. "For me," he admits, "public places on the U.S. East Coast are full of these nasty little moments of racist observation and then internal P.C. backlash."[12] Registering such "nasty little moments" of racism within his prose might not be enough to render Wallace a paragon of racial sensitivity, but it does speak to a broader sense of personal integrity, of attempting to lay bare one's own cognitive processes in an honest exchange with the reader. Indeed, Wallace's commitment to identifying his own shortcomings on many issues is done unsparingly, signaling a willingness to expose many of the more unflattering aspects of his internal monologue. *Signifying Rappers*, for instance, Wallace's early collaborative book on hip-hop, follows precisely this method, with many of his chapters exploring hip-hop's unique ability to provoke discomforting reflections on the listener's own racial positionality and gesturing toward some of the political and aesthetic implications that this positionality entails.[13]

This strategy demonstrates the subtle and insidious role that racialized assumptions have over our thoughts and actions, with Wallace's dramatization of such moments – in both his fiction and nonfiction – having the potential to prompt similar self-examinations on the part of his readers. Revealingly, Wallace understood his readership to be "mostly white, upper middle or upper class, [and] *obscenely* well educated," implying that the same kinds of racially problematic discoveries he could locate in himself would in all likelihood map on to his readers.[14] Wallace seems drawn to precisely these moments of sudden realization on race, which have the power to remind a predominately white readership of their own racial status, by making whiteness visible and thus raising it as an object for analysis. The short story "Oblivion," for instance, from Wallace's 2004 collection of the same name, also touches on racist perspectives via free indirect discourse. In one section, the narrator thinks about how an unwed mother has become "a kind of cautionary tale" to his daughter and her friends, with "one of her children being plainly interracial."[15] Indeed, if Wallace's literary voice in his essays and fiction really is "the voice in your own head," as A. O. Scott and other critics have claimed, then there is value in dramatizing the negative aspects of that voice, rather than merely the more laudable parts that readers have been eager to celebrate.[16] And since that internal voice speaks inside a patently *white* head, Wallace's work has the potential to show how various white internal voices can incorporate reflexive racist assumptions into their own self-narration. In such instances, Wallace enacts a critique of the white gaze not from a distant remove but from the inside. Such a strategy aligns with his broader focus on revealing how the self is imprisoned within structures and systems of various kinds, as well as the impossibility of ever fully escaping those systems.

Race and Irresolvability

The heavy demands that Wallace places on his reader also thwart any attempt at a straightforward reading of his racial representations. His project was centered on a particularly intense form of readerly engagement, with Wallace himself acknowledging that the "reader is going to have to put in her share of the linguistic work" in decoding the meaning of his texts. But beyond simply linguistic work, his writing invariably asks us to do our fair share of the interpretive work too, exerting considerable mental energy in formulating our own answers to various problems. This is because reading Wallace is a fundamentally collaborative and transactional exchange, and not simply a one-way form of communication. While scholars typically take Wallace's account of the reader's textual obligations to refer to the stylistic and syntactical complexity of his prose, we might also see them as applying equally to interpreting his work's partial and unresolved thinking around questions of race. In fact, readers are often asked to do the interpretive heavy lifting on such issues, with Wallace self-consciously stepping aside so that the reader can take up a line of thought where he leaves off. The Illinois State Fair piece, for instance, contains many observations on race that are left unexplored and uninterpreted, as for instance when Wallace notes that there are virtually no black fairgoers joining in the festivities: "Two of the kids are black," he writes, "the first black people I've seen anywhere on the Fairgrounds."[17] Such an observation is indicative of the way in which his journalism often contains odd moments of racial interaction, which Wallace chooses not to interpret. In this case, the observation is immediately overshadowed by a description of fair exhibits. Though there are surely many interesting reflections he could have made on the overwhelming whiteness of the state fair, and the implications it might have for the "conscious affirmation of real community" he sees elsewhere, Wallace instead hands the interpretive baton on to the reader.[18] He makes a similar gesture at a later point, in a brief observation on the fair's implicit celebration of whiteness that raises far more questions than it answers:

> There's an atmosphere in the room – not racist, but aggressively white. It's hard to describe. The atmosphere's the same at a lot of rural Midwest public events. It's not like if a black person came in he'd be ill-treated; it's more like it would just never occur to a black person to come in here.[19]

That the reader is left to extend an incomplete analysis at such moments could either be read as an unwillingness to think more deeply about such issues himself or as part of a deliberate attempt to place the interpretive burden on the reader. But in any case, there is something more complicated going on in such sections than we are usually willing to give Wallace credit for. *Signifying Rappers* works in this way too, with Wallace and Costello offering tentative gestures toward meaning ("The music's paranoia, together with its hermetic racial context, maybe helps explain why it appears just as vibrant and impassioned as it does alien and scary, to us, from outside," Wallace proposes early on) and opening up interpretive possibilities that can be taken up by the reader.[20] This resistance to offering coherent and neatly contained interpretations can at times be maddening, but it also liberates the reader to use the text as a jumping off point, rather than a final destination.

Strategies of Provocation

Another way of interpreting the reflections on race scattered throughout Wallace's fiction and journalism is in light of a persistent strategy of provocation. In many texts, Wallace seems to be deliberately raising the hackles of his readers, challenging their sensibilities and assumptions and casting himself as a figure more concerned with telling uncomfortable truths than with pandering to readers' sensibilities. Across his career, Wallace consistently saw himself as a gadfly-like provocateur, with a belief in the potentially redemptive value in causing offense. After all, "The View from Mrs. Thompson's" makes the extraordinary claim that the terrorists behind the 9/11 attacks were motivated not by geopolitical grievances or religious zeal but by a hatred of US irony and insincerity; "Back in New Fire" argues that the AIDS crisis is an unexpected "gift," with the power to "increase the erotic voltage of contemporary life"; while "Just Asking" – published only six years after 9/11 – makes the equally scandalous claim that we should think of the attack's victims as "sacrifices on the altar of freedom."[21] His fiction is often motivated by this same impulse, with Wallace admitting, for instance, that *Brief Interviews with Hideous Men* is "mean to just about everybody it's possible to be mean to."[22] Being aware of this strategy complicates our understanding of many of Wallace's portrayals, including the aforementioned Wardine section of *Infinite Jest*. This violent account of domestic abuse and poverty, set in the Brighton Projects and narrated in an urban black dialect, dates back to 1986 and, according to Burn's chronology, was the first chapter of the novel that Wallace wrote.[23] Various letters written around this time show that Wallace was extraordinarily proud of this extract, which he titled "Las Meninas" (presumably making a dark joke on the famous Velázquez painting, highlighting the disjuncture between Wardine and Clenette's squalid circumstances and that particular artwork's eponymous "Maids of Honor"). In fact, Wallace was so proud of this piece that in 1989, he asked his agent, Bonnie Nadell, to send it out to various literary magazines, including, for a lark, to the *New Yorker*.[24] His implication here is that the magazine's upper-middle-class, mostly white audience would be horrified by the story's graphic depiction of black poverty. This gesture recasts this much-maligned piece of fiction, revealing a more self-conscious side to Wallace's overt representations of race and again emphasizing the importance of racial provocations to his work. Marlon Bain's reflections, in *Infinite Jest*, contain a similarly provocative sentiment for an educated, middle-class white readership. Here, Bain instructs Helen Steeply to

> pay no attention to Orin's defense of football as a ritualized substitute for armed conflict. Armed conflict is plenty ritualized on its own, and since we have real armed conflict (take a spin through Boston's Roxbury and Mattapan districts some evening) there is no need or purpose for a substitute.[25]

Here, Wallace takes issue with a familiar interpretation of sport as violent ritual, pointedly reminding white readers of a form of violence in poor ethnic enclaves that in the mid-1990s was frequently sensationalized by the mainstream media. It also echoes his scathing interpretation of the media's conflation of hip-hop with black crime in *Signifying Rappers*, where he argues that the "media-We" view the emergence of this genre through "our own associative stereotypes – poverty, drugs, welfare, obscenity, gangs, entertainment, athletics, teen pregnancy, maleducation … and most of all crime."[26] Such examples reveal a more incendiary dimension to Wallace's treatment of race, in its attempt at exposing an unconscious privileging of white experience in contemporary US culture.

Moreover, his trenchant critique of "the tyranny of Political Correctness," a form of discourse that he elsewhere labeled "increasingly absurd and dogmatic," also fits within a larger project of provocation.[27] In Wallace's view, such usage obscures conditions of oppression rather than illuminating them. Having come through the university system at a time of increasing political correctness and affirmative action, Wallace seems to have instinctively rebelled against this discourse and to have found ways of using it for comic ends. ("Please know that I am both Caucasian and male," he told the hiring committee at the University of Illinois – an attempt at levity, but also an unmistakable critique of affirmative action.[28]) Wallace was particularly critical of the ways in which racial differences end up being preserved within this discourse. As he saw it, political correctness, with its "obsession with the mere forms of utterance and discourse," demonstrates "how effete and aestheticized our best liberal instincts have become."[29] For Wallace, such contorted language uses a logic of liberal self-congratulation instead of actually addressing the tangible problems at hand. During his time at the University of Illinois, Wallace paid a high price for these views, when he was asked to provide an official account of a classroom exchange with a student of color. Wallace's portrayal of this conversation is represented as a fundamentally pragmatic account of the ways in which Standard Written English – which Wallace acknowledged may as well be called "Standard *White* English" – is more authoritative and powerful than other dialectical forms.[30] As he later notes, "more than one colleague professed to find my spiel 'racially insensitive,'" and he also received an "official complaint" lodged by one "black undergraduate" who was offended by his account of such usage differences.[31] Although Wallace's essay goes to great lengths to mount a defense for such a "spiel," his classroom speech is nonetheless clumsily phrased and, as he later admits, "rhetorically naïve" about the complex investment of identity within all forms of language. However, if we fold this pragmatic approach back into a broader logic of provocation, we can see the ways in which Wallace was concerned with provoking both black and white assumptions alike.

Humor is an important aspect of many of these same portrayals. One of Wallace's recurring impulses was to make light of racial difference, and to use various kinds of provocations to generate comedy. His strategy mines the various uncomfortable racial tensions that are ambient within the culture for laughs, as in his *Saturday Night Live*-esque scene between a "resoundingly ... white" middle-aged nebbish and a group of "black guys" in a suburban mall, which he puts forward as a thought experiment in "Authority and American Usage":

> Imagine that two hard-core young urban black guys are standing there talking and I, who am resoundingly and in all ways white, come up and greet them with "Yo" and address one or both as "Brother" and ask "s'up, s'going on," pronouncing *on* with that NYCish oo-o diphthong that Young Urban Black English deploys for a standard o. Either these guys are going to think that I am mocking them and be offended or they are going to think I am simply out of my mind. No other reaction is remotely foreseeable. Q: Why?[32]

This thought experiment is obviously a comic exaggeration, but the joke operates as a kind of hyperbolic extension of the kinds of linguistic, cultural, and racial disconnects that structure everyday US life. (It also asks the reader for a direct response, in an even more overt way than the examples listed earlier.) This strategy is highly provocative, especially since the line between comedy and straight-out offense is notoriously hard to find. Wallace again found racial comedy in a scene between Ken Erdedy and Roy Tony in *Infinite Jest*, when he describes the former's discomfort at being instructed to hug "a tall heavy African-American fellow with a gold incisor and perfect vertical cylinder of African-American hairstyle."[33] Here, Wallace looks for the comic potential within American race relations, and the scene ends in slapstick, with Erdedy hugging Tony so enthusiastically that "it looked like [he] was trying to climb him."[34] Yet Wallace clearly crossed the line between humor and offense on many occasions, perhaps most obviously in one of the *Sabrina* parodies he wrote at Amherst, about mid-nineteenth-century students arriving to the college accompanied by their slaves, a piece that was protested by the university's Black Student Union.[35] A more complicated example of this approach occurs in the unmistakably racialized descriptions of Tibor (a Hungarian waiter) and Petra (an Asian cleaner) in "A Supposedly Fun Thing." Here, Wallace uses an odd mixture of sympathy and condescension to craft a complicated form of racial comedy. Throughout the essay, Wallace clearly exploits these two figures for laughs, but he also empathizes with their plight as low-wage service workers, in a way that makes it difficult to tease out the interwoven strands of sympathy and comedic exploitation. Both characters are racially marked in cartoonish ways: Tibor has a "pink and birdlike face" along with a mien that seemed "to sum up the whole plight of postwar Eastern Europe," while Petra's exoticism is portrayed via her "dimples and broad candid brow," along with an "epicanthically doe-eyed" expression.[36] In many ways, Petra and Tibor are used for comic relief, with their ESL solecisms and corporate humiliations providing fodder for laughs, yet Wallace's affection toward them is palpable, and he is clearly kinder to them than many of his fellow cruisers. A similar tension is present in his fictionalized account of the Eastern European immigrants who are rechristened with obscene names by a "psychotically jingoistic and sadistic" Ellis Island official in "Octet," a scene that once again mingles comic exploitation and sympathy.[37]

Another example of racialized comedy is present in the depiction of Solomon Silverfish, the eponymous protagonist of an early story, published in the *Sonora Review* in 1987.[38] The Jewish characters in this story speak like the most grotesquely stereotypical Jews from Hollywood entertainment, while the representation of Too Pretty, a black pimp and drug dealer, also conforms to negative racial stereotypes. In fact, Too Pretty's linguistic tics and flamboyantly ungrammatical interior monologue ("my man be gettin in you ass with his briefcase and these bad arms flying all over and a voice like the el train book by you ass on the platform, roar like to suck you in," he threatens at one point) foreshadow the aforementioned Wardine section of *Infinite Jest*, with several characters – including Wardine herself, and Reginald – appearing in both texts.[39] At numerous points, "/Solomon Silverfish/" teeters dangerously close to anti-Semitism, and it is unsurprising that Wallace's complex impersonations of Jewish identity rankled his Jewish MFA instructor at the University of Arizona, Jonathan Penner. But even here, the depiction is a complex one, since Silverfish himself is impersonating Jewishness: as a "secret Saxon, closet Celt," his ethnic masquerade mirrors Wallace's own, implying at least some level of self-awareness about the stakes of cultural appropriation. Hal experiments with a similar kind of racial impersonation at one point in *Infinite Jest*, echoing Silverfish's performance by briefly affecting a "Jewish-motherish" (908) persona while talking to Pemulis. Elsewhere in *Infinite Jest*, Wallace deploys several primitivist caricatures, as in Orin's theory that the paraphernalia surrounding American football masks deeper primordial fears, "because the bug-eyed native's lurking just under the surface, we know. The bug-eyed spear-rattling grass-skirted primitive, feeding virgins to Popogatapec and afraid of planes."[40] The short story "Another Pioneer," included in *Oblivion*, exploits similar primitivist tropes, with the narrator's description of a particularly macabre witch doctor rivaling even the most hyperbolic Hollywood representations of primitivism. This witch doctor is described as spending

> most of his time conducting private necromantic rituals that involve playing crude musical arrangements with human tibias and femurs on rows of differ-ently sized human skulls like sort of ghastly paleolithic marimbas, as well as apparently using skulls for both his personal stew pot and his commode.[41]

In such instances, Wallace redirects a postmodern emphasis on transgression and play toward racial stereotypes, in the attempt to craft an irreverent form of comedy. And while such representations might be viewed as merely taking a playfully postmodern logic of caricature to extreme ends, they nonetheless risk perpetuating pejorative stereotypes and cross-cultural misunderstanding.

Pop Anthropology and the Elision of Racial Difference

It is also important to situate Wallace's ambivalent approach to issues of race in light of his engagement with the structuralist anthropology of Joseph Campbell. Across his career, Wallace was clearly enamored with Campbell's reading of comparative mythology. Wallace quoted from *The Hero with a Thousand Faces* (1949) in his review of Apostolos Doxiadis's *Uncle Petros and Goldbach's Conjecture* (1992), and a heavily annotated copy of Campbell's *Myths to Live By* (1972) is included in his archives at the Harry Ransom Center. In the short story "Another Pioneer," Wallace borrowed liberally from Campbell's mythological lexicon, creating a story that updates Hegel's argument on the origins of self-consciousness in *Phenomenology of Spirit*. Campbell's work also influenced Wallace's approach to literary journalism. In *Signifying Rappers*, for instance, he deploys a similarly ethnographic gaze to explain hip-hop to white readers. Indeed, in many sections, the tone in this early book is that of an explorer bravely venturing inside an exotic culture to explain its appeal for privileged and distant outsiders. And in "Getting Away ...," Wallace takes this conceit even further, structuring his essay around an ethnographic excursion with a local informant, since "no anthropologist worth his pith helmet would be without the shrewd counsel of a colorful local, and I've brought a Native Companion here for the day."[42] The same faux-anthropological tonal qualities recur in many sections describing black characters in *Infinite Jest*, as when the narrator baldly states that "the couple of residents that are black are mingling with other blacks. ... Clennette Henderson clutches another black girl and laughs and says 'Girl!' several times."[43]

Yet what Wallace found most appealing about Campbell's work was his general approach to anthropological knowledge, which draws on an endlessly diverse set of spiritual and cultural traditions for what they might offer the Western subject, without being unduly troubled by questions of cultural fidelity. This approach is now widely shunned by anthropologists, with Robert Ellwood rightly pointing out that Campbell's project is an oddly "disembodied" one, attempting to uncover an entirely dehistoricized, "timeless story of eternal significance."[44] Yet just as Campbell's work implicitly regarded "all myths [as] equal and interchangeable," Wallace sought the broadest possible perspective on questions of religion, spirituality, and culture, looking for essential commonalities and "universal" spiritual truths, often at the expense of historical detail.[45] Such an approach naturally led into a similarly "disembodied" perspective on racial difference. Across his career, Wallace was inclined to look beyond what he saw as superficial racial variance to find the Campbell-like vantage point from which people of all races are essentially interchangeable actors in a "timeless story of eternal significance."

Indeed, Wallace's recurring impulse to elide various forms of difference stems from Campbell-like assumptions about race and culture. In much of his nonfiction and fiction, Wallace tried either to erase or else look past various identity markers, including those of language, class, culture, gender, and race. In terms of how this essentialist, and universalist, approach played out within his thinking around issues of race, there is a particularly revealing comment in Wallace's 2000 interview with Mark Schechner. After jokingly responding to Schechner's surprise at Wallace's admiration for the fiction of Cynthia Ozick ("We're both politically active Jewish females," Wallace quipped. "I don't see the problem"), he went on to talk about what he found most compelling in her work.[46] Wallace explained that Ozick's fiction differed from the work of other writers from unfamiliar racial or ethnic backgrounds in its ability to transcend cultural differences:

> In reading her I feel an utter erasure of difference, which does not happen to me with a lot of other writers from different cultural backgrounds. I can appreciate the peering across the chasm at another culture, but with Ozick that chasm just vanishes.[47]

This seemingly offhanded comment encapsulates a far more widespread approach to notions of identity, with Wallace's admiration for such an "erasure of difference" explaining his reluctance to explore the specific racial positions occupied by various characters. Across his career, Wallace was far less interested in exploring the particularities of ethnic identity by "peering across the chasm" than he was in making such particularities disappear. This may well be why non-white characters appear so infrequently throughout his writing and why, when such characters do appear, their representation – as in the aforementioned examples of Tibor, Petra, and Silverfish – rarely goes beyond preestablished tropes. It is also telling that in the notes for *The Pale King*, Chris Aquistipace is referred to at various points as being of wildly different races and ethnicities, with the point being that he is racially othered, rather than occupying a particular identity position that Wallace is keen to explore.[48] For Wallace, this strategy of minimizing differences of all kinds had crucial personal—as well as artistic—implications. In 1996, he told David Lipsky that learning to recognize such commonalities had saved his life: "The parts of me that used to think I was different or smarter or whatever almost made me die."[49] Though there are some obvious problems with thinking about racial difference – and other forms of difference – in these terms, we could potentially view it more positively, as a gesture toward the utter truthlessness of race itself. Under this logic, racial markers really are invisible and irrelevant, utterly emptied of content, and with no predictive or explanatory power. In fact, this is the utopian dream at the heart of the so-called post-race era, in which racialized thinking is rendered obsolete. Of course, many scholars have rightly critiqued this ideology, arguing that it is a deluded, optimistic notion, which conceals deeper forms of structural racism. As Terry Smith points out, it also functions as "a speech restraint on racial protest because whites are chronically 'exhausted' by issues of race."[50] Such complaints also apply to Wallace's strategy of minimizing racial differences, but we can also critique its latent utopianism and idealism. As many critics of Joseph Campbell and the structuralist school of anthropology have pointed out, so-called universal values are invariably rooted in suspiciously Western ideals. In any case, it is clear that many of Wallace's engagements with race fit within this logic of erasure, with his seemingly offhanded comment on Ozick's fiction encapsulating a far more widespread approach to notions of difference. Wallace's perspective on race is thus more unusual and also more complicated than it may initially appear, since it is in many ways the logical consequence of the beliefs about individual difference that proved productive for so much of his fiction. Paradoxically, this attempt to address broadly defined human problems – boredom, for instance, along with suffering and solipsism – is surely one reason why Wallace's work has found such a diverse global readership. Yet while this strategy makes his work accessible to a diverse audience, it also leads to a problematic approach to racial difference.

Conclusion: Taking the Long View

My aim in this chapter has been to set forth a more nuanced account of Wallace's engagements with race, which situates his many shortcomings in relation to broader artistic strategies. To do this kind of analysis is to recognize that many of the more problematic aspects of Wallace's work – those elements that we have the most misgivings about – are in fact intimately linked to broader aesthetic goals and agendas. The often uncomfortable use of racialized discourse, for instance, is the flip side of a more generalized approach to difference that proved artistically productive across his career. And the many racial provocations throughout Wallace's nonfiction go hand in hand with the recurring attempt to challenge readers' ideological assumptions. The potentially unsettling implication here is that much of what we most admire about Wallace's work is inextricable from those textual moments that we might well want to disavow, or at the very least view as regrettable. As readers and scholars of Wallace's work, we need to come to terms with both the achievements and the shortcomings of Wallace's literary career, finding middle ground between the twin poles of hagiography and reflexive dismissal. As Wallace's work continues to reach new audiences, comprised of more racially and ethnically diverse readers than he foresaw, it will be crucial to have an interpretive framework that can do justice to the complexity of racial representations throughout his work.

Notes

1. Samuel Cohen, "The Whiteness of David Foster Wallace," in Len Platt and Sara Upstone (eds.), *Postmodern Literature and Race* (Cambridge: Cambridge University Press: 2015), p. 239; Mark McGurl, "The Institution of Nothing: David Foster Wallace in the Program," *boundary 2* 41.3 (Fall 2014), p. 49; Clare Hayes-Brady, *The Unspeakable Failures of David Foster Wallace* (New York: Bloomsbury, 2016), p. 168.
2. Tara Morrissey and Lucas Thompson, "'The Rare White at the Window': A Reappraisal of Mark Costello and David Foster Wallace's *Signifying Rappers*," *Journal of American Studies* 49.1 (2015), p. 96.
3. David Foster Wallace, "Authority and American Usage," in *Consider the Lobster* (New York: Little, Brown, 2005), p. 102.
4. Mark McGurl, "The Institution of Nothing," p. 43.
5. Toni Morrison, *Playing in the Dark* (Cambridge: Harvard University Press, 1992), p. xi.

6. David Foster Wallace, *Infinite Jest* (Boston: Little, Brown, 1996), p. 384.

7. Ibid., p. 835.

8. David Foster Wallace, *The Pale King* (New York: Little, Brown, 2011), p. 287.

9. Brian McHale, "*The Pale King*, Or, The White Visitation," in Marshall Boswell and Stephen J. Burn (eds.), *A Companion to David Foster Wallace Studies* (New York: Palgrave Macmillan, 2013), p. 198.

10. Ibid., p. 272.

11. Ibid., p. 310.

12. David Foster Wallace, "A Supposedly Fun Thing I'll Never Do Again," in *A Supposedly Fun Thing I'll Never Do Again: Essays and Arguments* (Boston: Little, Brown, 1997), p. 272.

13. Wallace tells us early on that the book is motivated by the discovery that he and his coauthor, Mark Costello, "shared an uncomfortable, somewhat furtive, and distinctively white enthusiasm for a certain music called rap/hip-hop." The book is overwhelmingly concerned with tracing the contours of this discomfort, interpreting hip-hop as a contemporary indicator of the state of US race relations. Wallace and Costello, *Signifying Rappers*, p. 21.

14. David Lipsky, *Although of Course You End Up Becoming Yourself* (New York: Broadway Books, 2010), p. 82. Wallace's emphasis.

15. David Foster Wallace, "Oblivion," in *Oblivion* (New York: Little, Brown, 2004), p. 193.

16. A. O. Scott, "The Panic of Influence," *New York Review of Books* 47 (February 10, 2000), www.nybooks.com/articles/archives/2000/feb/10/the-panic-of-influence/.

17. Wallace, "Getting Away from Already Being Pretty Much Away from It All," in *Supposedly*, p. 88.

18. Ibid., p. 91.

19. Ibid., p. 125.

20. David Foster Wallace and Mark Costello, *Signifying Rappers: Rap and Race in the Urban Present* (New York: Ecco, 1990), p. 24.

21. David Foster Wallace, "Back in New Fire," in *Both Flesh and Not: Essays* (New York: Little, Brown, 2012), p. 172; Wallace, "Just Asking," in *Both Flesh and Not*, p. 321.

22. "David Foster Wallace (*Consider the Lobster*)," interview by Michael Silverblatt, Bookworm, KCRW, California, August 12, 1999.

23. Stephen J. Burn, *David Foster Wallace's* Infinite Jest: *A Reader's Guide* (New York: Continuum, 2003), p. xii.

24. Wallace, Letter to Bonnie Nadell (1989), Container 1.1, Bonnie Nadell's David Foster Wallace Collection, Harry Ransom Center, University of Texas at Austin.

25. Wallace, *Infinite Jest*, p. 1047.

26. Wallace, *Signifying Rappers*, p. 39.

27. Wallace, "Authority," p. 332; Wallace, "Joseph Frank's Dostoevsky," in *Consider*, p. 273.

28. D. T. Max, *Every Love Story Is a Ghost Story: A Life of David Foster Wallace* (New York: Viking, 2012), p. 174.

29. Wallace, "Dostoevsky," p. 273

30. Wallace, "Authority," p. 108.

31. Ibid., p. 110, p. 109, p. 116.

32. Ibid., p. 102.
33. Wallace, *Infinite Jest*, p. 505.
34. Ibid., p. 507.
35. See Max, *Every Love Story*, p. 312.
36. Wallace, "A Supposedly Fun Thing I'll Never Do Again," in *Supposedly*, pp. 296, 259, and 297. In a 1997 interview with Steve Paulson, Wallace spoke of the "luxuriousness" of the cruise in language that makes it seem like a pantomime of colonialism. As well as noting the ever-present "swarthy guys" who would fetch his towels, he described the natural beauty on show during the cruise as seeming as if "hordes of extremely low-paid third-world people worked frantically at night to make the thing as pretty as it was." Paulson, Interview with David Foster Wallace, Wisconsin Public Radio, 1997.
37. David Foster Wallace, "Octet," in *Brief Interviews with Hideous Men* (Boston: Little, Brown, 1999), p. 150.
38. David Foster Wallace, "/Solomon Silverfish/," *The Sonora Review*, 1987, 54–81.
39. Wallace, "/Solomon Silverfish/," p. 77.
40. Ibid., p. 243.
41. Wallace, "Another Pioneer," in *Oblivion*, pp. 125–126.
42. Wallace, "Getting Away," p. 88.
43. Wallace, *Infinite Jest*, p. 363.
44. Robert Ellwood, *The Politics of Myth: A Study of C. G. Jung, Mircea Eliade, and Joseph Campbell* (Albany: State University of New York Press, 1989), p. 130.
45. Ibid., p. 30.
46. David Foster Wallace, "Behind the Watchful Eyes of Author David Foster Wallace," by Mark Schechner, in Stephen J. Burn (ed.), *Conversations With David Foster Wallace* (Jackson: University of Mississippi, 2012), p. 108.
47. Ibid., 109.
48. David Foster Wallace, Materials related to *The Pale King*, Container 26.4, David Foster Wallace Papers, Harry Ransom Center, University of Texas at Austin.
49. Lipsky, *Although*, p. 217.
50. Terry Smith, *Barack Obama, Post-Racialism, and the New Politics of Triangulation* (New York: Palgrave Macmillan, 2012), p. 106.

14

JURRIT DAALDER

Wallace's Geographic Metafiction

Nostalgia for the Midwest runs deep in the American grain: for generations, the country's heartland has been the home of all Americans, even those who have never lived there but miss it all the same. For David Foster Wallace, too, the heartland was where home is. At least, that is what his editor Michael Pietsch implied when he described *The Pale King* as a novel that "comes home" to the Prairie State, to "this landscape of Illinois that was inside of" Wallace.[1] Couched in the language of homecoming that has colored our image of Middle America in the most literal sense since *The Wizard of Oz* premiered in 1939, Pietsch's comment shows how the region continues to be thought of as not only America's geographical middle but also its metaphorical interior. It seems fitting, then, to say of the Midwest what Michel Foucault said of "heterotopias" more generally, namely, that it is "simultaneously mythic and real" – an observation that Edward Soja would later translate into his concept of "real-and-imagined places."[2] This dual quality certainly did not escape Wallace's notice, for even his debut novel, *The Broom of the System*, offers a series of critical reflections on the Midwest, which it describes in similar terms as "a place that both is and isn't."[3]

Over the course of his writing career, Wallace would continue to explore the region's cultural meaning, and nowhere is this more immediately apparent than in his trio of personal essays, or rather, "autogeographies" about his home state.[4] The first of these three pieces, "Derivative Sport in Tornado Alley," recounts the author's real-and-imagined Midwestern boyhood; the second, "Getting Away from Already Being Pretty Much Away from It All," has Wallace putting on his metaphorical pith helmet to venture out into the 1993 Illinois State Fair; and the third essay, "The View from Mrs. Thompson's," depicts the writer's then home, Bloomington, Illinois, where we find him in the domestic security of his neighbor's living room, watching live footage of the 9/11 attacks. Based primarily on these three works of creative nonfiction in which "the operative word," as Charles

B. Harris observed, is definitely "*creative*," critics have begun to map out the Midwest's central place in Wallace's body of work.[5] Paul Giles, for instance, has examined the writer's oeuvre within the context of the information and communications technology that has turned the world into one "global village," arguing that Wallace's place-writing "tends to flatten th[e] distinction" between center and periphery.[6] Paul Quinn, on the other hand, has emphasized "the intensely dialectical nature of Wallace's topography" and claimed that his "tornadic" prose, much like the region it depicts, is "informed and deformed by wind."[7] Still, there is one thing that these critics all seem to agree on, which is that Wallace's regionalism, as Mark McGurl put it, "is one version at least of the next big move in the literary field."[8] But such broad claims inevitably raise questions, most important among them: is Wallace's regional poetics really that novel? The short answer, it is tempting to say, is that it both is and isn't.

More specifically, Wallace's writing about real-and-imagined places, be it fictional or nonfictional, is an example of what I will call "geographic metafiction." Such metafiction, I argue, is the spatial equivalent to what Linda Hutcheon has defined as "historiographic metafiction," a poetics in which "the intertexts of history and fiction take on parallel status in the parodic reworking of the textual past of both the 'world' and literature."[9] Wallace's writing about the heartland constitutes a similar parodic reworking, but one that enacts the views of postwar cultural geographers instead of historiographers. It offers a clear sense of place, but one that can only be known from its geographic intertexts, from the "myths" and "symbols" that, according to Henry Nash Smith's 1950 classic of American Studies, *Virgin Land*, make up our "collective representations" of any American region, including the Midwest.[10] In this case, it is place and text that take on parallel status, resulting in an ontological confusion that Brian McHale identified as the dominant of postmodernist writing – a state of confusion in which, to borrow an apt description from French "geocritic" Bertrand Westphal, "the place is then a text that is a place, or perhaps the text is a place that is a text."[11] It is no surprise, then, that the prose-poetic evocation of Peoria, Illinois, that opens *The Pale King* brings the place's features to our attention before extending the invitation: "Read these."[12]

Wallace himself, of course, did just that. Not only did he record his own "reading" of Peoria's landscape in a folder containing materials from his trips to Peoria County, but he also made a careful study of a range of Midwestern intertexts that he collected in his "Midwesternisms Notebook" as well as in his "Records" and "Evidence" notebooks.[13] Each of these binders, held at the Harry Ransom Center, contains a broad range of Midwestern phrases and idioms, as well as a collection of landscape descriptions that Wallace often lifted straight from the work of his Midwestern contemporaries, most notably Michael Martone and William H. Gass. Though these intertextual connections to his contemporaries are certainly worth their own in-depth study, this essay focuses on Wallace's reworking of a set of older intertexts, in particular two early twentieth-century "urtexts" of the Midwest and its regional literature: Sinclair Lewis's 1920 satirical realist novel *Main Street* and Sherwood Anderson's 1919 short story cycle *Winesburg, Ohio*. Both these classics were in the vanguard of the so-called "revolt from the village" and have done much to shape our collective representation of the Midwest that, as we shall see, is at the very heart of Wallace's geographic metafiction.[14]

To understand how Wallace's writing builds on these Midwestern urtexts, it is useful to consider Victoria E. Johnson's *Heartland TV*, which details what she has called the "Heartland myth."[15] This myth, Johnson argues, stereotypes the Midwest as a region of "all-American identification, redeeming goodness, face-to-face community, sanctity, and emplaced ideals."[16] In other words, it presents the Midwest as the "heart" of the country, and it is this shape that the region often assumes in the collective American imagination, especially in times of cultural upheaval or national trauma. Not unexpectedly, this "Heartland myth" figured prominently in the cultural response to 9/11. The November 19, 2001, issue of *Time* magazine, for example, included an article titled "The Culture Comes Home," which made the following observations about *The Corrections* by Jonathan Franzen, Wallace's fellow Midwesterner and friendly rival:

> On its release, the jacket art of *The Corrections* – a clean-cut family sitting at a holiday table laden with turkey, cranberry-jelly slices and radish rosettes – seemed like a Lynchian dig at Norman Rockwell Americana. Today the image just seems, well, nice. And before Sept. 11 a literary reader would most likely have identified with the novel's neurotic, sophisticated grown children. Today it's hard for even the most jaded not to feel more like Enid, hoping against hope and reality for one more normal holiday.[17]

With this case for the post-9/11 reappraisal of the square "Midwesternness" of the novel's Lambert family, the article is indicative of a surge in the popularity of the "Heartland myth."

Franzen's novel, however, predates the terrorist attacks, so the post-9/11 heartland mythology that would help elevate his book to the status of Great American Novel was mostly an accident of history. This is plainly not the case for Wallace's aforementioned autogeography, "The View from Mrs. Thompson's," which appeared in the October 25, 2001, issue of *Rolling Stone* and is a direct response to the terrorist attacks. One of the piece's working titles was "View from the Interior," which shows very clearly that Wallace sought to make deliberate use of the heartland's real-and-imagined qualities to create a space for thoughtful introspection.[18] Though this title was later abandoned, the final essay is no less up-close-and-personal in its account of the cultural impact of 9/11. It begins with Wallace puzzling over why, in the days following the attacks, everyone in Bloomington has American flags out. When he asks his neighbor Mr. N – why this is so, Mr. N – replies "(after a little moment of him giving [Wallace] the same sort of look he usually gives [his] lawn), 'to show our support towards what's going on, as Americans.'"[19] Another neighbor confirms that it is to "'show we're American and we're not going to bow down to nobody.'"[20]

In their local response to the national tragedy of 9/11, Wallace's neighbors define themselves primarily by their "Americanness," not by any distinct Midwestern sense of place. Far from unusual, this "sublation of regional identity for national representativeness" is entirely in keeping with a "Midwestern nationalism" that so closely identifies the Midwest with America at large that the region has, in fact, been called an "anti-region."[21] As we have already seen from the above *TIME* magazine article, this same Midwestern nationalism allows the nation to identify so easily with the Midwest. Wallace appears to have been well aware of this spatial dialectic of region and anti-region, which places the Midwest "both in the middle and on the fringe."[22] Indeed, he actually chose to preface "The View" with a short paragraph marked "**SYNECDOCHE**," thereby signaling to his readers that the locals' response to 9/11, which was reportedly "in true Midwest fashion," should at the same time be regarded as typical of the nation as a whole.[23]

It is here that we find the unmistakable traces of the first of our two Midwestern urtexts, for this preface resonates with the opening lines of Sinclair Lewis's *Main Street*. More so than any other text, it is *Main Street*'s portrait of Gopher Prairie, Minnesota, that established the myth of the archetypal prairie town, which has come to capture the popular imagination. Writers like Walt Whitman may have previously described the prairies and plains as "North America's characteristic landscape," but it was Lewis who made the region's typicality into the central theme of his work.[24] Already on its opening page, *Main Street* announces that "this is America – a town of a few thousand, in a region of wheat and corn and dairies and little groves."[25] The story's setting, we are told, may be Gopher Prairie, but "its Main Street is the continuation of Main Streets everywhere."[26] With these words, Lewis made the Midwestern small town synonymous with the interests of everyday people, and the term "Main Street" continues to function as a shorthand for these interests, especially when it is contrasted with Wall Street in the way that William Z. Ripley first did in his 1927 work, *Main Street and Wall Street*, for which Lewis personally sent him "his 'Godspeed.'"[27]

The broad influence of *Main Street*'s synecdochic Midwest would really become clear in 1929, which saw the publication of Robert Staughton Lynd and Helen Merrell Lynd's "total-situation study," *Middletown*.[28] Now regarded as a classic of sociology, this study put a small town in east central Indiana named Muncie on the global map for being exceptionally average, that is, a "Middletown" whose residents' behavior was deemed to be representative of larger statistical trends. Other places in the Midwest soon gained a similar reputation as America writ large, one of the more famous examples being Peoria, which, not coincidentally, serves as the main setting for Wallace's posthumous novel – a novel that even had as one of its working titles "*What Is Peoria For.*"[29] Wallace, moreover, also knew that Peoria's reputation had been immortalized in the well-known Midwestern saying "Will it play in Peoria?," given that his "Evidence Notebook" shows him carefully considering the phrase's literary potential, which surely indicates that he took a keen interest in the collective representation of the Midwest as a synecdoche of the nation.[30]

This synecdochic quality is central to "The View from Mrs. Thompson's" and its metafictional reworking of Bloomington, whose twin municipality of Normal could not be a more obvious reminder of the region's self-conscious averageness. In this portrait of a typical Midwestern town, the average townspeople are gathered in the living room of Mrs. Thompson, "one of the world's cooler seventy-four-year-olds," and as Wallace explains in one of his characteristic footnotes, these neighbors are "predominantly working-class Bloomington."[31] In other words, they are the same heartlanders whom Wallace had previously judged as "Kmart People" in his essay on the Illinois State Fair or ridiculed as residents of "pathetic-Christian-TV-viewer-land" in the closing pages of his debut novel.[32] Here, however, he refrains from taking any kind of "Lynchian dig" at them, and they are instead presented as "good people."[33] If taken at face value, this would suggest that Wallace eventually bought into the "Heartland myth" and developed a new appreciation for the rural inhabitants of Illinois. Christoph Ribbat has commented on such a "turn toward the Kmart People"; and Zadie Smith has likewise observed that, in the course of Wallace's career, "farmers and all kinds of down-home folks (usually from his home state of Illinois) receiv[ed] that warmness Wallace could never quite muster for hyper-reflexive intellectuals more or less like himself."[34]

But any argument for Wallace's straightforward embrace of the rural Midwest does not at all do justice to that very hyper-reflexive quality that makes "The View" a work of geographic metafiction. The essay achieves its strong emotional impact precisely by making strategic use of the powerful symbolism of Main Street and its evocation of the "Real America" – a symbolism that Edith Wharton already recognized in 1927, when she wrote about the ever-elusive Great American Novel and argued that such a nation-defining fiction "must always be about Main Street, geographically, socially, and intellectually."[35] Wallace offers a slight variation on the Main Street versus Wall Street juxtaposition: the precise moment that he identifies as "the start of a feeling of alienation" is, after all, one in which he explains to the old ladies at Mrs. Thompson's exactly where New York's Financial District and, therefore, the World Trade Center are located.[36] By drawing attention to this moment of alienation, he is able to bring into focus the enormous cultural distance between two real-and-imagined places: the small-town America of these provincial old ladies and the cosmopolitan America represented on the TV screen, which constantly reruns the horrific footage of the terrorist attacks.

This distance is further emphasized when Wallace marvels at the "lack of cynicism" in the room.[37] "Nobody's near hip enough," he observes, "to lodge the sick and obvious po-mo complaint: We've Seen This Before."[38] In making this observation, he creates a caricature of his unhip neighbors that, once again, brings us back to *Main Street*, to a scene where Dr. Kennicott compliments his Gopher Prairie neighbors by saying to his newly wedded wife Carol, "'I told you you'd like 'em. Squarest people on earth.'"[39] Yet Wallace's caricature of his neighbors as impossibly square Midwesterners is not meant to satirize them. On the contrary, these cartoonishly straight "good people" set the stage for Wallace's self-parody and ultimately self-criticism. His growing feeling of alienation emerges very clearly from two revealing comments in his handwritten draft of "The View," which specifies in what way, as Wallace put it in the published version, "these Bloomington ladies are ... innocent."[40] His neighbors, Wallace observes, have not buried their feelings under layers and layers of self-consciousness or self-protective mistrust; they simply wear their hearts on their sleeves.[41] For this reason, the author grudgingly admits that he finds them "taxing to be around," especially (judging by a comment in the margins of his manuscript) because the ladies' wholeheartedness aggravates his anxiety about his own inability to feel anything at all.[42]

Careful examination of this divide between Wallace's supposed apathy and the ladies' heartfelt sympathy reveals a sense of small-town estrangement that is central to the second of our two Midwestern urtexts, namely

Winesburg, Ohio by Sherwood Anderson, who receives a special mention in *The Pale King* as an "immortally great fiction writer."[43] Judging by his heavily annotated copy of *Winesburg, Ohio*, Wallace was intimately familiar with Anderson's tales, which all revolve around an alienated young man named George Willard who, as a kind of small-town Stephen Dedalus, feels he has to leave Winesburg to be able "to paint the dreams of his manhood."[44] But George is by no means the only disaffected Winesburgian. The story "Godliness," for example, centers on another villager named Jesse Bentley, whose feelings are more akin to that particular sense of alienation that Wallace dramatizes in "The View." In fact, Wallace wrote his initials "DW" in the margin next to the following description of Jesse's estrangement:

> As time passed and he grew to know people better, he began to think of himself as an extraordinary man, one set apart from his fellows. He wanted terribly to make his life a thing of great importance, and as he looked about at his fellow men and saw how like clods they lived it seemed to him that he could not bear to become also such a clod.[45]

It is hard not to see in this annotation some indication of the criticism that Wallace leveled against his alter ego in the published version of "The View."

That authorial alter ego, it should be noted, is as much of a caricature as those impossibly square Bloomington neighbors. It is only by strategically presenting the divide between Wallace and his neighbors as one between a self-confessed East Coast cynic and a room full of sincere "good people" that "The View" is able to lead up to its grand conclusion, which shows Wallace at his most critical both of himself and his implied cosmopolitan readership. "Part of the horror of the Horror," Wallace writes, "was knowing, deep in my heart, that whatever America the men in those planes hated so much was far more my America ... than it was these ladies'."[46] The terrorists' target, Wallace implies, was not the "Real America," that mythical heartland, but the America that betrayed those values. This conclusion is problematic for various reasons, but one in particular involves a paradox that is at the very heart of geographic metafiction – a paradox similar to that which Linda Hutcheon identifies in her account of historiographic metafiction.[47] In his parodic reworking of the popular myths and symbols that have shaped our collective representation of the Midwest, Wallace may have found an effective way to explore the cultural impact of 9/11, but at the same time he reproduces and enshrines these Midwestern myths and symbols. By playing around with stereotypes of the Midwest, Wallace ultimately ends up reinforcing that stereotypical notion of a cartoonishly straight heartland that is nothing like the lived reality of small-town America, whose divisions and social problems Lewis and Anderson, for instance, originally set out to expose.

Both Lewis and Anderson presented their critiques of the Midwest at a time when America still maintained the national mythology of Frederick Jackson Turner's 1893 "frontier thesis," which Wallace parodied in another one of his geographic metafictions, "Westward the Course of Empire Takes Its Way."[48] The cultivation of this myth is documented in *Middletown* as part of a widespread practice called regional "boosting," which the Lynds described as "the muzzling of self-criticism by hurling the term 'knocker' at the head of a critic and the drowning of incipient social problems under a public mood of everything being 'fine and dandy.'"[49] The "revolt from the village" was, in many ways, a revolt against precisely this practice, but *Middletown* inadvertently participated in boosterism's tendency toward selective representation, judging by one major reason that the Lynds gave for choosing Muncie. The town was chosen as a model for America because it had only a "small Negro and foreign-born population," which means, as Hugh Gusterson has rightly observed, that "America was normalized as white."[50] If, as we recall, a place is a text that is a place, then we might say that the Lynds effectively "read African Americans out of American society."[51] In much the same way, Walt Disney would later rework his boyhood home of Marceline, Missouri, into Disneyland's "Main Street, USA," which in the postwar years became symbolic of an all-American heartland where "urban life and culture, 'non-white' populations, and marked class differences" have no place.[52] With its noticeably, and often self-consciously, straight heartland populated by a uniform group of honest, God-fearing "good people," Wallace's "The View" is much closer in spirit to this Disneyfied version of Main Street, USA, than it is to Lewis's *Main Street*.

For one thing, the essay's only mention of a non-white resident is of the Pakistani owner of a convenience store named "KWIK-N-EZ," a store that reappears as a fictional setting in *The Pale King* and whose name is suspiciously similar to the "Kwik-E-Mart" in *The Simpsons*, which is owned by the Indian-American Apu. Surprisingly, however, Wallace's manuscript does present a much more socially and ethnically divided Bloomington. In his longhand draft, Wallace writes about a divide between the city's affluent east side and its much poorer west side, which houses the city's black community and has a large police presence. Signs posted around the town's perimeter may claim that there is no racism in Bloomington, Wallace continues, but the town's population has been quietly segregated along class and racial lines. Still, Wallace insists that the abovementioned signs are harmless since their message is in earnest; Bloomington's east-siders truly believe that there is no racism in their town because they never go to see the west side, not least because the stench of a nearby Purina plant keeps all non-residents away.[53] These notes, then, offer a fascinating insight into the town's local politics, yet not a single one of them made it into the published version of "The View," which means that Wallace, much like the Lynds, made a conscious decision to "read" any racial and socioeconomic differences out of his metafictional account of Bloomington. The tragic irony is that, in doing so, he ended up reinforcing the very idea that there is no racism here, for the reader never gets to see the west side of town.

Though his geographic metafiction since "The View" does little to correct this racial bias that is central to the "Heartland myth," the drafts that were published in 2011 as *The Pale King* do find other ways to push back against some of the stereotypes of a straight heartland – stereotypes from which, by the aforementioned paradox, Wallace nevertheless derives his creative energy. One particularly good example is the novel's chapters on Leonard Stecyk, a character whom Wallace uses to satirize that same popular image of Midwestern "good people" on which the whole of "The View" hinges. It is in the chapters that recount Stecyk's backstory, moreover, that Wallace's literary debts to Sherwood Anderson become fully apparent. In one of his longhand drafts of the story of Stecyk's childhood, for instance, Wallace describes Stecyk's compulsive niceness in terms that recall the opening story of *Winesburg, Ohio*, namely "The Book of the Grotesque," which for two years served as the working title of Anderson's entire story collection.[54] This introductory piece provides a window on Winesburg: it tells the story of an old writer who, while lying in his bed that is on a level with his bedroom window, has "a dream that [i]s not a dream."[55] In this real-and-imagined state of mind, he sees an entire "procession of grotesques" pass before his eyes, about whom he develops the following theory, which Wallace underlined in his own copy of the book: "It was his notion that the moment one of the people took one of the truths to himself, called it his truth, and tried to live his life by it, he became a grotesque and the truth he embraced became a falsehood."[56] In precisely this way, as Irving Howe observed, Anderson's Winesburgians "are subject to rigid monomanias" and embody "to fantastic excess a condition of psychic deformity."[57]

Just as this idea of the grotesque served as a prism through which Anderson filtered his criticism of regional boosting and the "Heartland myth," so too does psychic deformity appear to have been a central theme of Wallace's parodic reworking of the Midwest in *The Pale King*. Not yet a Hideous Man but certainly a Hideous Boy, Leonard Stecyk embodies to fantastic excess those popular notions of Midwestern niceness, neighborliness, and community spirit. These traits are already apparent from our first encounter with him in chapter 5 of the published novel, which depicts Stecyk as a volunteer member of his school's crossing patrol, "shepherd[ing] the lower grades' kids through the crosswalk outside school."[58] Later we see him as a hall monitor, proudly proclaiming that "he's here to serve, he feels, not run people down," which is an obvious allusion to the adult Stecyk's job at the Internal Revenue Service, or simply, "the Service."[59] Because of his obsession with niceness, however, no one really likes the boy. He gets bullied by his school's sixth-graders, who accost him just before Halloween and leave him "hanging from a stall's hook by his underpants' elastic."[60] Another psychologically painful moment is his "eleventh-birthday BLOWOUT BASH," to which only nine of the 322 invited children show up.[61] Even here, though, the young Stecyk shows himself to be an insufferable do-gooder, making sure to donate the staggering amount of leftovers to the Kent County Children's Home "via procedures and transport that the birthday boy has initiated even while the big Twister free-for-all is under way."[62]

But what could have made Stecyk into such a do-gooder? The published version of his backstory merely hints at some familial trauma involving his mother, who had a "terrible accident while cleaning the oven."[63] One of Wallace's character outlines, on the other hand, does offer a more detailed explanation that puts a darkly comic spin on the "home alone" scenario and takes direct aim, this time, at all-American domesticity and family life. Stecyk's worst childhood memory, Wallace writes, is of running home from kindergarten every day with the terrible fear that both parents had abandoned him. One day this nightmare becomes reality as he returns to an empty house and finds that his parents did not even bother to leave him a note. It turns out, Wallace explains, that Stecyk's mother had attempted suicide, then panicked and called her husband, who, in his rush to get her to the hospital, completely forgot to ask the neighbors to pick up Stecyk. Under the impression that he has been abandoned, the young Stecyk decides to get down on both knees and pray for his parents' return, promising that he will be a good boy from now on. Incidentally, the moment he finishes his prayer, the phone rings and it is his father calling. Relieved, Stecyk keeps up his end of the divine bargain and becomes that excessively nice kid we encounter in *The Pale King*.[64] When Stecyk makes his adult appearance in chapter 12 of the novel, going around his new Peoria neighborhood to hand out free copies of the "US Post Office's 1979 National Zip Code Directory," he is still that same do-gooder and his behavior is as unbearable to others – even, according to an unpublished piece of dialogue in Wallace's "Records Notebook," to his own dog, which reportedly hanged itself with its own leash.[65] Judging by this treatment of Stecyk, whose Midwestern niceness drives others to suicidal despair or near-murderous rage, it seems the gifted satirist in Wallace could not help but make sadistic fun of the cliché of square "Midwesternness" that he himself had reproduced in "The View from Mrs. Thompson's."

Such violent delight in tearing down the "Heartland myth" appears to have been the initial creative impulse behind even chapter 6 of *The Pale King*, which first appeared in the February 5, 2007, issue of the *New Yorker* as "Good People" and is often praised for its unironic, direct prose that reads "unlike anything else David ever wrote."[66] It centers on two young Christians, Lane Dean and his girlfriend Sheri Fisher, who are talking very awkwardly about whether to abort Sheri's pregnancy. In a supposed "*moment of grace*," Lane apparently sees into Sheri's heart: he sees that this girl, whom his mother thinks of as "good people," is "gambling that he is good" as well, and this leads him to decide to keep the baby and get married.[67] But Lane and Sheri were not always "good people," and different versions of the pregnancy scenario can be found throughout Wallace's manuscripts and notebooks. One such variation describes how an unnamed male character gets his girlfriend pregnant and then discovers, just when he is about to break up with her, that she faked the pregnancy. The man is left feeling extremely guilty, but what he does not know is that his girlfriend may have made the whole thing up precisely to get him to leave her.[68] And another scenario details how the male character, who is now described as possibly a Christian, refuses to marry his pregnant girlfriend, who therefore chooses to go ahead with the abortion. Unfortunately, the procedure goes horribly wrong and the girl dies, causing the young man to be so overwhelmed with guilt that he takes up the most miserable job he can think of.[69]

Of course that job, like Stecyk's, is with the IRS, on whose payroll we find a broad range of broken heartlanders, who are all, in their own way, parodies of Midwestern stereotypes. Likewise, the IRS itself parodies the spirit of the region. The novel's portrait of the Service's Regional Examinations Center, which provides nothing less than a haven for all those men in gray flannel suits, is a caricature of Peoria, whose "flannel plains," "blacktop graphs," and bland "monoculture" are all captured in the same shade of gray.[70] Seeing that, at one point, Wallace imagined Peoria's REC to be housed in an old mirror factory called "Mid West Mirror Works (sic)," we might even say that the REC holds up a mirror to the region, and a funhouse mirror at that.[71] Such a connection between region and REC adds further emphasis to the ways in which Wallace's geographic metafiction makes use of the Midwest. Much more than a mere backdrop or convenient setting, the region is an integral part of the novel.

This brings us to one final intertextual reference, not to either of the two urtexts that have been the focus of this essay, but to a piece by Wallace's contemporary Michael Martone, whose edited volume *A Place of Sense* was part of Wallace's personal library. Among the essays included in that 1988 volume is Martone's Midwestern autogeography "The Flatness," which Wallace underlined and annotated in his own copy of the book, perhaps in preparation for his own autogeography, "Derivative Sport in Tornado Alley," which appeared in Martone's 1992 volume *Townships*. "The Flatness" ends on a particularly strong note, with Martone observing that his native Midwest is "a landscape not often painted or photographed."[72] Instead, he suggests, "the place is more like the materials of the art itself – the stretched canvas and paper."[73] With these words, Martone manages to convey the essence of geographic metafiction, a regional poetics in which place is not simply out there for any regionalist to put it into writing, but it is the very material that the regionalist writes with. The geography of the Midwest, as Wallace himself observed in the margins of Martone's conclusion, is "not object but medium."[74] It is precisely this idea that his geographic metafiction brings home – home, which by popular convention, is in the heartland.

Notes

1. Michael Pietsch, interview by Geoffrey Ward, "Endnotes: David Foster Wallace," BBC Radio 3 (London, February 6, 2011), 40:30–40:31, 40:36–40:38.
2. Michel Foucault, "Of Other Spaces," (trans.) Jay Miskowiec, *Diacritics* 16.1 (1986), p. 24; Edward Soja, *Thirdspace: Journeys to Los Angeles and Other Real-and-Imagined Spaces* (Oxford: Blackwell, 1996), p. 13.
3. David Foster Wallace, *The Broom of the System* (New York: Penguin, 1987), p. 142.
4. For the source of this neologism, see Barrie Jean Borich "Autogeographies," in Margot Singer and Nicole Walker (eds.), *Bending Genre: Essays on Creative Nonfiction* (New York: Bloomsbury, 2013), pp. 97–101.
5. Charles B. Harris, "David Foster Wallace's Hometown: A Correction," *Critique* 51.3 (2010), p. 186.
6. Marshall McLuhan, *The Gutenberg Galaxy* (Toronto: University of Toronto Press, 2011), p. 25; Paul Giles, "Sentimental Posthumanism: David Foster Wallace," *Twentieth Century Literature* 53.3 (2007), p. 327.
7. Paul Quinn, "'Location's Location': Placing David Foster Wallace," in Marshall Boswell and Stephen J. Burn (eds.), *A Companion to David Foster Wallace Studies* (New York: Palgrave Macmillan, 2013), p. 87; David Foster Wallace, "Derivative Sport in Tornado Alley," in *A Supposedly Fun Thing I'll Never Do Again: Essays and Arguments* (Boston: Little, Brown, 1997), p. 5.

8. Mark McGurl, "The Institution of Nothing: David Foster Wallace in the Program," *boundary* 2 41.3 (Fall 2014), p. 28.

9. Linda Hutcheon, *A Poetics of Postmodernism: History, Theory, Fiction* (New York: Routledge, 1988), p. 124.

10. Henry Nash Smith, *Virgin Land: The American West as Symbol and Myth* (Cambridge, MA: Harvard University Press, 2000), p. xi.

11. See Brian McHale, *Postmodernist Fiction* (New York: Routledge, 1987); Bertrand Westphal, *Geocriticism: Real and Fictional Spaces*, (trans.) Robert T. Tally Jr. (New York: Palgrave Macmillan, 2011), p. 158.

12. David Foster Wallace, *The Pale King* (New York: Little, Brown, 2011), p. 4.

13. This Peoria binder, which contained a typescript draft of *The Pale King*'s prose-poetic opening, can be found in box 40, folder 4 of the Wallace Papers held at the Harry Ransom Center.

14. Carl van Doren, *The American Novel: 1789–1939* (New York: Macmillan, 1940), p. 295.

15. Victoria E. Johnson, *Heartland TV: Prime Time Television and the Struggle for US Identity* (New York: New York University Press, 2008), p. 5.

16. Ibid.

17. James Poniewozik, Jeanne McDowell, and Andrea Sachs, "The Culture Comes Home," *TIME* (November 19, 2001), p. 126.

18. Wallace qtd. in D. T. Max, *Every Love Story Is a Ghost Story: A Life of David Foster Wallace* (New York: Viking, 2012), p. 263. The first page of Wallace's manuscript of "The View" also includes a slight variation on this working title. See box 30, folder 11 of the Wallace Papers.

19. David Foster Wallace, "The View from Mrs. Thompson's," in *Consider the Lobster: And Other Essays* (New York, Little, Brown, 2005), p. 130.

20. Ibid.

21. William Barillas, *The Midwestern Pastoral: Place and Landscape in Literature of the American Heartland* (Athens: Ohio University Press, 2006), pp. 18, 19; Andrew R. L. Cayton, "The Anti-Region: Place and Identity in the History of the American Midwest," in Andrew R. L. Cayton and Susan Gray (eds.), *The American Midwest: Essays on Regional History* (Bloomington: Indiana University Press, 2007), p. 140.

22. Wallace, *Broom*, p. 142.

23. Wallace, "The View," p. 128.

24. Walt Whitman, "America's Characteristic Landscape," in *Collected Prose Works* (Philadelphia, PA: David McKay, 1892), p. 150.

25. Sinclair Lewis, *Main Street: The Story of Carol Kennicott* (New York: Penguin, 1985), p. 8.

26. Ibid.

27. William Z. Ripley, *Main Street and Wall Street* (London: Brentano's, 1927), p. vii.

28. Robert S. Lynd and Helen Merrell Lynd, *Middletown: A Study in American Culture* (London: Constable, 1929), p. 7.

29. Max, *Every Love Story*, p. 323, n. 17.

30. For further evidence of Wallace's interest in Peoria as America writ large, see p. 90 and p. 28 of his "Records Notebook," box 41, folder 7 of the Wallace Papers.

31. Wallace, "The View," pp. 135; 137, fn. 1.
32. David Foster Wallace, "Getting Away from Already Being Pretty Much Away from It All," in *A Supposedly Fun Thing*, p. 120; Wallace, *Broom*, p. 382.
33. Wallace, "The View," p. 139.
34. Christoph Ribbat, "Seething Static: Notes on Wallace and Journalism," in David Hering (ed.), *Consider David Foster Wallace: Critical Essays* (Los Angeles, CA: Sideshow Media Group, 2010), p. 194; Zadie Smith, "Brief Interviews with Hideous Men: The Difficult Gifts of David Foster Wallace," in *Changing My Mind: Occasional Essays* (London: Penguin, 2009), p. 283.
35. Edith Wharton, "The Great American Novel," in Frank Wegener (ed.), *The Uncollected Critical Writings* (Princeton, NJ: Princeton University Press, 1999), p. 152.
36. Wallace, "The View," p. 139.
37. Ibid.
38. Ibid. pp. 139, 140.
39. Lewis, *Main Street*, p. 36.
40. Wallace, "The View," p. 139.
41. See p. 5 of "The View" MS, box 30, folder 11 of the Wallace Papers, for the exact description of his Bloomington neighbors' ability to feel.
42. Wallace, "The View," 140; see the left margin of p. 6 of "The View" MS, box 30, folder 11, for Wallace's expression of his anxiety over his inability to feel.
43. Wallace, *The Pale King*, p. 73.
44. Sherwood Anderson, "Departure," in *Winesburg, Ohio* (New York: Penguin, 1978), p. 247.
45. Anderson, "Godliness: A Tale in Four Parts," *Winesburg, Ohio*, p. 69.
46. Wallace, "The View," p. 140.
47. Cf. Hutcheon, *A Poetics*, p. 126.
48. Frederick Jackson Turner, *The Frontier in American History* (New York: Dover, 1996), p. 4.
49. Lynd and Lynd, *Middletown*, p. 222.
50. Ibid. p. 8; Hugh Gusterson, "Introduction: Writing Race into *Middletown*," in Routledge M. Dennis, *Finding the African Americans that Middletown Left Out* (Lewiston, NY: Edward Mellen, 2012), p. xv.
51. Ibid.
52. See Steven Watts, *Magic Kingdom: Walt Disney and the American Way of Life* (Columbia: University of Missouri Press, 1997), p. 3; Johnson, *Heartland TV*, p. 115.
53. Wallace's exact descriptions of Bloomington's sociocultural and racial divisions, as well as his hand-drawn illustration of the antiracism signs, can be found on pp. 2–3 of "The View" MS, box 30, folder 11.
54. The exact phrase can be found on p. 2 of the MS stored in box 40, folder 7, subfolder 324 of the Wallace Papers. For a textual genesis of *Winesburg, Ohio*, see Walter B. Rideout, *Sherwood Anderson: A Writer in America* (Madison: University of Wisconsin Press, 2006), p. 209.
55. Anderson, "The Book of the Grotesque," *Winesburg, Ohio*, p. 22.
56. Ibid. pp. 23, 24.
57. Irving Howe, *Sherwood Anderson* (New York: William Sloane, 1951), p. 99.

58. Wallace, *The Pale King*, p. 29.
59. Ibid. p. 30.
60. Ibid. p. 35.
61. Ibid. p. 32.
62. Ibid. p. 33.
63. Ibid. p. 31.
64. For the exact details of this backstory, see Wallace's "Green Spiral Reward for Return Notebook," in box 41, folder 1.
65. See p. 221 of Wallace's "Records Notebook," box 41, folder 7.
66. "Rereading David Foster Wallace," *The New Yorker Festival*, October 6, 2012, 1:08:37–1:08:39, http://video.newyorker.com/watch/rereading-david-foster-wallace.
67. Wallace, *The Pale King*, pp. 42, 37.
68. See p. 157 of Wallace's "Records Notebook," box 41, folder 7.
69. For the exact description of this alternate scenario, see Wallace's MS draft in box 39, folder 6, subfolder 243.
70. See p. 69 and p. 126 of Wallace's "Records Notebook" for his exact description of what kind of refuge the IRS provides; Wallace, *The Pale King*, pp. 3, 271.
71. Wallace, *The Pale King*, p. 265. For further confirmation of Wallace's initial ideas of housing the Peoria REC in an old mirror factory, see his "Klimt Notebook," box 41 folder 6.
72. Michael Martone, "The Flatness," in Michael Martone, *A Place of Sense: Essays in Search of the Midwest* (Iowa City: University of Iowa Press, 1988), p. 33.
73. Ibid.
74. Wallace qtd. in Adam Kelly, "The Map and the Territory: Infinite Boston," *The Millions*, August 13, 2013, www.themillions.com/2013/08/the-map-and-the-territory-infinite-boston.html.

15

JOSEPH TABBI

David (Foster) Wallace and the (World) System

Notwithstanding Justice H. Harold Mealer's famous characterization, included in the Fourth Appellate Circuit's majority opinion on *Atkinson et al. v. The United States*, of a government bureaucracy as "the only known parasite larger than the organism on which it subsists," the truth is that such a bureaucracy is really much more a parallel world, both connected to and independent of this one, operating under its own physics and imperatives of cause. One might envision a large and intricately branching system of jointed rods, pulleys, gears, and levers radiating out from a central operator such that tiny movements of that operator's finger are transmitted through that system to become the gross kinetic changes in the rods at the periphery. It is at this periphery that the bureaucracy's world acts upon this one.

The crucial part of the analogy is that the elaborate system's operator is not himself uncaused. The bureaucracy is not a closed system: it is this that makes it a world instead of a thing.

The Pale King

As I said, human minds cannot communicate.
Niklas Luhmann, "How Can the Mind Participate in Communication"

By the time David Foster Wallace drafted the above fragment, one of hundreds that would be collected by his editor posthumously for presentation in *The Pale King*, he would have been aware that the term "systems novel" was being applied to his own work.[1] Yet even as he addressed himself specifically to the operations of bureaucratic systems, our understanding of the ways of the official world and the specific, bureaucratic location of one's own literary craft were themselves under reconsideration in contemporary systems theory. The early career essays Wallace had written – setting himself against irony as a default literary mode (overtaken from his postmodernist predecessors by television and advertising) and toward an endorsement by literary authors of "single-entendre values"[2] – were a prelude (as we'll soon see) to ever more verbal excess and inventive distributions of his own authorial voice. Wallace's self-consciousness about an author's personal location in systems, arguably, had only increased after he'd cleared the way for what would become (among his own generation) the embrace of a "New Sincerity,"[3] though his own practice may have been less of a departure than it seems from the postmodern aesthetic of his so-called "real enemies,"[4] such patriarchs for his patricide as Thomas Pynchon and John Barth. These are authors whose works, notably *The Crying of Lot 49* and "Lost in the Funhouse," themselves had been brought into the same academic curriculum that had become, in the United States, pretty much the only institution where writers of Wallace's generation could initiate and pursue a stable literary career. Mark McGurl, who addressed this particular re-situation of literary activity in his landmark book, *The Program Era*, portrays Wallace as not so much a rebel but more a "strong *student*" of his postmodernist predecessors with their "sprawling models" of world-spanning fiction.[5]

I want to suggest in the present chapter that the heightened self-consciousness and metafictional reflection in Wallace's later work differ significantly from what came before and his aesthetic shift can be seen as largely consistent with a conceptual shift in cybernetic thought at the time – away from informatic and dispositional communication toward more cognitive exchanges. Bruce Clarke (2011) articulates the shift away from a "first-order" cybernetics that had to do with problems of feedback between a system and its environment to a more self-referential, "second-order cybernetics" that takes into account the observer's influence on the systems under observation. Where first-order, first-generation cybernetics still regarded the "environment" as a source of information whose retrieval and analysis could help control a system's development, second-order approaches saw the feedback loop differently. "The disentanglement between informatics and cognition is key," notes Clarke, in the distinction between a first- and second-order cybernetics.[6] In such an approach, self-reflection is neither private nor necessarily pathologically involuted but is rather based on an individual's encounter with self-contained others, an encounter in which certain mental operations are shared, some reinforced and others corrected, and other things are left unknown, remaining part of the unexplored environment and keeping open the possibility for other concepts, other approaches to the materials at hand. (Hence the continued but qualitatively different expansiveness of Wallace, following the work of Pynchon and Barth, Joseph McElroy, Robert Coover, and some others.)

With the disentanglement of information and cognition, feedback happens not so much between a system and a never fully perceived or cognized environment as between one system and another, across boundaries that each partially share and all can only partially understand: that is, any meaningful exchange of information (when it does occur) happens some-place very much like Wallace's "periphery" where (in governmental systems) "the bureaucracy's world acts upon this one."

Understood this way, by Wallace in this chapter's epigraph no less than his contemporaries in the field of systems theory, a second-order cybernetic approach emerges not so much as a model of control over subjects as a mode of *worlding*. The self that is addressed by bureaucratic systems is not "itself uncaused" and neither is the bureaucracy "a closed system: it is this that makes it a world instead of a thing." As Wallace has his near namesake "David Wallace" remark in an "Author's Foreword" (an appar-ently completed chapter that is placed 68 pages into *The Pale King*[7]), part of the compulsion of an emerging writer in the 1990s might have been precisely to *avoid* the drudgery of bureaucratic systems whose expansion in the United States was unprecedented and would extend into hitherto private as well as official channels. So there's "the autobiographical fact," cited by David Wallace, "that like so many other nerdy, disaffected young people of that time, I dreamed of becoming an 'artist,' i.e., somebody whose adult job was original and creative instead of tedious and dronelike. My specific dream was of becoming an immortally great fiction writer à la Gaddis or Anderson, Balzac or Perec, & c." Except that the greatness of each of these authors, much like the greatness aspired to by David Foster Wallace (himself, not necessarily his personified near namesake) lies largely in their embrace of systems, their respective submission to constraints of the system that would emerge not so much through the author's semiautonomous imagination as through a concerted encounter with bureaucratic but also enabling systems and vocalizations. Gaddis and Anderson had achieved something along these lines in narratives constructed largely (like those of Dos Passos also, as we'll see) of the "everyday speech of Americans."[8] Balzac, who abandoned a career in law because of its tedium, was in this respect similar; and so was Perec in his generative conceit of "Life" as nothing more (or less) than a "User's Manual" and in his willing embrace of technical constraints, such as the drafting of an entire novel without using the letter *e* (*La Disparition*, 1968, translated as *A Void* by Gilbert Adair in 1995, *A Vanishing* by Ian Monk, *Vanish'd!* by John Lee, and *Omissions* by Julian West).[9]

That last example indicates a way, literally, for an author to become himself or herself a part of "the intricate branching system," not of machinic mechanisms as such but of language that is also constructed organically over extended periods of time, not mechanically, whether it be written or thought, spoken to others or held in mind. Indeed, the question of how or even whether one's mental experiences are communicable is itself a crucial part of the analogy with systems drawn here by Wallace. It is after all in the epigraph from which I began, an "operator's finger," not the mind, that engages with systems at the "periphery." An engagement that is as much operative as it is psychic or social is for Wallace (David Foster, no less than David) the "crucial part of the analogy" that conjoins the parallel world systems of modern bureaucracies and literary fictions.

The literally "digital" implementation of second-order systems, hinted at in this reference to an "operator's finger," were pretty well anticipated in the foreword's "cultural present of 2005," when David Wallace refers to the erasing of "any clear line between personal and public, or rather between private vs. performative. Among obvious examples are web logs, reality television, cell-phone cameras, chat rooms ... not to mention the dramatically increased popularity of the memoir as a literary genre."[10] *The Pale King* itself, according to David Wallace in the foreword, is also "a kind of vocational memoir. It is also supposed to function as a portrait of a bureaucracy – arguably the most important federal bureaucracy in American life – at a time of enormous internal struggle and soul-searching, the birth pains of what's come to be known among tax professionals as the New IRS."[11]

To appreciate how close Wallace came to realizing this ambition seamlessly to enter (and admit one's implication within) systems, one needs to move past the "nerdy" outlook that conceives the arts as an outside to systems, an autonomous realm of creativity separate from either bureaucratic or academic programs, or somehow separate from the publishing world, which at the time when Wallace's career was starting (the period in the 1980s when *The Pale King* is set) was itself undergoing a vast transformation. The apotheosis of "memoir," the fetishizing of truth telling (and subsequent cashing in on the shock after eventual revelations of an author's lies) are clearly noted and pretty thoroughly undermined by the appearance of "David Wallace" in *The Pale King* – starting with his opening assertion, "Author here,"[12] of authorial presence and absolute sincerity: "All of this is true. This book is really true."[13] Against decades of Derridean deconstruction of authorial "presence" (any author, of any literary period and whether speaking or writing), we have an objective resurgence in the publishing world of the memoir genre and (the character) David Wallace's determinedly forthcoming assertion of his own presence and sincerity – at such length and with so many "irksome"[14] paradoxes requiring such lengthy analysis and clarification that Wallace achieves with his "occasional 'author' appositive thing"[15] nothing less than an ironic reassertion of Derrida's position and a compelling demonstration (through overkill) of the philosopher Donald Davidson's insight that there can be no convention for sincerity.

At the same time, David Wallace's characterization of systems as themselves "tedious and dronelike" reinforces commonplace cybernetic assumptions that Wallace's contemporaries in literary and systems theory were rethinking, even as Wallace himself came eventually to write in parallel with bureaucracies (notably in parts of *Oblivion* and throughout the unfinished fragments of *The Pale King*). As the youthful Wallace in the mid-1980s could only conceive of a career in a federal bureaucracy "as little more than one tiny ephemeral dronelike cog,"[16] systems theory itself was often viewed at this time (in the words of Cary Wolfe) as "just a grim technocratic functionalism or a thinly disguised apology for the status quo, a kind of barely camouflaged social Darwinism. In this view, systems theory … gets assimilated to the larger context of post-World War II society's obsession with management, command-and-control apparatuses, informatic reproduction, homeostasis, and the like."[17] As for "the daunting difficulty of the theory itself," particularly as it was formulated by Niklas Luhmann, this too can be seen, in retrospect, to be something that Wallace shared. Luhmann is said (by Wolfe) to have given

> seasoned readers of [literary] theory pause with [his work's] extraordinary abstraction and rigor; its head-on engagement with problems of paradox, self-reference, and the like; its systematically counterintuitive findings; and its relative lack of creature comforts along the way of those who have signed on for the journey of what Luhmann unabashedly calls "super-theory."[18]

As Dietrich Schwanitz, a near contemporary of Luhmann, once put it: "Systems theory is anything but mechanistic."[19] Its move to instantiate paradox, unceremoniously as a ground for any conceptual system (not a conundrum to be endlessly dissected), might also help to explain Wallace's awareness of the limits to his own tendency toward verbal excess and involution, and why these are, in *The Pale King*, so clearly attributed to a character in fiction – a comedic authorial construction sharing aspects of Wallace's voice, character, and work life and certainly offering insights into his aesthetic but determinedly not speaking "for" the book's author.

Not that Wallace was ever any less committed than Luhmann to an overarching ambition: his at once world weary and thoroughly *worldly* fiction can be said to reconstruct established narrative genres in much the same way that a "super-theory" resituates metaphysics in professional practices and functionally differentiated realms of knowledge. In Wallace's case, the terms of preference have been more numerous but no less overarching: His expansiveness has been called "encyclopedic,"[20] an "art of excess," and "mastery."[21] Critical terms of preference, such as Frederick Karl's "Mega-novel,"[22] Franco Moretti's "modern epic,"[23] and Tom Leclair's "systems novel," have been consolidated by Stefano Ercolino under the generic formulation "Maximalist

Novel," a term that is itself notably varying and flexible enough so as to include a variety of works (and not exclusively books by white males from the United States). The "experimentalism" of such fiction, for Ercolino, by Zadie Smith and Roberto Bolaño no less than Pynchon and Wallace, "is measured not across the totality of each novel, but at the level of single characteristics. As a result, we will have novels that are longer, novels that are more encyclopedic, novels that are more polyphonic, novels that are more digressive, novels that are more paranoid, novels that are more inter-semiotic than others."[24] The sprawling nature of such novels encourages Ercolino "to speak of a *chaos function* and a *cosmos function*" that produces "a dialectic between centrifugal and centripetal forces within the narrative, in which traits such as 'length,' 'encyclopedic mode,' 'dissonant chorality,' and 'diegetic exuberance' … will play a common role *against* traits such as 'completeness,' 'narratorial omniscience,' and 'paranoia.'"[25] He goes further and finds (in Wallace in particular) an "ethical commitment," "hybrid realism," and "intersemioticity,"[26] terms that are consistent with the dialogism that, for Adam Kelly, "[brings] a range of voices into" Wallace's texts, making them "a forum for competing ideas."[27]

Each of these approaches, Ercolino's (Hegelian/Marxist) dialectic and Kelley's (Bakhtinian) dialogic, convey important aspects of Wallace's aesthetic, though they might just as readily describe maximalist tendencies in the unattributed dialogue favored by William Gaddis or (a generation earlier) Dos Passos's conception of the US nation-state as nothing more (nor less) than the "the speech of Americans." But dialogue and diatribe in Wallace have a much different feel; his characters, unless they are gathered in a stalled elevator at their place of work for the explicit purpose of debate,[28] rarely speak openly and unaffectedly to one another, as they do throughout Gaddis's *J R* (1973), for example, and there is nothing approaching the "Camera Eye" and "Newsreel" projections of human consciousness in Dos Passos, which are basically stream of consciousness interludes that are perhaps notionally but nonetheless effectively associated with the emerging, filmic technology of the achieved modernist era. The prologue to the *USA Trilogy*, unlike the foreword to *The Pale King*, is owned by John Dos Passos, and his novels display a similar (constructed, though easily naturalized) presentation of characters – as when he narrates the thoughts of Fainy McCreary (Mac) or J. Ward Moorehouse, their actions, and the actions of the women in their lives when they discover they are pregnant. The working-class Mac, after some urging, will do the right thing by Maisie; Moorehouse, for his part, isn't told by his upper-class love interest, Annabelle Strang, that she intends to have an abortion. The thoughts leading to Annabelle's decision (and Ward's response), are presented through a third-person indirect narration:

> She went to a very famous specialist for women's diseases who agreed that on no account should she have a baby at this time. An immediate operation was necessary and would be a little dangerous as the baby was so far along. She didn't tell Ward and only sent word from the hospital when it was over. It was Christmas day. He went immediately to see her. He heard the details in chilly horror. He'd gotten used to the idea of having a baby and thought it would have a steadying effect on Annabelle. She lay looking very pale in the bed in the private sanatorium and he stood beside the bed with his fists clenched without saying anything. At length the nurse said to him that he was tiring madame and he went away.[29]

Cognitive and affective aspects for each of the characters are stated and described, not detailed in direct presentations of a character's thought stream at the moment the thoughts are experienced – as they are for example in Wallace's depiction of Lane Dean, Jr. and "his girlfriend," Sheri Fisher, who are faced with a similar decision. Dos Passos's wording, in reference to a doctor who "agreed" with the patient rather than having offered an independent diagnosis, suggests collusion. And Ward in any case had reason to doubt that the baby was his: he'd asked Annabelle, "How long is it since you . . . noticed?"

> Her eyes were suddenly black and searching in his again. They stared at each other and hated each other. "Quite long enough," she said and pulled his ear as if he was a child.[30]

The *Pale King* dialogue between Lane Dene and Sheri is by contrast entirely open, up front, and trusting. They're sincere with one another, and the reader overhears Lane's thoughts rather than observing the couple as they watch one another and work out the arrangements at length. "One thing Lane Dean did was reassure her again that he'd go with her [to the abortion clinic] and be there with her. It was one of the few safe or decent things he could really say. The second time he said it again now she shook her head and laughed in an unhappy way that was more just air out of her nose. Her real laugh was different. Where he'd be was in the waiting room, she said."[31] We don't so much see Sheri shaking her head (in the way Dos Passos has us observe, cinematically, Annabelle's "black" eyes), as we observe Lane observing her; instead of easing the burden, Lane's promise to be there at the clinic makes Sheri feel all the more hopeless at the prospect of her being alone in the operating room.

Both are from the same congregation – it is where they met: "they'd prayed on it and talked it through from every angle. Lane said how sorry she knew he

241

was, and that if he was wrong in believing they'd truly decided together when they decided to make the appointment she should please tell him. . . . She did not reply. . . .. He said the appointment could get moved back."[32] No aspect of the decision is neglected, both the young man and his girlfriend are open and honest with one another; the thoughts of one concerning how the other must feel are shared completely (with one another and, in turn, with the reader), and nothing is communicated.

I know of no better illustration in contemporary literature than this chapter early in *The Pale King,* of Luhmann's credo that minds cannot communicate, not even to communicate our own thought to ourselves:

> It was still so early in it, they both knew that, he said. This was true, he felt this way, and yet he also knew he was also trying to say things that would get her to open up and say enough back that he could see her and read her heart and know what to say to get her to go through with it. He knew this without admitting to himself that this is what he wanted, for it would make him out to be a hypocrite and a liar.[33]

He did not go to their pastor "or the prayer partners at campus ministries, not his UPS friends" where he works "or the spiritual counselling available through his parents' old church. But he did not know why Sheri herself had not gone to Pastor Steve – he could not read her heart. She was blank and hidden. He so fervently wished it never happened. He felt like he knew now why it was a true sin and not just a leftover rule from past society" (41–42). The necessity of convention, the need to trust in an authority and respect a consensus, religious or professional or even bureaucratic, the need to follow recognized rules in society is of "personal concern" precisely because there are no conventions for sincerity and no way of knowing what's in another person's mind or heart, not even that of one we love – or might not know we love since this is no more communicable than any other autoaffection:

> There is a mower cutting grass someplace off behind them. It will be a terrible, make-or-break gamble born out of the desperation in Sheri Fisher's soul, the knowledge that she can neither do this thing today nor carry a child alone and shame her family. Her values block the way either way, Lane can see this ... Lane Dean Jr. sees all this, and is moved with pity and with also something more, something without any name he knows, that is given to him to feel in the form of a question that never once in the long week's thinking and division had even so much as occurred – why is he so sure he doesn't love her? Why is one kind of love any different? What if he has no earthly idea what love is?[34]

Wallace is here taking conventional "leftover" value systems, that the characters also know, systems designed to preclude thought, and putting these systems directly in touch with the thought of his characters, which is itself, oddly, disturbingly inconsequential. Sheri's own silence is itself an assertion (more presumably than Wallace ever would allow himself to assert) that Lane, the male, was the one who needed to decide, if they should stay or go, have the child, or keep their appointment at the clinic. (The decision is not communicated in this chapter, but the girl's silence prevails and, like Fainy and Maisy before them, Wallace's working-class couple are married, not particularly happily in later chapters.)

An aspect of Wallace's maximalism, not yet fully explored by any of Wallace's critics (or myself in this chapter), may be grounded in the unknowable yet maximally distributed nature of consciousness as this is currently understood.[35] Adam Kelly suggests Wallace's departure from both the modernist and postmodernist paradigms when he notes how "speakers in Wallace's fiction are often desperate for genuine dialogue, but find that their overwhelming need to predict in advance the other's response blocks the possibility of finding the language to get outside themselves and truly reach out to the other."[36] The one exception, published in Wallace's lifetime and placed by the editor toward the end of the novel, is the chapter that takes place at a Friday happy hour for the mostly recent recruits to the Peoria tax service. Had Meredith Rand not sought out Shane Drinion specifically, the one male among her colleagues who is never made "nervous or uncomfortably quiet"[37] by her beauty, her personal life story would not have been conveyed so openly (not even to herself). Even so, her narrative is more of a monologue, albeit one that is not so much interrupted as inflected and moved forward by Drinion's close but never self-interested attention and an un-self-consciousness that at moments causes him to levitate.

Such self-consciously staged dialogues in Wallace, in my view, can only reinforce the counterintuitive (and surely polemical) assertion by Luhmann that human minds cannot communicate. The distinction between "consciousness" and "communication" that underlies Luhmann's claim has long been a guiding principle not only in systems theory but (as Wolfe notes) in any deconstructive project that regards authorial self-presence as a production, not the communication of an a priori intention. Luhmann in this respect is no more dismissive of communicative practice than Derrida, who similarly gets us to question the "autoaffection" of "the voice-as-presence and the valorizing of speech (as an index of the self-presence of consciousness to itself) over writing (a recursive domain of iterative communication that is, properly understood, fundamentally ahuman or even antihuman)."[38] Understood this way, any wholly successful, mind-to-mind communication – of the type achieved by Meredith Rand and Shane ("Mr. X") Drinion – is a production of presence about as likely as levitation.

What is more likely and certainly more frequent in Wallace's fiction is the staging of a single consciousness as it takes us through its own self-interrogation. If that sounds solipsistic, it may appear less so if we only take seriously the "ahuman or even antihuman"[39] influences on our thought that Wallace engages, arguably more openly than any of his maximalist forebears. As we've seen in the authorial address from "David Wallace," these autoaffective performances are deflected at every turn by (for example) publishing protocols, legal constraints, academic programs, and numerous other functionally differentiated systems that may have been devised by humans but by now operate semiautonomously, employing human consciousness for mostly operational, not communicative, purposes. The incorporation of persons into such systems, as employees, citizens, or (what supplants citizenship from the point of view of the Reagan-era "New IRS") bureaucratic subjects – all that depends on the training of consciousness toward focused, preformulated tasks. Dull as such tasks may be, our incorporation by systems does not make us "cogs" or "drones" so much as faithful subjects who, more and more often, are disposed (and expected) to trust and *believe* in the system.[40] As "David Wallace" notes toward the end of the foreword, members of the tax service, in particular, end up "negotiating boredom as one would a terrain, its levels and forests and endless wastes." The "ahuman or even antihuman"[41] dimensions of our ever more disengaged official lives create in Wallace a somewhat different sense of our embeddedness in the world. "Maybe," he writes, "it's because the subject is, in and of itself, dull ... only then we're again right back where we started, which is tedious and irksome. There may, though, I opine, be more to it ... as in vastly more, right here before us all, hidden by virtue of its size."[42]

And this, in my opinion, is an aspect of *The Pale King*'s maximalism that is yet to be addressed by Wallace criticism. Just as the physical, material, and informatic world becomes familiar to consciousness, so too has an official, corporate system – humanly constructed – become so familiar as to be a world in itself, one that is ever present and immediate. Though our corporations, too, are abstractions that require belief for their perpetuation, they are now (like the world they've supplanted) available for representation but also, definitively in literary practice, for defamiliarization. Even as "the stone," in Russian Formalist Viktor Shklovsky's formulation, is made to feel "stoney" again through artistry, the world system for Wallace is made invisible "by virtue of its size," and it is the function of literary arts to make us see and feel the presence of systems in our own conscious experience. What distinguishes the current phase of corporate enterprise, as Wallace knew as well as anyone, is the expansion of systems operations into cognitive realms. And the cognitive fictions that are so particular to Wallace ought to at once help to identify but also delimit the reach of our own consciousness within the corporate lifeworld.

Notes

1. Tom LeClair's essay "The Prodigious Fiction of Richard Powers, William Vollmann, Davis Foster Wallace" had already appeared in 1996 in *Critique: Studies in Contemporary Fiction* 38.1.
2. David Foster Wallace, "E Unibus Pluram: Television and U.S. Fiction," *The Review of Contemporary Fiction* 13.2 (Summer 1993), p. 192.
3. Although Wallace's essay of 1993, "E Unibus Pluram," was eagerly embraced by authors of his generation who were calling for a "New Sincerity," Wallace himself seems to have grasped, as the philosopher Donald Davidson argued in "Communication and Convention" (1985), that one cannot ground an aesthetic practice in "single-entendre values" (Wallace) any more than one can assert, in spoken or written communication, a "convention for sincerity" (Davidson).
4. See "An Expanded Interview with David Foster Wallace" by Larry McCaffery in Stephen J. Burn (ed.), *Conversations With David Foster Wallace* (Jackson: University of Mississippi, 2012).
5. Mark McGurl, "The Institution of Nothing: David Foster Wallace in the Program," *boundary 2* 41.3 (Fall 2014), p. 30.
6. Bruce Clarke identifies the 1970s, the period of Wallace's adolescence and the setting for *The Pale King*, as a seminal moment when second-order cybernetics and autopoietic systems theory converge to posit a noninformatic conception of cognition. Systems theory of this era, as we'll see, generalizes this shift to include technological and bureaucratic systems, which are "anything but mechanistic" (Schwanitz). Clarke's summary appears in *Neocybernetics and Narrative* (Minneapolis: University of Minnesota Press, 2014), p. 2.
7. The placement of the foreword is evidently David Foster Wallace's intention, observed by his editor. As we're told by "David Wallace": "The Foreword's having now been moved seventy-nine pages into the text is due to yet another spasm of last-minute caution on the part of the publisher." (It opens on page 68 of the published text.)
8. Prologue to *The USA Trilogy* (1938; New York: The Library of America, 1996).
9. Mark McGurl, as we will see, finds a similar concern with "The Institution of Nothing" in Wallace and the creative writing programs where he studied and taught. McGurl had previously applied systems thought to the emerging program; however, he doesn't seem to want to extend to Wallace the "neutral" sociology stance he has in *The Program Era* (Boston: Harvard University Press, 2011). McGurl won't condemn MFA programs for standardizing American literature and killing originality, yet one of their most original, if odd, "products" (DFW) is marked not as "the ultimate success story of the program" (p. 34) but rather as "office-bound" (p. 54) and out of touch with the "war going on" (p. 54) between creditors and debtors. McGurl takes no notice, however, of "David Wallace's" citation of the problem of debt undertaken by university students specifically, a thematic that was cited by another Wallace scholar, William Deresiewicz, and has turned into one of the most powerful critiques of the turn taken toward greater

diversity but diminished content or critical perspective on offer at elite universities in the United States. See Deresiewicz "On Political Correctness: Power, Class, and the New Religion" in *The American Scholar*, spring 2017; and note how "David Wallace" describes the "leftist piety" of the liberal college he attended, "a veritable temple of mammon" in *The Pale King*, pp. 77, 78.

10. Wallace, *The Pale King*, p. 82.

11. Ibid., p. 72. Later the "New IRS" is (helpfully) "distilled to its essence," namely, "to what extent the IRS should be operated like a for-profit business." Like so many "New" practices in so many disciplines, not least the "New Sincerity" of the post-postmodernist return to narrative realism, the "newness" turns out to be consistent with neoliberal (or, if one prefers, neoconservative) extensions of the for-profit and universally professionalized model of doing business, even in traditionally not-for-profit areas such as government and academia and formerly publicly held industries.

12. Ibid., p. 68 and again at p. 258 when Wallace informs us in a note that he "won't keep saying this each time that I, the living author, am actually narrating." Wallace, in another chapter (located, reasonably by the editor toward the end) before signing off again, reminds us in another note "why this occasional 'author' appositive thing is sometimes necessary" (p. 416). A notation by Wallace himself indicating that the character "David Wallace disappears – becomes a creature of the system" (*The Pale King*, appendix, p. 546) is seen by Brian McHale in "*The Pale King*, Or, The White Visitation" (also cited by McGurl, p. 48) as "unsettling" in light of the author's death; see Marshall Boswell and Stephen Burn (eds.), *A Companion to David Foster Wallace Studies* (New York: Palgrave Macmillan, 2013), p. 203. Might it also measure the distance between periodic displacements of the literary self, namely, Wallace's self-conscious absorption of his authorial persona in "systems" and earlier denials of literary aspiration – notably T. S. Eliot's "personal talent" that strives to be absorbed by tradition and Thomas Pynchon's carefully constructed paranoid connectivity that's overwhelmed, inevitably by entropic wastes.

13. Ibid., pp. 68, 69 and then again with such statements as "Here is the real truth" (p. 71); "*The Pale King* is basically a nonfiction memoir, with elements of reconstructive journalism" (p. 75) that might include, for example, interviews and releases "authorizing the use of certain audiovisual recording" (p. 74). These, "as an aggregate ... have provided reminiscences and concrete details that ... have yielded scenes of immense authority and realism, regardless of whether this author was actually corporally right there on the scene at the time or not" (p. 74). All of this "might appear to set up an irksome paradox" (p. 69) when we're given, for example, the author's reasons for including his own fore-word under the publisher's disclaimer overleaf from the title page concerning "the characters and events in this book." Clearly, however, Wallace has no interest in resolving paradoxes with so many (conflicting) truth claims; rather, like his contemporaries in systems theory and deconstruction, he is arguably *grounding* his literary aesthetic in paradox, and so it becomes not just "tedious and irksome" (p. 87) but also generative.

14. Ibid., pp. 69, 87.

15. Ibid., p. 416.

16. Ibid., p. 81.

17. Cary Wolfe, *What Is Posthumanism?* (Minneapolis: University of Minnesota Press, 2010), p. 3.
18. Ibid., p. 5.
19. "Systems Theory According to Niklas Luhmann – Its Environment and Conceptual Strategies," *Cultural Critique* 30 (Spring 1995), p. 146. Cited in Wolfe, p. 10.
20. Stephen J. Burn, "The Collapse of Everything: William Gaddis and the Encyclopedic Novel," in Joseph Tabbi and Rone Shavers (eds.), *Paper Empire: William Gaddis and the World System* (Tuscaloosa: University of Alabama Press, 2007), pp. 46–62.
21. Tom LeClair, *The Art of Excess: Mastery in Contemporary American Fiction* (Urbana: University of Illinois Press, 1989).
22. Frederick R. Karl, *American Fictions: 1940–1980: A Comprehensive History and Critical Evaluation* (New York: Harper and Row, 1983).
23. Franco Moretti, *Modern Epic: The World System from Goethe to Garcia-Marquez*, (trans.) Quentin Hoare (1994; London: Verso, 1996).
24. Stefano Ercolino, *The Maximalist Novel: From Thomas Pynchon's* Gravity's Rainbow *to Roberto Bolaño's 2666* (London: Bloomsbury, 2014), p. xv.
25. Ibid., pp. xv–xvi.
26. Ibid., p. xvi.
27. Adam Kelly, "David Foster Wallace and the Novel of Ideas," in Marshall Boswell (ed.), *David Foster Wallace and "The Long Thing": New Essays on the Novels* (New York: Bloomsbury, 2014), p. 5.
28. Wallace, *The Pale King*, ch. 19.
29. Dos Passos, *USA Trilogy*, p. 175.
30. Ibid., p. 172.
31. Wallace, *The Pale King*, p. 39.
32. Ibid., p. 41.
33. Ibid., p. 41.
34. Ibid., pp. 44–45.
35. Stephen J. Burn, in "'A Paradigm for the Life of Consciousness: *The Pale King*,'" acknowledges that "one of the unifying mechanisms" in *The Pale King* "is Wallace's career long fascination with consciousness"; in Boswell (ed.), *David Foster Wallace*, p. 151. Burn also hints at how Wallace's fascination differs from that of past authors, when he recasts a formulation by Melville: "On the subject of analogies," Burn writes, "Herman Melville noted halfway through *Moby Dick* that: 'not the smallest atom stirs or lives in matter, but has its cunning duplicate in mind.'" Burn then goes on to argue "that the unifying analogies in *The Pale King* reverse Melville's dictum, to search in the external world for 'a paradigm for the life of consciousness'," p. 162; Burn is citing Frank Bidart, *Desire* (New York: Farrar, Straus, and Giroux, 1997), p. 9.
36. Kelly, "David Foster Wallace," in Boswell (ed.), *David Foster Wallace*, p. 7.
37. Wallace, *The Pale King*, p. 449.
38. Wolfe, *What Is Posthumanism?*, p. 6.
39. Ibid.
40. And for those who would wish for an alternative, the advice offered not by the character but by the author David Foster Wallace, in his address to the 2005

graduating class of Kenyon College, has struck at least one commentator, Ralph Clare, as close to "Monkish" in its advocacy of "the really important freedom [that] involves attention, and awareness, and discipline, and effort." (*This Is Water*, p. 120, cited in Clare, "The Politics of Boredom and the Boredom of Politics," in Boswell, *David Foster Wallace*, p. 204.)

41. Wolfe, *What Is Posthumanism?*, p. 6.
42. Wallace, *The Pale King*, p. 87.

Selected Critical Studies

Boswell, Marshall. *Understanding David Foster Wallace*. Columbia: University of South Carolina Press, 2009.

Burn, Stephen J. *David Foster Wallace's* Infinite Jest: *A Reader's Guide*. Second Edition. New York: Continuum, 2012.

Carlisle, Greg. *Elegant Complexity: A Study of David Foster Wallace's* Infinite Jest. Los Angeles: SSMG Press, 2007.

Den Dulk, Allard. *Existentialist Engagement in Wallace, Eggers, and Foer*. New York: Bloomsbury, 2016.

Hayes-Brady, Clare. *The Unspeakable Failures of David Foster Wallace: Language, Identity, and Resistance*. New York: Bloomsbury, 2016.

Hering, David. *David Foster Wallace: Fiction and Form*. London: Bloomsbury, 2016.

Severs, Jeffrey. *David Foster Wallace's Balancing Books: Fictions of Value*. New York: Columbia University Press, 2017.

Thompson, Lucas. *David Foster Wallace and Global Literature*. London: Bloomsbury, 2017.

Edited Collections and Special Journal Issues

Bolger, Robert K. and Scott Korb, eds. *Gesturing toward Reality: David Foster Wallace and Philosophy*. New York: Bloomsbury, 2014.

Boswell, Marshall, ed. *David Foster Wallace and "The Long Thing": New Essays on the Novels*, ed. Marshall Boswell. New York: Bloomsbury, 2013.

Boswell, Marshall and Stephen J. Burn, eds. *A Companion to David Foster Wallace Studies*. New York: Palgrave Macmillan, 2013.

Burn, Stephen J. and Mary K. Holland, eds. *Approaches to Teaching the Works of David Foster Wallace*. New York: The Modern Language Association of America. Forthcoming.

Cahn, Steven M. and Maureen Eckert. *Freedom and the Self: Essays on the Philosophy of David Foster Wallace*. New York: Columbia University Press, 2015.

Cohen, Samuel and Lee Konstantinou. *The Legacy of David Foster Wallace*. Iowa City: University of Iowa Press, 2012.

Coleman, Philip, ed. *Critical Insights: David Foster Wallace*. Ipswich, MA: Salem Press, 2015.

Hering, David, ed. *Consider David Foster Wallace*. Los Angeles: SSMG Press, 2010.

Herman, Luc and Toon Staes, eds. "Unfinished: Critical Approaches to David Foster Wallace's *The Pale King*." Special issue of *English Studies* 95.1 (2014): 1–93.

Selected Uncollected Essays and Book Chapters on Wallace

Aubry, Timothy. *"Infinite Jest* and the Recovery of Feeling," in *Reading as Therapy: What Contemporary Fiction Does for Middle-Class Americans.* Iowa City: University of Iowa Press, 2011, pp. 97–126.

Boswell, Marshall. "The Rival Lover: David Foster Wallace and the Anxiety of Influence in Jeffrey Eugenides's *The Marriage Plot.*" *Modern Fiction Studies* 62.3 (Fall 2016): 499–518.

Cioffi, Frank. "'An Anguish Become a Thing:' Narrative as Performance in David Foster Wallace's *Infinite Jest.*" *Narrative* 8.2 (2000): 161–181.

Cohen, Samuel. "The Whiteness of David Foster Wallace," in *Postmodern Literature and Race*, eds. Len Platt and Sara Upstone. Cambridge: Cambridge University Press, 2015, pp. 228–243.

Fest, Bradley. "The Inverted Nuke in the Garden: Archival Emergence and Anti-eschatology in David Foster Wallace's *Infinite Jest.*" *boundary* 2 29.3 (2012): 125–49.

Freudenthal, Elizabeth. "Anti-interiority: Compulsiveness, Objectification, and Identity in *Infinite Jest.*" *New Literary History* 41.1 (2010): 191–211.

Giles, Paul. *The Global Remapping of American Literature*. Princeton, NJ: Princeton University Press, 2011, pp. 161–180.

"Sentimental Posthumanism: David Foster Wallace." *Twentieth Century Literature* 53.3 (Autumn 2007): 327–44.

Goerlandt, Iannis. "'Put the Book Down and Slowly Walk Away': Irony and David Foster Wallace's *Infinite Jest.*" *Critique: Studies in Contemporary Fiction* 47.3 (2006): 309–28.

Harris, Charles B. "The Anxiety of Influence: The John Barth/David Foster Wallace Connection." *Critique: Studies in Contemporary Fiction* 55.1 (2014): 103–126.

Hayles, N. Katherine. "The Illusion of Autonomy and the Fact of Recursivity: Virtual Ecologies, Entertainment, and *Infinite Jest.*" *New Literary History* 30.3 (Summer 1999): 675–697.

Holland, Mary K. "'The Art's Heart's Purpose:' Braving the Narcissistic Loop of David Foster Wallace's *Infinite Jest*," in *Succeeding Postmodernism: Language and Humanism in Contemporary American Literature.* New York: Bloomsbury, 2013, pp. 57–89.

"'By Hirsute Author': Gender and Communication in the Work and Study of David Foster Wallace." *Critique: Studies in Contemporary Fiction* 58.1 (2017): 64–77.

Kelly, Adam. "David Foster Wallace: The Death of an Author and the Birth of a Discipline." *Irish Journal of American Studies Online* 2 (Summer 2010). Web. April 15, 2017. www.ijasonline.com/Adam-Kelly.html

"Dialectic of Sincerity: Lionel Trilling and David Foster Wallace." *Post* 45, October 17, 2014.

Jacobs, Timothy. "The Brothers Incandenza: Translating Ideology in Fyodor Dostoyevsky's *The Brothers Karamazov* and David Foster Wallace's *Infinite Jest*." *Texas Studies in Language and Literature* 49.3 (2007): 265–292.

Konstantinou, Lee. "How to Be a Believer," in *Cool Characters: Irony and American Fiction*. Cambridge, MA: Harvard University Press, 2016, pp. 163–216.

"The World of David Foster Wallace" *boundary* 2. 40.3 (September 2013): 59–86.

LeClair, Tom. "The Prodigious Fiction of Richard Powers, William T. Vollmann, and David Foster Wallace." *Critique: Studies in Contemporary Fiction* 38.1 (1996): 12–37.

McGurl, Mark. "The Institution of Nothing: David Foster Wallace in the Program." *boundary* 2 4.3 (September 2014): 27–54.

McLaughlin, Robert. "Post-postmodern Discontent: Contemporary Fiction and the Social World." *Symploke* 12.1–2 (2004): 53–68.

Miley, Mike. "... And Starring David Foster Wallace as Himself: Performance and Persona in *The Pale King*." *Critique: Studies in Contemporary Fiction* 57.2 (2016): 191–207.

Morrissey, Tara and Lucas Thompson. 'The Rare White at the Window': A Reappraisal of Mark Costello and David Foster Wallace's *Signifying Rappers*." *Journal of American Studies* 49.1 (2015): 77–97.

Smith, Zadie. "Brief Interviews with Hideous Men: The Difficult Gifts of David Foster Wallace," in *Changing My Mind: Occasional Essays*. New York: Penguin, 2009, pp. 255–297.

Szalay, Michael and Richard Godden. "The Bodies in the Bubble: David Foster Wallace's *The Pale King*." *Textual Practice* 28.7 (2014): 1273–1322.

Veggian, Henry. "Anachronisms of Authority: Authorship, Exchange Value, and David Foster Wallace's *The Pale King*." *boundary* 2 39.3 (2012): 389–408.

Williams, Iain. "(New) Sincerity in David Foster Wallace's 'Octet.'" *Critique* 56 (2015): 299–314.

Biography

Max, D. T. *Every Love Story Is a Ghost Story: A Life of David Foster Wallace*. New York: Viking, 2012.

Selected Print, Video, and Audio Interviews

Burn, Sephen J., ed. *Conversations with David Foster Wallace*. Jackson: University Press of Mississippi, 2012.

"David Foster Wallace." Interview by Charlie Rose, PBS, March 27, 1997. www.youtube.com/watch?v=hm94gUBCih8

David Foster Wallace: The Last Interview and Other Conversations. Brooklyn, NY: Melville House, 2012.

"David Foster Wallace (*Consider the Lobster*)." Interview by Michael Silverblatt, *Bookworm*, KCRW, March 2, 2006. www.kcrw.com/news-culture/shows/bookworm/david-foster-wallace-consider-the-lobster-and-other-essays

Lipsky, David. *Although of Course You End Up Becoming Yourself: A Road Trip with David Foster Wallace*. New York: Broadway Books, 2010.

McCaffery, Larry. "An Interview with David Foster Wallace." *Review of Contemporary Fiction*. 13.2 (Summer 1993): 127–151.

On the World Wide Web

The David Foster Wallace Archive at the Harry Ransom Humanities Research Center, University of Texas at Austin: http://norman.hrc.utexas.edu/fasearch/findingAid.cfm?eadid=00503

The David Foster Wallace Literary Trust: www.davidfosterwallacebooks.com/contact.html

The David Foster Wallace Research Group at the University of Glasgow's DFW Secondary Sources Bibliography: https://davidfosterwallaceresearch.wordpress.com/

The Howling Fantods Website: www.thehowlingfantods.com/dfw/

The International David Foster Wallace Society: www.dfwsociety.org

WORKS BY DAVID FOSTER WALLACE

NOVELS

The Broom of the System. New York: Penguin, 1987.
Infinite Jest. Boston: Little, Brown, 1996.
The Pale King: An Unfinished Novel. Ed. Michael Pietsch. New York: Little, Brown, 2011.

STORY COLLECTIONS

Girl with Curious Hair. New York: W. W. Norton, 1989.
Brief Interviews with Hideous Men. Boston: Little, Brown, 1999.
Oblivion: Stories. New York: Little, Brown, 2004.

NONFICTION

Signifying Rappers: Rap and Race in the Urban Present. Coauthored with Mark Costello. New York: Ecco, 1990.
A Supposedly Fun Thing I'll Never Do Again: Essays and Arguments. Boston: Little, Brown, 1997.
Everything and More: A Complex History of ∞. New York: W. W. Norton/Atlas Books, 2003.
Consider the Lobster: Essays. New York: Little, Brown, 2005.
McCain's Promise: Aboard the Straight Talk Express with John McCain and a Whole Bunch of Actual Reporters, Thinking about Hope. New York: Back Bay, 2008.
This Is Water: Some Thoughts, Delivered on a Significant Occasion, about Living a Compassionate Life. New York: Little, Brown, 2009.
Fate, Time, and Language: An Essay on Free Will. New York: Columbia University Press, 2010.
Both Flesh and Not: Essays. New York: Little, Brown, 2012.

SELECTED UNCOLLECTED WORKS

"Solomon Silverfish." *Sonora Review* 16 (Autumn 1987): 54–81.
"Order and Flux in Northampton." *Conjunctions* 17. Ed. Bradford Morrow. New York: Bard, 1991: 91–118.

"The Fifth Column – A Novel: Week Eleven." *Village Voice* 41.7 (February 13, 1996): 50–51.

AS EDITOR

The Best American Essays 2007. Boston: Mariner/Houghton Mifflin, 2007.

SMORGASBORD

The David Foster Wallace Reader. Eds. Karen Green and Michael Pietsch. New York: Little, Brown, 2014.

INDEX

Cambridge Companions to ...

AUTHORS

TOPICS